A Virtuous Circle

Is the process of political communications by the news media and by parties responsible for civic malaise? *A Virtuous Circle* sets out to challenge this conventional wisdom. Based on a comparison of the role of the news media and parties in postindustrial societies, focusing in particular on western Europe and the United States, this study argues that rather than mistakenly 'blaming the messenger', we need to understand and confront more deep-rooted flaws in representative democracy.

The book outlines appropriate standards for evaluating the performance of the news media and compares changes in the news media, including the rise of the Internet and the development of postmodern election campaigns. Norris shows that although negative news can erode public support for specific policy issues, in general there is a consistently positive relationship between attention to the news media and political knowledge, trust, and participation. The theory of a 'virtuous circle' is proposed to account for the main findings.

For more information on the book, please visit the author's website at www.pippanorris.com.

Pippa Norris is Associate Director (Research) of the Joan Shorenstein Center on the Press, Politics and Public Policy at Harvard University, and she lectures at the Kennedy School of Government. A political scientist, she focuses on comparing political communications, elections, and gender politics. Her recent books include *On Message: Communicating the Campaign*; *Critical Elections: Voters and Parties in Long-Term Perspective*; and *Critical Citizens: Global Support for Democratic Governance*. Professor Norris is author of more than 100 articles and chapters on comparative political behaviour, and has served on the editorial boards of many journals, including *Electoral Studies*, the *European Journal of Political Research*, and *Political Communication*.

COMMUNICATION, SOCIETY, AND POLITICS

Editors

W. Lance Bennett, *University of Washington*

Robert M. Entman, *North Carolina State University*

Politics and relations among individuals in societies across the world are being transformed by new technologies for targeting individuals and sophisticated methods for shaping personalized messages. The new technologies challenge boundaries of many kinds – between news, information, entertainment, and advertising; between media, with the arrival of the World Wide Web; and even between nations. Communication, Society, and Politics probes the political and social impacts of these new communication systems in national, comparative, and global perspective.

A Virtuous Circle

POLITICAL COMMUNICATIONS IN
POSTINDUSTRIAL SOCIETIES

Pippa Norris
Harvard University

 CAMBRIDGE
UNIVERSITY PRESS

PUBLISHED BY THE PRESS SYNDICATE OF THE UNIVERSITY OF CAMBRIDGE
The Pitt Building, Trumpington Street, Cambridge, United Kingdom

CAMBRIDGE UNIVERSITY PRESS
The Edinburgh Building, Cambridge CB2 2RU, UK
40 West 20th Street, New York, NY 10011-4211, USA
10 Stamford Road, Oakleigh, VIC 3166, Australia
Ruiz de Alarcón 13, 28014 Madrid, Spain
Dock House, The Water Front, Cape Town 8001, South Africa

http://www.cambridge.org

First published 2000

Printed in the United States of America

Typefaces Minion 11/13 pt. and Centaur   *System* QuarkXPress [BTS]

A catalog record for this book is available from the British Library.

Library of Congress Cataloging in Publication Data
Norris, Pippa.
A virtuous circle : political communications in postindustrial societies / Pippa Norris.
p.   cm. – (Communication, society, and politics)
Includes bibliographical references and index.
ISBN 0-521-79015-8
1. Communication in politics.   2. Communication – Political aspects.   3. Press and
politics.   4. Political parties.   I. Title.   II. Series.
JA85.N67   2000
320'.01'4 – dc21   00–023673

ISBN   0 521 79015 8   hardback
ISBN   0 521 79364 5   paperback

Contents

Contents

CONCLUSIONS

Tables

Figures

Preface

When I began writing this book I had an agnostic position towards popular theories of media malaise. The belief that political communications have contributed towards civic disengagement has become so prevalent among journalists and scholars, a mantra of pessimism repeated by media commentators, that the challenge for this book seemed to be to say anything new about this phenomenon. Whether the problem du jour was school shootings, world poverty, or cynicism about Congress, one branch or other of the media was, apparently, to blame. Journalists happily self-flagellated. Politicians contributed. After all, why not blame the media when, given a free press, we can do so little about it? A perfect do-nothing strategy. Yet as more and more evidence accumulated that proved contrary to prevailing expectations, I became increasingly skeptical and doubtful about the conventional wisdom. The literature, though plentiful in recent years, often slides too easily from discussing real changes in the news industry (which have occurred) to the assumed effects of these changes on public opinion (which have not). In searching for evidence to support or refute the thesis, several avenues that initially seemed promising eventually proved false leads. As with any study relying upon existing data, the available evidence was often limited. No single indicator presented in this book can be regarded as definitive. But by the end of the chase, the sheer weight of evidence that has accumulated over successive chapters, using a variety of surveys, in different years and in different countries, including the United States, has led to skepticism about the standard view of the impact of political communications on the public. It's just plain wrong.

Journalism is often venerated as a beacon of light that helps to sustain democracy, a force for freedom lying between venal government and the citizens, a protector of the innocent. Then we are shocked, *shocked*, to discover that in fact hacks and scribblers have to turn a penny by selling their wares. A more realistic view of the news industry, and more limited claims about the responsibility of journalism for all the sins of the world, would do us all good.

This book would not have been possible without the encouragement and stimulation provided by colleagues at the Joan Shorenstein Center on the Press, Politics and Public Policy at the John F. Kennedy School of Government, Harvard University. In particular, Marvin Kalb, Director of the Shorenstein Center during the period of writing, deserves thanks for his continuous encouragement and support. Many colleagues helped by providing feedback and criticisms of earlier drafts. Lance Bennett, Stephen Earl Bennett, Jay Blumler, Derek Bok, Tami Buhr, Timothy Cook, Ivor Crewe, Wolfgang Donsbach, Mark Franklin, Doris Graber, Anna Greenberg, Christina Holtz-Bacha, Edie Holway, Marion Just, Anthony Mughan, Ken Newton, Nancy Palmer, Richard Parker, Tom Patterson, Susan Pharr, Robert Putnam, Fred Schauer, and Holli Semetko all deserve special mention in this regard, for listening to my thoughts and reading my arguments at different stages as the book progressed.

The ideas presented in this study were developed over many years in conjunction with a series of projects. Any book using large-scale data sets inevitably accumulates many heavy debts. I am most grateful to the DG X.A2 Public Opinion section at the European Commission, and in particular to Anna Melich and Agnes Hubert, for access to the content analysis in *Monitoring Euromedia* and for the invaluable series of Eurobarometer surveys. The Central Archive at the University of Köln, the ICPSR at the University of Michigan, and the Data Archive at Harvard University helped obtain the myriad data sets. Work on the 1994 Eurobarometer 41.1 was conducted in conjunction with Mark Franklin, Hermann Schmitt, Jacques Thomassen, Richard Katz, Bernhard Wessels, Michael Marsh, and others who formed part of the 1994 European Election Study. I am also indebted to Andy Kohut at the Pew Center for the People and the Press for access to surveys of online users in 1995, 1996, and 1998.

Some of the core ideas in this book originated from an earlier study of the role of the news media in the context of the 1997 British election,[1] developed with John Curtice, David Sanders, Margaret Scammell, and Holli Semetko. The 1997 British election campaign panel study (BES) was funded by the Economic and Social Research Council

(ESRC) (H552/255/003). The BES panel was developed in conjunction with John Curtice, Anthony Heath, Roger Jowell, Alison Park, Katarina Thomson, Geoffrey Evans, Bridget Taylor, and others associated with the Centre for Elections and Social Trends (CREST). CREST is an ESRC Research Centre linking Social and Community Planning Research (SCPR) and Nuffield College, Oxford. Earlier research findings on political trust and support for government, and on the Internet, were stimulated by the Visions of Governance project, led by Joseph Nye, Jr., and Elaine Kamarck at the John F. Kennedy School of Government.[2]

More details about this project and related publications, classes, and data sets are all available on the Web at www.pippanorris.com.

Lastly, I would like to thank the reviewers for their excellent suggestions and Alex Holzman, Lew Bateman, Lance Bennett, and Robert Entman, the editors who have worked with me on this volume.

Harvard University, Cambridge
May 2000

PART I

The News Media and
Civic Malaise

CHAPTER 1

The News Media and Democracy

Recent years have seen growing tensions between the ideals and the perceived performance of democratic institutions.[1] While there is no 'crisis of democracy', many believe that all is not well with the body politic. Concern in the United States has focused on widespread cynicism about political institutions and leaders, fuelling fears about civic disengagement and a half-empty ballot box.[2] The common view is that the American public turns off, knows little, cares less, and stays home. Similar worries echo in Europe, particularly at the supranational level. Commentators have noted a crisis of legitimacy, following the steady expansion in the power and scope of the European Union despite public disengagement from critical policy choices.[3] An important indicator is plummeting turnout in European elections, falling to less than half the electorate in 1999, down from three-quarters two decades earlier. The growth of critical citizens is open to many explanations, as explored in a previous study,[4] including the failure of government performance, changing cultural values, and problems of institutional effectiveness.

One common explanation concerns developments in political communications. During the past decade a rising tide of voices on both sides of the Atlantic has blamed the news media for growing public disengagement, ignorance of civic affairs, and mistrust of government. This idea has developed into something of an unquestioned orthodoxy in the popular literature, particularly in the United States. A related viewpoint, more prevalent in Europe, regards the growth of professional political marketing by parties as also contributing towards greater public cynicism.

But is the conventional wisdom correct? This book, based on a systematic examination of the role of political communication in postindustrial societies, argues that the process of political communications by the news media and by parties is not responsible for civic malaise. Rather than mistakenly 'blaming the messenger', we need to understand and confront more deep-rooted flaws in systems of representative government.

THE CONVENTIONAL CRITIQUE OF POLITICAL COMMUNICATIONS

Let us first outline popular accounts of 'media malaise' or 'videomalaise' that have become so pervasive and then consider the alternative perspective developed in this book. The political science literature on this topic originated in the 1960s, developed in a series of scholarly articles in the post-Watergate 1970s, and rippled out to become the conventional wisdom in the popular culture of journalism and politics following a flood of books in the 1990s. The chorus of critics is loudest in the United States, but similar echoes can be heard in Europe. There is no single theory or canonical text.

In this book, the term *media malaise* refers to accounts claiming that common practices in political communications by the news media and by party campaigns hinder 'civic engagement', meaning citizens learning about public affairs, trust in government, and political activism.[5] That is, all the theories we consider, by definition, make two core assumptions: (1) that the process of political communication has a significant impact upon civic engagement, and (2) that this impact is in a negative direction.

Accounts differ widely in the reasons given for this phenomenon. One school blames trends in journalism. *Structural perspectives* emphasize institutional developments common to many postindustrial societies, such as economic pressures moving the news industry downmarket, the erosion of public-service broadcasting, and the emergence of a more fragmented, multichannel television environment. *Cultural accounts* stress historical events specific to journalism in the United States, notably the growth of a more adversarial news culture following Vietnam and Watergate. Others blame politics: *Campaign accounts* focus on the growth of political marketing with its attendant coterie of spin-doctors, advertising consultants, and pollsters, reducing the personal connections between citizens and representatives. The earliest theorists made restricted claims, focused primarily upon common practices in television news. Later versions extended the scope far more widely to blame a news culture shared across many types of journalism.

Yet others focus upon the social impact of the *mass* media more generally, including everything from Hollywood movies to TV entertainment, advertisements, and rap music, which fall well outside the scope of this study.

Multiple interpretations therefore cluster within this perspective. Irrespective of these important differences, what all media malaise accounts share, by definition, is the belief that public disenchantment with the political process is due, at least in part, to the process of political communications.

There is nothing particularly novel about these claims. Throughout the nineteenth century, critics expressed concern about the popular press contributing to moral decline as newspapers became more widely available.[6] The phenomenon of the 'yellow press' in the 1890s caused worry about its possible dangers for public affairs. In the 1920s and 1930s, the earliest theories of mass propaganda were based on the assumption that authoritarian regimes could dupe and choreograph the public by manipulating radio bulletins and newsreels.[7] Recent decades have seen multiple crusades against the supposed pernicious influence of the mass media, whether directed against violence in movies, the 'wasteland' of television, the impact on civic engagement of watching TV entertainment, the dangers of tobacco advertising, or the supposedly pernicious effects of pop music.[8] Though all that is hardly new, what is different today is that an unquestioned orthodoxy has developed as a chorus of complaints has decried the impact of political communications on public life.

THE AMERICAN LITERATURE ON MEDIA MALAISE

The modern idea of media malaise emerged in the political science literature in the 1960s. Kurt and Gladys Lang were the first to suggest a connection between the rise of network news and broader feelings of disenchantment with American politics. TV broadcasts, they argued, fuelled public cynicism by overemphasizing political conflict and downplaying routine policy-making in Washington. That process, they suggested, had its greatest impact on the 'inadvertent audience', who encountered politics because they happened to be watching TV when the news was shown, but who lacked much interest in, or prior knowledge about, public affairs.[9] The Langs proved an isolated voice at the time, in large part because the consensus in political communications was that the mass media had only minimal effects on public opinion.

5

The idea gained currency in the mid-1970s because it seemed to provide a plausible reason for growing public alienation in the post-Vietnam, post-Watergate era. Michael Robinson first popularized the term 'videomalaise' to describe the link between reliance on American television journalism and feelings of political cynicism, social mistrust, and lack of political efficacy. Greater exposure to television news, he argued, with its high 'negativism', conflictual frames, and anti-institutional themes, generated political disaffection, frustration, cynicism, self-doubt, and malaise.[10] Robinson saw this process as most critical during election campaigns, when viewers were turned off, he argued, by TV's focus on the 'horse race' at the expense of issues, analysis rather than factual information, and excessive 'bad news' about the candidates.[11] Many others echoed those claims over the years.[12] According to Samuel Huntington, in a widely influential report for the Trilateral Commission, the news media had eroded respect for government authority in many postindustrial societies, contributing towards a widespread 'crisis' of democracy evident on the streets of Washington, DC, Paris, and Tokyo.[13] Others argued that the problem was rooted less in TV news than in mainstream entertainment. According to Gerbner, TV drama about violent crime and urban conflict cultivated fear, alienation, and interpersonal mistrust.[14] The prevailing view in the early 1980s was expressed by Austin Ranney, who thought that television, while not solely responsible for civic disengagement, was a major contributing factor. TV, Ranney claimed, 'has altered the culture by intensifying ordinary Americans' traditional low opinion of politics and politicians, by exacerbating the decline in their trust and confidence in their government and its institutions, and by helping to make them even less inclined to vote than they used to be.'[15]

During the 1990s, the trickle of complaints about the news media, from voices within and outside journalism, became a popular deluge. This reflected a new mood of angst about the vitality of democracy at a time of widespread cynicism about political leaders and government institutions, and there were stronger claims about media effects. For Entman, the free press falls far short of its ideals, leaving too much of the American public ignorant of, and disconnected from, politics.[16] For Neil Postman, the major networks, driven by their hemorrhage of viewers to cable, have substituted entertainment-oriented, crime-, celebrity-, and consumer-obsessed tabloid television for serious political coverage of national and world affairs. The result is endless coverage of Hollywood, the 'health beat', and sports, rather than the problems facing America, so that we are 'entertaining ourselves to death'.[17] For Roderick Hart, television charms the modern voter into an illusion of political participation and information, while encouraging couch-potato passivity, thereby seducing America.[18] Neal Gabler echoes those claims, arguing that entertainment has come to be the predominant value in television news, with the result that the political process has been repackaged into show business. Serious political debate, serious policy problems, and serious election coverage have become marginal-ized in an entertainment-driven celebrity-oriented society where the only standard of value is whether or not something can grab and hold the public's attention.[19]

Larry Sabato warns of the dangers of pack journalism, with all of the press corps focusing obsessively on a few sensationalized stories (O.J., Diana, Lewinsky), producing a 'feeding frenzy'.[20] For Thomas Patterson, the press, in its role as election gatekeeper, has become a 'miscast' insti-tution, out of order in the political system. The core reason, he suggests, lies in the post-Vietnam, post-Watergate adversarial culture of Amer-ican journalism, combined with the rise of interpretive journalism.[21] As a result, he suggests, echoing Robinson and Sheehan,[22] today campaign coverage by all the news media (not just TV) focuses excessively on the poll-driven horse race ('who's ahead, who's behind'), on conflictual and negative news (bad news), and on strategic game frames (the insider 'scoop' about what's behind a proposal). Because of a cultural shift, the routine campaign news frame for American journalists, he believes, routinely criticizes politicians for shifting positions, wavering on tough decisions, pandering to groups, and making promises they do not intend to keep. Cappella and Jamieson stress that the strategic news frames for politics activate cynicism about campaign politics, govern-ment, and public policy.[23] Dautrich and Hartley conclude that the news media 'fail American voters', because many citizens believe that jour-nalists place too much emphasis on campaign strategy and tactics, coverage is politically biased, and too little attention is devoted to infor-mation about political issues.[24]

James Fallows is concerned that down-market trends have led to the relentless pursuit of sensational, superficial, and populist political reporting on network news, in an attempt to maintain ratings before surfers click to other channels.[25] All this breathless flimflam, Schudson argues, comes at the expense of detailed and informed debate about policy issues and 'hard' (real) news. The result is that although there is more information available for Americans than ever before, this does not create informed citizens.[26] Hachten complains that public affairs journalism, in particular, has been trivialized and corrupted by a mélange of entertainment, sensationalism, celebrity-watching, and merchandising driven by advertising, PR, and corporate profits.[27] Coverage of international affairs has been one of the primary casualties, many argue, as America has turned away from the complexities of the post–Cold War world.[28] Marvin Kalb has drawn attention to the 'new news', with commercial journalism driven further down-market because of new technology and economic restructuring in the industry.[29] The role of public television in the United States, long underfunded as a poor cousin, has been unable to compensate for the relentless drive for ratings by network and cable TV.[30] Many have concluded that the news media can be blamed for a host of political ills assumed to be plaguing America, such as widespread ignorance about government and public-policy issues, declining electoral turnout, and cynicism about government institutions. Such criticisms have moved well beyond the halls of academe: many U.S. journalists share the opinion that something is seriously wrong with their profession in terms of traditional standards of accuracy, fairness, and balance.[31] The Committee of Concerned Journalists, led by Tom Rosensteil and Bill Kovach, has debated potential reforms to the profession.

THE EUROPEAN LITERATURE ON MEDIA MALAISE

In the European literature, similar, although perhaps less strident, voices can be heard. European accounts emphasize structural developments in the news industry and in party campaigning. Many fear that growing competition from commercial channels has undermined the quality and diversity of public service television. The proliferation of media outlets, seeking to capture the mass-market audience with low-cost, low-quality programming, is believed to have reduced the choice of program types.[32] This development may have eroded the audience's ability to make sense of public affairs, and, echoing Habermas, there is widespread concern from commentators like Dahlgren that the displacement of public-service television by commercial channels has impoverished the public sphere.[33] During the 1980s, the public sector experienced a massive wave of privatization throughout western Europe. During the same era, the growth of alternative commercial channels, breaking down the monopoly of public-service broadcasting, undermined the rationale for subsidizing television through state resources. Schulz argues that in Germany the decline of public-service broadcasting and the rise of commercial channels, with the latter emphasizing the more sensational and negative aspects of political news, may have increased public cynicism.[34] Kaase fears that these developments may produce audiences segmented according to the amount of political information to which they are exposed, possibly reinforcing a 'knowledge gap'.[35]

In the print sector, there is widespread concern that increased competition for readers has increased the pressure on the traditional standards for news, leading to 'tabloidization' or 'infotainment'. 'Yellow journalism' in the 1890s had routinely highlighted the moral peccadilloes and sexual proclivities of the rich and famous. Sensationalization of crime and scandal in newspapers is hardly new, providing a popular alternative to the dull business of politics.[36] But today we routinely have front-page news about government scandals, seemingly more than in previous decades – whether concerning sleaze in Britain, Tagentopoli in Italy, Recruit and Sagawa in Japan, or the Clinton-Lewinsky affair in America.[37] Such coverage is believed to corrode the forms of trust underpinning social relations and political authority. The process of 'tabloidization' seems to have gone further in Europe than in the American or Japanese press, with papers like the *Sun* and *Der Bild* leading the pack, each with many millions of readers. But similar phenomena are evident in the chase for ratings among local TV news and 'all talk, all the time' cable news 'magazines' in the United States.

Many hope that the Internet can escape these problems, but others fear that this new medium may reinforce political cynicism. Davis and Owen have concluded that the Internet will provide new sources of information for the politically interested, but given the uneven levels of access there are good grounds to be skeptical about its transformative potential for democratic participation.[38] Murdock and Golding[39] argue that the new medium may merely reproduce, or even exacerbate, the existing social biases in conventional political participation. Hill and Hughes believe that the Internet will not change people, but will simply allow them to do the same things in a different way.[40] Moreover, because of the speed of transmission of news on the Internet, and the absence of gatekeepers to exercise professional standards of editorial accuracy, it may lead to anarchy, with rumor replacing fact. The pace of breaking headlines on the Net may in turn undermine journalistic standards in the old media, just as the *Drudge Report* on the Web scooped *Newsweek* in breaking the first Lewinsky story. The Net also provides a platform that may amplify the voices of those well outside of mainstream democratic politics, from white-supremacy groups to bomb-making terrorists.

A related stream of European literature attributes the problems of political communications primarily to the practice of 'professional marketing'. One of the most striking developments in many countries has been the declining importance of the 'premodern' campaign involving local party meetings, door-to-door canvassing, and direct voter–candidate contact. The rise of the 'modern' campaign is characterized by widespread adoption of the techniques of political marketing.[41] Strategic communications feature a coordinated plan that sets out party objectives, identifies target voters, establishes the battleground issues, orchestrates consistent key themes and images, prioritizes organizational and financial resources, and lays out the framework within which campaign communications operate. This is part of the 'professionalization' of campaigning, giving greater roles to technical experts in public relations, news management, advertising, speech-writing, and market research.[42]

The rise of political marketing has been widely blamed for growing public cynicism about political leaders and institutions. The central concern is that the techniques of 'spin', selling, and persuasion are undermining the credibility of political leaders.[43] If everything in politics is designed for popular appeal, with 'catch-all' parties adopting whatever slogan, message, or image will resonate with focus groups, then people may become more reluctant to trust the messages or messenger. The attempt to manage the news is nothing new, but more stories are being published about this process, so that the language of 'spin-doctors' and 'image consultants' has entered the popular lexicon, drawing increased attention to these developments. Although lacking direct evidence of public opinion, Bob Franklin provides one of the clearest statements of this thesis, decrying the 'packaging of politics', the manipulation of the public by official government advertising campaigns, and the ascendancy of image over substance in British election campaigns.[44] Some regard the adoption of strategic communications as just one more way for parties to connect with voters in modern campaigns.[45] Yet many others have expressed concern about the 'Americanization' of election campaigning in Britain, Germany, and Scandinavia and the possible impact this may be having on public confidence in political parties.[46] The use of 'negative' or 'attack' advertising by parties and candidates has also led to fears that this practice may demobilize the electorate.[47]

Along related lines, Jay Blumler suggests that a 'crisis of civic communication' is afflicting Western Europe.[48] In increasingly complex societies, Blumler argues, governing has become more difficult, popular support more contingent, and mass communications more vital. Yet at the same time, structural failures in the news media have reduced their capacity to function in a way that would promote civic communications and strengthen the public sphere. The core problem, for Blumler, lies in the more adversarial relationship that has developed between politicians and journalists. In their struggles to control the news agenda, parties have increasingly tailored their messages to journalistic formats, news values, and predilections, whereas in response the reporters have intensified their efforts to put their own stamp on the 'political story', to expose what politicians are really 'up to'. The net result, Blumler argues, has impoverished the campaign coverage and decreased the quality of public debate about serious policy issues facing the country.

The number of skeptics questioning the evidence for all these claims has been growing in recent years. Earlier studies by the author found that, contrary to a pattern of media malaise, although TV watching was related to some signs of apathy, attention to the news media was associated with positive indicators of civic engagement in the United States and Britain as well as in other countries.[49] In Britain, Kenneth Newton reported that the practices of reading a broadsheet newspaper and watching a lot of television news were associated with greater political knowledge and interest and a better understanding of politics.[50] Christina Holtz-Bacha found similar patterns associated with attention to the news media in Germany,[51] while Curtice, Schmitt-Beck, and Schrott reported similarly positive findings in a five-nation study of elections in the early 1990s.[52] The most recent examination of the American National Election Survey (NES) evidence, by Stephen Earl Bennett and his colleagues, found that trust in politics and trust in the news media went hand-in-hand, with no evidence that use of the news media was related to political cynicism.[53] But so far such findings have appeared primarily in scattered scholarly publications and continue to be drowned out by the Greek chorus of popular lament for the state of modern journalism. The claims about the negative effects of news coverage on the public deserve a thorough reexamination. A chorus of voices can therefore be heard, a few optimistic, but most decrying the impact of modern political communications. Before we all jump on the media malaise bandwagon, is the conventional critique correct? This book seeks to provide an alternative interpretation that sees recent developments in a far more positive light.

THE CORE ARGUMENT

The overall plan of the book can be summarized as follows. Chapter 2 discusses the normative standards that are available to evaluate the functions of the news media. Conceptions of representative democracy suggest three basic roles for the news media: as a *civic forum* encouraging pluralistic debate about public affairs, as a *watchdog* against the abuse of power, and as a *mobilizing agent* encouraging public learning and participation in the political process. These concepts provide normative benchmarks, rooted in Schumpeterian theories of representative democracy, that are available to compare media performances.

Chapter 3 discusses the methods available to examine how well the news media meet these standards. Three approaches have been common in the literature. *Longitudinal analysis* has compared trends in the content of news coverage and public opinion at the macro-level. *Experimental studies* have analyzed differences between groups of news users exposed to different stimuli. *Survey analysis* has examined the individual-level relationship between news exposure and indicators of civil engagement, using cross-sectional or panel studies. After discussing the pros and cons of these different approaches, Chapter 3 then describes the multimethod research design and the triangulated sources of evidence used throughout the book. Part II of this book compares the structural trends in all of the Organization for Economic Cooperation and Development (OECD) member states, twenty-nine countries that have similar levels of political and economic development, yet with political and media systems that differ in important respects, such as the role of public-service television, the degree of penetration by cable or satellite television, and the regulations for election broadcasting and advertising. The aim for this part of the book is to see whether there are common trends transforming the news environment and campaign communications across postindustrial societies. Subsequent chapters then use content analysis and survey data to compare the effects of news exposure on civic engagement in the fifteen member states of the European Union. Because much of the impetus for the media malaise thesis originated in the United States, Chapter 13 will use fifty years of NES data to examine similar patterns in American public opinion.

Structural Changes in the News Industry

The central argument developed in this book distinguishes among the *production, content,* and *effect* of political communication. The process can be seen as a sequential-systems model, beginning with the development of political messages, progressing through the content of news-media coverage, and ending with the effects on the public (Figure 1.1).

Part II examines how the structure of the news industry has evolved in response to technological, socioeconomic, and political developments in the postwar era. Since the 1950s, the print press has experienced increasing concentration of ownership and a reduction in the number of independent papers, although at the same time total newspaper sales have remained stable, not declined as some had feared. During the 1980s, public television, which had enjoyed a state monopoly throughout much of western Europe, faced increasing competition from the proliferation of new broadcast, cable, and satellite television channels. Since the mid-1990s, the explosive growth of the Internet has challenged the dominance of television, a pattern most advanced in Scandinavia. Thus the news industry underwent major structural changes during the late twentieth century, although postindustrial societies continue to bear the imprint of their historical origins, showing important contrasts even within the European Union, as well as between the United States and Europe.

The Content of Political Coverage

Yet it is not immediately obvious that developments in the communications environment have necessarily transformed political coverage for the worse. Commentators have expressed concern about a long-term decline in hard news, such as coverage of international affairs, public-policy issues, and parliamentary debates. In its place, many suggest, news has been 'dumbed down' to become 'infotainment', focusing on human-interest stories about scandal, celebrities, and sex. 'Tabloid' papers in Britain, the 'boulevard press' in Germany, and local television news in the United States share many common characteristics.

The available comparative evidence suggests two important trends, each with important implications for the claims of media malaise. First, the new information environment has greatly expanded the opportunities to learn about public affairs from a wider variety of channels, programs, formats, and levels. Since the 1970s, the amount of news and current-affairs broadcasting on public-service television in OECD

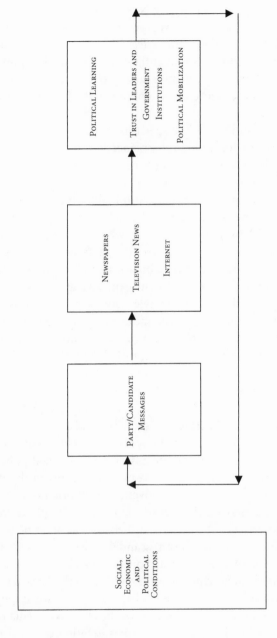

Figure 1.1. Schematic model of political communications.

countries has more than tripled. During the past three decades the proportion of Europeans who read newspapers every day has almost doubled, and the proportion watching television news every day has risen from one-half in 1970 to almost three-quarters in 1999. Access to the Internet has grown phenomenally. By the late 1990s, about one-fifth of all Europeans and half of all Americans and Scandinavians were online, surfing the Web. Getting news is one of the most popular uses of the Internet in the United States and Europe. In short, news consumption is up. We often tend to generalize on the basis of the American literature on the subject, but compared with other postindustrial societies, the United States rates exceptionally low in consumption of newspapers and TV news. Moreover, the formats have become diversified beyond the standard flagship evening news programs and current-affairs programs, incorporating 24-hour rolling news, on-the-hour radio headlines, and TV magazines and talk shows, as well as the panoply of online news sources. It has become easier to bump into the news, almost accidentally, than ever before, and this entire process has broadened the background of the news audience.

Second, rather than seeing an inexorable downward erosion in the standards of serious journalism, which has been termed the 'tabloidization' of news, or the growth of 'infotainment', it seems more accurate to understand trends during the 1980s and 1990s as representing a *diversification* of the marketplace in terms of levels, formats, and topics. 'Soft' news and 'infotainment' undoubtedly have increased in some sectors of the market, but the availability of serious coverage of political events, international affairs, and financial news has been steadily expanded elsewhere. Endless Senate debates shown on C-SPAN coexist today with endless debates about sex and personal relationships on the *Jerry Springer Show*. The *Sun* can be found on the same newsstands as the *Economist*. News.bbc.co.uk is as easily available as Amsterdam pornography sites. Diversification does not mean that the whole of society is being progressively 'dumbed down' by trends in the news media. By focusing only on excesses in the popular end of the market, such as the wasteland of endless punditry on American cable TV talk shows, or 'if it bleeds, it leads' on local American TV news, we overlook dramatic changes, such as the ability to watch live legislative debates, to witness Kosovo refugees at the moment they crossed the border, or to find online information about local government services. Potentially, diversification could lead to another danger, namely, greater division between the information haves and have-nots. But chapters also demonstrate that in fact the audience for news has greatly expanded in size and broadened socially during the past quarter-century, not narrowed.

The evidence remains limited, and systematic data are lacking to confirm or deny whether other assumed long-term changes in the news culture have occurred in postindustrial societies – for example, whether there has been a growth in negative coverage of politicians during election campaigns, or whether a more adversarial relationship has developed between journalists and governments. The available studies, however, strongly suggest that developments in political coverage observed in particular countries often are highly contextual, rather than representing trends common across postindustrial societies.[54] For example, the most comprehensive comparison of news cultures in twenty-one countries, based on surveys of journalists, found almost no consensus about professional roles, ethical values, and journalistic norms.[55] Rather than showing the emergence of a single prevalent model of journalism, based on American norms, this suggests considerable diversity worldwide.

Political campaigns have been transformed by the diversification in the news industry, and also by the widespread adoption of political marketing techniques. Other countries have not simply imported American campaigning practices lock, stock, and barrel. But politicians in many democracies often are paying more attention to formal feedback mechanisms like polls and focus groups, with expanding roles for campaign professionals from marketing and public relations. Comparative surveys have found that in the 'shopping' model, parties adopt whatever techniques seem best suited for their particular environment, supplementing but not discarding older forms of electioneering.[56] Even in America, as Chapter 13 demonstrates, traditional forms of grassroots voter contact have been maintained, alongside newer forms of campaign communications. Rather than decrying the 'black arts' of spin-doctors, we can regard the professionalization of political communications as an extension of the democratic process *if* these techniques bind parties more closely to the concerns of the electorate. The key issue is less the increased deployment of marketing techniques per se, which is not in dispute, than their effect upon politicians and voters, which is.

THE IMPACT ON CIVIC ENGAGEMENT

This brings us to the issue at the heart of the book: whether changes in political communications have contributed towards civic disengagement. The fundamental flaw in the accounts of media malaise concerns not the claims about developments in the news industry and political campaigns and their impact on the content of political coverage, but rather the assumptions about the audience. Theories of media malaise argue that exposure to the news media discourages learning about politics, erodes trust in political leaders and government institutions, and dampens political mobilization. The net result, it is argued by proponents, has been a decline in active democratic citizenship.

Part III of this book presents extensive evidence from a battery of surveys in Europe and the United States, as well as experiments in Britain, that cast strong doubt upon these claims. Instead, this book indicates that, contrary to the media malaise hypothesis, use of the news media is positively associated with a wide range of indicators of political knowledge, trust, and mobilization. People who watch more TV news, read more newspapers, surf the Net, and pay attention to campaigns are consistently more knowledgeable, trusting of government, and participatory. Far from being a case of 'American exceptionalism', this pattern is found in Europe *and* the United States. Repeated tests using a variety of data sets in different countries and across different time periods during the past half-century have confirmed this positive relationship, even after controlling for factors that characterize the news audience, such as their education and prior political interest. The public is not simply responding passively to the political communications being presented to them, as in a naive stimulus–response model; instead, they are critically and actively sifting, discarding, and inter-preting the available information. A more educated and literate public is capable of using the more complex range of news sources and party messages to find the information they need to make practical political choices. True, Chapter 9 demonstrates that a persistent pattern of crit-ical coverage of the euro in the European news media was associated with a decline in public support for this policy issue. But that repre-sented 'normal' politics, rather than a crisis of support for democracy per se. The survey evidence indicates that news exposure has not been associated with civic disengagement at diffuse level in America and Europe.

Why should we find a positive link between civic engagement and attention to the news media? There are three possible answers.

One interpretation concerns *selection effects*. In this explanation, those who are most predisposed to participate politically (for whatever reason) could well be more interested in keeping up with current affairs in the news, so the direction of causation could be one-way, from *prior attitudes* to *use of the news media*. This view is consistent with the 'uses-and-gratification' literature, which suggests that mass-media habits reflect prior predispositions in the audience: People who love football turn to the sports pages, people who invest in Wall Street check the business pages, and people interested in politics read editorials about government and public policy.[57] But if we were to assume a purely one-way selection effect, that would imply that even if one repeatedly turned to the news about public affairs, one would learn nothing whatever from the process, a proposition that seems inherently implausible.

Another answer could involve *media effects*. In this explanation, the process of watching or reading about public affairs (for whatever reason) can be expected to increase our interest in and knowledge about government and politics, thereby facilitating political participation. The more we watch or read, in this interpretation, the more we learn. News habits can be influenced by many factors, such as leisure patterns and broadcasting schedules: People may catch the news because it comes on after a popular sitcom, or because radio stations air headline news between music clips, or because the household subscribes to home delivery of a newspaper. In this view, the direction of causality would again be one-way, but in this case running from *prior news habits* to *subsequent political attitudes*.

Each of these views could logically make sense of the associations we establish. One or the other could be true. It is not possible for us, any more than for others, to resolve the direction of causality from cross-sectional polls of public opinion taken at one point in time. But it seems plausible and more convincing to assume a *two-way interactive process*. The conclusion argues that over the long term, through repeated exposure, like the socialization process in the family or workplace, there may well be a 'virtuous circle' whereby the news media and party campaigns serve to further activate the active. Those who are most interested and knowledgeable pay the most attention to political news. Learning more about public affairs (the policy stances of the candidates and parties, the record of the government, the severity of the social and economic problems facing the nation) reduces the barriers to further civic engagement. In this interpretation, the ratchet of reinforcement thereby moves in a direction that is healthy for democratic participation.

In contrast, the news media have far less power to reinforce the disengagement of the disengaged: Given the easy availability of the multiple alternatives now available, and minimal political interest, when presented with news about politics and current affairs this group is habitually more likely to turn over, turn off, or surf to another Web page. If the disengaged do catch the news, they are likely to pay little attention. And if they do pay attention, they are more likely to mistrust media sources of information. Repeatedly 'tuning out' political messages inoculates against their potential impact. This theory cannot be proved conclusively from the available cross-sectional survey evidence, any more than can theories of media malaise, but it does suggest a plausible and coherent interpretation for the different pieces of the puzzle found in this study.

To substantiate this argument, the study uses multiple sources of evidence. Trends in the structure of the news industry since 1945 are analyzed using data from UNESCO, the most authoritative source monitoring worldwide patterns of news consumption. To compare news coverage, the analysis draws upon systematic content analysis of newspaper and television news about the European Union in the mid-1990s in the fifteen member states of the EU. To compare patterns of public opinion, the study draws on the thirty-year series of Eurobarometer surveys produced by the European Commission, which monitored public opinion from 1970 to 1999 in EU member states. Those surveys measured the uses of newspapers, television and radio news, and, more recently, the Internet, as well as attention to political campaigns and various indicators of political knowledge, trust, and mobilization. To attempt to unravel the complex issue of the direction of causality, this study examines some experimental research on the effects of positive and negative television news conducted in Britain, involving more than 1,000 subjects.

For analysis of the American case, Chapter 13 utilizes a half-century of National Election Surveys in the United States, running from 1948 to 1998. Because so much of the media malaise literature is American, we pay particular attention to examining both specific and diffuse effects there. At individual level, Chapter 13 establishes that, as in Europe, those Americans most exposed to the news media proved the most politically knowledgeable, active, and trusting. At diffuse level, the timing of long-term secular trends across a range of indicators of civic engagement since the early 1950s fails to fit with media malaise

THE NEWS MEDIA AND CIVIC MALAISE

accounts. Instead, the patterns showed either broad stability over time (such as in attention to election news and campaign activism) or, alternatively, a temporary plateau during the heated politics of the 1960s, both preceded and followed by slightly lower levels (such as in turnout for presidential elections and the level of political interest). According to these indicators, there is little evidence for civic malaise in America, let alone malaise caused by changes in the culture of the news media.

For reasons that will be explained fully in subsequent chapters, the claims of media malaise are methodologically flawed, so that they are at best unproven, to use the Scottish verdict, or at worst false. As a result, too often we are 'blaming the messenger' for more deep-rooted ills of the body politic. This matters not only because we need to understand the real causes of civic disengagement in order to advance our knowledge but also because the correct diagnosis has serious implications for public-policy choices. This is especially important in newer democracies struggling to institutionalize a free press during the transition from authoritarian rule. 'Blaming the messenger' can prove a deeply conservative strategy, blocking effective institutional reforms, especially in cultures that idealize the independence of the press and its protection from public regulation.

This book does not seek to claim that all is for the best in the best of all possible political worlds. Though not 'broken', there are many deep-rooted flaws embedded in the core institutions of representative democracy; we are not seeking to present a Panglossian view. But consider just some of the many contemporary challenges to democracy: In Russia, widespread corruption and political instability threaten to undermine fragile electoral gains. In America, the sea of special-interest money in politics and the unending campaigns, combined with legislative do-nothingism, fail to serve the public well. In the European Union, the lack of transparency and accountability in the policy-making process and the increasing power and scope of EU institutions are leading to a worrying disconnect from the European public. Ethnic conflict, violence, and intense poverty continue to plague many emerging democracies in Africa. Worldwide, women's voices continue to be underrepresented in the decision-making process. The list could go on and on. The important point for this argument is that these and many other related political problems have deep-seated structural causes. If we stopped blaming the news media's coverage of politics and directed our attention to the problems themselves, perhaps remedies would be more forthcoming. The media malaise thesis is not just misleading; it is also deeply conservative. The concluding chapter summarizes the core findings, expands on the theory of a virtuous circle, and considers the implications for public policy and for strengthening democratic governance.

CHAPTER 2

Evaluating Media Performance

Commentators often have suggested that newspapers or television should fulfill certain obligations, such as raising public awareness about AIDS, encouraging interest in international affairs, or stimulating community activism. Many believe that during election campaigns the news media have a particular responsibility to help strengthen democracy by providing political coverage that will educate the public about the major issues, inform citizens about the contenders for office, and mobilize people to turn out. If judged by those standards, the news media have largely failed in their democratic functions, media malaise theories suggest. Embedded in these claims are certain normative assumptions about what political coverage the news media *should* provide. But what are the appropriate standards for evaluating the roles of the news media?

This chapter starts with the theory of representative democracy developed by Joseph Schumpeter and Robert Dahl, based on the concepts of pluralistic competition, public participation, and civil and political rights. We then consider the benchmarks available to evaluate journalism that flow from this understanding. The strategy we use follows the idea of a democratic audit, developed to evaluate how institutions like elections, legislatures, and the judiciary work in any particular society.[1] Our approach identifies three core political functions of the news media system – as a civic forum, as a mobilizing agent, and as a watchdog. Based on these functions, we develop more specific benchmarks, or a checklist, that can be used to audit the performance of the news media system in any democracy. Subsequent chapters go on to examine the evidence for media performances judged against these standards.

DEMOCRATIC THEORIES OF THE NEWS MEDIA

Following the Schumpeterian tradition, we can define representative or liberal democracy in terms of its structural characteristics.[2] Understood in this way, democracy involves three dimensions:

(1) *pluralistic competition* among parties and individuals for all positions of government power,
(2) *participation* by citizens in the selection of parties and representatives through free, fair, and periodic elections, and
(3) *civil and political liberties* to speak, publish, assemble, and organize, as the conditions necessary to ensure effective competition and participation.[3]

This definition focuses particularly on how democracies function through elections – their primary mechanism for holding governments accountable for their actions. Representative democracies require competition for elective offices, allowing citizens to choose from among alternative candidates and parties. Information should be available from parties and from the news media so that citizens can understand the electoral choices and estimate the consequences of casting their ballots. Citizens need opportunities to formulate their preferences, signify their preferences, and have their preferences weighted equally in the conduct of government. Free and fair elections should be held at regular intervals to translate votes into seats and to allow for alternation of parties and officeholders. If these conditions are met, then citizens can exercise an informed choice, hold parties and representatives accountable for their actions, and, if necessary, 'kick the rascals out'. Of course, many other definitions are available, especially those based on alternative conceptions of direct or plebicitory democracy, but the Schumpeterian perspective reflects one of the most widely accepted understandings of democratic institutions.[4] It has the advantage of having been used extensively for cross-national and longitudinal comparisons.[5] The Schumpeterian conceptualization has been operationalized and measured with the Gastil index, which Freedom House has published annually since the early 1970s, ranking countries worldwide.[6]

On this basis, we can identify three political functions for the news media system during election campaigns – as a *civic forum* for pluralistic debate, as a *watchdog* for civil and political liberties, and as a *mobilizing agent* for public participation – that flow from this understanding of representative democracy (Figure 2.1). Obviously, many other crite-

Conditions for Representative Democracy	Pluralistic Competition	Public Participation	Civil Liberties and Political Rights
Role of the News Media	Civic Forum	Mobilizing Agent	Watchdog
Performance Indices	Availability and balance of news in terms of: • Stopwatch balance • Directional balance • Agenda balance	Civic engagement of news users in terms of: • Practical knowledge • Political interest • Civic activism	Independence and effectiveness of the news media in terms of: • Abuses of power • Public scandals • Government failures
Measurement of Performance	**Content analysis:** Amount and balance of news coverage	**Mass surveys:** Knowledge, interest, and activism of news users	**Case studies:** The role of the news media in exposing abuses of power, public scandals, and government failures

Figure 2.1. Standards of media performance.

ria for evaluating the performances of the mass media are available, such as those concerning educational or cultural goals.[7] But only the core political functions for the news media that we have identified are central to the Schumpeterian understanding of representative democracy. What does this conceptualization imply for evaluating the performances of the news media?

THE NEWS MEDIA AS CIVIC FORUM

The concept of the news media as a civic forum is most closely associated with the work of Jürgen Habermas, who has been widely influential, although our argument does not depend upon his conceptualization. Habermas's ideal notion of a public sphere was predicated on the notion of widespread discussion about public affairs in civic society.[8] A 'public sphere' represents a meeting place or debating forum mediating between citizens and the state, facilitating informed deliberation about the major issues of the day. In the eighteenth century, a diverse range of intellectual journals and public affairs periodicals among fashionable society were regarded as providing the ideal media in this process, and there were meeting places in the political salons and coffee houses of London, Paris, and Vienna.

In the late nineteenth century, changes in the nature of liberal democracy – particularly expansion of the franchise beyond the bourgeois elites, the growth of the popular press, and the increasing specialization and complexity of government – transformed the conditions that sustained the traditional channels of elite political discussion and enlarged the public sphere. Habermas deplored the effects of developments in the news media, including the growing role of the mass-circulation popular press, the concentration of corporate ownership in large media groups, and the rising power of advertisers, a process that, he argued, would lead to a homogenization of political information and a shift from 'real' to 'virtual' political debate.

Despite those developments, today the ideal of the press as a civic forum for pluralistic debate, mediating between voters and government, remains highly influential.[9] Traditional meeting places have been altered, but not beyond recognition: Venues such as newspapers ('op-ed' features, editorial columns, and letter pages), public affairs magazines, and newer outlets (talk-radio programs, CNN's *Larry King Live*, the BBC2's *Newsnight*, *Meet the Press*, and Internet discussion forums) all provide regular opportunities for political debate among a network of politicians, government officials, journalistic commentators, advocacy-group spokespersons, think-tank analysts, and academic policy experts, in addition to providing opportunities for public input through phone-in or studio discussions.

As a civic forum, it is widely assumed that the news media should function at the most general level as a conduit providing the government and the governed with opportunities to communicate effectively with each other.[10] In this regard, the news media provide an essential linkage connecting horizontally between political actors and vertically between these actors and the electorate. The central priority in this process should be accorded to the parties, which are the core representative institutions that aggregate interests, nominate candidates, and provide collective responsibility for government. Parties attempt to influence newspapers and television headlines, and thereby reach 'downward' towards the electorate, through activities such as news conferences, photo opportunities, and professional political marketing techniques. Equally important, to make sure that electoral choices reflect public priorities, citizens need to be able to express their concerns and convey their preferences 'upward' to parties and elected representatives. Opinion polls, focus groups, and traditional doorstep canvassing are all ways by which representatives can learn about the preferences of the electorate, but often politicians rely on the news media as a proxy for public opinion. This process is important at any stage of the political cycle, but particularly so during election campaigns, when citizens have their greatest opportunity to influence the political process and choose the government.

Opportunities for Civic Debate

If we accept that the news media should function as a civic forum, then specific indicators can be used to audit how well the media perform in this capacity. We assume that the news media, to prove effective, should provide extensive political coverage that is widely and easily available to all sectors of society. A rich information environment, with multiple sources of regular news about politics available from different outlets, is most likely to promote effective government communications, to provide multiple venues for public debate, and to reduce the costs of becoming informed about public affairs. In contrast, if, as some claim, there has been a decrease in the amount of political coverage because of trends such as the decline of public-service broadcasting or the rise of 'infotainment', then civic affairs may be impoverished.

Yet the amount of political news tells us nothing about its quality. Pluralist theory emphasizes that as a civic forum the news-media system should reflect the political and cultural diversity within a society, providing a fair and impartial balance, so that all voices can be heard in political deliberations. 'Balance' can be defined in terms of either external or internal diversity.

Notions of *external* diversity stress competition between different media outlets. In Britain, for example, although direct financial links between parties and newspapers have weakened, the press remains broadly partisan in its political leanings. Papers like the *Daily Telegraph* and *Daily Mail* have long sympathized with the Conservative party, while the *Daily Mirror* and *Guardian* have provided a more left-liberal slant to news and editorial commentary. Although the overall balance of the press in the postwar era has traditionally leaned towards the right, competition between papers, offering voters choices of alternative political perspectives at the newsstand, preserves pluralism. The role of the news media as a civic forum becomes problematic if most major news outlets consistently favour only one party or viewpoint, if they systematically exclude minor parties or minority perspectives, or if citizens rely upon only one news source.

The alternative conception emphasizes the *internal* diversity of reporting. In this model, typified by the American press, each paper provides multiple and contrasting perspectives within its columns, often balancing liberal and conservative op-ed commentary. Internal diversity preserves pluralism, even with a restricted choice of newspapers within a particular market. The monopoly once enjoyed by public broadcasters meant that most emphasized the need for strict partisan balance in news coverage, especially during election campaigns. Television editors and producers commonly stress the need for equidistant coverage of the main political parties, balancing favourable and unfavourable stories about each party, as well as evenhandedness in coverage of all sides of an issue.[11] The typical story in this regard tends to present one party's policy proposals or record, followed by a rebuttal from opponents, in a familiar 'on the one hand, and on the other' sort of format. Studies have found that balance, or 'expressing fairly the positions on both sides of a dispute,' is one of the most common ways for journalists to understand objectivity, especially in the United States and Britain.[12] Many broadcasters seek to ensure that the major parties or candidates are given equal, or proportional, airtime during election campaigns. This is also the principle commonly used for allocating time to political or election broadcasts,[13] as well as for the time rules governing presidential debates. A comparison of election coverage in the early 1990s found that the British and Spanish press displayed greater external diversity, while in contrast the American and Japanese press, and broadcast news in most countries, displayed higher internal diversity.[14] A potential danger with internal diversity is a possible bias towards middle-of-the-road coverage, excluding the radical left and right. The multiple and conflicting signals in news coverage may also complicate the process of trying to use the news media as cue-givers in political choices, thus reducing the ability of the news media to mobilize voters.[15]

To what extent the news media meet these standards can be tested by examining the amount and direction of news coverage of major controversies on the policy agenda. For example, in the context of the European Union, Chapter 9 analyzes television and newspaper coverage of the debate about the Economic and Monetary Union (EMU) and the adoption of the single currency (the euro). If the European news media system worked well as a civic forum for those issues, then we would expect to find extensive political coverage of the EMU debate available in the news, and this coverage would provide a platform balancing different political and cultural viewpoints for and against monetary union. On the other hand, the news media can be seen to have failed by this standard if serious political coverage of Europe was driven out by 'infotainment' values, 'soft' news, and 'tabloidization', if news systematically excluded major voices from the public debate, or if only one perspective for or against monetary union was given a platform.

WATCHDOG OF THE POWERFUL

Equally important, a viable democracy requires that there be extensive political rights and civil liberties, to protect the interests of minorities against abuses of power. In their watchdog function, it has long been recognized that the news media should scrutinize those in authority, whether in government institutions, in nonprofit organizations, or in the private sector, to hold officials accountable for their actions.[16] Since the time of Edmund Burke, the 'fourth estate' has traditionally been regarded as one of the classic checks and balances in the division of powers. In this role, investigative reporters seek to expose official corruption, corporate scandals, and government failures. In the more popular notion, the press is seen as a champion of the people, guarding the public interest, taking up grievances, and challenging government authorities.[17]

In political coverage, the watchdog role implies that journalists and broadcasters should not simply report on political speeches, campaign rallies, or photo opportunities 'straight' or unfiltered from politicians to the public without also providing editorial comment, critical analysis, and interpretive evaluations of political messages to help readers and viewers place these events in context. Critical coverage can help to safeguard effective political competition by ensuring that claims, for example, about the government's record or a candidate's qualifications for office, are open to external scrutiny and evaluation. Analyses of party strategy and tactics can also be regarded as part of this watchdog role, for contextual information about the aims of spin-doctors and campaign managers can help citizens to evaluate the reliability and meaning of political messages. The watchdog role can also be seen as vital for the protection of civil liberties and political rights, exposing the actions of governments and major corporations to the light of public scrutiny.

Clearly there is the potential for conflict between the need for the news media to act as a pluralistic civic forum, setting the platform and rules of engagement for others to debate public affairs, and for journalists to function as active watchdogs of the public interest. The conventional distinction between 'factual' reporting on the front pages and 'editorial' commentary in the middle of the paper is one way to make this distinction, although the line between 'reporting' and 'interpretation' often becomes blurred in practice. To see how journalists balance these different functions, we can examine case studies of the coverage of issue debates or election campaigns. The key issue is whether the news media act as independent, fair and impartial critics of powerful interests or whether abuses of public standards go unchecked.

THE NEWS MEDIA AS A MOBILIZING AGENT

We now come to the issue at the heart of this book, which is concerned above all with unraveling the impact of political communications on public engagement. The roles of the news media as civic forum and as watchdog essentially ensure the appropriate conditions for maintaining political competition at the elite level. As defined earlier, public participation through free, fair, and periodic elections is the third Schumpeterian precondition for representative democracy. By this criterion, the news media succeed if they encourage *learning* about politics and public affairs so that citizens can cast informed ballots, if they stimulate grassroots *interest* and discussion, and if they encourage the public to *participate* through the available channels of civic engagement, including voting turnout. For classical liberals, like John Stuart Mill in *Representative Government* and *On Liberty*, one of the major reasons for extending the franchise to the working classes was to encourage civic education, because he believed that citizens could best learn about public affairs through active engagement with the democratic process.

Does the news media system perform according to these expectations? As discussed earlier, media malaise theories blame the news for widespread apathy about public affairs, cynicism about political leaders and institutions, ignorance about the basic facts of politics, and low turnout at the ballot box. Recent decades have seen an erosion of support for the core institutions of representative government in many advanced industrialized societies, and support for parliaments, parties, and political regimes remains low in many new democracies.[18] Many hold the common practices in journalism responsible for this situation, particularly the way that routine news headlines often are dominated by 'negativism', conflict, personalization, and crime and violence, with political coverage characterized by a focus on horse-race polls and insider strategy, rather than political issues.[19] Yet, as will be discussed further in Part III, the evidence that exposure to the news media has deleterious effects on political learning, interest, and participation remains a matter of considerable debate.

In this chapter, as the basic premises for my argument, we begin with three simple assumptions about the ideal conditions for acquisition of political knowledge. The empirical evidence supporting these propositions will be examined in Part III. First, there is much controversy as to whether or not the public learns enough from the news media to cast an informed ballot, because there is no consensus on what counts as 'political knowledge'. We start with the premise that what voters need for effective citizenship, and therefore what the news media should provide, is *practical knowledge about the probable consequences of their political actions*. To cast an informed vote, citizens need to be able to minimize uncertainty and predict the results of their political decisions, such as whether voting for X or Y will maximize their preferences.[20] As discussed later, practical knowledge is only one form of knowledge – it focuses on prediction, not on explanation or analysis such as is characteristic of knowledge in the natural sciences. For example, understanding the principles of the internal-combustion engine, while of intrinsic interest for engineers, provides no practical guidance to a driver wanting to know how to accelerate a car. In the same way, a civics-class understanding of how a bill becomes law, or of all the details of the government's transport policy, or of party manifestos on regional aid, is of little help for citizens who want to know what will happen to the issues they care about if they vote for a particular party of the left, center, or right. We therefore assume a distinction between prediction and explanation: We can explain without necessarily being able to predict, and predict without necessarily being able to explain.

Second, in seeking practical knowledge, we further assume that *the type of information most useful for citizens is contextual to the electoral decisions they face.* The reason is that the information most relevant for voting choices will depend on the kinds of electoral and party systems. There is no single 'gold' standard. In parliamentary general elections contested by programmatic parties, for example, voters need information about political issues, party platforms, and the government's record, which may well prove useful in predicting the consequences of casting a ballot. But in other contexts, different kinds of knowledge may also help citizens predict the consequences of their actions. For example, information from opinion polls about party rankings is useful to guide tactical voting choices. Insights into communication strategies may help voters to evaluate the reliability and meaning of party messages. Analysis of the strengths and weaknesses and the personal background and experience of candidates can prove invaluable in presidential primaries. Therefore, although information about policy issues can provide the basis for practical knowledge, voters may seek many alternative types of information to guide their decision-making, depending upon the context.

Third, we assume that *the news media should provide citizens with political information at a variety of different levels,* ranging from the most technical and thorough details to the most simple accounts. The reason is that citizens come to politics with different backgrounds, interests, and cognitive skills. Some may seek detailed policy briefings and analysis, provided by journals such as *The Economist,* newspapers like the *New York Times,* or radio programs like the BBC World Service *News Hour.* Others may require information in more popular or accessible formats, typified by sources like tabloid newspapers, brief radio news bulletins presented 'on the hour' by music stations, or local television news. The hurdles preceding informed choices are exceptionally high in some contexts, such as examining the pros and cons concerning ballot initiatives about protecting the environment or electoral reform. The information barriers are relatively low in others, as in deciding how to cast a ballot in a parliamentary general election contested by only two major parties. Given the different skills, experiences, and understandings that voters bring to the forum, we assume that news should be available at different levels, rather than one format being ideal for all. The serious image of the gray columns of the *Wall Street Journal* may well suit the political cognoscenti within the beltway or East Coast establishment, but we assume it will thereby exclude many other types of voters. In this regard, the down-market tabloids can be seen as playing a legitimate role in democracy by reaching groups who are uninterested in the up-market broadsheets. Just as democratic elections require competition for office, we assume that there should be pluralistic competition at different levels for various types of information.

Lastly, the role of the news media as mobilizing agent assumes that journalists share some responsibility, along with parties, for stimulating interest in public affairs and encouraging the different dimensions of civic engagement. Citizens have many opportunities for political participation, ranging from following events during the campaign to discussing the options with friends and family, voting in elections and referendums, and engaging in party work like fundraising and canvassing, helping in voluntary organizations, new social movements, or community associations, as well as 'unconventional' activities like direct action. Ever since the early studies by Paul Lazarsfeld and colleagues, traditional theories of the news media have emphasized their mobilizing potential in election campaigns.[21] More recently in the United States, the decline in voter turnout has commonly been blamed on negative campaign coverage in the news media, and Putnam has argued that television is largely responsible for a long-term erosion of social capital in the baby-boom generation.[22] The conception of the news media as a mobilizing agent – generating practical knowledge, political interest, and civic engagement – is therefore widely accepted, although many doubt its capacity to perform up to the ideal.

CONCLUSIONS: EVALUATING PERFORMANCE

There are many approaches to defining appropriate standards that can be employed to evaluate the performances of the news media. Discussions are commonly based on certain middle-range ethical principles understood as given ends in themselves. Debate often revolves around the priority that should be given to different values, such as 'balance', 'freedom of expression', 'objectivity', 'accuracy', 'independence', 'impartiality', and 'diversity' in the news.[23] Blumler, for example, identifies certain general values underlying public-service broadcasting in Western Europe, including program quality, the maintenance of regional, linguistic, and political diversity, the protection of cultural identities, the welfare of children, the independence of program producers, and the integrity of civic communication.[24] Gurevitch and Blumler argue that the news media should perform eight different functions for the political system, including agenda-setting, providing platforms for advocacy, and holding officials to account.[25] Arguably these are all important standards, but it is difficult to rank these values, when they conflict, in the absence of any broader theoretical principles. Moreover, these values are accorded different priorities by those who lean towards the libertarian view and those espousing the social-responsibility view of the news media.[26]

Others have attempted to identify common features in the principles embedded in public-policy regulations, or in the values held by different journalistic cultures, but it has proved difficult to find generally agreed standards in such sources. Within western Europe, communications policies differ significantly in their relative emphasis on broadcasting independence, diversity of access, protection of national languages and cultures, and promotion of the local media.[27] Worldwide, the sharp contrasts between the free market and developmental vision of the role of the media were illustrated by the heated debate that erupted in the mid-1980s over UNESCO's proposed 'New World Information and Communication Order'.[28] American, British, and German journalists place different priorities on core values such as 'objectivity'.[29] Any attempt to specify certain 'universal' yardsticks to evaluate the functions of the news media therefore runs the risk of ethnocentrism – assuming one set of cultural values that may be seen as inappropriate elsewhere. An important reason for the lack of consensus about appropriate standards for the political performances of the news media is that values often are only loosely linked to broader notions embedded in democratic theory.

The premise for the argument advanced here begins with certain general propositions about the nature of representative democracy and the role of the news media in that context, which serve as normative assumptions for the book. We then develop certain specific indices of media performance that we argue flow from these premises. To summarize the argument, in the Schumpeterian tradition we define representative democracy procedurally as a set of institutions that function to allow pluralistic competition for power, public participation through free, fair, and periodic elections, and civil rights and political liberties. If this conception of representative democracy is accepted as a starting point, it is then argued that the following specific indicators can be used to audit the performances of the news media in any political system:

In order to facilitate *pluralistic competition*, we assume that the news media should act as a *civic forum* for debate. As such, to judge its performance we can ask the following:

- Do the news media provide extensive coverage of politics and government, especially during election campaigns?
- Over time, has the total amount of political coverage diminished, for example due to the decline of public-service broadcasting and newspaper sales, or has it increased and diversified across different media outlets?
- Do the news media provide a platform for a wide plurality of parties, groups, and actors?
- Do the news media provide equal or proportional political coverage for different parties?

The most appropriate way to evaluate whether the news media system meets these standards is systematic content analysis of the amount and type of news and current-affairs coverage, comparing media outlets like newspapers and television over time and across different countries.

In order to preserve the conditions for *civil rights and political liberties*, we assume that the news media should act on behalf of the public as a *watchdog* holding government officials accountable. To see how well the news media fulfill this function, we can ask the following:

- To what extent do the news media provide independent, fair, and effective scrutiny of the government and public officials?

The most effective way to explore this issue is with historical case studies describing the role of the news media in classic examples of the abuse of power, public scandal, and government corruption, to see how far journalists have acted fairly and independently in the public interest to hold officials to account.

Lastly, to promote conditions for *public participation*, we assume that the news media system should act as a *mobilizing agent* to encourage political learning, interest, and participation. To evaluate how well the news media function in this regard, we can ask the following:

- How far do the news media succeed in stimulating general interest in public affairs?
- How far do the news media encourage citizens to learn about public affairs and political life?
- How far do the news media facilitate and encourage civic engagement with the political process?

The media malaise thesis casts doubt on the capacity of the news media to function according to these standards. If the public remain stubbornly unaware of the political facts of life and choose to stay home on election day, if civic debate about the major issues of the day degenerates into a dialogue of the deaf, incivility, and personal name-calling, and if abuses of public standards go unchecked, then often the news media are blamed. Before we can start to evaluate the empirical evidence, we need to consider the methodological approaches available to analyze these issues.

CHAPTER 3

Understanding Political Communications

Although there is an abundance of heated rhetoric and conjecture, and everyone who watches television seems to have a view about the issue, it has been surprisingly difficult to find systematic evidence that proves the media malaise hypothesis. There is a broad consensus that the process of political communication has changed, but it remains questionable whether this has had a major impact on the contents of election news, still less influenced public attitudes and behavior. Unfortunately, discussions of the perceived problems of the news media often fail to distinguish between criticisms based on unsystematic observations and those based on more solid ground. Many recent books on the news media, in discussing phenomena such as trends towards 'soft' or 'infotainment' news, have simply assumed that the content of news coverage must influence the public, in a simple 'hypodermic-syringe model', with no prior evidence. But this model has been largely abandoned in communications research as we have come to realize that the public actively react to, deconstruct, and interpret what they watch and read, rather than simply absorbing messages like passive sponges.[1] The attempt to understand the political influence of the news media raises difficult theoretical and methodological challenges. Previous studies exploring whether political coverage in the news media contributes towards civic malaise have generally employed trend analysis, experimental designs, or cross-sectional surveys, and each of those methods has certain advantages and disadvantages.

TREND ANALYSIS: DIFFUSE THEORIES OF MEDIA MALAISE

One approach has been to compare trends in the content of news coverage with trends in public opinion. Popular accounts often assume a causal connection if negative news about government has grown in recent years along with public cynicism about political institutions. Content analysis provides a systematic description of the media land-scape, and monthly polls monitor the pulse of public opinion.[2] The media are then believed to exert a diffuse, long-term, and cumulative influence on the political culture. It is the steady repetition of messages over and over again, not individual exposure, that is thought to entrench mainstream orientations in most viewers. Robinson and Sheehan first suggested the linkage between declining trust in Ameri-can government institutions and the rise of television news.[3] As encap-sulated by Austin Ranney: 'It is hard not to put two facts side by side: one is the fact that the age of television began in the 1950s and reached its presen dominance by the mid-1960s; the other is the fact that the rise in public cynicism has been continuous through the same period. . . . These two facts do not prove that television portrayal of politics explains all the decline in confidence, but it is not unreasonable . . . to conclude that television has made a major contribution to that decline.'[4] Similar studies in Germany, Sweden, and Japan have shown that increased coverage of scandals and negative news has accompanied declining confidence in political leaders.[5]

That approach was exemplified in an influential study in which Thomas Patterson argued that there had been a shift in the culture and values of American television journalism in the post-Vietnam, post-Watergate era that had gradually infected the rest of the news media.[6] For evidence, that study examined the evaluative tone of coverage of American presidential elections in *Time* and *Newsweek* since the 1960s, and it found increasing negativity in election news: The proportion of 'bad news' in news magazines accounted for about one-quarter of cam-paign coverage in 1960. That grew to about 40% in presidential elec-tions from 1964 to 1976, and then rose to about 50–60% in elections from 1980 to 1992. The data followed a pattern of stepped plateaus, rather than a steady linear rise. Although we lack direct evidence mon-itoring the culture of journalism in this period, Patterson argued that Vietnam and Watergate were seminal events that transformed Ameri-can news, as the press turned against politicians.

While intuitively plausible, time-series analysis faces two main chal-lenges before it can be accepted as fully convincing. First, can we assume that there has been a substantial change in the content of news over time, with the growth of 'negative news' or 'infotainment'? The evidence available from the United States is limited, and Patterson's data from those sources may be unrepresentative of the broad range of news media.[7] Dalton, Beck, and Huckfeldt's analysis of campaign coverage in a nationwide sample from the U.S. press in the 1992 elections found that the contents were fairly neutral, with local papers presenting their readers with multiple messages about each party and candidate, or a diverse set of evaluative viewpoints, rather than predominantly negative coverage.[8] Systematic content analysis that could compare long-term trends in typical news coverage across many countries is lacking, and, as discussed in the next chapter, the existing evidence from Britain and Germany challenges the common assumption of growing tabloidization in these countries.[9] The declinism thesis may be falling into the trap of assuming a 'golden age' of journalism that in fact, proves mythical. 'Tabloidization' refers simultaneously, and thereby ambiguously, both to news formats and to subjects. As discussed in detail in the next two chapters, one possible interpretation of developments in recent decades is that perhaps the news may have diversified into both more popular and more serious formats, rather than simply having moved down-market in terms of the types of stories covered.

Even if we accept the presumed changes in the content of news, with the growth of tabloid or negative news in the United States and Europe, as a working assumption, we still face a large inferential leap before we can establish the impact of news coverage on public opinion. The evidence in the macro-level studies is open to many alternative interpretations.

Any parallel trends over time may in fact be independent. There may be no systematic linkage between the type of coverage and the public's response. Studies have found that even when political news on American networks has used a conflict frame, for example in covering the debate between the president and Congress over the issue of gays in the military, the public tended to discount such framing, instead interpreting the story in terms of the underlying events or the merits of particular policy proposals.[10] Even if news proves negative or conflictual, therefore, content analysis may provide a misleading picture of how the public respond and construct their understandings from the messages they see.

Or the association may prove spurious, as the result of other causal factors: An increase in the incidence of government corruption, for example, might logically produce both more negative media coverage and greater public cynicism about politicians. In the cultural account, it is particularly important that the timing of events in Vietnam and Watergate should relate systematically to changes over time in political coverage; otherwise, many factors could be said to have driven trends in the news in recent decades.[11] The increased focus on strategy in American campaign news during the 1970s and 1980s, for example, might plausibly be explained by actual changes in electioneering, such as the rising importance of primaries, the lengthening of the campaign season, the declining salience of many of the hot-button issues of the 1960s and the accompanying generational and cultural conflict, and above all the growth of professional political marketing. Campaign news may have changed to reflect the fact that election strategy has become more important, and substantive policy issues have become less important, in determining election outcomes.

Equally plausibly, the direction of causality might be reversed: If political news seems more cynical, that might be the result rather than the cause of cynicism in the wider political culture. As Robinson and Sheehan note, television journalists are part of a broader set of norms and values in society:[12] 'To some degree the entire process must be circular, with the networks affecting the public and the public affecting the networks in return.' They argue that the media influences the public, because in several instances, such as civil rights, the networks have been ahead of the prevailing view.[13] But this argument fails to explain certain apparent major anomalies, situations in which the news media charged ahead like cavalry, but the poor bloody foot soldiers failed to follow. For example, media malaise theories need to account for how the endless onslaught of 'scandal' coverage in the news frenzy that afflicted the second term of the Clinton presidency failed to damage his long-term public popularity, and indeed probably boosted it. If this prolonged saturation coverage did not erode support for the president, then it seems implausible to expect that more transient 'scandals' would have major impacts on public opinion. As John Zaller suggests, we need to understand the conditionality of media effects, both when coverage of scandal matters for public opinion and when it does not.[14] As Lance Bennett concluded, after a lengthy critique of the time-series data presented by Putnam, a circular process may be at work: 'The well documented political uses and abuses of television are as much a response to, as primary causes of, societal breakdown, individual isolation, and generalized discontent with politics.'[15]

Given these potential problems, the best that can be said about trend analysis is that it generates interesting hypotheses that deserve further examination, but essentially the case remains unproven, more faith than fact.

EXPERIMENTAL STUDIES

Another approach is through experiments that monitor the process of short-term individual-level opinion changes in response to specific media messages. Such experiments take the form of 'if X, then Y', and, in principle, if people are randomly allocated to groups, and the analysis compares differences between groups, the prior backgrounds, attitudes, and values of subjects should not influence the results.[16] The logic of such experiments is disarmingly simple: If some are shown negative news, for example news highlighting political scandals, government waste, or policy failures, while others watch clips featuring positive news, how do both groups react? This method potentially should provide some of the most convincing and rigorous evidence, evidence that might settle the media malaise debate.

Such experiments have long been used to examine the media malaise perspective. In the mid-1970s, Michael Robinson showed 212 subjects a single controversial documentary, *The Selling of the Pentagon*, and he found differences in internal political efficacy after exposure to the program.[17] Cappella and Jamieson conducted perhaps the most thorough experimental work on political cynicism. Their study argues that strategic coverage of policy debates has come to predominate; winning and losing become the central concerns; the language of wars, games, and competition predominates; there is discussion of performers, critics, and voters; there is much emphasis on the performances and styles of candidates; and great weight is given to polls and their latest rankings in evaluating candidates. Of course, there is little that is new in all this; after all, elections are primarily about who wins and forms the government, not simply a civics debate to educate the public. But their study argues that over the years this framing has come to predominate in campaign coverage.[18]

To test for the effects of such developments, Cappella and Jamieson conducted experiments involving 350 subjects in six media markets. One group was exposed to news in the print and broadcast media framed strategically, where winning or losing was the predominant way of characterizing the motivations of the candidates. Another group was shown substantive news about health care framed in terms of issues, where the stories concerned problems facing society and proposed solutions. The study found that those who saw the strategic frame were more likely to have cynical responses, meaning that they saw self-interest as the primary motivation of politicians: 'A story can be framed in terms of the advantages and disadvantages for the candidate's chances of election or in terms of the advantages and disadvantages for the constituency. Mistrust of politicians and their campaigns arises when strategy framing dominates.'[19] The study concluded that American network news was guilty of sensationalizing and oversimplifying complex policy issues like health care, emphasizing the political game over substantive debate, contributing towards a 'spiral of cynicism' among the public.

Such experiments certainly come closer than many other methods to nailing down causal effects in a rigorous manner, but they face the common problem of how far one can generalize from experimental results to the real world. Experiments may involve a large number of participants who are allocated to stimulus and control groups wholly at random. Yet the findings can be strongly influenced by the particular methodology used, including the stimulus messages that are presented, the means used to measure political attitudes like 'cynicism', and other artifactual elements in the design. For example, in the Cappella and Jamieson study, nonstandard measures of political cynicism limited replicability with other research, and the operationalization of these items may also have been subject to problems of circularity.

The problem of excessive coverage of strategy represents one dimension of the media malaise case. Another important aspect concerns the impact of 'negative' news, which can be regarded as critical or damaging from the perspective of one particular actor. In an influential study, Ansolabehere and Iyengar demonstrated that watching negative or 'attack' television advertising discouraged voter turnout and decreased political efficacy in the United States.[20] Yet parallel studies in Britain came to a different conclusion. Experiments on the impact of negative and positive television news, conducted in the 1997 British general election campaign among 1,125 subjects, found that negative news failed to damage, while positive news served to boost, levels of party support.[21] As will be discussed further in the concluding chapter, that pattern proved significant even after the use of a wide range of controls. The contrasting findings from the experimental studies of the effects of negative television news in Britain, and Ansolabehere and Iyengar's study of negative TV ads in the United States, may be attributable to any of three reasons: variations in the specific conditions under which they were conducted (such as their operationalization and measurements of negativity and party support); the repetitive 30-second TV ads and the longer TV news stories may have influenced viewers in different ways; people may have reacted differently in the U.S. and British media, electoral, and political contexts. Experimental studies may be able to provide precise findings that can address the issue of causality in media effects, but it can be difficult to generalize from the necessarily artificial conditions of an experiment to the real world.

SURVEYS: SPECIFIC THEORIES OF MEDIA MALAISE

Perhaps the most common approach has been to look for individual-level evidence from cross-sectional national surveys. Behavioral research has focused on understanding the conditions of media exposure believed to produce certain individual-level effects, including variations in source, content, channel, receiver, and destination. Several studies have compared the attitudes and behaviours of regular users of different types of media, such as newspapers and television news, or viewers of television debates and campaign ads.

This approach was exemplified by Michael Robinson, who used American NES survey data from the sixties to show that those who relied on television news had lower political efficacy, greater social distrust and cynicism, and weaker party loyalties than those who relied on newspapers, radio, and magazines for their political news.[22] Experimental data from 212 subjects were used to confirm the direction of causality. For Robinson, the media malaise story runs as follows: In the 1950s and 1960s television news developed a mass audience, reaching an 'inadvertent audience' who watched the news although they were otherwise inattentive to political information. The inadvertent audience is theorized to be particularly vulnerable to the messages in what they watch and prone to believe in the credibility of the networks. American television journalism is said to have certain characteristics, namely, a tendency to present interpretive, negativist, and anti-institutional news. The result is that viewers, particularly those of the inattentive audience who lack other forms of political information, respond to such content by growing more cynical, frustrated, and despairing about public affairs and more disenchanted with social and political institutions. The main evidence that Robinson presented, in addition to the experimental findings already mentioned, were simple cross-tabulations of the 1968 NES data on internal political efficacy scores, subdivided into those relying solely on TV for information, those relying mainly on TV, and those relying on some other news medium. Robinson concluded that those who relied solely on TV had less confidence that they could have an effect in the political system: 'Those who rely upon television in following politics are more confused and more cynical than those who do not. And those who rely totally upon television are the most confused and cynical of all.'[23]

Robinson theorized that five factors are involved in the explanation of those relationships: the size of the television news audience; public perceptions of the credibility of the networks; the interpretive character of television news; the emphasis on conflict and violence; and the anti-institutional theme in network news. In later work, he suggested that network television news was strongly influenced by the prestige press, notably the *New York Times*, the *Washington Post*, and the *Wall Street Journal*, with greater focus on 'inside-the-beltway' strategic analysis, rather than on the traditional coverage of politics by the regional press and wire services.[24] In the post-Watergate era, after the standard NES indicators of trust in American politicians experienced free-fall, the thesis that television news was responsible for civic malaise seemed plausible to many. Others broadened the critique: An early study by Miller and associates linked the content of newspapers, particularly critical political coverage, with feelings of political disaffection experienced by their readers.[25]

More recently, Robert Putnam analyzed American survey data and reported that the heaviest users of television entertainment were least socially trusting and least willing to join community groups.[26] Putnam related the dramatic transformations in our leisure patterns associated with the rise of TV to broader trends in civic engagement: As television began to saturate American homes in the 1950s, that produced a post-civic generation. This could help to explain the new cohort patterns of political mobilization and why generational cohorts raised in this new cultural environment are less likely than their parents to trust others, to join voluntary associations, and to vote. It has been shown that social participation, such as belonging to clubs, attending church, or working on community projects, can be strongly and consistently predicted by TV use, and such participation is down among those who say that they habitually depend upon television as their primary form of entertainment. In short: 'More television-watching means virtually less of virtually every form of civic participation and social involvement.'[27] The reasons for that pattern are not entirely clear, though Putnam suggests that time spent on television may displace other recreational activities and community involvement outside the home, and watching prime-time entertainment television may also foster passivity.[28] Whatever the reason, television entertainment (which does account for the vast bulk of TV watching) although not TV news, is thereby indicted for the dramatic erosion of civic engagement and social capital in America.

Analysts of cross-sectional surveys face four major challenges in interpreting the available evidence. The most important is that cross-sectional surveys carried out at only one point in time make it difficult to resolve the classic chicken-and-egg direction of causality. Is there a selection bias? Does political interest cause us to turn on *Meet the Press* or *Nightline*? Or is there a media effect? Does watching these programs make us more politically interested? In the same way, does watching television sitcoms and prime-time dramas produce less social trust and less community involvement? Or do people who don't trust others and are not engaged in their community simply prefer, as a matter of personal choice, to stay home and watch TV? We cannot tell from cross-sectional survey data. The uses-and-gratifications approach argues that we choose to watch programs that are most in tune with our prior predispositions and tastes.[29] In this view, our exposure to the new media may tend to reinforce our political views (which is still an important effect) rather than change our political attitudes.

Second, people often generalize about 'newspaper readers', 'television viewers', or even 'Internet users' as though we all had a single experience of these media. In practice, with the modern proliferation of television channels, my TV experience (*Nightline*, C-SPAN, and *ER*) probably is far removed from your TV experience (*Monday Night Football*, MTV, and *Oprah*). Ideally, we need to compare the effects of variance in the media messages so that we can see whether people who consistently use one distinctive source (such as crime-focused local TV news) differ from those who use others (such as right-wing talk radio). Unfortunately, in practice it is often difficult to disentangle news sources through survey research: Our measures of media habits are often diffuse and imprecise. (How many hours per day do I usually watch the news?) Often there is little variation in the content of mainstream sources like television news on different channels, so we cannot easily contrast the effects of watching ABC or NBC. We usually have multiple and overlapping uses of different media. For example, tabloid readers often are also fans of popular TV; broadsheet readers often listen to current-affairs programs; people who watch TV news often are newspaper readers; and so on. One way to monitor media use is to ask the standard question long employed in American polls: Where do you get most of your news – from the newspapers or radio or television or magazines or talking to people, or where? But that question is poorly designed, for it is akin to asking electors what influenced their votes, rather than analyzing this process indirectly. That question seeks a simple trade-off answer, but given our multiple uses, most of us are unable to provide a sensible answer. I get most of my news from Internet newspapers and online TV bulletins, from National Public Radio (NPR) and the BBC World Service, and, depending upon the topic, from occasional programs like *Nightline* and *Meet the Press*. What reply should I give? The alternative is to ask about habitual reliance on a series of different sources, such as how many days per week one usually listens to the radio, or watches the TV evening news, or reads a paper. Such self-reports of media exposure are also unsatisfactory, because they take no account of one's degree of attention, but they provide a more reliable indicator than a simple trade-off question. Our case can be strengthened if we can establish a significant and consistently positive relationship between this weak measure of media use and the indicators of civic engagement.

Moreover, there is no consensus in the literature, for other studies based on survey analysis have challenged the media malaise claims. Earlier studies strongly indicated that heavy use of television was associated with certain indicators of political apathy, as Putnam suggested, both in America and in other postindustrial societies.[30] But that was not a problem of television *news* per se: People who often watched TV news and current-affairs programs were among those most involved in a wide range of civic activities, such as voting, campaigning, and organizational membership.[31] Recently, Stephen Bennett has also challenged the theory of the pernicious effects of American TV news, concluding that media-exposure measures are not significant predictors of trust in government.[32] In series of studies involving several countries it has been found that regular viewers of television news and readers of broadsheet papers have higher-than-average levels of political information, interest, and engagement.[33]

Lastly, individual-level survey analysis is concerned with monitoring the specific influence of media malaise on particular groups of news media users. But that does not address the diffuse version of the media malaise thesis. If the whole country has been affected by similar trends, for example if American journalists are collectively overtaken by

Monica madness, then it becomes almost impossible to disentangle the effects of different media sources on the public. Like the air we breathe, if daily news about political scandals or government failures is all around us, from the *New York Times* to the *New York Post*, from the *Drudge Report* to *Larry King Live*, we cannot tell if the public is cynical because of this endless diet from the media or whether journalists are simply feeding the voracious public appetite for such headline news, or both. Only stringent comparative designs for studies across countries can allow us to explore cross-cultural differences.

COMPARATIVE STUDIES

This leads to the conclusion that the impact of the news media ideally needs to be studied using a triangulated research design within a cross-national setting. As Blumler, McLeod, and Rosengren argue, comparative research can allow us to overcome national and time-bound limitations on the generalizability of our theories, assumptions, and propositions.[34] At present, the bulk of the existing research has been conducted within the United States, and it remains unclear to what extent the patterns found in these studies are evident in other countries.[35] As discussed in Chapter 13, many features of the news environment in the United States may be products of 'American exceptionalism'. Despite the formidable problems facing comparative research, and the serious limitations of data, such a strategy is worthwhile because it can begin to counteract both 'naïve universalism' (assuming everywhere is the same as us) and 'unwitting parochialism' (assuming everywhere is different to us).[36]

COMPARING POSTINDUSTRIAL SOCIETIES

The comparative framework adopted for this book focuses on postindustrial societies, defined as the twenty-nine member states of the Organization for Economic Cooperation and Development. This comparison includes most of the major developed economies and established democracies in the world, including all G7 and European Union (EU) states. The advantage of this design is that it allows us to compare a wide range of advanced industrialized societies and democratic states that are reasonably similar in terms of their levels of economic, social, and political development. This follows the classic logic of the 'most-similar-system' design that assumes that the factors common to relatively homogeneous societies are irrelevant to explaining their differences.[37] The common levels of literacy, education, and affluence in postindustrial societies mean that we can discount these factors in searching for explanations for civic participation. At the same time, there remain significant contrasts in the news environments, in the political systems, and in the dependent variables concerning levels of political knowledge, interest, and civic engagement among citizens in these states. At the broadest level, we are seeking to move from an analysis of nations towards an analysis of types of political communication systems. The analysis of newspaper-centric and 'television-centric' media systems presented in Chapter 4 is one example of this approach.[38]

The basic economic and social indicators for the countries in this comparison are summarized in Table 3.1. The OECD includes more than a billion people in large and small states, ranging from the United States, Japan, Mexico, and Germany at one end of the population spectrum down to Luxembourg and Iceland at the other. Many of the most affluent societies in the world, characterized by a GDP per capita of over $30,000, are members of the OECD, such as Switzerland, Japan, the United States, and the Scandinavian states, although at the lower level of economic development the OECD has countries with GDP per capita below $10,000, including member states in southern, central, and eastern Europe, as well as Mexico.[39] All these post-industrial economies are overwhelmingly based on the service sector, which accounts for two-thirds of civilian employment and roughly the same proportion of contribution to GDP. Just over one-quarter of jobs in the OECD states remain in manufacturing industries, and less than one-tenth are in agriculture. The only countries with more than one-fifth of the work force in agriculture are Greece, Mexico, Poland, and Turkey. The size of the public sector varies substantially between countries, whether measured by government expenditure as a percentage of GDP or by the size of public sector employment. The largest public sectors are found in the countries of Scandinavia and northern Europe, especially in small welfare states with a strong social-democratic tradition, such as Sweden and The Netherlands. In contrast, the levels of public sector spending are far lower in Japan and South Korea. Lastly, the indicators show that OECD societies are among the most literate and best educated in the world, with, on average, over one-fifth of their working-age populations attaining some higher education. Thus comparisons among OECD member states should allow us to detect any significant differences in their news environments, for example between countries with

Table 3.1. *Social and economic indicators, OECD countries, mid-1990s*

Country	Area (square miles)	Pop. (1000's) 1996	GDP per capita 1996 ($)	Service Sector	Size of Public Sector		Educational Indicators	
				Contribution to GDP % Services 1996	General Government Expenditure % of GDP Mid-1990s	Government Employment % of Total Employment 1996	% Pop. with at Least Upper-Secondary Educ (25–64-year-olds) 1996	% Pop. with at Least Higher Educ (25–64-year-olds) 1996
Australia	7687	18,289	21,375	69.5	35.6	16.0	52.8	24.3
Austria	84	8,060	28,384	67.9	48.6	22.8	69.5	7.9
Belgium	31	10,127	25,409	70.2	51.7	19.0	53.5	24.6
Canada	9976	29,964	19,330	72.1	45.8	19.6	75.2	46.9
Czech Rep	79	10,316	5,445	58.4	40.5		83.4	
Denmark	43	5,262	33,230	72.1	59.6	30.7	62.0	20.4
Finland	338	5,125	24,420	64.9	55.9	25.2	65.4	20.5
France	549	58,380	26,323	71.7	51.6	24.9	68.4	18.6
Germany	357	81,877	28,738	68.4	46.6	15.4	83.7	22.6
Greece	132	10,465	11,684	67.9	52.1		42.5	17.4
Hungary	93	10,195						
Iceland	103	270	27,076	68.5	35.1	19.9		
Ireland	70	3,621	19,525	54.7	36.9	13.4	47.2	19.9

Italy	301	57,473	21,127	65.5	49.5	16.1	34.9	
Japan	378	125,864	36,509	60.0	28.5	6.0		
Korea, S.	98	45,545	10,644	50.9	15.7		59.8	
Luxembourg	3	418	40,791	74.9	45.0	12.0	29.3	
Mexico	1973	96,582	3,411	69.5				
Netherlands	41	15,494	25,511	69.8	50.0	11.9	61.2	
NZ	269	3,640	18,093	66.6		22.1	59.1	25.3
Norway	324	4,370	36,020	65.5	45.8	30.8	81.2	28.6
Poland	313	38,618					73.7	13.1
Portugal	92	9,935	10,425	62.9	42.5	15.3	20.1	11.0
Spain	505	39,270	14,894	64.8	41.2	15.7	28.0	16.1
Sweden	450	8,901	28,283	70.5	63.8	31.2	74.7	28.3
Switzerland	41	7,085	41,411	63.5	47.7	14.0	82.2	21.1
Turkey	781	62,695	2,894	52.5			23.0	
UK	245	58,782	19,621	70.8	42.3	14.1	75.9	21.5
US	9373	265,557	27,821	71.9	34.3	13.4	85.8	33.3

Source: OECD.

predominantly commercial or public sector television, or between those with high and low levels of newspaper circulation, controlling for reasonably common levels of social and economic development.

The basic features of the political systems are listed in Table 3.2. The OECD contains most of the world's major established democracies, as well as three newer democracies that have joined the organization more recently: Hungary, Poland, and the Czech Republic. The only exceptions to this generalization are Mexico and Turkey, which can best be classified as semi-democracies. In Mexico, the Partido Revolucionario Institucional (PRI) has held power at the federal level since 1929, although under increasing electoral challenge in recent years, and it has certain authoritarian characteristics. Turkey currently lacks important political rights and civil liberties and has had a mixed and unstable record of democratic development.[40] The Gastil index, provided by Freedom House every year since 1973, has monitored worldwide levels of political rights and civil liberties on two scales, ranging from 1 (most free) to 7 (least free). By the mid-1990s, most of the nations in our comparison fell into the 'free' column, with the exceptions of Mexico and Turkey, which were classified as 'partly free'.

As shown in Table 3.2, the countries compared in this book, though all democracies, feature a wide range of different types of political institutions. The electoral system is one of the most important aspects of any constitution, and the OECD countries range from proportional representation using national or regional party lists, as in The Netherlands and Sweden, through mixed systems, such as those in Germany and Italy, to plurality and majoritarian systems, like the first-past-the-post systems in the United Kingdom and the United States. Their party systems also vary substantially, and these are classified on the effective number of parliamentary parties elected to the lower house (ENPP) in the early and middle 1990s. This allows us to distinguish among predominantly one-party systems (characteristic of Mexico and Japan), two-party or two-and-a-half-party systems (found in Australia and the United States), the moderate multiparty pluralism (with between 2.5 and 4.5 ENPP) common in many European systems, and fragmented multiparty pluralism (with ENPP greater than 4.6).[41] The remaining columns in Table 3.2 indicate the opportunities for electoral participation within each system, including popular contests for the upper house in bicameral legislatures, direct votes for the presidency, and the frequency of national referendums. The comparison of OECD nations also reveals important differences in the news environments

Table 3.2. *Political systems, OECD countries, mid-1990s*

Country	Electoral System for Lower House 1996	Number of Members Lower House 1996	Number of Effective Parliamentary Parties 1991–95	Type of Party System 1991–95	Popular Election for Upper House 1996	Popular Election for President 1996	National Referendums N. 1945–95	Political Rights Index 1997	Civil Liberties Index 1997	Type of Democracy 1997
Australia	AV	148	2.42	Two party	Yes	No	23	1	1	Free
Austria	PR	183	3.40	Moderate pluralism	No	Majority-runoff	1	1	1	Free
Belgium	PR	150	7.95	Fragmented pluralism	Indirect	No	1	1	2	Free
Canada	Plurality	295	2.35	Two party	No	No	1	1	1	Free
Czech Rep	PR	200	4.85	Fragmented pluralism	Yes	No		1	2	Free
Denmark	PR	179	4.70	Fragmented pluralism	Unicameral	No	13	1	1	Free
Finland	PR	200	4.88	Fragmented pluralism	Unicameral	Majority-runoff	1	1	1	Free
France	Majority-runoff	577	2.96	Moderate pluralism	Indirect	Majority-runoff	12	1	2	Free
Germany	Mixed	656	2.78	Moderate pluralism	No	No	0	1	2	Free
Greece	PR	300	2.17	Two party	Unicameral	No	4	1	3	Free
Hungary	Mixed	386	2.89	Moderate pluralism	Unicameral	No	5	1	2	Free
Iceland	PR							1	1	Free
Ireland	STV	166	3.48	Moderate pluralism	Mixed	AV	20	1	1	Free
Italy	Mixed	630	7.45	Fragmented pluralism	Yes	No	29	1	2	Free
Japan	Mixed	500	3.95	Moderate pluralism	Yes	No		1	2	Free
Korea, S.	Plurality	299	2.70	Moderate pluralism	Unicameral	Plurality	6	2	2	Free

Table 3.2. (cont.)

Country	Electoral System for Lower House 1996	Number of Members Lower House 1996	Number of Effective Parliamentary Parties 1991–95	Type of Party System 1991–95	Popular Election for Upper House 1996	Popular Election for President 1996	National Referendums N. 1945–95	Political Rights Index 1997	Civil Liberties Index 1997	Type of Democracy 1997
Luxembourg	PR							1	1	Free
Mexico	Mixed	500	2.28	One party predominant	Yes	Plurality	0	4	3	Partly free
Netherlands	PR	150	5.38	Fragmented pluralism	No	No		1	1	Free
NZ	Mixed	120	2.16	Two party	Unicameral	No	10	1	1	Free
Norway	PR	165	4.15	Moderate pluralism	Unicameral	No	1	1	1	Free
Poland	PR	460	3.85	Moderate pluralism	Yes	Majority-runoff	5	1	2	Free
Portugal	PR	230	2.55	Moderate pluralism	Unicameral	Majority-runoff		1	1	Free
Spain	PR	350	2.67	Moderate pluralism	Yes	No	4	1	2	Free
Sweden	PR	349	3.51	Moderate pluralism	Unicameral	No	3	1	1	Free
Switzerland	PR	200	5.60	Polarized pluralism	Yes	No	275	1	1	Free
Turkey	PR	550	4.40	Moderate pluralism	Unicameral	No	4	4	5	Partly free
UK	Plurality	659	2.26	Two party	No	No	1	1	2	Free
US	Plurality	435	2.00	Two party	Yes	Elec. college/plurality	0	1	1	Free

Sources: Political rights, civil liberties, and type of democracy: *Freedom Review*, 'Index of Freedom', January 1998, 28(1). Electoral system: Lawrence LeDuc, Richard Niemi, and Pippa Norris. 1996. *Comparing Democracies*. London: Sage. Plurality systems, first past the post; AV, alternative vote; PR, party list; mixed, combination of plurality and party list systems. Number of effective parliamentary parties defined as those with at least 3% of seats in the lower house in the most recent election. Type of party system based on ENPP in the latest election available: 0–2.5, two party; 2.6–4.5, moderate pluralism; 4.6+, fragmented pluralism.

within this wide range of advanced postindustrialized economies and democratic states.

CONTENT ANALYSIS OF EU NEWSPAPERS
AND TELEVISION

For aggregate trends, UNESCO is the most authoritative source for official statistics worldwide, such as data on the numbers of television sets and the circulation of newspapers. When we turn to content analysis of the news media, however, we focus on the available data from the fifteen member states of the European Union. The content analysis used in this book is derived from *Monitoring Euromedia*, a monthly report published by the European Commission from January 1995 to September 1997.[42] The company that carried out the research, Report International, used quantitative and qualitative methods to study coverage of the EU in newspapers in all 15 member states, and television in six member states, providing the most comprehensive cross-national content-analysis data set that is currently available. *Monitoring Euromedia* examined the contents of 189 newspapers every month, including all the national papers and the most important regional papers in all member states. The detailed list of sources is provided in the Technical Appendix at the end of the book. The survey included heavyweight broadsheets like *Le Monde*, the *Financial Times*, and the *Frankfurter Allgemeine Zeitung*, as well as large-circulation tabloids like *Der Bild* and the *Sun*. The weekly magazine press was also included, such as the *Economist* and *L'Express*, as well as dailies and Sunday papers. The average monthly report identified some 11,000–12,000 articles selected as containing information on the EU and its policies. The study then selected a random sample of 50% of the articles to be analyzed every month, or some 5,000–6,000 articles. Over the whole thirty-three-month period the study therefore analyzed the contents of just under 200,000 articles.

Each article was coded according to the source, country, date, and type of information contained (facts, opinions, or comment).

Articles were also assigned two or three different 'topic' codes, because most covered more than one subject. These categorized topics such as foreign policy, monetary policy, EU institutions, and enlargement of the EU.

A selection of stories was also coded on whether the topic was evaluated positively or negatively. This can be termed the 'directional' code or tendency, which was scaled from 1 (very negative) through 2 (slightly negative), 3 (neutral), and 4 (slightly positive) to 5 (very positive). When the positive and negative evaluations balanced, stories were given a neutral code. Supervisors checked for inter-coder reliability and consistency of coding practices.

Most research on news balance has concentrated on the extent to which election news has been evenhanded in terms of partisanship or ideology, such as in the amount of coverage of different candidates or issues.[43] But elections are special cases: Practices in broadcasting often are strictly regulated by explicit fair-treatment regulations, as in allocating equal time to all sides in leadership debates and equal airtime for party broadcasts; in contrast, newspaper partisanship often increases during campaigns. While it is particularly important that campaign coverage be balanced, it is difficult to generalize from patterns found in this context to the daily editorial practices in newsrooms. Other comparative research has focused on how a particular dramatic event was reported in different countries, such as a positive or negative frame when reporting the Persian Gulf War or the downing of the Korean airliner over Russia. Only a couple of studies have attempted to compare typical daily news coverage across different countries.[44] This analysis of routine coverage of the EU over a thirty-three-month period provides a unique look at how the concept of directional balance operates in newspapers and television outside of election campaigns. By comparing the amount and balance of EU coverage in different member states over time, we can analyze whether or not the news media have provided an effective civic forum, as discussed in Chapter 2, encouraging public debate about the EU.

The monthly content analysis for television was based on daily news and current-affairs programs in six countries (Belgium, France, Germany, Italy, Spain, and the United Kingdom). The study recorded the main news programs in each of those countries, with details as given in the Technical Appendix, analyzing 500–600 programs per month. During the course of the thirty-three-month period the study therefore analyzed some 16,000–20,000 programs in total. *Monitoring Euromedia* included the main news bulletins in each country, such as the *6 O'Clock News* and *9 O'Clock News* on BBC1 and *Newsnight* on BBC2 in Britain, the 6:30 A.M., 8:00 P.M., and midnight *Telegiornale* on RAI1 in Italy, and the *Desayunos de RN* and *Telediario* on TVE in Spain. The study examined the extent to which news stories in these programs contained information on the European Union and its policies, and

54

around 300 EU-related stories were coded every month, following the same process used for newspaper articles. *Monitoring Euromedia* also compared coverage of EU special events (notably the Turin Inter-Governmental Conference, IGC, and the Florence and Dublin councils) in all member states by 73 public and commercial television stations. These sources therefore allow us to compare the topics and directions of coverage of the EU by a wide range of newspaper and television outlets for each month. We can monitor how news coverage changed during these years in response to political developments, such as the 1996 Turin IGC, the process of moving towards Economic and Monetary Union, and events like the British beef crisis caused by 'mad-cow' disease. Using this data set, we can examine the amount and tone of the news about the EU, making comparisons between countries and over time. If coverage of EU policies and institutions became more negative in some member states than in others, for example with the European ban on British beef generating splash Euroskeptic headlines in the British tabloids, while generating more popular support for the EU in the French press, we can assess whether or not that led to changes in public opinion about the EU that differed across member states.

Inevitably, having to rely on secondary data limits our ability to examine certain important questions raised by theories of media malaise. Most importantly, we lack any direct evidence whether or not there has been a long-term change in the news culture since the 1970s, as some suggest, for example whether there has been an increase in negativity, or more frequent disdainful commentary by reporters, or a shift from a substantive to a strategic frame in news stories. Nor can we use this data set to examine many of the subtle nuances of news coverage of the EU, such as the extent to which the media present national political leaders, EU officials, and members of the European Parliament (MEPs) speaking at length, in context, rather than having journalists provide their interpretations of events, or the extent to which national frames, as one would expect, dominate stories about Europe. Such features of news stories may well play key roles in shaping the content of news coverage about Europe.

What we can do in this study, however, is examine certain long-term effects. If we assume that this typical content of news has changed over time and that this has contributed to public disenchantment with the political process, as media malaise theories hypothesize, then we should see changes in public opinion as monitored by the long-term series of surveys we examine. This study analyzes the American public using the

NES series from 1948 to 1998, and European public opinion using the Eurobarometer series from 1970 to 1999. Media malaise theories suggest two alternative hypotheses that we shall discuss in detail and test in subsequent chapters. One possibility is that if changes in news coverage have increasingly turned off all the public or a major segment of the public, then that should be evident in a shrinkage in the size of the news audience. In that scenario, many people disgusted with negative journalism would be expected to turn to other channels or to cease buying newspapers. Another possibility is that people may have continued to watch TV news and read newspapers, perhaps because of habitual leisure patterns, but over time those who have paid the most attention to the news have become increasingly cynical and disenchanted with government institutions and political leaders. If we assume that news did become more negative in the United States in the 1960s and early 1970s, as many assert, and that this fuelled public disenchantment with politics, then we should see a changed relationship between attention to the American news media and a range of indicators of civic malaise.

A second potential problem is that coverage of European affairs, involving distant, complex, and low-salience issues, may differ in certain important respects from news about domestic politics. The latter may well provide more coverage of the drama, personalities, and salient issues more relevant and immediate to the lives of citizens. This is true, but in principle it can be argued that these conditions should maximize the potential impact of the news media's coverage. For domestic politics, the public has multiple sources of information. For example, people can evaluate the economic performance of the government on the basis of their own pocketbooks, the economic conditions of their friends, colleagues, and neighbours, and news reports of the trade gap, the rate of inflation, and the growth of jobs. Given all these sources, people may choose to discount some of the information provided by the news media. In contrast, in regard to European affairs, though some EU policies may have direct and visible impacts, most are conducted at such an abstract and technical level that citizens have to rely almost wholly on the news media for their information, along with cues from opinion-leaders and personal discussions. In this regard, coverage of the EU can be regarded as comparable to how public opinion is shaped towards other foreign-policy issues, such as conflict in Kosovo, trade with China, or the Gulf War. Plausibly, if we find few systematic effects on public opinion from coverage of the EU, then we might expect to find even weaker effects from news coverage of domestic politics.

Lastly, the content analysis provides no direct evidence regarding coverage in the 'new' news, meaning television magazines, live discussion programs, and talk radio, let alone the flourishing sources of news on the Internet. This is a valid criticism, up to a point. The content analysis we use draws heavily on the mainstream evening news programs on television. But it does also include leading current-affairs magazines like the BBC's Sunday *Breakfast with Frost* and BBC2's *Newsnight*, as well as German ARD's *Europa-magazin* and *Presseclub* and France 2's Sunday *Revue de Presse*. These can be seen as roughly equivalent to American television magazine programs like *Meet the Press*, *Nightline, 20/20*, and *Dateline*. If the 'new' news has infected traditional standards of mainstream journalism, as some suggest, then this should be picked up by our analysis. In addition, it remains unclear whether there is a distinct 'new' news sector in Europe. In Britain, for example, one of the oldest BBC radio programs, *Any Questions*, now forty years old, and the direct descendant of television's *Question Time*, has always involved live discussion of public questions and debate between political leaders. News magazines, in different formats, have been popular since the 1960s. Certainly there are some equivalents to the American 'new' news in Europe, such as the Spanish *tertulias*, twenty-four-hour radio talk channels, and Internet magazines, but their audience currently remains limited. The content analysis of television and newspapers used in this study, while less than ideal in terms of long-term time-series data, and while limited to the 15 European OECD countries, therefore does provide a suitable basis for a comparative study of typical news coverage of European affairs across the EU.

PUBLIC OPINION

Content analysis, no matter how comprehensive, remains silent about the effects of coverage. To understand the impact of attention to the news media on the public, we draw on two decades of Eurobarometer surveys ranging from the first European Community Study in 1970 to the most recently available survey in March–April 1999. Surveys were conducted two to five times per year, with about 1,000 face-to-face interviews in each member state, with reports published on a biannual basis for the European Commission. These studies have been supplemented since January 1996 by Europinion surveys (European continuous-tracking surveys) that have sought to monitor public opinion about key issues and institutions via telephone interviews each week, with results released on a monthly basis. These rich data sets allow us to monitor whether people who are most attentive to newspapers, television and the Internet differ in any significant ways in their political attitudes, opinions, and behaviours towards the European Union, in terms of its institutions and its policies in the fifteen member states. When there are key events – such as the Maastricht agreement, the introduction of the euro, and the resignation of the Santer European Commission – these sources allow us to compare coverage in the news media with public opinion. Because EU policies often involve fairly complex and technical issues with which ordinary people have had no direct experience, this provides a strong test of the learning effects of the news media. It is difficult for European citizens to know much about these issues except via the news media, so if journalism fails in its informational role, then that may have important implications for European Union governance, raising widespread concern about a 'democratic deficit'. Within this context we can explore the role of the news media system as a mobilizing agent and the effects of media use on political knowledge, interest, and activism in different European member states.

One potential criticism of using European data is the 'American exceptionalism' argument. Much of the media malaise literature originated in the United States, and many of the claims about changes in news journalism may relate to specific historical and cultural factors peculiar to America. As we shall see, the news environment in the United States is more television-centric (and with far more commercially oriented TV) than those in most European countries. The predominant liberal political culture in America may also be more mistrustful of government than is the more social-democratic tradition in the smaller European welfare states. To test whether or not patterns found in European public opinion were also evident in the United States, we drew on half a century of data from the American National Election Studies (NES) from 1948 to 1998. Obviously there are some important differences between the NES and the Eurobarometer, including the specific questions that monitor media use and civic engagement, as well as the electoral context of the NES. Nevertheless, by matching functionally equivalent, if not identical, measures, we can examine the impact of attention to the American news media on similar indicators of political knowledge, trust, and participation. As mentioned earlier, the NES also has the advantage of allowing us to monitor trends from 1952, before the television age became established, until 1998, representing the early years of the Internet age.

The next chapter goes on to use official statistics from UNESCO and other international bodies to examine some of the most important structural trends in the news environment in postindustrial societies since the end of World War II,[45] including the following: *press diversity*, such as the number of national daily newspapers being published, changes in circulation and sales figures, and concentration of ownership; *television diversity*, including the structure of competition between public-service and commercial channels, regulation of broadcasting, and the availability and penetration of cable, satellite, and other new communications technologies; and *Internet usage*, a development that has proceeded far faster in some countries than in others. Given an understanding of those matters, we can then start to consider what impact these differences might have on the content of the news and its potential effects on the public.

PART II

Trends in Political Communications

CHAPTER 4

The Decline of Newspapers?

There is widespread concern that newspapers face an uncertain future, and many fear a long-term decline due to the rise of the electronic media, economic pressure from a loss of advertising share and increasing costs of production and distribution, and falling sales. Changes in the newspaper industry are believed to have led to concentration of ownership, erosion of news standards, and narrowing of the readership. To address these concerns, this chapter focuses on four interrelated issues: In the postwar era, have the electronic media gradually replaced newspapers, as some fear, so that the press is heading towards the technological graveyard, rather like hand-cranked phonographs, vinyl long-playing records, and post-office telegraphs? Second, have sagging sales in the print sector fuelled down-market pressures towards tabloid sensationalism in the pursuit of readers and a decline of traditional journalistic standards? Third, has greater concentration of newspaper ownership led to fewer choices and less diversity for consumers? And lastly, does the press continue to reach all sectors of society, or is readership increasingly concentrated among the more affluent, well-educated, and older population?

The belief that newspapers are in decline has triggered major alarm-bells, because, as argued earlier, it is assumed that the news media can best fulfill their functions in a democracy if there is a rich and pluralistic information environment that is easily available to all citizens. There is a large body of American literature suggesting that if TV has taken over from the press as our main source of news, that may be limiting our capacity to learn about public affairs; newspapers are believed to be far more effective than television for conveying the detailed information necessary to understand complex and detailed policy issues, such as the background to the conflict in Kosovo, proposals about Social

Security reform, and negotiations over the 'general agreement on trade and tariffs' (GATT).[1] Robinson's original videomalaise thesis blamed the increasing reliance on television, not newspapers, for the deterioration of trust and confidence in government.[2] There is also widespread concern that if newspapers fail to reach large sections of the community, particularly younger and less well educated readers, that may reinforce a growing gap between the information-rich and information-poor. Ben Bagdikian, for example, argues that commercial pressure from advertisers for short-term profits has meant that, despite the loss of readers, American newspapers have not seriously tried to address the needs of one-third to one-half of the population, especially low-income and ethnic minority groups.[3] Lastly, if ownership of newspapers is concentrated in the hands of a few multinational corporations that remain unaccountable to the public, and if citizens face a more restricted range of different sources of news, that may limit the conditions for pluralistic civic debate.[4]

Yet many of the popular fears about the inexorable decline of the print press are misplaced or exaggerated, and the cross-national picture is far more complex than media malaise accounts commonly suggest. The United States has a particularly television-centric media system, and thus it is an outlier from the pattern for OECD countries. In many other societies, particularly the smaller European welfare states, newspapers retain a far stronger role. Rather than declining, the press is reaching a wider readership than in previous decades.

FALLING NEWSPAPER SALES?

Concern about traditional standards of journalism has been fuelled by major changes in the newspaper industry during the postwar era. In the United States, the daily press has experienced dwindling readership and sales, especially among the younger generations, a loss of advertising market share to the electronic media, and growing concentration of ownership in larger multiple-newspaper chains or a few multimedia conglomerates.[5] Those developments have had a major impact on the profitability and economic viability of the print sector, particularly for smaller outlets. Similar trends have been noted throughout Europe,[6] and UNESCO suggests that most postindustrial societies have seen declining newspaper sales.[7] The conventional explanation for this phenomenon is the rise of alternative news sources, whether radio in the 1920s, television in the 1950s, or the Internet in the 1990s, all of which are believed to have been gradually displacing the traditional role of the print press.

Although the demise of newspapers has been predicted for decades, we should not underestimate their continuing popularity and their technological adaptation to new forms of production and distribution. If we compare postwar trends in circulation, controlling for population growth, the evidence shows that sales of the daily press in most postindustrial societies has not been affected by the increasing availability of electronic media. The long-term trend in per capita newspaper sales in OECD countries has remained fairly stable (Figure 4.1). Average circulation over all OECD states was 271 per 1,000 in 1950, and that rose modestly in 1980 before subsiding slightly to 263 per 1,000 in 1996. Despite the massive surge in the availability of television during the last fifty years, also shown in Figure 4.1, about one-quarter of the population continues to buy daily newspapers and readership figures are even higher. The electronic media have therefore increased the choice and diversity of news outlets and formats, but at the same time they have not killed sales of the printed press. Because of the increasing educational levels and the affluence characteristic of postindustrial societies, consumption of news has not proved a zero-sum game.

The newspaper market varies greatly by country due to such factors as long-standing historical and cultural traditions in each region; levels of social development in terms of education, literacy, and income; the news industry's organization, economics, production and distribution system; and the overall structure of public subsidies, government regulations, and national levels of democratization.

Circulation figures per 1,000 population in the mid-1990s in OECD countries (Figure 4.2) show that newspapers were most popular in Scandinavia and Japan, countries that also had the sharpest surge in sales since the 1950s. Despite intensive penetration by television, Japan has the largest-circulation papers in the world, usually sold by household subscription, including the big three: *Yomiuri Shimbun* (with regular sales of 12.4 million copies per day), *Asahi Shimbun* (12.6 million), and *Mainichi Shimbun* (6 million). The country has over 120 newspapers, ranging from local through regional to national, with average daily circulation reaching 580 per 1,000 persons. Competition for readers is fierce, in part because of substantial dependence on sales for income, but nevertheless there is little variation in their content and format, in the social backgrounds of their readers, or in the political leanings of the newspapers, because of their heterogeneous national

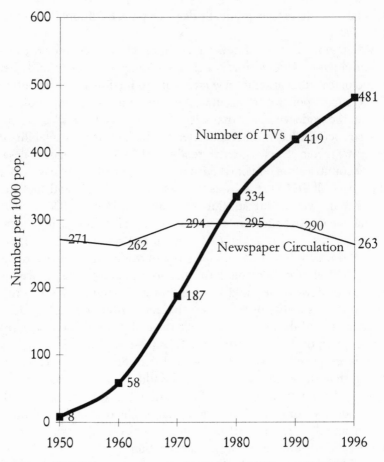

Figure 4.1. Trends in newspapers and television, 1950s to mid-1990s.
Source: UNESCO.

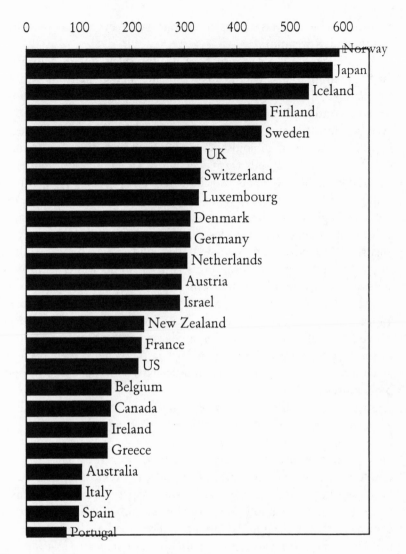

Figure 4.2. Newspaper circulation by nation, 1996.

audience. The Japanese press is characterized by factual reporting, avoiding interpretation.[8]

Scandinavian countries also have healthy sales, but in contrast to Japan, their markets include many smaller newspapers. In Norway, for example, there are approximately 100 daily papers, mostly regional or local, and with subscription services most households take on average almost two newspapers every day.[9] The largest Norwegian papers are national tabloids based in Oslo, including *VG (Verdens Gang)*, *Aftenposten*, and *Dagbladet*, all with circulation figures of 200,000–400,000. Sweden is also characterized by high newspaper readership, again with a predominantly regional and local press. One reason for such high sales relates to pricing, because many Swedish papers enjoy direct public subsidies, designed to maintain consumer choice by ensuring that more than one newspaper will serve each local community.[10] Indirect support to the press is given in all western European states, most commonly in the form of preferential rates for the value added tax (VAT), lower postal rates, or tax breaks for investment, and a number of states have also subsidized the price of newsprint. These forms of financial aid often are largely indiscriminate, although in states such as Italy, France, and Austria the benefits have been targeted towards supporting the economically weaker papers to preserve press pluralism.[11]

Societies with moderate circulation figures include many of the western European countries, like the United Kingdom, Germany, and Austria. In Britain, the eleven national weekday papers, and their Sunday counterparts, dominate the market. Since the 1890s, with the development of the mass-circulation 'penny' press, the industry has been split between broadsheet or 'quality' papers, providing extensive coverage of national and international news, public affairs, and serious commentary, and the popular tabloids.[12] The broadsheet papers include the *Times*, the *Independent*, the *Guardian*, the *Financial Times*, and the *Daily Telegraph*, with combined sales of about six million copies. The tabloid sector includes most notably the *Sun*, with sales of about 3.5 million per day and about 10 million readers, along with the *Daily Mirror* on the left and the more middle-brow *Daily Mail* on the right. Although there has been a decline in the number of provincial evening papers and local weeklies, some remain strong, notably the London *Evening Standard*. There is also a distinctive market in Scotland, led by the *Scotsman* and *Glasgow Herald* and Scottish editions of the national papers. Although there is a segmented national market, with different papers appealing to slightly different readerships defined by partisan-ship, class, age, and gender, competition in both sectors has been fierce. With many readers comparing papers headline to headline across the eleven national papers in newsagents and newsstands, a popular front-page splash, such as an investigative special, can trigger a sudden surge in sales.

The German press has experienced considerable postwar growth in sales but also marked constriction in terms of the number of news-paper titles and concentration in terms of the number of independent owners.[13] The number of local papers in Germany appears substantial, but in fact most of them are only side editions of regional papers based in large towns, with little editorial independence. In the mid-1990s, about 40% of Germans lived in towns or cities dominated by a single local paper. The German papers with the largest national distribution include the tabloid right-wing populist *Bild,* with a circulation of 5 million per day, the highly prestigious independent weekly paper *Die Zeit* (circulation 500,000), the conservative *Frankfurter Allgemeine Zeitung* (400,000), the left-liberal *Suddeutsche Zeitung* (300,000), and *Die Welt* (200,000). Germany also has a flourishing and diverse weekly magazine and periodical sector, notably *Der Spiegel* (cir-culation one million), the more flashy *Focus,* and the general-interest *Stern.*

In contrast, North America has relatively weak newspaper sales. The federal structure and physical size for both Canada and the United States have hindered the development of a national press widely dis-tributed coast-to-coast. The United States has many provincial and regional daily papers (1,520 in 1996), although the pool has shrunk substantially in recent decades, so that today little local competition remains, with 98% of all American cities having only one daily news-paper.[14] There has been increasing concentration of ownership, whether due to multiple ownership of different newspapers, cross-media own-ership of newspapers along with television or radio stations, or con-glomerates owning newspapers along with other types of businesses. By the mid-1990s, 80% of America's daily papers were controlled by regional or national chains such as Thomson Newspapers, Gannett, or Knight-Ridder.[15] The only American papers with legitimate claims to a national readership are the *Wall Street Journal* (1.8 million), *USA Today* (1.7 million), the *New York Times* (1.1 million), the *Los Angeles Times* (1.1 million), and the *Washington Post* (0.8 million), although others like the *Chicago Tribune,* the *Boston Globe,* and the *Miami Herald* dominate their regional media markets.[16] Only the weekly news magazines have large national readerships, including *Time* (4.3 million), *Newsweek* (3.2 million), and *U.S. News and World Report* (2.2 million). Over 1950–98, average readership of weekday papers plummeted from 78% to 59% of the adult population.[17]

Lastly, southern Europe also typically has low newspaper readership. Many factors may have contributed towards this pattern, including the levels of education and literacy in these societies, the slower transition to democracy in Spain, Portugal, and Greece, problems of effective distribution and transportation networks outside of the major cities, and low subscription sales.[18] Greece, for example, has 16 national dailies printed in Athens, along with four national financial and five national sports newspapers. But in that country of ten million citizens, the combined sales for all dailies in the mid-1990s was just over half a million, and circulation has been declining during the past decade. The press traditionally is highly partisan, favouring PASOK or the New Democratic party, and the government has strong links with newspapers through forty million ECU of annual subsidies.[19] Southern Mediterranean countries have also lacked a popular tabloid sector; in Italy, for example, the attempt to launch *Telegiornale* in 1995, a paper modeled after the *Sun* and *Der Bild*, failed within weeks. The contrasts in news habits between EU regions are striking; according to the 1996 Eurobarometer survey, about a quarter of all citizens in southern Europe read a paper every day, compared with half of all those in western Europe, and two-thirds of those in northern Europe.

GROWING TABLOIDIZATION?

Where countries have experienced declining newspaper circulation, what have been the consequences? One of the greatest concerns lies in the potential threat to traditional standards of journalism. Many fear that fierce competition for readers and profits in the news industry has fuelled a down-market slide towards the popular tabloid market.[20] If the bottom line has come to dominate the decisions of newsroom executives, and profitability is the only criterion of corporate success, that may erode older standards of news journalism. 'Tabloidization' is a murky and often confused phrase bandied about for anything people disapprove of in the news media,[21] but it has at least three distinct meanings.

The term 'tabloid' can refer most simply to the production *format* for the newspaper, designed to be physically smaller and more manageable than broadsheet papers.

The second meaning, more relevant to this study, concerns the *style* of journalism, referring to an emphasis on simple and concrete language, light, bright, and vivid writing, shorter stories, and extensive use of photographs and graphics. Front-page colorful images are accompanied by dramatic splash headlines, with stories conveyed in a vivid and direct style. The length and language of news stories, and the use of photographs, can be used to gauge this sense of tabloidization. But it is not obvious why we should be concerned about a tabloid style per se, for as any good politician knows, the use of pithy language, personal anecdotes, and effective humour can leaven the dry stuff of politics and make it more accessible to a popular audience. Short and tight journalism, even for complex stories, often can be preferable to lengthy, prolix writing. And since at least the time of Victorian lithographs of the Crimean War, editors have realized, to use the cliché, that a single picture is worth a thousand words.

The last meaning, which has aroused the greatest concern, refers to the distinctive *subject* of news stories, where the mass-circulation tabloid press is characterized above all by a focus on scandals involving minor celebrities, entertainment stories, sexual shenanigans, crimes, sports, and lurid 'victim' or disaster stories as their staple fare, accompanied by giveaway games. 'Exclusives' about the lives of the semi-rich and semi-famous are endemic.[22] The more populist press incorporates 'soft' porn into its daily mix. This pattern of coverage is not confined only to newspapers, as many commentators have noticed similar tendencies in 'tabloid television', especially the local news and talk shows in America.[23] The concern about tabloidization can be concentrated either on a distinct sector of the news media, or as a general approach to news stories infecting all the mainstream news media. Typically, such trends are measured by comparing the number of news stories about international affairs, government, and politics and the number of stories dealing with human-interest topics and entertainment. It is widely assumed that the inclusion of tabloid stories may thereby produce a downgrading of 'traditional' news about current affairs, policy issues, the arts, and foreign affairs, pushing these out of prime time or out of the headlines and thereby impoverishing public life.

Yet whether we should be concerned about the effects of growing tabloidization of subject matter, as some suggest, remains an open question. After all, there is nothing new in this phenomenon: The staple fare of the 'penny press' *New York Sun* (1833) and *New York Herald* (1835) was violent crime and human-interest stories.[24] One of the most notorious Sunday scandal sheets in Britain, the *News of the World*, was established in 1843. Tabloids also have strong roots in the 'yellow press' that expanded rapidly in the 1890s. In Britain, that included the creation of popular mass-circulation national newspapers such as the *People* (1881), *Daily Mail* (1896), *Daily Express* (1900), and *Daily Mirror* (1903).[25] The equivalent papers in the United States were James Gordon Bennett's New York *Herald*, Joseph Pulitzer's New York *World*, and William Randolph Hearst's New York *Morning Journal* (1895).[26] Fun and lighthearted human-interest stories, along with bloody crimes and sexual intrigues, have always been staple fare in the tabloids. Much of the current attack on the tabloid press echoes long-standing debates over the encroachment of popular culture into high culture and taps deep-rooted ideological divisions between 'giving the public what it wants' and the desire to educate, reform, and improve.[27] Rather than an inexorable drive down-market, developments in the tabloid sector can best be understood as cyclical phenomena driven by periods of intense competition.

Although the tabloid sector thrives today in some countries, notably *Der Bild* in Germany, the *Sun* and *Daily Mirror* in the United Kingdom, and the *New York Post* in the United States, tabloids are not widely established in every country, especially not in their more graphic manifestations. In Germany the influence of the *Bild* is declining, and the quality political newspapers and magazines have been able to increase their circulation in recent years.[28] With a few exceptions, the mainstream daily press in the United States, Italy, France, and The Netherlands continues to lack distinct major tabloid sectors.

In the mainstream media in many countries, the jury is still out on whether there are systematic trends that may have changed the traditional subject of news, with increasing focus on crime, sex, and entertainment, as is assumed by some critics. What seems equally plausible across OECD countries is an expansion of both lowbrow and highbrow news media in recent decades, representing a diversification of the market. A recent review of the comparative literature by Kees Brants concluded that the few available content-analysis studies provide an ambiguous and sometimes contradictory picture of the growth of 'infotainment' news in different countries, rather than showing a uniform pattern: 'Where for the European countries as a whole we might see a slight tendency towards the popularization of news, there is little evidence that politicians and politics are dramatically [more] personalized and sensationalized than before.'[29] Brants found that the available content analysis shows a mixed picture of the growth of 'infotainment' news in different European countries, rather than a uniform trend. Frank Esser concluded that there were marked contrasts among Germany, Britain, and the United States in the popularity of tabloid news and that the nature and degree of competition in a particular media market were the decisive factors explaining the degree of tabloidization.[30] Moreover, systematic research on long-term trends in British newspapers from 1952 to 1997 found that the amount of political coverage in the tabloid sector had not declined over time, as many critics assume. Instead, the tabloid press in Britain has expanded its coverage of entertainment, but also has maintained its coverage of political news during the past half-century.[31] In this sense, European daily newspapers are far removed from the 'Men from Mars Kidnap Liz Taylor' weekly exposé at the supermarket checkout counter in the United States.

If the issue of expanding tabloidization is one for which we lack systematic longitudinal research in most countries, we know even less about the effects of tabloid news on the public. The focus on political and social scandals may produce greater cynicism among readers; but on the other hand the characteristic style of tabloids may make politics more understandable and accessible for a less well informed or less well educated readership. Political coverage in the tabloid press is believed to exert an important influence on its readers.[32] If the choice is between reading tabloids that contain some political fare, combined with news about pop stars, violent crime, and football results, or not reading any newspaper, then arguably the former is preferable.

GROWING CONCENTRATION OF NEWSPAPER OWNERSHIP?

Therefore, across all postindustrial societies, newspaper circulations have remained largely stable during the postwar era, but at the same time the range of papers published in OECD states has contracted. The number of daily newspapers published in OECD nations fell, on average, by 15% during the postwar era, from 160 per country in 1960 to 130 in 1996, producing greater concentrations of readership for the fewer outlets. Many countries have introduced measures to maintain press diversity, on the assumption that we need diverse outlets for an effective civic forum. Antitrust regulations have attempted to ensure competition in the ownership of the press, such as by limiting the proportion of cross-media ownership by a single company, administered by fair-trade bodies like the British Monopolies and Merger Commission or the German Federal Cartel Office. As mentioned earlier, other societies, such as Sweden and Norway, have used press subsidies as a policy instrument to protect the financial viability of the more vulnerable sectors of the press.[33] Countries with provincial and localized newspaper markets like the United States and Germany have proved particularly prone to media mergers and acquisitions, reducing pluralism and competition in many cities (Figure 4.3). Papers in smaller countries like Austria and Belgium often have experienced takeovers or closure because of limited domestic markets and imports from neighbouring states with a shared language.

Concentration of ownership in the hands of a few multinational corporations with multimedia empires has become increasingly common, notably Rupert Murdoch's News International and the vast holdings of Bertelsmann in Germany and Fininvest in Italy.[34] Rupert Murdoch, who started with two small Australian newspapers, built an empire in News Corp. that includes 20th Century Fox films, the Fox TV network, a number of U.S. television stations, 50% ownership of Sky TV, a majority interest in the STAR Asian satellite, ownership of the *Sun* and the *Times* in Britain, additional television stations in Latin America, and the book publisher HarperCollins, as well as investments in Internet companies. In the United States, Time Warner's purchase of Turner Broadcasting Systems (including CNN) in 1996 created the largest media firm in the world, with strong print, cable, and programming divisions. The Walt Disney Company's acquisition of Capital Cities/ABC for $19 billion in 1995 created the second largest media conglomerate, with movie, TV, cable, and Internet interests, although the purchase proved costly, because ABC's balance sheet moved sharply into the red four years after the acquisition. Conrad Black's acquisition of Southam in Canada in 1996 gave his company, Hollinger Inc., control of two-thirds of the newspapers in that country. Many commentators like Ben Bagdikian fear that media mergers have concentrated excessive control in the hands of a few multinational corporations that remain unaccountable to the public and that only greater economic competition can

change that situation.[35] Study of that problem has led to the understanding that economic controls can constrain the media just as significantly as can political controls. There is nothing new about such
concern, which often was expressed during the interwar era of the press
barons, when proprietors like Beaverbrook and Rothermere actively
intervened to further their political ambitions.

Yet other commentators like Robert Picard remain more sanguine
about recent developments, arguing that we need to distinguish
between concentration defined by the number of media outlets held
by a dominant firm and concentration defined by dominance in a geo-
graphical market.[36] It is the latter – which can harm consumers by producing fewer choices, poorer services, and higher prices – that is
important for the availability of alternative sources of political information in a democracy. A monopoly in a local market for ideas can be
harmful for pluralism. Nevertheless, it must be recognized that we need
to look beyond any single media sector to evaluate any harmful political effects of concentration, because consumers use and have access to
multiple sources of news and information, from newspapers to radio,
television and the Internet. Moreover, the trends towards greater concentration are not universal, as some OECD countries have seen a significant expansion in the circulation and range of daily newspapers
being published in the postwar era, particularly states like Mexico and
Greece, where educational and literacy rates have been rising sharply,
and more modest growth is evident in newer democracies like Hungary,
the Czech Republic, and South Korea (Figures 4.3 and 4.4).

Many are concerned that greater concentration of ownership may
inhibit freedom of the press, for with greater power owners and advertisers might be emboldened to intervene to constrain reporters.[37] Yet a
comparison by Freedom House suggests that press freedom remains
fairly robust in most OECD nations. Freedom of the press is measured
by Freedom House according to the degree to which journalists remain
independent, free from government restriction, political influence, economic influence, and actual incidents of violation of press autonomy.
The 1997 survey compared 187 nations worldwide and estimated that
two-thirds of them had a free or partly free press, while one-third
remained not free.[38] In total, 24 of the 29 postindustrial societies being
compared in this book were given high rankings for press freedom in
1997 (Table 4.1). The exceptions were France, Greece, Hungary, and the
United Kingdom, which were classified by Freedom House as 'partly
free', while Mexico and Turkey were categorized as 'not free' because of

Table 4.1. *Newspaper indicators, OECD countries, mid-1990s*

Country	Number of National Daily Newspapers 1950	Number of National Daily Newspapers 1996	Number of National Daily Newspapers Change 1950–1996	Newspaper Circulation per 1000 People 1950	Newspaper Circulation per 1000 People 1996	Newspaper Circulation per 1000 People, Change 1950–1996	Press Freedom Ranking 1997	Press Freedom Classification 1997
Australia	54	65	11	416	105	−311	90	Free
Austria	35	17	−18	200	294	94	88	Free
Belgium	39	30	−9	384	160	−224	88	Free
Canada	95	107	12	246	159	−87	88	Free
Czech Rep	13	21	8	137	256	119	82	Free
Denmark	127	37	−90	366	311	−55	95	Free
Finland	64	56	−8	269	455	186	90	Free
France	151	117	−34	239	218	−21	77	Partly free
Germany	598	375	−223	242	311	69	90	Free
Greece	68	156	88	71	153	82	75	Partly free
Hungary	21	40	19	128	189	61	72	Partly free
Iceland	5	5	0	439	535	96	88	Free
Ireland	8	6	−2	237	153	−84	82	Free
Italy	107	78	−29	.	104	.	80	Free
Japan	186	122	−64	374	580	206	78	Partly free
Korea, S.	45	60	15	50	394	344	72	Partly free
Luxembourg	5	5	0	436	327	−109	92	Free

Country								Status
Mexico	131	295	164	.	97	.	45	Not free
Netherlands	108	38	−70	249	305	56	87	Free
NZ	43	23	−20	358	223	−135	93	Free
Norway	96	83	−13	396	593	197	93	Free
Poland	22	55	33	.	113	.	80	Free
Portugal	32	27	−5	64	75	11	87	Free
Spain	104	87	−17	67	99	32	87	Free
Sweden	145	94	−51	445	446	1	93	Free
Switzerland	127	88	−39	300	330	30	92	Free
Turkey	.	57	−59	31	111	80	38	Not free
UK	114	99	−15	573	332	−241	77	Partly free
US	1786	1520	−266	342	212	−130	85	Free
G7	433	345	−88	336	273	−34	82	Free
EU-15	114	81	−32	274	250	−24	85	Free
OECD Total	153	130	−23	271	263	−8	82	Free

Notes: Press freedom was scaled by Freedom House on the basis of press freedom vis-à-vis laws and practices, political influence over media content, economic influence over media content, and actual violations of press freedom. The Freedom House score out of 60 was converted into a percentage, where 0 = lowest and 100 = highest press freedom. The press-freedom scale was then categorized where low through 59 = not free, 60 through 79 = partly free, and 80+ = free. See text for details.

Sources: Number of daily newspapers: *UNESCO Statistical Yearbook*. Paris: UNESCO (annual volumes). Circulation of daily newspapers: *UNESCO Statistical Yearbook*. Paris: UNESCO (annual volumes). Press freedom: Derived from Leonard R. Sussman (ed.). 1997. *Press Freedom 1997*. Freedom House (www.freedomhouse.org/Press/Press97).

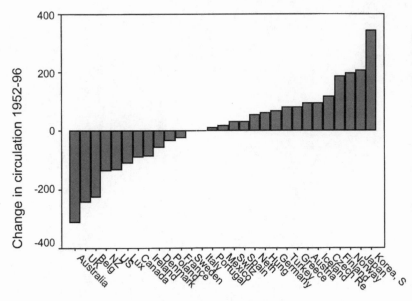

Figure 4.3. Changes in newspaper circulation, 1952–96.

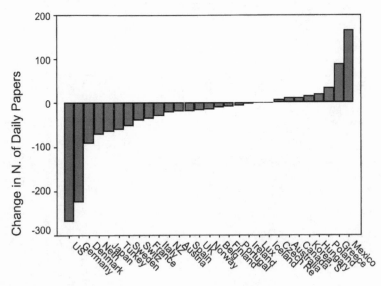

Figure 4.4. Changes in the numbers of daily newspapers, 1952–96.

serious restrictions on free speech and government pressures on jour-nalists. Thus, we can conclude that in most OECD states the structure of the newspaper industry has experienced greater concentration of ownership and a reduction in the range of independent local and regional outlets, but nevertheless during the postwar era the overall sales figures have remained fairly stable, and most OECD countries maintain a relatively high level of press freedom.

CONCENTRATION OF NEWSPAPER READERSHIP?

As discussed earlier, considerable concern has been expressed that falling sales in the United States may have led to a greater *concentration of readership* among the more highly educated and more affluent sec-tions of society, with particularly marked hemorrhage of readers among the younger generations. If that pattern were to be found across postin-dustrial societies, that might produce a long-term generational slide in newspaper use and also reinforce the gap between the information-rich, who are most likely to participate in politics, and the information-poor, who tend to tune out. It also may be the case that poorer sections of communities are being inadequately served because of the need to target affluent consumers to attract advertising revenue.

We can examine the typical demographic profile of newspaper readers using the 1999 Eurobarometer survey for the fifteen EU member states and the 1998 NES for the United States. Newspaper readership was measured using the five-item scale 'About how often do you read the news in daily papers? Every day, several times a week, once or twice a week, less often, or never?' 'Regular' readers were defined as those who each read a paper every day.[39] It should be noted that this subjectively reported indicator of media use in the Eurobarometer correlated strongly at the national level with the independent official record of per-capita newspaper sales ($R = 0.86$, significance, $p = 0.01$), thus increas-ing confidence in the reliability of the survey measure. The comparison shows that overall, almost half of all Europeans said that they read a daily paper every day, in contrast to only a third of Americans. As expected, readership proved to be strongly associated with regional cul-tures: Compared with southern Europe, there were about twice as many readers in western Europe, and almost three times as many readers in northern Europe. Confirming our earlier observations, the lowest daily readership proved to be in Portugal (17%), while the highest was in Sweden (75%). In comparison, use of television news tended to be far

Table 4.2. *Regular sources of news, Europe and the United States, 1999*

Country	Regular Newspaper (% 'read every day')	Regular TV News (% watch 'every day')	Regular Radio News (% listen 'every day')	Online Users (% with access)
Austria	54	63	67	11
Belgium	30	66	42	11
Denmark	56	76	65	44
Finland	69	82	49	39
France	26	58	37	9
Germany	63	68	56	8
Greece	17	80	19	7
Ireland	44	66	64	14
Italy	29	82	23	14
Luxembourg	53	71	60	22
Netherlands	61	76	56	32
Portugal	16	62	27	5
Spain	27	70	32	8
Sweden	58	63	47	61
UK	49	71	45	22
US	34	53	29	49
Northern Europe	60	71	57	48
Western Europe	48	70	52	17
Southern Europe	22	74	25	9
EU-15	*45*	*71*	*47*	*20*

Notes: Eurobarometer measures: see source note for NES equivalent. Regular newspaper: reads the news in daily papers 'every day'. Regular television news: watches the news on television 'every day'. Regular radio news: listens to the news on the radio 'every day'. Northern Europe: Denmark, Finland, and Sweden. Western Europe: Austria, Belgium, Germany, France, Ireland, Luxembourg, The Netherlands, and the UK. Southern Europe: Italy, Greece, Portugal, and Spain.
Sources: Eurobarometer 51.0, spring 1999; American NES, 1998.

more uniform across postindustrial societies; the lowest viewing rates were found in France and the United States,[40] where just a bare majority watched TV news, and the highest audiences were in Italy and Finland (Table 4.2).

The regression models used to predict how often people read newspapers were based on a range of demographic factors, including education, gender, age, left–right self-placement, urban residency, harmonized income scale, and socioeconomic status.[41] Nationality was also included, to see if that factor remained significant after controlling at the individual level for social background. The pattern for 1999 shows that all the demographic indicators proved to be significant predictors of newspaper use, in the expected direction: Readership was higher among men and among the better-educated, older middle class and the more affluent sectors of society (Table 4.3). Readership was also higher among those who regularly tuned into television and radio news. The fact that nationality continued to prove significant even after social controls were introduced, showing lower-than-average use in the Mediterranean countries, suggests that cultural and historical legacies continue to influence the news market in each country, even after controlling for differences in socioeconomic development.

To see if the social biases in readership had strengthened over time, as some fear, the models were run again for 1970, 1980, and 1999 for France, Germany, Belgium, The Netherlands, and Italy, where we had comparable time-series data. In fact, the results in Table 4.4 show the contrary pattern: Compared with 1970, readership of newspapers in the late 1990s was less strongly predicted by education, gender, and ideology, although the influences of age, class, and income remained stable. The decline of the gender gap in readership has been dramatic in the past twenty-five years, probably reflecting changing lifestyles and the way that newspapers have been more successful at widening their market to reach more women. Readership of newspapers has always been strongly associated with other media habits, such as regular use of television and radio news. Compared with the European average, the national differences have slightly increased over time, confirming the pattern we have already noted at the aggregate level. The overall lesson from this analysis is that social background continues to be an important predictor of who does and who does not regularly read the press, but educational and gender differences have diminished gradually over time.

Overall, the size of the audience for news has substantially expanded in Europe. If we analyze attention to the news media in our EU-5, for which we have comparable figures, the results in Table 4.5 show that since the 1970s, use of newspapers and television news has risen sharply. The proportion of Europeans who each have read a paper 'every day' has almost doubled during the past three decades, to almost half the population. Over the same period, the proportion of those who have watched TV news every day has risen from half to almost three-quarters of all citizens. These figures may even provide an underestimate of the picture across Europe, because the numbers of regular viewers and readers in all 15 EU member states were even higher. The only medium for which regular use has been stable is radio news.

Table 4.3. *Models predicting readership of newspapers, 1999, EU-15*

	Predictors of Newspaper Readership 1999	Sig.	Operationalization
DEMOGRAPHICS			
Education	0.08	**	Age finished full-time education
Gender: Male	0.10	**	Male (1) Female (0)
Age	0.11	**	In years
Left-Right Ideology	−0.01		10-point scale: From left (1) to right (10)
Socioeconomic Status	0.07	**	Manual (0) or Nonmanual (1) HoH
Household Income	0.11	**	Harmonized income scale
USE OF OTHER MEDIA			
TV News Use	0.18	**	5-point scale
Radio News Use	0.15	**	5-point scale
Online User	0.01		No (0)/Yes (1)
NATION			
Austria	0.02		
Belgium	−0.12	**	
Denmark	−0.04	**	
Finland	0.03	*	
France	−0.14	**	
Germany	0.03		
Greece	−0.20	**	
Ireland	−0.03	**	
Italy	−0.09	**	
Netherlands	−0.01		
Portugal	−0.22	**	
Spain	−0.12	**	
Sweden	0.02		
UK	−0.05	*	
Constant	0.65		
R^2	*0.30*		
N.	16179		

Notes: The table reports the standardized beta coefficients predicting frequency of reading newspapers based on ordinary least-squares regression models. The dependent variables are the 5-point scales measuring frequency of use of newspaper and television news, where 5 = 'everyday use' and 1 = 'never use'. HoH = head of household. Significance: **$P > 0.01$; *$P > 0.05$. The Luxembourg dummy variable is excluded as a national predictor in the models.

Source: Eurobarometer 51.0, spring 1999.

Table 4.4. *Models predicting readership of newspapers in 1970, 1980, and 1999, EU-5*

	Predictors of Newspaper Readership 1970	Sig.	Predictors of Newspaper Readership 1980	Sig.	Predictors of Newspaper Readership 1999	Sig.	Operationalization
DEMOGRAPHICS							
Education	0.16	**	0.16	**	0.04	*	Age finished full-time education
Gender: Male	0.25	**	0.15	**	0.08	**	Male (1) Female (0)
Age	0.16	**	0.13	**	0.15	**	In years
Left-Right Ideology	−0.04	**	−0.04	**	0.01		Scale: From left (1) to right (10)
Socioeconomic Status	0.08	**	0.04	**	0.08	**	Manual (0) or Nonmanual (1) HoH
Household Income	0.09	**	0.10	**	0.12	**	Harmonized income scale
Urbanization	0.02		0.10	**	0.01		Rural (1), Small town (2), Large Town/City (3)
USE OF OTHER NEWS MEDIA							
TV News Use	0.11	**	0.19	**	0.18	**	5-point scale
Radio News Use	0.15	**	0.12	**	0.16	**	5-point scale
NATION							
Belgium	−0.17	**	−0.07	**	−0.21	**	
France	−0.12	**	−0.25	**	−0.23	**	
Italy	−0.14	**	−0.27	**	−0.16	**	
Netherlands	−0.01	**	−0.01	**	−0.05	*	
Constant	0.56		0.63		0.74		
R^2	0.22		0.24		0.25		
N.	8567		6521		6218		

Notes: The table reports the standardized beta coefficients predicting frequency of reading newspapers based on ordinary least-squares regression models. The dependent variables are the 5-point scales measuring frequency of use of newspaper and television news, where 5 = 'everyday use' and 1 = 'never use.' HoH = head of household. Significance: $**P > 0.01$; $*P > 0.05$. The German dummy variable is excluded as a predictor in these models.

Sources: European Community Study, 1970; Eurobarometer 13.0, April 1980, weighted for EU-6; Eurobarometer 50.1, March–April 1999, weighted for EU-6.

Table 4.5. *Expansion in the size of the news audience, EU-5, 1970–96*

	Read Newspaper (%)		Watch TV News (%)		Listen to Radio News (%)	
	1970	1999	1970	1999	1970	1999
Every Day	27	45	49	72	44	46
Several Times a Week	14	17	20	18	16	18
One or Two Days a Week	13	13	11	6	10	8
Less Often	17	14	8	3	13	14
Never	29	12	12	2	18	13
Change in 'Everyday' Use	+18		+23		+2	

Notes: For consistent comparisons over time, media use is compared only in Belgium, France, Italy, The Netherlands, and Germany. Media use in all the EU-15 member states in 1999 was about 5–8 percentage points higher than these figures.
Sources: Eurobarometers, 1970, 1999.

COMPARING NEWS ENVIRONMENTS

How can we compare and conceptualize these systematic differences in news environments? Following the work of Siebert, Peterson, and Schramm in the mid-1950s, distinctions have conventionally been drawn among four ideal models of the mass media: the libertarian, social responsibility, authoritarian and Soviet communist ideal types.[42] This typology is based largely on regulations governing broadcasting and the press, ranging from a free market to a symbiotic relationship. Others have adapted and modified this framework. For example McQuail also identified developmental and 'democratic-participant' models,[43] and Hachten added the concepts of revolutionary and developmental and categorized 'Western' news media as a single group.[44]

Yet these attempts to classify macro-level government–media relations seem increasingly outdated and inadequate in the post–Cold War era. In central and eastern Europe the traditional Soviet model has been transformed, and authoritarian control of television by the state is found in far fewer nations today.[45] Positing a single model of the media to cover 'developing' countries as diverse as Singapore, India, and Nigeria seems equally inadequate. Postindustrial societies have moved towards 'mixed' systems, blending elements of public-service television with increasing numbers of commercial channels. The older black-and-white Cold War models do not capture these more subtle distinctions.[46]

Yet major structural differences in national news environments, such as patterns of newspaper sales and ownership, which can be expected to influence the roles and content of the news media in each country, continue to differentiate nations.

To understand these differences more systematically, postindustrial societies can be classified into different groups based on their use of traditional media. Newspaper consumption (measured by the percentage circulation figures in each country) can be compared with the use of television (measured by average hours spent watching all types of television, mostly TV entertainment). In the 1990s, the OECD countries clustered into four distinct types (Figure 4.5).

Newspaper-centric societies are characterized by extensive reading of the press and relatively little attention to TV entertainment. This category includes all the Scandinavian nations and many smaller European welfare states like Switzerland, Austria, and The Netherlands, as well as the Czech Republic and South Korea. Although the rate of newspaper reading is significantly higher in the more affluent and educated societies,[47] the countries that cluster in this group cannot be explained simply in terms of levels of socioeconomic development, access to television sets, common language skills, or even a simple Scandinavian regional culture.

Television-centric societies, in contrast, feature intensive use of TV entertainment and low newspaper circulation. This group includes the United States, Mexico, and the Mediterranean cluster of Greece, Spain, Italy, and Turkey, as well as Poland and Hungary. Some western European states like Germany and France are located roughly in the middle of the spectrum, along with Canada and Australia. Again, there are few characteristics in common in the nations that cluster within the TV-centric category, which cannot be explained as the result of a common regional or cultural background or low levels of socioeconomic development.

There are also some societies that do not fit this pattern, like Portugal, which is low on both indicators. Japan is also a distinct outlier, with by far the highest combined use of newspapers and television, and the United Kingdom is slightly higher than average on both scales.

Yet a slightly different pattern becomes evident if we analyze cross-national differences in Europe and the United States regarding use of television news, rather than all types of television watching. Figure 4.6 compares the proportion watching television news every day with the proportion reading newspapers every day (based on Table 4.2). The

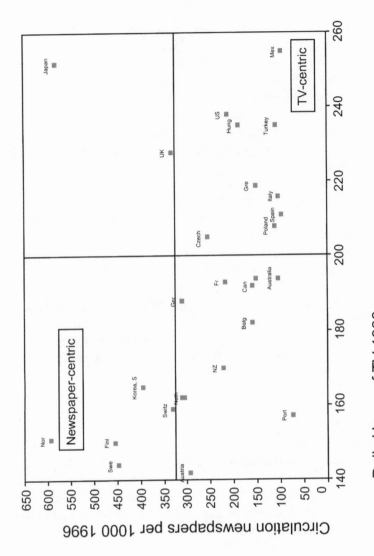

Figure 4.5. Typology of media use.

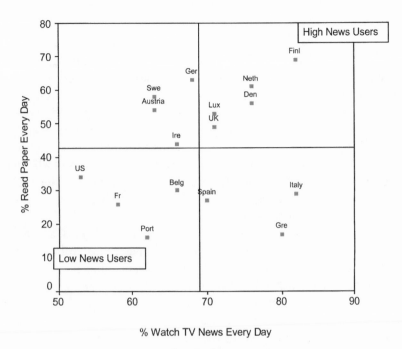

Figure 4.6. News use, EU-15 and United States, 1999.

highest news users are the Scandinavian countries such as Finland and Denmark, the smaller European welfare states like The Netherlands and Luxembourg, and the UK. Countries where the public is least attentive to the news are the United States, France, Portugal, and Belgium. The United States therefore watches a great deal of TV, but not news and current affairs per se.

The overall pattern demonstrates that there remain major differences in the use of different types of media, despite an apparent convergence of technological developments in recent decades. The United States has the highest number of television sets per capita, and the highest average viewing time (almost 4 hours per day, or one-quarter of all the waking hours), but compared with Europe the United States proves relatively low in news consumption. In contrast, in Scandinavia the newspapers continue to play a more important role, and although Scandinavians typically watch few hours of TV, they are among the most regular users of TV news. Later chapters go on to explore the consequences of these structural differences for civic engagement and public opinion.

CONCLUSIONS: DIVERSIFICATION OF THE NEWS MEDIA

This chapter has explored four interrelated trends that are assumed to have produced a decline in the newspaper industry in recent decades: whether there has been a widespread slump in newspaper circulations and sales; whether declining revenues have fuelled down-market pressures towards tabloid sensationalism in the pursuit of readers and a decline of traditional journalistic standards; whether greater concentration of media ownership, has reduced consumer choice; and whether there has been greater concentration of readership among the more educated and affluent sections of society, with a particularly marked hemorrhage of readers among the younger generation.

We can conclude that despite similar social, technological, and economic trends that have affected the newspaper industry in postindustrial societies, there continue to be significant differences in news environments; anyone moving from Portugal to Sweden, or from the United States to Germany, would experience very different types of newspaper markets. Cultural and historical legacies have left distinct imprints on each country. What are the implications of these structural differences for the process of political communication in a democracy? Many assume that in the postwar era technological and economic developments have altered the main sources of news about government and public affairs. In particular, commentators have suggested that there has been widespread erosion in readership of newspapers and periodicals across advanced industrial societies. The use of news has been envisaged as a zero-sum game, so that given their limited time and energy, people began to turn from newspapers to radio in the 1920s, then to television news in the 1950s, before starting to surf for Internet news in the mid-1990s. It has been contended that use of newspapers has declined and that the public is no longer exposed to detailed, analytical stories that are common in the printed press, such as those about international affairs and the global economy. Television news is believed to have 'dumbed down' traditional standards of journalism because of its emphasis on dramatic images over dry analysis, on the simple and timely over the complex and long-term, and on 'infotainment' over civic affairs and parliamentary debate.

Yet on the basis of the evidence in this chapter we can conclude that postindustrial societies have experienced a more complex pattern of development, or the emergence of what can be termed 'postmodern communications', in which the news media are characterized by diversification of outlets and levels. In most societies the electronic media have supplemented existing sources of news, not undermined the market for newspapers. The United States has proved to be something of an outlier among postindustrial societies and is far more television-centric than any of the other countries in this comparison. In contrast, many smaller northern and western European states continue to have flourishing newspaper markets and to rely far less on television. To understand why that is the case, and to explore its consequences, we shall go on to examine developments in the electronic media in recent decades, beginning with the rise of broadcasting in the 1950s and the subsequent challenge of the Internet in the 1990s (in Chapters 5 and 6), and the ways in which parties have responded to these developments (in Chapters 7 and 8).

CHAPTER 5

The Rise (and Fall?) of the Television Age

Just as there are serious concerns about the future of newspapers, many believe that in recent decades the traditional standards for television news and public-affairs coverage have come under threat from technological and economic developments. The critical factors transforming broadcasting include the following: proliferation of channels on broadcast, cable, satellite, digital, and now broadband services, fragmenting the mass audience; the crises of identity and funding facing public-service television, which once enjoyed a monopoly throughout most of Europe, following the rise of myriad commercial competitors; the more recent technological convergence with the digitization and compression of images, sounds, and data that has produced a new multimedia environment, breaking down the traditional boundaries between telecommunications, the audiovisual industries, and computers.

These trends have affected the OECD countries to different degrees, with their impact and timing strongly mediated by the existing communications landscape. In the Thatcherite 1980s, deregulation and privatization had profound influences on public-service broadcasters throughout western Europe.[1] Following the fall of the Berlin wall, the transition to democracy in the early 1990s produced an even more radical jolt to public television in central and eastern Europe.[2] Meanwhile, in the United States, the traditional domination of the three major networks experienced an equivalent coup d'état, cut down in the 1980s by myriad competitors on cable and satellite.[3] Despite the long-standing contrasts between the commercially dominant major networks in the United States and public television in Europe, in recent years they have faced strikingly similar multiplications of outlets and fragmentation of television audiences, raising new concerns about the standards of programming.

As a result of the new multichannel television environment there is apprehension that both the amount and the quality of news coverage of public affairs have been diminishing, so that many countries are experiencing the rise of what has been termed 'tabloid TV', 'soft news', or 'infotainment', emphasizing human-interest stories and gaudy sensationalism rather than government affairs and public policy. The rise of the Internet since the mid-1990s and cross-media convergence as traditional newspapers and television have become easily available via the Web have added another layer of complexity to this process. The previously separate telecommunications, computer, and audiovisual technologies, with different modes of distribution and regulatory environments, are rapidly converging and thereby transforming the nature of the news media.[4]

To evaluate whether or not these developments should raise concern, this chapter focuses on three issues with important implications for the role of the electronic media in representative democracies: First, given that most television systems have moved towards a 'mixed model', combining elements of commercial and public-service broadcasting, do major structural differences continue to differentiate broadcasting systems in OECD countries today? Second, has there been a widespread decline in public-service broadcasting of news and current affairs, as some fear, following greater competition from commercial channels? Third, given the fragmentation of channels and programs that have become available in recent decades, does television news continue to reach a mass audience or only certain sectors of society, such as the more highly educated and the politically interested? Based on this analysis, the following chapter goes on to consider whether use of the Internet seems set to supplement or to replace older forms of TV broadcasting.

STRUCTURAL DIFFERENCES IN BROADCASTING SYSTEMS

Given the patterns of transatlantic convergence in recent years, do structural differences continue to distinguish the TV systems in the United States and Europe? From the 1920s until the early 1980s, a public-service monopoly characterized all broadcasting systems in Europe, with the significant exceptions of the British duopoly system (with the heavily regulated but commercial ITV established in 1955) and Luxembourg (established from the start as a commercial service).[5] In 1980, western Europe had thirty-six public and only three commercial broadcast channels (Table 5.1). Public television also predominated

Table 5.1. *Numbers of national terrestrial television channels, Europe and the United States, 1980–97*

Country	Public Channels 1980	Commercial Channels 1980	Public Channels 1997	Commercial Channels 1997
Austria	2	0	2	0
Belgium	4	0	4	4
Denmark	1	0	3	2
Finland	2	0	2	2
France	3	0	3	3
Germany	3	0	5	9
Greece	2	0	3	5
Ireland	2	0	2	0
Italy	3	0	3	6
Luxembourg	0	4	0	4
Netherlands	2	0	3	6
Norway	1	0	2	3
Portugal	2	0	2	2
Spain	2	0	3	3
Sweden	2	0	2	3
Switzerland	3	0	4	0
UK	2	1	2	3
US	1	3	1	4
Total Number	37	8	46	59
Total Percentage	82%	18%	44%	56%

Source: Denis McQuail and Karen Siune. 1998. *Media Policy: Convergence, Concentration and Commerce.* London: Sage (table 3.1).

in Japan (NHK), Canada (CBC), and Australia (ABC). Public regulation of broadcasting originated with licensing of radio stations, introduced to avoid chaotic overcrowding of the analog airwaves, given the technical scarcity of frequencies. Initially conceived as a state monopoly, like the provision of railroads, telephones, and electricity, television was seen as part of the package of public goods the state should provide. In Europe, financial regulation of radio, and then television, usually fell under the influence of traditional postal, telegraph, and telephony authorities. At least until the early 1980s the traditional characteristics of public-service television included six main features:[6]

- an emphasis on *universal access*, making the same services freely available to everyone,
- *comprehensive coverage*, catering to all tastes and interests, including everything from drama and news to sports and education,

- *pluralistic diversity*, including programming for linguistic, ethnic, cultural, and political minorities,
- *cultural vocation*, catering to the national community with local arts,
- *noncommercialism*, meaning universality of payment, often through license fees,
- *independence*, meaning freedom from government interference, although the degrees varied among systems.[7]

Three primary types of regulatory authorities existed. Some public broadcasting organizations are governed by independent *public corporations*, or quangos, like the British Broadcasting Corporation. The Corporation for Public Broadcasting in the United States also fits this model, as a nonprofit agency that distributes a modest government subsidy to help fund PBS and National Public Radio, along with private and corporate donors.

In *corporatist* systems, an independent body, representing the major social and political sectors in civil society, regulates public broadcasting, as in Germany, Sweden, and The Netherlands. For example, German public broadcasting corporations are governed by independent broadcasting councils at Länder level whose members are selected from groups such as political parties, business and labour organizations, churches, farmers, sports bodies, women's groups, and so on. Parties have a strong influence, and television executives and sometimes journalists are selected along proportional party lines.[8]

Lastly, in *state-dependent* systems, public broadcasting organizations were initially tied fairly closely to the government, as in Greece, Italy, and France, although throughout Europe public broadcasters have become increasingly autonomous over the years. In France, for example, Radiodiffusion–Television de France (RTF) was established as a state monopoly in 1945 and was closely supervised by the government via the Ministry of Information. The medium was freed from direct government influence only after reforms that started with the events of May 1968, although controversy about the role of the appropriate regulatory body for French public broadcasting has continued until recent years.[9] In Greece, the electronic media have served as propaganda tools during non-democratic periods. More recent attempts to separate the public media from direct government control have proved problematic, although the growth of independent private channels in the 1990s has created more overall political balance on Greek television.[10]

As late as the 1970s there remained a captive television audience in Europe; viewers in most countries had only one or two public channels. Deregulation of the television industry and expansion of commercial channels, eroding the public-service monopoly, occurred fairly rapidly during the 1980s in western Europe, followed by central and eastern Europe in the 1990s.[11] If we compare only terrestrial channels (excluding satellite and cable) in the 17 European countries listed in Table 5.1 from 1980 to 1997, the number of public channels rose from 36 to 46 (a significant expansion). But during the same period the number of commercial channels surged from 3 to 59, to become the dominant type. By 1997 the only European countries left with pure public-service television on terrestrial channels were Austria, Ireland, and Switzerland, largely because of initial financial difficulties in establishing viable commercial stations, rather than public-policy restrictions.

Cable and satellite stations have expanded rapidly. The market share for subscription television (such as cable and satellite services, and direct-pay TV) has increased at double the rate of that for television paid for by a universal license fee or advertising.[12] As shown in Table 5.2, by 1997 half of all households in OECD countries had cable or satellite TV, although the proportion varied substantially, from the most intensively cabled smaller urbanized countries like The Netherlands and Belgium, with over 90% penetration, down to a quarter or less of all households in southern European nations. The predominance of public-service monopolies has been broken in nearly every country, and the major challenge facing public-service television today is to find its function and role in a multichannel environment after losing its traditional hold over a captive audience. There is widespread concern that public broadcasters face a crisis of identity, finance, and organization, and that this could have particularly serious consequences for the informational role of television in democracy.[13]

Yet Table 5.2 shows that despite the deluge of commercial alternatives, the public channels have remained popular; on average, across all OECD states, public channels maintain a 42% share of the television audience. This varies substantially, however, by country. Public television RAI1 and TVE1 remain market leaders in Italy and Spain, while NRK in Norway and SVT in Sweden have had most of the best-rated shows in their countries. In contrast, public TV has a far smaller share in some other societies, such as PBS (3%) in the United States and NHK (18%) in Japan.[14] Today OECD states can be classified into three major types: those that remain predominantly *public* systems (based on an audience share for

Table 5.2. *Television indicators, OECD countries, mid-1990s*

Country	TV Sets per 1000 1960	TV Sets per 1000 1996	Viewing Times per Person (min.) 1998	Audience Shares of Public Channels 1997	Dominant Type	Audience Share of the Leading Channel % 1997	% TV Households with Cable or Satellite 1997	Year Regular TV Broadcasts Began	Broadcasting Freedom Index 1997	Broadcasting Freedom Classification 1997
Australia	109	554	194					1956	93	Free
Austria	27	518	142	61.5	Public	ORF2 37.1	75	1956	92	Free
Belgium	68	463	182	25.9	Private		92	1959	95	Free
Canada		714	192					1952	93	Free
Czech Rep	58	534	205	34.3	Private	Nova 53.5	32		87	Free
Denmark	119	592	162	67.0	Public	ETV 39.7	69	1954	90	Free
Finland	21	605	150	47.0	Mixed	MTV3 42.0	46	1956	85	Free
France	41	591	193	45.3	Mixed	TF1 34.4	20		80	Free
Germany	83	564	188	41.1	Mixed	RTL 16.1	84	1952	92	Free
Greece		238	219	8.2	Private	ANT1 22.9	0		80	Free
Hungary	10	438	235	62.8	Public	MTV1 45.5	58		77	Partly free
Iceland	17	354		43.0	Mixed	Sj 43.0	30		92	Free
Ireland		411	194	53.0	Mixed	RTE1 37.0	43	1961	87	Free
Italy	43	524	216	48.9	Mixed	RAI1 23.0	5	1954	75	Partly free
Japan	73	684	252	26.0	Private	NHK 26.0	26	1953	88	Free
Korea, S.	0	337	165						87	Free
Luxembourg	23	387				RTL	88		92	Free
Mexico	19		255			RTL 58.3			68	Partly free

Table 5.2 (cont.)

Country	TV Sets per 1000 1960	TV Sets per 1000 1996	Viewing Times per Person (min.) 1998	Audience Shares of Public Channels 1997	Dominant Type	Audience Share of the Leading Channel % 1997	% TV Households with Cable or Satellite 1997	Year Regular TV Broadcasts Began	Broadcasting Freedom Index 1997	Broadcasting Freedom Classification 1997
Netherlands		514	162	36.0	Private	RTL4 21.3	99	1953	90	Free
NZ	1	521	170						97	Free
Norway	13	460	151	43.2	Mixed	NRK1 40.8	57	1957	98	Free
Poland	14	337	208	53.7	Mixed	Polsat 31.0	48		75	Partly free
Portugal	5	336	157	39.7	Private	SIC 48.1	23		85	Free
Spain	8	406	211	51.9	Mixed	TVE1 25.8	10	1956	82	Free
Sweden	156	499	144	48.6	Mixed	SVT2 27.8	64	1956	92	Free
Switzerland	24	443	159	31.9	Private	SF1/TSR1 27.0	91	1958	93	Free
Turkey	0	333	235	3.0	Private	Kanal D 19.0	11	1972	53	Not free
UK	211	516	228	42.8	Mixed	ITV 33.5	31	1936	87	Free
US	412	805	238		Private		72	1950	92	Free
G7	32	628	214	41	Mixed	27	39		87	Free
EU-15	4	478	183	45	Mixed	33	50		86	Free
OECD Total	8	480	181	42	Mixed	34	49		86	Free

Notes: 'Dominant type' was determined on the basis of the audience share captured by the public channels: 0–39% = private dominant; 40–59% = mixed; 60–100% = public dominant. 'Broadcasting freedom' was scaled on the basis of press freedom of laws and practices, political influence over media content, economic influence over media content, and actual violations of press freedom. The Freedom House score out of 60 was converted into a percentage where 0 = lowest and 100 = highest broadcasting freedom. The broadcasting-freedom scale was then categorized such that low through 59 = not free, 60 through 79 = partly free, and 80+ = free.

Sources: TV sets per 1000: UNESCO Statistical Yearbook 1998. Paris: UNESCO. Households with cable or satellite: Television 98. IP Deutschland (www.ip-deutschland.de). Audience shares of public channels: Television 98. IP Deutschland (www.ip-deutschland.de). Year regular TV broadcasts began: Lawrence LeDuc, Richard G. Niemi, and Pippa Norris. 1996. Comparing Democracies. London: Sage. Broadcasting freedom: Derived from Leonard R. Sussman (ed.). 1997. 'Press Freedom 1997.' Freedom Review. Freedom House (www.freedomhouse.org/Press/Press97).

public channels of 60% and above), *mixed* systems (with a public share of 40–59%), and predominantly *private* systems (with a public share of less than 40%). Where we have comparable data, today only three OECD nations can be categorized as predominantly public (Austria, Denmark, and Hungary), eleven represent mixed systems, and ten can be classified as predominantly private systems. Although there has been convergence over the years, nevertheless broadcasting systems continue to bear the distinct imprints of their origins from radio in the 1920s, as can be seen by contrasting case studies of the continuing public-service model exemplified by Sweden, the mixed model that has existed for many decades in Britain, and the commercial model as developed in the United States.

THE PUBLIC-SERVICE MODEL OF BROADCASTING: SWEDEN

The Swedish Broadcasting Corporation was established in 1956 as the national radio and television monopoly. The corporation was reorganized in 1979 and again in 1992, so that today there are three separate and autonomous state-owned corporations, operating radio, television, and educational broadcasting services. Sveriges Television operates two national TV networks, SVT1 and SVT2. Sveriges Radio runs four national public services, each with a distinct profile focusing on talk and news, classical music, minority and educational services, and youth-oriented music and information, and there are regional stations and network programs for an older audience. Parliament decides the annual license fee paid by every household with a television set and allocates the revenue to all services. Advertising is not allowed on any of the public services, although they can raise some revenue through sales of programs and technical services, as well as sponsorship. The Swedish Broadcasting Corporation includes representatives from various mass organizations, such as churches, consumer groups, unions, civic associations, and publishing organizations, representing a corporatist cross section of Swedish civic society.[15]

Until recently, commercial television was prevented by the Radio Act, which banned advertising. The first two channels to break the public monopoly were TV3 and Filmnet, both established via satellite in 1987. These were quickly followed in 1989 by the American-owned Kanal 5, and in 1990 by TV4, the only licensed terrestrial commercial channel in Sweden. By 1997 Swedish viewers could therefore access two public and one commercial terrestrial channels, while satellite and cable added another six channels paid by advertising and four paid by subscription. The Swedish model is typical of Scandinavian countries, with its monopoly of public television until the late 1980s. The ethos of public-service broadcasting remains widely accepted, meaning the provision of comprehensive programming, with considerable emphasis on the provision of news and current affairs, as well as a mix of entertainment, culture, and education. The past decade has seen a radical shake-up in the broadcasting environment in Sweden, with the rise of a range of commercial alternatives, although public television continues to be well supported. The continued popularity of public television is shown by the fact that in the mid-1990s SVT1 and SVT2 maintained an average daily share of around half the audience. Almost two-thirds of the people feel that the license fee is good value for their money (at 1,476 SKr), and 40% are against advertising, with these proportions slightly strengthening in recent years.[16]

THE MIXED MODEL OF BROADCASTING: BRITAIN

The BBC exemplifies the mixed or 'dual' model, characterized by a long history of combining public and commercial television within a carefully regulated environment.[17] In Britain, encouraged by the radio manufacturing industry, the Post Office established the British Broadcasting Company in 1922 as a commercial cooperative, wholly funded by the broadcast license fee payable by all citizens who owned radio sets. In 1927 the private monopoly was transformed into a public corporation, as the British Broadcasting Corporation, and was granted a Royal Charter, which ensured the principle of its freedom from direct parliamentary control. From the start, Lord Reith's classic definition of the core responsibility of the BBC was to 'entertain, inform and educate' the nation, as a public service mediating between Parliament and the people, an ethos widely adopted in other European countries. Although the predominance of public television has been eroded over the years, these core principles continue to be reflected in the ethos and standards guiding public television. The director general of the BBC reports to the Board of Governors, appointed as an independent body, and the level of the license fee is reviewed by Parliament at regular intervals. The BBC originally enjoyed a monopoly of broadcasting, and as a result regulations held broadcasters accountable to ensure the quality and diversity of programming, including the universality of service provision throughout the British Isles. The first regular public television service was started by the BBC in 1936, to a restricted audience. Service was suspended during the war, only to resume (with exactly the program it was transmitting when it left the air) in 1946.

Commercial competition was introduced relatively early in Britain. Independent Television (ITV, subsequently termed Channel 3) was established in 1955 as a federal system of companies, each serving different regional areas within a framework regulated by successive bodies, currently the Independent Television Commission (ITC).[18] The ITC allocates franchises for a ten-year term according to the 'public interest', including programming standards such as high quality, diversity, original productions, news, regional productions, equal opportunities, provision for the disabled, and provision of party political broadcasts.[19] The ITC also regulates the content, amount, and placing of advertisements that can be broadcast. The organization monitors standards and complaints and can impose penalties on broadcasting companies, ranging from warnings to fines and revocation of licenses. The ITV companies aimed for a popular audience, but also competed with the high journalistic and cultural standards established by the BBC.

This dual system was expanded in 1964 with the establishment of BBC2, a second public-service channel originally designed for quality programming for minority groups, followed by Channel 4 in 1992, a second commercial channel also designed to cater to minorities, and Channel 5 in 1997, the latter reaching a limited audience. Thus the British system subsidized the BBC wholly from the annual license fee paid by all owners of television sets and allowed ITV companies to finance their operations from advertising. Channel 4 received an annual subscription paid by the ITV companies, who then sold the advertising for the channel. As a result of these arrangements, instead of a free market, the competition for advertising revenue was strictly limited. The system was designed to ensure a range of quality programming and popular programming on public and commercial channels. There was rivalry for ratings, as much for status as for revenue, but the financial viability of each channel did not depend wholly on its audience share. Cable and satellite services have been picking up subscriptions in recent years, especially Sky TV, but despite such availability, fewer than one-third of households subscribe, and average audience ratings are well below that figure. Despite some recent changes, mainly because of the evening lineup on ITV following the cancellation of *News at Ten*, the BBC continues to hold an average audience share of about 43%.

THE COMMERCIAL MODEL OF BROADCASTING:
THE UNITED STATES

The history of broadcasting in the United States and Latin America took a route different from that in Europe, with significant consequences for its subsequent development.[20] Regular radio broadcasting started in the United States with commercial companies in the early 1920s, as in Britain, but within a few years the local stations were funded by advertising revenue. Local radio stations had trouble filling all their airtime, so they joined together to share programming. The market became dominated by the National Broadcasting Company (NBC), the Columbia Broadcasting System (CBS), and the American Broadcasting Company (ABC), sending programs sponsored or produced by advertisers to their affiliated stations all over the country. The main regulatory body to allocate frequencies of the airwaves is the Federal Communications Commission (FCC), created in 1934. The work of the FCC concerns limiting concentration of power and laying down some loose guidelines for programming and content, but it remains very weak compared with equivalent European bodies like the British ITC. Commercial television was built on this network-affiliate structure, with the first regular service being offered in the late 1940s. Because of increasing costs, multiple advertisers were needed to pay for programs, and the networks took over responsibility for program content. Initially the networks provided only fifteen minutes of news per day, in straight bulletin format, but that expanded in the late 1950s to 30 minutes, inclusive of commercials. That move was prompted by the need to refurbish the reputations of the networks, badly damaged by revelations about dishonest and rigged quiz shows. The three major networks air news at the same time slot in the early evening, leaving local stations and cable to broadcast news at other times. Facing increasing competition from cable and satellite, the audience for network news has steadily plummeted; from 90% of the audience watching TV at that hour in the 1960s down to less than half by 1999. Today the United States has about 11,000 radio stations, four national terrestrial television networks, twenty national radio networks, 1,000 local television stations, and 6,000 cable television systems.[21]

In the United States, educational television was started with some pioneer stations just after the war, but public broadcasting per se was established on a widespread basis only after the Public Broadcasting Act of 1967, as what one account termed 'the under funded afterthought',[22] by which time the dominant ethos of American broadcasting had already been established. Federal, state, and local governments provide 47% of the Public Broadcasting System (PBS) budget, the rest being contributed by viewers (23%), corporate sponsors (15%), and foundations (6%). PBS programming is distributed to more than 350 affiliates. Unlike the situation in Europe, PBS was established to fill a particular educational and cultural function, such as children's programs, music concerts, science programs, and documentaries, rather than to provide a comprehensive service covering the complete gamut of programs designed for the mass audience. Given this remit, not surprisingly, although widely available across the country, PBS is watched by a limited audience of around 3% of all viewers, whereas the popularity of National Public Radio (NPR) has been growing in recent years, and in the 1998 Pew survey 15% of Americans reported regularly listening to NPR.

Cable services began to penetrate the market in the mid-1960s, but it was only in the 1980s that increasing competition from cable and satellite made sharp inroads into the three major networks' share of the audience. Today, more than two-thirds of American homes have cable or satellite access, well above the European average. The expansion in competition has led to a host of channels directed towards niche marketing, specializing in travel, weather, religion, sport, home shopping, and judicial proceedings. The multichannel environment has produced a revolution in American news habits. The 1998 Pew Center survey of 'regular' use of the news media showed that the most common activities, engaging about two-thirds of the American public, continued to be reading a daily newspaper (68%) and watching the local evening TV news (64%), and the majority (52%) also regularly listened to radio news at some time during the day.[23] In contrast, network news has suffered a significant loss of its audience; in 1998 only 38% of Americans said they were 'regular' viewers. The proliferation of cable and satellite stations has produced a Balkanization of the TV audience.[24] To some extent that simply reflects dispersion of the network audience, as people may now find MSNBC or CNBC or CNN on cable more convenient for their schedules than early evening network news. Obviously that phenomenon has set off alarm bells within the major networks.[25]

THE IMPACT ON NEWS AND
CURRENT-AFFAIRS PROGRAMMING

The structure of the television industry has moved towards greater transatlantic convergence over the years, but nevertheless, following a path-dependent model, broadcasting systems today continue to bear the imprints of traditions established by radio in the 1920s, with marked contrasts in the roles of public and commercial television in Sweden, Britain, and the United States. What are the consequences of those changes in the structures of the television industry for the availability and content of news coverage of politics and public affairs? There is a consensus that the fragmentation of the audience and the proliferation of channels have had profound consequences for broadcasting, although there is little agreement as to whether these developments are proving positive or negative for the diversity of program choices offered to the public.

Some would argue that the traditional ethos of public-service broadcasting ensured a wide range of programming, including news, current affairs, documentaries, talk shows, drama, games, children's programming, soap operas, music, culture, and sports. In most European countries, until recently few channels were available, as in Sweden, but precisely because of this monopoly, public-service broadcasting was regulated to ensure that it provided comprehensive programming. There is widespread concern that the introduction of new channels via cable and satellite will reduce the quality of broadcasting, because commercialization will impose greater emphasis on low-cost productions, U.S. imports, and repeats. The expansion in the number of broadcast outlets has produced a surge in demand for programs, driving up costs. Any vacuum among the airwaves often has been filled by the already available, low-budget, low-quality off-the-shelf entertainment, with minimum production values, exemplified by imported soaps and sitcoms in Europe, telenovellas and game shows in Latin America, and talk shows and tired repeats in the United States. For example, the individual programs attracting the highest audience share in 1998 in individual countries included *Jurassic Park* in Panama, *Miss Universe 98* in Venezuela, *Father Ted* in Ireland, *Friends* in Australia, and *Donald Duck* in Sweden. If we compare the audience shares for the top ten programs in 1998, World Cup football (soccer) was included throughout most of Europe and Latin America. One-third of the programs in the top-ten lists were soap operas, and half the films ranked in those lists were American movies.[26]

The major producers of television shows, including the three major U.S. networks and public broadcasters in Europe, are able to reap rewards from sales of their programming to other channels, but they also face rising production costs, erosion of their base audiences, and therefore threats to either advertising revenues or the level of their license fees. This may produce a 'leveling-down' of broadcasting, so that even the public channels may abandon serious programming on public affairs. The common fear is that more television may have expanded consumer choice in theory but reduced the actual diversity of content in practice, the well-known phenomenon of 100 channels and still nothing on TV.[27] As Weymouth and Lamizet encapsulated these fears: 'A possible and ironic danger for the receivers and users of information in Western Europe is that, in spite of the massive increase of capital investment, and the equally extraordinary multiplication of media outlets, they may well end up with a reduced choice of programme type, as well as with a lower quality of information.'[28]

This general process may have particularly serious consequences in downsizing news divisions, for two reasons: First, commercial companies may abandon anything more than headline coverage of news and current affairs in favour of mass-appeal entertainment. Indirectly, that might increase the pressure on public-service broadcasters to compete for their share of the audience by also going down-market and reducing the amount and quality of public-affairs coverage. That might produce a shift from an informational function of television, essential to the democratic needs of the people, towards 'infotainment' and the development of tabloid television. Fears have been expressed about the eroding market share of American network television news, faced with multichannel competition from cable and satellite stations, which may increase the amount of soft news focusing on human interest.[29] Of course, there is nothing particularly novel in the observation that television news blends information with entertainment; in the 1970s, commentators like Ed Diamond and David Altheide deplored the way that American news programs emphasized style over substance and used excessive 'hype' to maintain ratings.[30] But over the past decade, critics charge, trends in the economics of television news production and the chase for ratings have exacerbated this tendency, so that entertainment values have come to dominate on mainstream channels.[31]

But has the new environment produced a sharp down-market shift towards tabloid television in many countries, as popular accounts claim, or has it instead produced a diversification of available programming? After all, the influx of new satellite and cable channels includes some devoted to news and current affairs, such as Sky TV, the BBC World Service, and CNN International, as well as channels devoted to documentaries about the natural world, history, and the arts. In contrast with previous decades, today presentation of national and local legislatures on channels like C-SPAN in the United States and the Parliamentary. Channel in Britain allows the public to see the work of their representatives firsthand. So, has the new broadcasting environment reinforced the distinctive mandate of public-service television, or has it forced those channels to abandon news for more popular fare?

One way to examine the evidence concerning this issue is to compare the content of public-service broadcasting in 1971, before the rise of commercial competition in most European countries, and the content of programming in the mid-1990s. We can use two indicators. The average amount of time devoted to broadcasting a given category of programs, such as news or entertainment, indicates the *availability* of this type of coverage for the audience. This can address the question: If people want to watch news, is it less, or more, widely available on public-service channels today? In contrast, the *proportions* of time devoted to different types of programs indicate the priorities of the schedulers, and how much news or entertainment people would see if they watched only public-service television. Arguably the latter measure is less significant for the function of public-service broadcasting in a democracy, because, as argued in Chapter 2, what is most important is to provide the public with extensive coverage of public affairs. If there has been an erosion of the quality of broadcasting in the public-service sector, we would expect to find reductions in the number of hours and the proportion of time devoted to its 'informational' function, notably, presentation of news, current affairs, and documentaries, as well as reductions in educational and cultural programming such as music, arts, and drama, and, in contrast, we would expect increases in the number of hours and the proportion of time devoted to popular entertainment and advertising.

If we compare the contents of public-service broadcasting, shown in Table 5.3, it is clear that the total number of hours devoted to news and current-affairs programs has expanded substantially during the past twenty-five years, in part because of the greater number of public-

Table 5.3. *Changes in the amounts of news and entertainment broadcast on public television, 1971–96*

Country	Change in the Number of Hours of News and Current-Affairs Broadcasting 1971–96	Change in the Number of Hours of Entertainment Broadcasting 1971–96
Australia	+931	+42
Austria	+2,489	+5,105
Belgium	−507	+2,321
Czech Rep	+2,648	+5,848
Denmark	+21	+1,391
Finland	+1,051	+2,474
France	−464	+6,448
Greece	+2,709	+5,324
Hungary	+3,412	+2,296
Ireland	+592	+4,655
Italy	+7,300	+12,945
Korea, S.	+2,751	+5,195
Netherlands	+963	+2,243
Norway	−115	+1,342
Poland	+4,195	+3,698
Portugal	+2,634	+12,051
Spain	−238	+2,469
Sweden	−1,069	+992
Switzerland	+4,251	+8,315
Turkey	+7,259	+14,699
EU-15	*+1,290*	*+4,868*
OECD Total	*+2,041*	*+4,992*

Note: For the full range of categories see Table 5.4.
Source: Calculated from *UNESCO Statistical Yearbook*. Paris: UNESCO (1971–98).

service channels available. For the twenty OECD countries from which we have consistent UNESCO data, the data show that the average number of hours per week of news broadcasting on public-service television rose in fifteen states, most notably in Italy, Poland, and Turkey, whereas the hours were cut in five states (Belgium, France, Norway, Spain, and Sweden). Overall, from 1971 to 1996 in OECD countries the amount of time that news and current-affairs programs were broadcast almost tripled, from 1,168 to 3,042 hours. That was a massive increase, making far more television news available to the audience. Over the same time period, there was an even greater increase in the average time devoted to entertainment, which quadrupled from 1,505 to 6,020 hours. This expansion followed a relatively uniform pattern across all the

OECD countries, but it was especially marked for Italian, Portuguese, and Turkish public TV. Overall, the increase in the number of public-service channels, and the total hours per day they broadcast, facilitated increases in the amounts of both news and entertainment they presented, rather than only feeding the public more soaps, variety shows, and sitcoms, as some have contended.

If we analyze the *proportion* of time devoted to news on public television in the countries for which we have comparable data, the picture looks slightly different (Table 5.4). In 1996, news and current affairs accounted for, on average, one-quarter of all the programming broadcast on public-service television, with most of the remainder accounted for by entertainment (47%), culture (10%), education (8%), and advertisements (2%). News and current affairs were particularly prominent on public television in Germany, the United Kingdom, and Finland, with a greater entertainment balance in France and Belgium. The proportion seems to have dropped most significantly in some of the Scandinavian countries, which suggests that public TV has changed its balance of coverage most in these nations.

As to whether the content of news coverage has also changed in terms of subject matter and style, we have a wealth of speculation, but little systematic evidence. As discussed in Chapter 4, 'tabloidization' and 'soft news' refer to both stories and formats, and these separate dimensions are often confused. Changes in the length or style of presentation of news stories, for example, may be completely unrelated to changes in their contents. In the United States there is evidence for the growth since the early 1970s of 'soft' news on the national networks, meaning human-interest stories, as compared with news about public-policy issues, public events, and social controversies.[32] But there has been little comparative analysis of the stories shown on television news, with the exception of a study of public-service news in eight countries by Heinderyckx.[33] Systematic time-series data comparing the contents of news in OECD nations is unavailable. The separate country studies in Europe that are available provide an ambiguous picture of trends. One recent review of the available literature concluded that, contrary to expectations, news and current-affairs programs on public channels had not been moved outside of prime time to better compete with the popular entertainment on commercial channels.[34] Moreover, when commercial channels were first established, they tended to marginalize political news, but that is no longer the case. For example, in Germany, Barbara Pfetsch found that both commercial and public channels had

Table 5.4. *Changes in the proportions of news coverage in public-service broadcasting, 1971–96*

Country	Total Hours 1971	Total Hours 1996	News + Current Affairs % 1996	News + Current Affairs Change % 1971–96	Enter-tainment % 1996	Enter-tainment Change % 1971–96	Edu-cation % 1996	Edu-cation Change % 1971–96	Culture % 1996	Culture Change % 1971–96	Ads % 1996	Ads Change % 1971–96
Australia	4,186	6,280	25	9	47	–22	22	20	3			
Austria	4,394	13,779	28	–4	44	22	3	–8	7	–11	4	1
Belgium	5,174	5,597	19	–11	53	40	5	–14	6	–3	1	–2
Canada	3,151	.										
Czech Rep	3,120	15,336	27	–23	39	32	4	–8	17	10		–11
Denmark	1,976	2,956	25	–11	54	43	2	–2	13	–10		–2
Finland	2,756	7,228	30	–11	48	10	7	—	8	3		
France	7,982	17,923	13	–22	47	21	1	–20	25	13	5	3
Germany	.	6,024	36		56				4		1	
Greece	1,898	11,187	27	6	56	2	4	4	4	–4	1	1
Hungary	2,964	11,559	34	14	30	–10	7	–9	7	–2	2	
Ireland	2,860	9,528	14	–12	60	22	6	–8	4	2	8	
Italy	5,720	31,860	28	–1	43	25	5		16	11	2	–14
Japan	1,523	.										
Korea, S.	4,316	18,596	20	–5	37	–3	18	17	9	—	5	–1

Table 5.4 (cont.)

Country	Total Hours 1971	Total Hours 1996	News + Current Affairs % 1996	News + Current Affairs Change % 1971–96	Entertainment % 1996	Entertainment Change % 1971–96	Education % 1996	Education Change % 1971–96	Culture % 1996	Culture Change % 1971–96	Ads % 1996	Ads Change % 1971–96
Luxembourg	.	838	43		26		3		10		3	
Netherlands	4,514	8,578	27	–3	46	8	6	–2	12	9	4	
NZ	3,380	.										
Norway	2,002	3,518	24	–24	52	27	3	–3	8	5		
Poland	4,186	15,944	33	5	35	–11	11	–5	8		2	2
Portugal	3,332	21,374	14	–1	61	26	17	11		—	1	–14
Spain	5,997	7,661	21	–9	63	23	3	2	5	–10	2	–1
Sweden	4,691	6,668	7	–26	48		10	10	27	27		
Switzerland	8,948	31,827	16	4	40	–9	1	–4	7	–11	2	–1
Turkey	780	32,684	22	–5	45	7	18	6	10	–5		
UK	10,296	21,144	37		33		6		25		0	0
US	.	6,500	19		36		29		16		0	0
G7		18,602	26		26		49		14		3	
EU-15		10,800	24		24		51		11		3	
OECD Total		13,042	25		47		8		10		2	

Source: Calculated from *UNESCO Statistical Yearbook.* Paris: UNESCO (1971–98). U.S. public television calculated from *PTV Programming Survey.* Washington, DC: Corporation for Public Broadcasting. Data for Britain for network (not regional) television estimated from the BBC Annual Report, 1997/98 (http://www.bbc.co.uk/info/report98).

increased their political information since the mid-1980s: 'Our findings show that the similarities in the appearance of politics on television in 1993 in public and commercial news [were the results] of an alignment on two levels: private channels caught up with public channels regarding the contents of political information, while public channels caught up with commercial stations in their presentation formats. Eventually these programme strategies will lead to a pretty similar portrayal of politics in television news.'[35]

Some studies in Belgium, Sweden, and Denmark[36] have reported greater sensationalism and 'soft' news on commercial channels, as compared with public television, although it remains to be seen if that change in political coverage will be part of a longer-term trend in Europe. It is also unclear whether or not it is commercialization per se that has produced a significant 'tabloidization' in mainstream TV news bulletins. In Britain, for example, most contemporary observers believed that the introduction of commercial competition from ITN news in the mid-1950s improved the pace, presentation, and quality of the rather staid BBC broadcasts at the time.[37] By 1997, the campaign coverages on the flagship evening programs, the BBC 9 O'Clock News and ITN News at Ten, were very similar in terms of the proportion of the evening news devoted to the election (about half for each program), the range of issue stories versus campaign stories, and the positive-versus-negative balance towards each major party.[38] A study classifying the topics of stories on the main evening news programs on British television during a six-month period in the late 1990s found that the BBC1's 9 O'Clock News showed a higher proportion of 'hard' news stories about international affairs and policy issues than did ITN's News at Ten, but the commercial Channel 4 7 O'Clock News showed the highest proportion of any channel, as well as the lowest proportion of entertainment, sports, and human-interest news.[39] Rather than showing a clear-cut public-service–commercial division, television news in Britain has diversified into several market segments reaching different audiences.

A glance at the schedules suggests that what seems to have occurred in many countries is increased diversification of news formats and styles, with the expansion of 'vox-pop' discussion programs, 24-hour repetitive rolling news, brief hourly news headline bulletins, and infotainment 'talking-heads' magazines, as well as a faster pace of traditional news coverage. None of these formats is novel; indeed, some of them, such as discussion programs in front of a live audience, are among the most venerable in broadcasting, and all have become more widely available, probably because production of those types of programs is relatively inexpensive.

One of the distinguishing features of 'hard' news is its focus on international coverage. To compare differences between private and public television sectors more systematically we can examine how European television covered the politics of the European Union, drawing on content analysis of the coverage of three key events: the Turin Inter-Governmental Conference (29–30 March 1996), the Florence Council (20–22 June 1996), and the Dublin Council II (13–14 December 1996). During these events, *Monitoring Euromedia* analyzed coverage of the EU and its policies by all regular news and current-affairs programs on seventy-three television stations in total, almost equally divided between commercial (thirty-six) and public-service (thirty-seven) channels. (Full details of the methodology can be found in the Technical Appendix.) Overall, during these events, *Monitoring Euromedia* found 1,012 stories referring to the European Union and its policies across all fifteen EU member states. The content-analysis data have been summed across all three events to increase the reliability of the results.

The data in Figure 5.1 confirm a major difference in European coverage by sector: Public-service television news aired 626 stories about the EU, almost twice as many as commercial stations (386). But at the same time, there was considerable variation within each sector. Public television's greater coverage was due in large part to a few major channels, notably Germany's ZDF, Italy's RAI1,[40] Finland's TV1, Austria's ORF2, Britain's BBC1, and Germany's ARD. Some of the commercial channels also devoted considerable coverage to those events, surpassing many public stations, notably Finland's MTV3, the United Kingdom's ITV, and France's LCI. If we can generalize from these findings, they suggest that public-service television does devote more attention to international news; nevertheless, the proliferation of public and private channels has produced considerable differentiation across the airwaves. Some public channels, notably those with stronger cultural or arts orientations, provided relatively little coverage of EU politics, while at the same time the private channels that were news-oriented gave considerable priority to coverage of Community affairs. That implies that news coverage does vary by sector, but the difference is one of degree rather than kind.

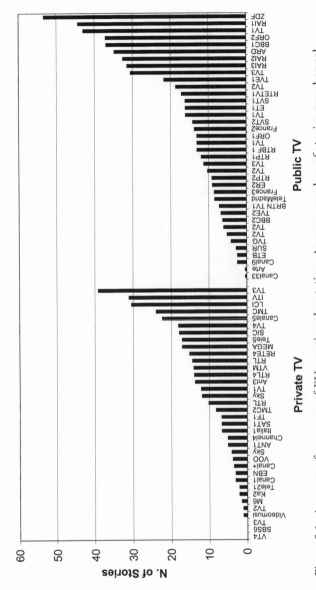

Figure 5.1. Amount of coverage of EU meetings by station: Average number of stories per channel covering the Turin IGC, Florence Council, and Dublin Council II. *Source:* Calculated from *Monitoring Euromedia,* 1995–97. Brussels: European Commission.

THE END OF THE MASS AUDIENCE FOR
TELEVISION NEWS?

Another major concern about the growth of the multichannel environment is that television news will become a minority interest, leading to a growing divide between the information haves and have-nots. Those who are already interested in politics will be able to find out more about events because of the growing numbers of twenty-four-hour rolling-news channels like Sky TV, BBC World Service, and CNN International, although those who are uninterested may simply tune out public life. Russell Neuman has suggested that we may be experiencing the 'end of the mass audience' as we move towards niche markets or 'narrowcasting' in the new multichannel and multimedia environment.[41]

Despite such fears, some news and current-affairs programs still rank in the lists of the most popular broadcasts, with high audience shares, year after year. They include *19 Heures* and *Journal televise* in south Belgium, *TV Uutiset Ja* in Finland, *20 Heures* in France, *Heute* and *Tagesschau* in Germany, the *9 O'Clock News* in Ireland, *Kveldsnytt* in Norway, *Tagesschau* and *Schweiz Aktuell* in German Switzerland, and *60 Minutes* in the United States. With the exceptions of *20 Heures* in France, *19 Heures* in Belgium, and *60 Minutes* in the United States, they all air on public-service television.[42] The mainstream news can still routinely attract a large audience, in both Europe and America, and a much larger audience in the event of dramatic breaking news.

We can examine the late-1990s social profiles of European viewers who regularly watch television news and those who read newspapers to see whether demographic factors can predict the audience for television news. Regression models based on the spring 1999 Eurobarometer allow us to examine the effects of education, socioeconomic status, income, gender, age, left–right ideology, region of residence, and nationality on regular use of television news. The findings can be compared with the social profile for newspaper readers shown in Table 4.3.

Table 5.5, reporting standardized beta coefficients, shows that demographic factors can explain little of the variance in patterns of watching television news. The strongest social predictor was age, with older generations far more likely to watch, a phenomenon that previous studies had found to be associated with general patterns of leisure

Table 5.5. *Predictors of use of television news, EU-15, 1999*

	Predictors of Watching TV News	Sig.	Operationalization
DEMOGRAPHICS			
Education	−0.03	*	Age finished full-time education
Gender	0.02	*	Male (1) Female (0)
Age	0.15	**	In years
Left-Right Ideology	0.03	*	10-point scale: From left (1) to right (10)
Socioeconomic Status	0.01		Manual (0)/Nonmanual (1) HoH
Household Income	0.02		Harmonized income scale
USE OF OTHER MEDIA			
Newspaper Use	0.22	**	5-point scale
Radio News Use	0.11	**	5-point scale
Online	0.01		No (0)/ Yes (1)
REGION			
Northern Europe	−0.05		Denmark, Finland, and Sweden
Southern Europe	0.07	*	Italy, Greece, Portugal, and Spain
NATION			
Austria	−0.06	**	
Belgium	−0.01		
Denmark	0.02		
Finland	0.04		
France	−0.05	*	
Germany	−0.03		
Greece	0.11	**	
Ireland	0.01		
Italy	0.07	**	
Netherlands	0.02		
Portugal	0.01		
Spain	0.03		
Sweden	−0.06	*	
UK	0.01		
Constant	3.65		
R^2	0.12		
N.	16,179		

Notes: This table reports the standardized beta coefficients predicting use of the news media based on ordinary least-squares regression models. The dependent variables include a 5-point scale measuring frequency of use of television news, where 5 = 'everyday use' and 1 = 'never use'. HOH = head of household. Significance: **$P > 0.01$; *$P > 0.05$. The western European region was excluded from the 'Region' categories. *Source:* Eurobarometer 50.1, March–April 1999.

time.[43] In addition, those who regularly read a newspaper or listened to the radio news were more likely to tune in to television news. The regional trends in newspaper use reported in Chapter 4 have been reversed: People in southern Europe proved more likely to watch TV news than those in the north. Some of the national variables remained significant, even after controlling for major region, suggesting that broadcasting systems and cultural habits continue to play roles in predicting viewing habits. The overall pattern suggests that among newspaper readers there was a clear social bias in favour of the more affluent middle class, but with the exception of the older viewers, those who watched TV news proved to be a far more representative cross section of European society.

If we turn to trends over time we can monitor the backgrounds of viewers in the smaller group of countries (France, Germany, Belgium, The Netherlands, and Italy) included in EU surveys in 1970,[44] 1980, and 1999. This period was selected to allow comparison of television viewing in 1970, when public-service television dominated in Europe, and in the late 1990s, after commercial channels had made major inroads into the mass audience. If the fragmentation of stations and the commercialization of television has produced widening disparities between the types of people who tune in to news and those who tune out, that should be evident in this comparison. Similar regression models were run as before.

We have already observed, in Table 4.5, that the regular audience for TV news (those who watch every day) has expanded during the past three decades from half to three-quarters of all Europeans. Not surprisingly, the data in Table 5.6 show that in Europe the social profile of those who watch the news has broadened over the same period. Age has always been the strongest indicator of use of TV news, and there is no trend showing a strengthening of the age gap (Figure 5.2). Most importantly, that suggests a life-cycle effect rather than a generational effect in television habits. The most plausible reason is that older people usually turn to more sedentary pusuits such as television viewing, as they have more leisure time and less active hobbies. Despite the advent of MTV, movie channels, and similar alternatives, younger viewers are as likely to watch TV news now as they were in the 1970s. The other coefficients show no widening social gap regarding who watches TV news, but rather, if anything, the reverse pattern: The gender gap and income gap evident in 1970 had disappeared by 1980. Use of TV news continues to be strongly associated with reading newspapers and listening to radio news,

	Predictors of TV News Viewership 1970	Sig.	Predictors of TV News Viewership 1980	Sig.	Predictors of TV News Viewership 1999	Sig.	Operationalization
DEMOGRAPHICS							
Education	-0.07	**	-0.03	**	-0.03		Age finished full-time education
Gender	0.04	**	0.01	*	0.00		Male (1) Female (0)
Age	0.16	**	0.09	**	0.14	**	In years
Left-Right Ideology	-0.01		0.05	**	0.04	*	Scale: From left (1) to right (10)
Socioeconomic Status	0.01		-0.05	**	0.01		Manual (0)/Nonmanual (1) HoH
Household Income	0.08	**	0.01	**	0.01		Harmonized income scale
USE OF OTHER MEDIA							
Newspaper Use	0.13	**	0.21	**	0.21	**	5-point scale
Radio News Use	0.01		0.16	**	0.08	**	5-point scale
NATION							
Belgium	-0.13	**	-0.02	*	0.01		
France	-0.11	**	-0.06	**	-0.04	*	
Italy	-0.18	**	0.15	**	0.12	**	
Netherlands	0.01		-0.03	*	0.05	*	
Constant	3.3		3.25		3.65		
R²	*0.08*		*0.12*		*0.11*		
N.	8,567		8,827		6,218		

Notes: This table reports the standardized beta coefficients predicting the frequency of reading newspapers based on ordinary-least-squares regression models. The dependent variables are the 5-point scales measuring frequency of use of newspapers and television news, where 5 = 'everyday use' and 1 = 'never use'. HoH = head of household. Significance: $**P > 0.01$; $*P > 0.05$. The German dummy variable is excluded as a predictor in these models.

Source: European Community Study, 1970; Eurobarometer 13.0, April 1980, weighted for EU-6; Eurobarometer 50.1, March–April 1999, weighted for EU-6.

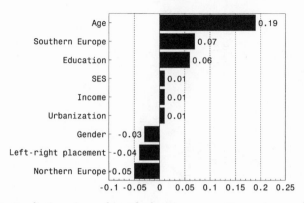

Figure 5.2. Predicting viewership of television news: Regression-analysis standardized beta coefficients using a 5-point scale for frequency of use of TV news as the dependent variable. *Source*: Eurobarometer 1996.

suggesting a self-selecting mechanism at work, and there has been a slight strengthening of this relationship since the 1970s. More people are therefore using multiple sources of news, supplementing newspapers with TV. There were also some important shifts at the national level. For example, fewer people than the EU average watched TV news in Italy in the 1970s, but this pattern had been sharply reversed by the mid-1990s. Overall, the social profile for users provides no support for the idea that television news is moving into a specialized niche audience, as some fear, rather than continuing to reach a mainstream mass audience in Europe. And television news continues to reach certain sectors of the European public that newspapers fail to reach.

THE IMPLICATIONS OF STRUCTURAL CHANGES

On the basis of this discussion we can conclude that despite gradual convergence over the years, major structural differences continue to distinguish broadcasting systems in OECD societies. Reading the newspaper, watching television, and even surfing the Internet are likely to prove quite different experiences for dissimilar audiences, depending on the communications environments in countries like Sweden, Britain, and the United States. Public-service television, which once enjoyed a monopoly in many countries, has moved into a multichannel world, but it retains a considerable share of the audience and has expanded its news and current-affairs broadcasting. Television news is far more easily available than in previous decades, and it continues to appeal to a broad cross section of the public, more so than newspapers or the Internet. As discussed in the next chapter, use of the Net has grown by leaps and bounds in the past few years, but outside of Scandinavia and the United States, access remains restricted, although that seems likely to change in the next decade. The overall findings tend to reinforce the conclusions of the preceding chapter, namely, that postindustrial societies have experienced the emergence of what can be termed 'postmodern communications', characterized by greater diversification and multiplication of news *sources* and leading towards a richer and more pluralistic news environment.

The diversification of news sources is a widely noted phenomenon, notably the breakdown of public-service television monopolies throughout Europe and the end of the dominance of the major networks in the United States, due to the proliferation of rival services on cable, satellite, digital, and now broadband Internet. Many deplore these developments, fearing that the new technology will render the older forms of communication redundant – if the struggle for control of mass communications in a society is a zero-sum game. There is widespread angst in the journalism profession that tried and trusted forms of authority are toppling, new ones are not taking their place, and familiar institutions like network TV in the United States and public television in Europe are in a precarious state of flux. Technological and economic changes have produced a climate of uncertainty about the future of the old media like newspapers and television.

Yet in almost every case we find that new media, such as the Internet, tend to supplement rather than replace the old media of newspapers and television. There may be some trade-offs involved. For example, television surged in the 1950s during a decade of declining box-office sales at the movies. Some media do completely replace older technologies, such as CDs driving out vinyl records. Nevertheless, this chapter demonstrates that the predominant trend during the twentieth century was one of an expanding range of news media outlets, so that now we commonly tend to read newspapers as we also listen to radio news in the background, or we catch the CNN headlines online as we also surf the Net. In short, the evidence we have examined for postindustrial societies shows that as we begin the twenty-first century, more sources of news are available than ever before, news consumption has increased, and the audience has broadened.

Most can accept the fact that there has been a diversification of news sources. Nevertheless, there remains widespread concern that the general trend has been towards a down-market popularization and homogenization of news standards. This process is believed to have led to a gradual reduction in quality journalism, replaced by the tabloid press and tabloid TV. Yet, rather than seeing the news as moving in a single downward direction, it seems more plausible to suggest that there has been greater diversification in the levels and formats of news. So at one end of the spectrum there has been an expanding popular audience in the United States for such things as the talk shows hosted by Oprah Winfrey, Jerry Springer, and Howard Stern, with emphasis on the sensational, on celebrities, and on personal problems, along with 'soft news' in news magazines and local news. Yet at the same time, more political information has become available at the 'quality' end of the market, with serious coverage of international affairs from such sources as C-SPAN, CNN, and NPR. In Europe, cable and satellite carry music videos, porn, and violent action movies to a broader audience than ever before, but they also facilitate services such as the BBC World Service, Sky TV, and the Discovery Channel, as well as stations devoted to parliamentary or public-affairs coverage. And the Internet offers an even wider diversity of contents, formats, and outlets.

There is legitimate concern that the development of niche markets may exacerbate the division between the information-rich and the information-poor. In the 1970s, the dominant network news in the United States and the evening news on European public broadcasting channels was designed to reach a mainstream middle-brow audience. In many cases that was a captive audience, because of the limited number of channels. At the turn of the century, in contrast, the pattern of newly abundant news outlets operating at a variety of popular and serious levels seems likely to cater quite well to the diverse needs of different groups of people. Some people may prefer to immerse themselves in public affairs, and others will opt to catch two minutes of radio news headlines on the hour every hour between the pressures of shopping, work, and children. Some readers want serious broadsheet papers, while others opt for tabloids. Some surf channels, while others surf the Net. At least in Europe, the mainstream middle-brow evening news programs reach more people, and a broader cross section of the public, than in the 1970s. If we accept the contention that political learning is facilitated, or even driven, by prior interest, then the plurality of outlets and levels can be regarded as largely healthy for democracy. Before we explore the impact of the use of television on political campaigns, we must first attempt to understand the phenomenon of the Internet and its possible consequences for traditional news media and the political system.

CHAPTER 6

The Emerging Internet Era

L ike earlier periods witnessing the rise of radio and then television, the birth of the Internet era has generated extensive speculation about the potential consequences of this development for the older news media, for political campaigns, and for civic society.[1] As the Internet has taken off, research has begun to explore the possible consequences for parties, candidates, and election campaigns; for new social movements, interest groups, and organizational activism; and for the policy-making process and governing in an information age.[2] Despite the growing literature in America, we know less about who surfs in other societies.

This chapter compares the social characteristics of Net users in western Europe and the United States, examining the evolution of the information society and the online community since the mid-1990s.[3] We focus on two issues: At the national level, is the information society expanding throughout postindustrial societies, or is a new cleavage emerging between the information-rich and information-poor? And at the individual level, is the Internet community 'normalizing' throughout society, or are clear disparities emerging between the more affluent and better educated and the rest of society? The conclusion of this chapter summarizes the core findings and considers the implications for understanding political communications in the emerging Internet era.

MOBILIZATION AND REINFORCEMENT THEORIES OF THE INTERNET

The explosion in Internet use in postindustrial societies appears to be leading to a sweeping transformation in the major sources of political news, with the rise in online newspapers, broadband television and radio, and new forms of political interaction like online political discussion groups. Interpretations about the potential for expanding social equality through use of the Internet differ sharply. On the one hand, *mobilization theories* claim that 'virtual democracy' promises a cornucopia of empowerment in a digital world; Schwartz emphasizes the potential for a virtual community.[4] Rheingold argues that bulletin-board systems are democratizing technologies and are being used to exchange ideas, to mobilize the public, and to strengthen social capital.[5] Lawrence Grossman anticipates great opportunities for shrinking the distance between the governed and the government using the new communication technology.[6] Ian Budge argues that the Web will facilitate direct democracy.[7] The strongest claims of mobilization theories are that Net activism represents a distinctive type of political participation that differs in significant ways from conventional activities like working for political parties, organizing grassroots social movements, or lobbying elected officials. By sharply reducing the barriers to civic engagement, leveling some of the financial hurdles, and widening the opportunities for political debate, for dissemination of information, and for group interaction, it is said that the Net may reduce social inequalities in public life. For enthusiasts, the Net promises to provide new forms of horizontal and vertical communication that can facilitate and enrich deliberation in the public sphere.

If mobilization theories are correct, and if information on the Net reaches those who have conventionally tuned out from traditional media or have been less involved in public affairs, such as young people, or people in isolated communities, or minority political groups, then such developments should have the capacity to expand civic engagement in important ways. By directly linking citizens worldwide, and reducing communications costs, the Net may also foster new types of international mobilization by non-governmental organizations (NGOs) around the globe, such as the campaign against the use of land mines. At the societal level, the new technology may also prove a boon to economic development in societies like Malaysia and India, facilitating the move from a semi-agricultural economy to a service economy, as in Singapore. Bill Gates claims that the information society may thereby reduce global inequalities between rich and poor nations.[8]

Yet, in contrast, *reinforcement theories* suggest that use of the Net will strengthen, not radically transform, the existing patterns of social inequality and political participation. From that more skeptical perspective, this new medium threatens to reinforce, and perhaps even widen, the participation gap between the haves and have-nots. Davis and Owen have concluded that though the Internet does provide new sources of information for the politically interested, because of the uneven levels of access there are good grounds to be skeptical about its transformative potential for democratic participation.[9] Murdock and Golding warn that the familiar socioeconomic biases that exist in nearly all conventional forms of political participation seem unlikely to disappear on the Net, even if access gradually widens to the electronically disadvantaged.[10] At the societal level, the north–south divide may be exacerbated in a situation in which most of the world's population lacks basic access to a telephone, let alone a computer.[11] The gains in productivity that are facilitated by the new technology may increase the differences in economic growth between the most affluent societies and those that lack the skills, resources, and infrastructure to invest in the information society.[12]

To examine these issues, this chapter compares different groups of *Net users*, defined as those who report using or having access to the Internet or the World Wide Web.

THE EVOLUTION OF THE INFORMATION SOCIETY

The first issue to consider is whether the information society will develop anywhere near equally across postindustrial societies. If the reinforcement thesis is correct, we should expect to find that existing differences between information-rich and information-poor nations will be exacerbated by the growth of the Internet. As in the ancient injunction 'To those who have, it shall be given', the more affluent and most advanced postindustrial economies can be expected to be able to make the investments in skills, technology, and infrastructure that will allow them to continue as leading players in the global information society, whereas poorer states almost surely will lag further behind. Far from promoting greater equality among nations, the Net could allow the more advanced economies to pull further ahead.

We can compare the spread of the information society in Europe during the middle 1990s and the late 1990s, encompassing a wide range of mediated and interpersonal communications technologies. These can be categorized as *computer*-related (including access to a computer, CD-ROM, and modem facilities, and the Internet), *television*-related (such as access to cable and satellite television, decoders for paid television programs, teletext news services on television, the use of video

Table 6.1. *Trends in the use of communications technologies, EU-15, 1996–99*

	% with Access/Use				Increase
	1996	1997	1998	1999	1996–99
COMPUTER-RELATED					
Computer	31	30	35	40	*+9*
CD-ROM	13	16	25	26	*+13*
Modem	8	8	12	23	*+15*
Internet/WWW Connection	5	6	12	20	*+15*
TELEVISION-RELATED					
Video Recorder (VCR)	72	73	74	73	*+1*
Teletext on TV	50	52	59	60	*+10*
Satellite TV	17	18	18	20	*+3*
Decoder for Pay TV, e.g. Canal+	10	11	11	10	*0*
TELEPHONE-RELATED					
Fax Machine	19	N/a	N/a	19	*0*
Minitel or Videotex System	5	5	3	3	*−2*

Note: The Eurobarometer question: 'Do you have access to, or do you use, . . . ?'
Sources: Eurobarometers: 44.2, spring 1996; 47.0, spring 1997; 50.1, fall 1998; 51.0, spring 1999.

recorders, or VCRs), and *telephone*-related (such as use of Minitel or other videotex service without TV, and fax machines).

The comparison in Table 6.1 shows a dramatic explosion in use of the new information technologies, but the pattern across postindustrial nations, even within the EU, has proved highly uneven thus far. The trends in Europe from the middle to late 1990s show that among all of the communications technologies, the growth in computer-related formats has easily outstripped those for other systems. Over just four years, the proportion of Europeans with access to computers rose from 31% in the spring of 1996 to 40% in the spring of 1999. Even more dramatically, during that same period the proportion of European Internet users quadrupled from 5% to 20%. In the late 1990s, the Internet moved from margin to mainstream in Europe, reaching more people than many traditional media outlets. There was a related surge in the number of those with access to CD-ROM on their computers or with modem connections. In contrast, during the same years, demand remained flat for the use of television-related technologies like VCRs, satellite TV, and decoders for paid TV; only access to televisions with teletex news increased, in large part because this feature became fairly

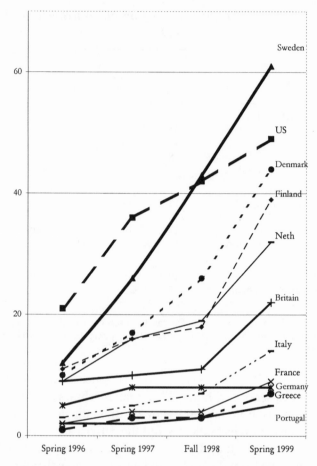

Figure 6.1. Percentages of Internet users, EU and United States, 1996–99.

standard among TV manufacturers. About two-thirds of all television households in Europe now have access to a VCR and to teletex, and half have cable or satellite TV (see Table 4.2). The purely telephone-related technologies also remained fairly stable (with the exception of the all-pervasive, jangling mobile phone, not shown here),[13] whereas the use of older Minitel systems, largely confined to France, declined during this period.

The overall surge in the reach of the Internet, however, disguises major contrasts between certain European states (Table 6.2, Figure 6.1). The level of penetration is highest in Sweden, where almost two-thirds (61%) of the adult population are online, followed by Denmark and Finland. In the middle ranks, from one-fifth to one-third are online in

Table 6.2. *Proportions of Internet users, EU and United States, 1996–99*

	Spring 1996	Spring 1997	Fall 1998	Spring 1999	Increase 1996–99
Sweden	12	26	43	61	+49
U.S. (a)	21	36	42	49	+28
Denmark	10	17	26	44	+34
Finland	11	16	18	39	+28
Netherlands	9	16	19	32	+23
Luxembourg	5	13	16	22	+17
Britain	9	10	11	22	+13
Northern Ireland	4	8	10	20	+16
Italy	3	5	7	14	+11
Ireland	4	5	9	14	+10
Austria	4	10	7	11	+7
Belgium	3	6	8	11	+8
France	2	4	4	9	+7
Germany West	5	8	8	8	+3
Germany East	2	4	5	8	+6
Spain	2	2	5	8	+6
Greece	1	3	3	7	+6
Portugal	2	2	3	5	+3
EU-15	*5*	*9*	*12*	*20*	*+15*

Notes: The Eurobarometer question: 'Do you have access to, or do you use, the Internet or World Wide Web?' There is some ambiguity in these items: whether they refer to use at home or at work or both. It should be noted that Eurobarometer 50.1 asked users whether they had access at home or at work to different types of technology, such as a computer. The data suggest that in the other surveys respondents based their answers on their home use. If so, this measure may considerably underestimate the total proportion of computer users and online users in western Europe. The Pew Center question: 'Do you ever go online to access the Internet or World Wide Web or to send and receive e-mail?'
Sources: Eurobarometers: 44.2, spring 1996; 47.0, spring 1997; 50.1, fall 1998; 51.0, spring 1999. (a) United States: Successive surveys by the Pew Research Center for the People and the Press. See www.people-press.org.

The Netherlands, Luxembourg, Britain, and Northern Ireland. The laggards in Internet use are countries in southern Europe, notably Spain, Greece, and Portugal. The patterns of Net users are closely correlated, not surprisingly, with access to computers (Table 6.3 and Figure 6.2). Again Sweden leads the way in computer users, followed by Denmark, Finland, and The Netherlands. But affluent Germany and France remain low on both indicators, and Greece and Portugal are the least wired to the information society. The importance of the north–south divide, already observed in European use of TV and news-

Table 6.3. *Proportions of computer users, EU and United States,*
1996–99

	Spring 1996	Fall 1997	Spring 1999	Increase
Sweden	43	62	73	*+30*
U.S. (a)	60	66	69	*+9*
Denmark	49	61	65	*+16*
Netherlands	54	61	64	*+10*
Finland	36	43	52	*+16*
Luxembourg	41	49	48	*+7*
Britain	41	47	45	*+4*
Northern Ireland	25	34	39	*+14*
Italy	31	32	37	*+6*
Belgium	28	32	37	*+9*
Austria	23	41	33	*+10*
Spain	25	29	33	*+8*
Ireland	23	27	31	*+8*
France	25	34	30	*+5*
Germany West	31	32	29	*−2*
Germany East	27	32	27	*0*
Portugal	21	20	22	*+1*
Greece	12	19	17	*+5*
EU-15	*31*	*38*	*40*	*+9*

Notes: The Eurobarometer question: 'Do you have access to, or do you use, a computer?'
Published estimates of the numbers of computer users differ considerably. There are
also important differences in the question wording, as well as in the fieldwork, in the
U.S. and European sources that hamper strict comparability. Items have been selected
that are functionally equivalent, although not identical. Nevertheless, comparisons of
Eurobarometer and Pew Center surveys over time should increase the reliability of the
estimates of change. The Pew Center question: 'Do you use a computer at your workplace, at school, or at home on at least an occasional basis?'
Sources: Eurobarometers: 44.2, spring 1996; 47.0, spring 1997; 50.1, fall 1998; 51.0,
spring 1999. (a) United States: successive surveys by the Pew Research Center for the
People and the Press. See www.people-press.org.

papers, is reinforced when we examine trends in access to computers
and the Internet (Table 6.2). The pattern shows by far the highest levels
of Net users in northern Europe, where 39% were online in the spring
of 1999, in contrast to southern Europe, where only 8% surfed.

Accurate comparisons between the United States and Europe are difficult, because measurement protocols differ and the various estimates
of the proportion of Internet users that are available often vary considerably (see for example http://www.nua.ie/). If we turn to the estimates in the regular Pew Center surveys of online users, by January 1999
almost half (47%) of all Americans said that they had gone online at

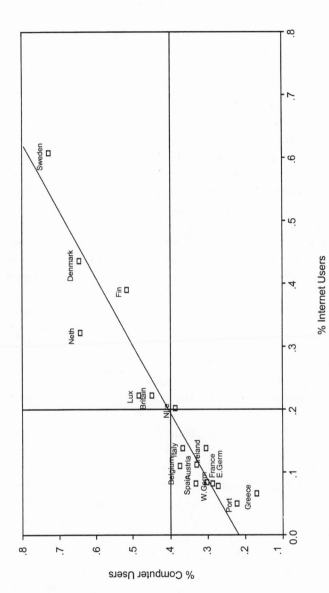

Figure 6.2. Use of computers and Internet, EU, 1999.

least once to access the Internet or World Wide Web, up from 14% in June 1995, and 23% in July 1996.[14] Like access, regular use has also surged dramatically in just a few years. The Pew Center estimated that by January 1999 two-thirds of all Americans (69%) used computers, either at home or at work. The overall rate of growth has been phenomenal: The number of Americans using online and Internet services has been doubling every 12 months for the past three years.

There are many possible reasons for these cross-national variations. Levels of socioeconomic development can be expected to have played a role: Societies with a large white-collar service sector facilitate Internet access in the workplace, and those with experience of higher education are likely to have acquired computer skills. At the national level, use of the Net was significantly correlated with levels of affluence and education.[15] Participation in the Internet requires telephone or broadband cable facilities, computer and software skills, literacy, and a certain standard of living. When Europeans were asked in the Eurobarometer why they were not interested in getting certain services over the Internet, cost proved a major factor. Yet the level of economic development can provide only a partial explanation for the observed patterns. After all, the low rates of access to the Internet in Greece and Portugal cannot simply be blamed on the education and skills of the work force nor on the size of the service sector, for Austria, France, and Germany also have few Net users.

Another reason may lie in linguistic skills. Surveys of Web sites indicate that the Net remains an overwhelmingly English-language-dominated medium.[16] If so, then we would expect that the level of Internet use would reflect a society's familiarity with English as its primary or secondary language. That could help to explain the size of the online community in Scandinavia, The Netherlands, Britain, and Ireland, as compared with Germany or France.

Lastly, technological developments, government policies, and private sector initiatives within each country work to structure the opportunities for Internet use and access, including investments in scientific research, programs to facilitate Internet connections via public libraries and schools, computer training, and communications policies regulating telephone charges, cross-media ownership, and online server companies.

We can conclude that at present the information society has not spread evenly throughout postindustrial economies. Instead, there are major differences between leaders and laggards, even within the European Union. There is a strong correlation at the national level between patterns of newspaper readership and use of the Net.[17] Far from equalizing the playing field for all European societies, the adoption of new technology has thus far exacerbated a north–south divide that already existed in the use of the traditional mass media.

THE CHARACTERISTICS OF THE ONLINE COMMUNITY

Is the online community disproportionately composed of more affluent and better-educated people, men rather than women, and the younger generation rather than the older? Does it draw from those who are already heavy users of newspapers and television news? Will the online community become 'normalized' over the years if Internet usage gradually widens and broadens into mainstream society?

Based on what we know about the characteristics of the online community in the United States, we would expect to find that Net users would be drawn disproportionately from the more affluent and better-educated sectors of society, from the male population, from younger generations, and from those most attentive to the traditional news media.[18] In these respects, except for age, the online community reflects the socioeconomic biases common in conventional forms of political participation.[19] The literature also suggests that we would expect to find that the online community would include those already most engaged with, and knowledgeable about, public affairs. With the important exception of age, if the profile for Net users is similar to the profile for those already most likely to participate politically, the Internet may function to reinforce rather than transform the existing social inequalities in civic society.

Table 6.4 and Figure 6.3 compare European Internet users on the basis of social background and use of traditional news media in the spring of 1996 and the spring of 1999. For multivariate analysis, these variables were entered into a logistic regression model, shown in Table 6.5, along with each nation (coded as dummy variables), to examine the effects of the societal-level variations already observed. The typical profile for Internet users shows that, as expected, they are more similar to newspaper readers than to television viewers. The demographics of Net use show that the strongest predictors for this group are age, education, and region; Internet users in Europe are far more numerous among the younger generation (in marked contrast to TV news viewers), the better educated, and those living in northern Europe.

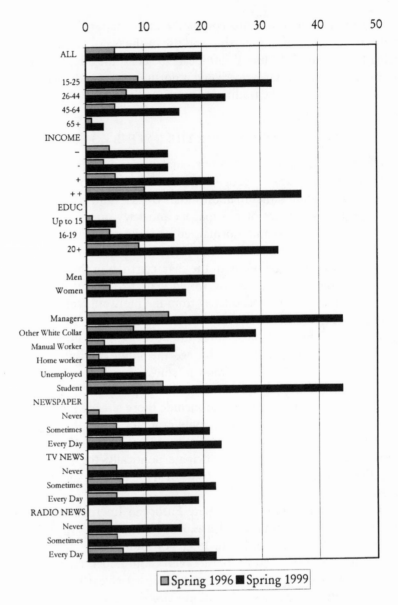

Figure 6.3. Online community, EU-15.

Table 6.4. *Social profile for Internet users, EU-15, 1996–99*

	% Online Spring 1996	% Online Spring 1999	Change
ALL EU-15	5	20	+15
AGE			
15–25	9	32	+23
26–44	7	24	+17
45–64	5	16	+11
65+	1	3	+2
HH INCOME CATEGORY			
—	4	14	+10
–	3	14	+11
+	5	22	+17
++	10	37	+27
AGE FINISHED EDUC			
Up to 15	1	5	+4
16–19 Years	4	15	+11
20+	9	33	+24
GENDER			
Men	6	22	+16
Women	4	17	+13
OCCUPATIONAL STATUS			
Managers	14	44	+30
Other White Collar	8	29	+21
Manual Worker	3	15	+12
Home Worker	2	8	+6
Unemployed	3	10	+7
Student	13	44	+31
READ DAILY NEWSPAPER			
Never	2	12	+10
Sometimes	5	21	+16
Every Day	6	23	+17
WATCH TV NEWS			
Never	5	20	+15
Sometimes	6	22	+16
Every Day	5	19	+14
LISTEN TO RADIO NEWS			
Never	4	16	+12
Sometimes	5	19	+14
Every Day	6	22	+16

Sources: Eurobarometers: 44.2, spring 1996; 51.0, spring 1999.

Table 6.5. *Predictors of use of the Internet, EU-15, 1999*

	Using Internet R	Sig.	β	Operationalization
DEMOGRAPHICS				
Age	−0.168	0.000	−0.642	In years
Education	0.153	0.000	0.609	Age finished FT education
Income	0.141	0.000	0.439	Harmonized HH income scale
Class	0.077	0.000	0.574	Manual (0)/Nonmanual (1) HoH
Gender	0.052	0.000	0.327	Male (1) Female (0)
USE OF MEDIA				
Newspaper Use	0.044	0.000	0.139	5-point scale
Radio News Use	0.031	0.315	0.092	5-point scale
TV News Use	0.000	0.315	−0.031	5-point scale
NATION				
Greece	−0.073	0.000	−1.72	0/1
Germany	−0.067	0.000	−1.30	0/1
France	−0.057	0.000	−1.24	0/1
Spain	−0.055	0.000	−1.36	0/1
Portugal	−0.054	0.000	−1.44	0/1
Belgium	−0.052	0.000	−1.20	0/1
Austria	−0.041	0.000	−0.93	0/1
Italy	−0.036	0.000	−0.91	0/1
Ireland	−0.029	0.000	−0.73	0/1
UK	0.000	0.432	0.23	0/1
Netherlands	0.021	0.000	0.45	0/1
Finland	0.035	0.000	0.65	0/1
Denmark	0.049	0.000	0.89	0/1
Sweden	0.099	0.000	1.77	0/1
Cox-Snell R^2	0.278			
Nagelkerke R^2	0.431			
% Correct	83.8			

Notes: This table reports the coefficients predicting use of the Internet based on logistic regression models. Use of the Internet is measured as a dichotomy, where 1 = yes, 0 = no. HoH = head of household. Luxembourg, which is close to the European mean, is excluded from the national dummies.
Source: Eurobarometer 51.0, spring 1999.

Users also tend to be higher in socioeconomic status and income, and there is a familiar gender gap, with women slightly less active on the Net than men. The pattern by occupational status was clearly defined, with 44% of managers online, compared with 15% of manual workers, and only 10% of the unemployed. Once we control for region, then the large disparities by nation are reduced in strength. In terms of use of the traditional news media, just as in the United States, European online users were more likely than the average to read a newspaper and listen to radio news, although there was no significant relationship with use of TV news. Although there was much overlap in media use, those on the Internet typically tended to differ in some important regards, particularly by age, from those who most often relied on television news. The generation gap in the patterns of media consumption probably will have important consequences for future developments in the news industry. The familiar social biases in the online community that had been widely observed in the United States were also present in western Europe.

The multivariate analysis in Table 6.5 confirms that all these variables proved significant. After controlling for individual-level social background and media use, the societal-level variations we had already observed remained significant. That suggests that the pattern regarding higher use of the Net in Scandinavia was not just a product of the educational and occupational backgrounds of the populations in these countries, but reflected broader societal patterns of access. That is, a white-collar college graduate in Portugal would still be less likely to be online than would a Swedish equivalent.

If we compare the changes shown in Table 6.5, as use of the Internet expanded from the middle 1990s to the late 1990s, it is apparent that the social division between Net users and non-users has widened. The groups who have flocked most readily to the Net are the young, the most affluent, and the well educated, whereas other groups have registered far more modest increases. For example, the proportion of managers online shot up by 30%, double the average rate of increase. The profile of online users may flatten again in a few years if Net use spreads more widely throughout society (e.g., if the price of equipment and access drops), as seems likely, but during the emerging Internet period it is the younger generation with the educational skills and financial resources to get online who have taken most advantage of the opportunities on the Internet. The gap between the information-rich and information-poor has widened substantially, at both individual and societal levels, in the emergent Internet era.

CONCLUSIONS: REINFORCING THE INFORMATION GAP

Many exaggerated hopes and fears surround 'virtual democracy'. Internet research is sometimes in as much danger of 'irrational exuberance' as the NASDAQ index. Much debate revolves around whether the distinctive structure and interactive format of the Internet will provide a genuinely new form of political mobilization, enticing the disengaged and apathetic into public life and producing a more egalitarian democracy, or whether its primary function will be to reinforce the dominance of those who are already most active in the conventional channels like social organizations, community groups, and political parties. At present, we often lack systematic evidence, and much of the more speculative theoretical literature seems to treat the Internet as a Rorschach test, broadly reflecting technophile or technophobe beliefs about the future.

Mobilization theories would suggest that by sharply reducing some of the barriers to political participation, lowering some of the financial hurdles, and widening the opportunities for political debate, for dissemination of information, and for group interaction, Net activism may have the potential to broaden involvement in public life. For enthusiasts, the Net promises to provide new forms of horizontal and vertical communication that can facilitate and enrich deliberation in the public sphere and produce a more egalitarian politics.

Yet an emerging consensus in American research on Net users seems to favor the reinforcement view: In the early stages of the Internet era, the online community in America is being drawn from the more affluent and better-educated social strata, and Net activists share many of the characteristics of conventional activists.[20] If so, the new medium may merely reinforce the division between the information-rich and information-poor.

The conclusion from my earlier analysis of the social and political characteristics of Net activists in the 1996 and 1998 American elections, based on Pew Center surveys of online users and of the general public, serves to confirm an overall pattern of *reinforcement* rather than mobilization: Net political activists were already among the highly motivated, most interested, and best-informed people in the American electorate.[21] In this sense, during these campaigns, politics on the Net was essentially preaching to the converted. The Internet still provided a valuable service in broadening the range of information that was easily available to the online community during the campaign. But the Web was used more often as a means to access traditional news sources, like the *New York Times*, rather than as a radical new source of unmediated information and communication between citizens and their elected leaders.

While the reinforcement pattern does seem to characterize Internet users in past American elections, if use broadens and evolves over the years it remains to be seen whether or not that pattern will be maintained in subsequent campaigns. The Internet era is still in its adolescence: The first packet-switching network started in the UK in 1968, and the University of California at Los Angeles (UCLA) launched ARPANET the following year, but it was only in 1992 that the World Wide Web was born, followed by an explosion of use and the launch of Mosaic and Netscape in 1993–94.[22] Mobilization theorists will argue that it will take more than a few years for the Net to level the playing field and transform the established patterns of political participation, and the social profile for Internet users could well change over time. Just as the early, more affluent television audience of the 1950s had moved mainstream by the 1960s, in a process of 'normalization', so the massive surge in Web access and the declining costs may mean that the early users will prove to be atypical of the larger number of later participants. Whether or not the Internet will have the appeal to reach beyond the active group, and beyond traditional news sources, as access gradually ripples out to broader groups in the electorate and political uses of the Web evolve in new ways, remains an open question at this stage.

This chapter confirms that the patterns of reinforcement within the context of American political campaigns can also be found in this broader comparison of postindustrial societies. The familiar social biases observed among American users in the early years of Internet expansion are also evident in western Europe, notably the appeal of the Net for the more affluent and better-educated public. The mobilization of the younger generation in the online community provides some evidence counter to that trend, for they are the ones who have been least involved in many traditional forms of political activism such as voting and who also have been least likely to watch television news. Over the longer term, that may provide some support for the mobilization thesis. At the societal level, the north–south divide in the information society is marked and seems likely to reinforce existing cross-national differences in the use of the print and electronic news media. The European nations that are proving most receptive of the Internet tend to be those in which there is already heavy consumption of the print press, whereas the Mediterranean region, which has been slowest to move online, is characterized by a television-centric mass audience. It remains to be seen whether this pattern will be evident more generally in other postindustrial societies. The next chapter goes on to consider the consequences of the Internet for campaigns and elections, and Chapter 12 examines the mobilizing effects for 'virtual democracy' in the Internet age.

CHAPTER 7

The Evolution of Campaign Communications

M any accounts have noted the decline of traditional forms of party campaigning, such as local rallies and door-to-door canvassing, and new developments like the growth of spin-doctors and political consultants. A growing series of case studies has documented these trends in a range of established and newer democracies.[1] Different accounts have interpreted these changes in various ways: as the 'rise of political marketing', if the techniques have been borrowed from the private sector, or as the 'Americanization of campaigning', if these forms of electioneering originated in the United States.[2] Building upon this literature, the core argument of this chapter is that such changes in campaign communications can best be understood as evolutionary processes of *modernization* that simultaneously transform party organizations, the news media, and the electorate. This typology is illustrated schematically in Table 7.1 and Figure 7.1.

In this theoretical framework, *premodern campaigns* are understood as having three basic characteristics: The campaign organization is based upon direct forms of interpersonal communications between candidates and citizens at the local level, with short-term, ad-hoc planning by the party leadership. In the news media, the 'partisan press' acts as core intermediary between parties and the public. And the electorate is anchored by strong party loyalties. During this era, local parties selected the candidates, rang the doorbells, posted the pamphlets, targeted the wards, planned the resources, and generally provided all the machinery linking voters and candidates. For citizens, the model is one that is essentially *local-active*, meaning that most campaigning is concentrated within local communities, conducted through relatively demanding political activities like rallies, doorstep canvassing, and party meetings.

Table 7.1. *Typology of the evolution of campaigning*

	Premodern Mid-19thC to 1950s	Modern Early 1960s–late 1980s	Postmodern 1990s+
Campaign Organization	Local and decentralized party volunteers	Nationally coordinated with greater professionalization	Nationally coordinated but decentralized operations
Preparations	Short-term, ad hoc	Long campaign	Permanent campaign
Central Coordination	Party leaders	Central party headquarters, more specialist advisors	Special party campaign units and more professional consultants
Feedback	Local canvassing and party meetings	Occasional opinion polls	Regular opinion polls plus focus groups and interactive Web sites
Media	Partisan press, local posters and pamphlets, radio broadcasts	Television broadcasts through main evening news	Television narrow casting, targeted direct mail, targeted ads
Campaign Events	Local public meetings, whistle-stop leadership tours	News management, daily press conferences, controlled photo-ops	Extension of news management to routine politics and government
Costs	Low budget	Moderate	Higher costs for professional consultants
Electorate	Stable social and partisan alignments	Social and partisan dealignment	Social and partisan dealignment

Source: Adapted from Pippa Norris. 1997. *Electoral Change since 1945.* Oxford: Blackwell. Figure 9.1.

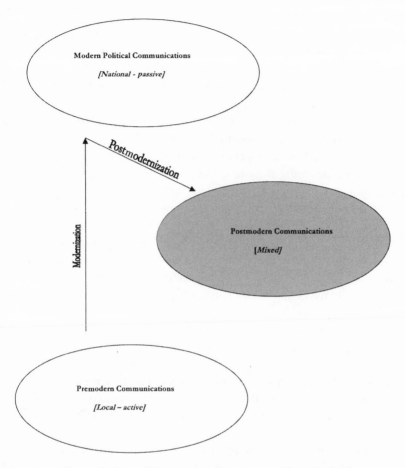

Figure 7.1. The evolution of campaign communications in postindustrial societies. *Source*: Adapted from Ronald Inglehart. 1997. *Modernization and Postmodernization: Cultural, Economic and Political Change in 43 Societies.* Princeton, NJ: Princeton University Press (fig. 3.1).

Modern campaigns are defined as those with a party organization coordinated more closely at a central level by political leaders, advised by external professional consultants like opinion pollsters. In the news media, national television has become the principal forum for campaign events, supplementing other media. And the electorate has become increasingly decoupled from party and group loyalties. Politicians and professional advisors conduct polls, design advertisements, schedule the theme du jour, leadership tours, news conferences, and photo opportunities, handle the press, and battle to dominate the nightly television news. For citizens, the typical experience of the election becomes more passive, in the sense that the main focus of the campaign is located within national television studios, so that campaigns have become more distant from most voters, leaving them disengaged spectators outside the process.

Postmodern campaigns are understood as those in which the coteries of professional consultants on advertising, public opinion, marketing, and strategic news management become more coequal actors with politicians, assuming a more influential role within government in a 'permanent' campaign, in which they coordinate local activities more efficiently at the grassroots level. The news media system is fragmenting into a more complex and incoherent environment of multiple channels, outlets, and levels. And the electorate becomes more dealigned in their voting choices. For some citizens, the election may represent a return to some of the forms of engagement found in the premodern stage, as the new channels of communication potentially allow greater interactivity between voters and politicians.

The essential features of this model can be expected to vary from one context to another. Rather than claiming that all campaigns are inevitably moving into the postmodern category, this view emphasizes that contests can continue to be arrayed from the premodern to the postmodern, due to the influence of a range of intermediary conditions, such as the electoral system, campaign regulations, and organizational resources. And instead of seeing the development of a specifically American pattern, with practices like negative advertising, personalized politics, and high campaign expenditures that are subsequently exported to other countries, it seems more accurate to understand the changes in campaigning as part of the modernization process rooted in technological and political developments common to many postindustrial societies. This chapter aims to develop the main elements in this theoretical framework and then to compare evidence of the main channels of direct and mediated campaigning to see how far we can characterize contemporary elections along these dimensions. To attempt to understand longitudinal trends, the next chapter builds on this framework by comparing case studies from the United States and Britain illustrating how campaigns have evolved since the war. We can then summarize the conclusions and consider the implications of these developments for the core issues of political trust and civic engagement that lie at the heart of this book.

THE PREMODERN CAMPAIGN

Premodern campaigning originated in the nineteenth century with the expansion of the franchise and continued in recognizable form in most postindustrial societies until at least the 1950s, when the advent of televised campaigns and the regular publication of opinion polls began to transform the process. In general elections, the premodern era was characterized by a campaign organization with a party leader at the apex, surrounded by a few close political advisors, running a relatively short, ad-hoc national campaign. The party base was a loose organizational network of volunteers dispersed in local areas. The party organization was predominantly constituency-oriented, involving politicians, party workers, and citizens in direct face-to-face contact through activities like town-hall hustings, canvassing, and branch-party meetings. In national-party/branch-party organizations (or 'mass–branch' parties) the grassroots membership provided the unpaid labour, helping the local candidate, advised by an agent from the national party. Premodern campaigns relied heavily on the partisan element of the press as the main source of mediated information, either directly owned and subsidized by party elements or independently owned and managed but providing sympathetic partisan spin through editorial columns and political commentary. Newspapers were indirectly supplemented in the 1920s by radio and newsreels at the movies, important sources of news in the interwar period, and these media began to nationalize the campaign even prior to the age of television. The classic theories of voting behaviour have stressed the stability of the electorate during this era, anchored by social and party loyalties. Lipset and Rokkan stressed that European parties were based on stable sectoral cleavages in the electorate, with divisions based on class, religion, and region providing the solid bedrock of electoral support.[3] The earliest studies of campaign communications in America, by Lazarsfeld and colleagues, emphasized that the primary impact of elections was to reinforce partisan supporters, rather than to produce new converts.[4] The classic accounts of American electoral behaviour by V. O. Key[5] and Campbell and associates[6] have argued that voters were guided by partisan identification, representing an enduring loyalty or 'standing decision' that influenced those votes over successive contests. If voters were largely stable, the main function of party organizations was to energize and mobilize their traditional base of electoral support.

Today these direct forms of campaigning have essentially been supplemented, but not replaced. The traditional campaign, built on personal networks of volunteers and face-to-face candidate–voter communications, continues to be common when mobilizing voters in no-frills contests for local, municipal, and state-level elected offices, as well as for minor parties without generous financial resources, as well as in countries like Britain where mass-branch party organizations maintain networks of active party members.[7] Electoral systems where politicians compete in multimember seats with others within the same party often emphasize the importance of local campaigning to maintain support. This pattern is evident in Ireland under STV, as well as in Japan, where LDP politicians, when competing under STNV, traditionally relied upon a local association, or *koenkai*, acting as an election machine maintaining contact with voters.[8] Direct campaigning also remains characteristic of elections in developing countries like India and South Africa, where there are relatively low levels of literacy and television access. Even in the United States, 'retail' politics continues in the New Hampshire primaries, in district and state caucuses, and in general elections, with candidates meeting activists in local living rooms and diners, and displays of yard signs and bumper stickers.[9] Huckfeldt and Sprague have emphasized the political importance in presidential elections of local mobilization efforts, party canvassing, and discussion networks within American communities.[10] In Chapter 13 we shall examine long-term trends in the proportions of Americans engaged in campaign activism, and the results show no consistent or substantial decline across most dimensions (other than the display of buttons and bumper stickers). Figure 7.2 shows no decline in the proportion of the electorate contacted by the major U.S. parties, either face-to-face or, more commonly today, by telephone; if anything, recent indicators point towards more contacting activity. Nevertheless, technological changes, notably the rise of television and of opinion polls, have meant that in postindustrial societies direct forms of campaigning have become ancillary in general elections to mediated channels of party–voter communication.

THE MODERN CAMPAIGN

The gradual evolution of the modern campaign from the early 1950s to the mid-1980s was marked by several related developments: the move from dispersed state and local party organizations to a nationally coor-

I:Premodern Campaigns

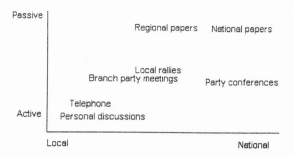

II: Modern Campaigns:

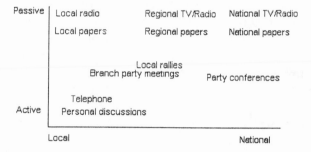

III: Postmodern Campaigns:

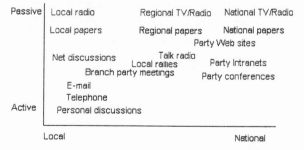

Figure 7.2. The typology of campaign communications.

dinated strategic campaign; from party officials and volunteers contributing time and labour to paid professional consultants specializing in communications, marketing, polling, and campaign management; the shift from more partisan newspapers towards national television news; and the development of a more detached and instrumental electorate, less strongly anchored to party loyalties and social cleavages. The 'long campaign' that lasted for the year or so before polling day gradually became as important strategically as the short 'official' campaign.

In most postindustrial democracies the critical shift towards the modern campaign developed with the rise of television and the regular publication of opinion-poll results during the 1950s. This process gradually shifted the primary locus of political communications from the print media towards broadcasting, particularly the mainstream national evening news on the major television channels. The print press remains politically important, particularly in newspaper-centric systems, and as we discussed in Chapter 4, the per-capita circulation levels for newspapers in OECD countries have not declined. Nevertheless, there is evidence to suggest that many countries have experienced a dealignment in traditional press–party linkages, as newspapers have become increasingly politically independent, selecting news on the basis of commercial logic to maximize sales, rather than following the political logic of party support.[11]

In The Netherlands, for example, at least until the 1960s there were strong sectoral cleavages, producing 'pillarization', as people within various communities attended the same schools and churches, joined the same social clubs, sports clubs, and community associations, tended to vote for the same party, and therefore bought the party newspaper. The *zuillen* or pillars of that system were built on Protestant, Catholic, and labour mass movements that mobilized for political purposes in the early twentieth century at the same time as mass-circulation newspapers were developing in The Netherlands – all of which contributed to the creation of stable cleavage subcultures. Limited numbers of papers represented the Protestant, Catholic, and Socialist pillars.[12] A process of de-pillarization began in the mid-1960s, and one major consequence has been the decline of the partisan press in The Netherlands. Many other countries seem to have followed similar processes, leading to greater internal diversity within the newspaper sector, such as balanced pro–con op-ed columns, but thereby reducing the degree of external diversity between the newspaper sector and other print media. As will be discussed later, even Britain, which had long exemplified the partisan press, began to experience press–party dealignment in the 1990s.

Like the more direct forms of personal communication, newspapers did not necessarily decline in importance as sources of political communication, but increasingly they became supplemented by television. The main effort of party campaign organizations, from the morning party press conferences through the day's events, visits, and photo opportunities to the evening rallies and speeches, became increasingly focused on achieving favourable coverage on the mainstream evening news, current-affairs programs, and leadership debates on television. That trend was reinforced by the fact that the mainstream audience was virtually captive to such programs, given that until the early 1980s there were only two or three television stations broadcasting in most OECD countries, major news programs occurred at regular prime-time slots in the evening rather than on a twenty-four-hour cyclical basis, and most countries offered no opportunities for paid political advertising on television. To a large extent, therefore, what was reported on the flagship news programs on Britain's BBC and ITN, on Sweden's SVT, or on Japan's NHK, to a largely captive electorate, *was* the heart of the modern election campaign, setting the agenda for the following morning's newspapers. The role of television news strengthened the party leadership's control over the campaign, which became increasingly national.

Commentators have suggested that the focus on the television campaign has intensified the spotlight on party leadership, moving the campaign from cleavage-based and issue-based conflict towards 'personalization' of politics.[13] Case studies suggest that such a trend is particularly marked for presidential elections, such as those in Latin America, but it is apparent in parliamentary elections as well, such as recent elections in Israel,[14] Germany, and Italy.[15] It seems plausible that the shift in emphasis from newspapers to television probably has heightened the visibility of leaders, especially those like Tony Blair and Bill Clinton who seem most comfortable in this medium, although we lack systematic evidence to confirm whether this is a general trend in western democracies. Moreover, it is not clear from the available research whether the focus on party leaders in campaign coverage is necessarily leading to an increasing importance of party leaders in determining votes in parliamentary systems.[16]

In the modern campaign, following the rise of television, parties increasingly developed coordinated national and regional campaigns, with communications designed by specialists skilled in advertising, marketing, and polling. The adoption of such practices did not occur overnight. A recent study of European political marketing has termed that process a 'shopping model', in which parties grafted particular practical techniques that had seemed useful or successful in other campaigns onto the existing machinery on an ad-hoc basis.[17] Party adaptation was particularly evident following extended periods out of power. The move from amateur to professional campaigns was marked by more frequent use of specialist consultants, public-relations experts, and professional fund-raisers influencing decisions formerly made by candidates or party officials.[18] Ever since the expansion of the franchise there have been 'professional' campaigners, in the form of full-time local agents or party managers, along with permanent staff like press officers, at central headquarters. The new professionals, however, were essentially 'hired guns' external to the party organization, often working on campaigns in different countries, such as the advertising consultants Saatchi and Saatchi. Increased use of paid consultants, public-opinion polls, direct mail, and professional television broadcasts during the long campaign led to rising costs and the shift from labour-intensive to capital-intensive campaigns.

The professionalization of the political-consultant industry has developed furthest in the United States, with demand fuelled largely by the traditional weakness of American party organizations, the rise of the candidate-centered campaign in the 1960s, the capital-intensive nature of advertising-driven campaigns, and the number and frequency of American primary and general elections.[19] Outside of America, the rise of independent political consultants has been slower, mainly because parties have incorporated professionals within their ranks,[20] but recent years may have seen the development of a more distinctively European style of political marketing.[21] Organizations like the International Association of Political Consultants (IAPC) and the World Association of Public Opinion Research, along with regional affiliates, bring together polling experts, advertising specialists, and campaign consultants.

The rise of the modern campaign was also related to major changes in the electorate. Many studies have highlighted how dealignment eroded traditional social cleavages and partisan loyalties and produced a more instrumental electorate supporting parties on a more contingent basis, based on their policies and performance. The familiar cleavages along lines of class and religion, which had long anchored the

European electorate, proved weaker predictors of voting behaviour in many countries as party competition over issues, images, and leadership became increasingly important.[22] In the new campaigns the electorate became less likely to encounter the more demanding forms of local political communication, such as direct face-to-face discussions on the doorstep or in local meetings, and were more likely to experience elections via more passive and indirect forms of spectatorship, like watching television. Earlier theories suggested that dealignment was largely a product of long-term socioeconomic and secular trends that were gradually transforming the mass public, stressing rising levels of education, class mobility, and cross-cutting cleavages along lines of race and gender, whereas more recent accounts have emphasized that parties have both contributed to and sought to benefit from these changes in the electorate by developing 'catch-all' strategies designed to attract voters from outside their core constituency.[23] The modern campaign evolved into a familiar pattern from the early fifties until the mid-eighties, with similar, although not identical, changes becoming evident in many general elections across postindustrial societies.

THE POSTMODERN CAMPAIGN

Accounts commonly identify only two steps in this historical sequence, regarding the age of television as the culmination of the modernization process. But during the past decade we can identify the transition from this familiar world to the 'postmodern' campaign marked by several related developments: the fragmentation of television outlets, with the shift already discussed from national broadcasting towards more diverse news sources, including satellite and cable stations, talk radio, and twenty-four-hour rolling news bulletins; the opportunities for newer forms of party–voter interaction offered by the rise of the Internet; and the attempt by parties to reassert control in a more complex, fragmented, and rapidly changing news environment through strategic communications and media management during the permanent campaign, with the continuous feedback provided by polls, focus groups, and electronic town meetings to inform routine decision-making, not just campaigns. This last stage of the modernization process remains under development, and it is more clearly evident in some societies than in others, but it seems likely to represent the future direction of political campaigning in postindustrial societies. Like another layer of the onion, news forms supplement, rather than displace, older forms of campaigning.

In the extensive literature on 'postmodernism', the concept is understood as a complex phenomenon, open to multiple interpretations.[24] Yet the commonalities of postmodernism are usually understood to include greater cultural pluralism, social diversity, and fragmentation of sources; increased challenges to traditional forms of hierarchical authority and external standards of rational knowledge; and a more inchoate and confused sense of identity. For these reasons, the term does seem to capture many of the developments that are currently transforming the context and process of political campaigning in postindustrial societies.

In anticipating potential ambiguities, two points of clarification need to be made to this argument. First, the conceptualization in this book refers to campaign, not societal, modernization. As Swanson and Mancini argue,[25] many other factors may well be transforming society in general, such as a greater differentiation of roles, rising educational levels and cognitive skills, and more complex social identities, but these factors remain well outside the scope of this book. The focus here is restricted to developments within political communications, defined narrowly in this chapter as communications in election campaigns.

Second, many others have characterized the recent changes as culminating in the rise of political marketing, placing primary emphasis on the strategic activities of parties, politicians, and campaign advisors in their attempts to maintain or expand their share of the electorate. The heart of the political-marketing concept is a shift from sales of existing products (advertising party policies, leaders, and images) to a focus that puts the 'customer' first, using research into voters' needs, wants, and drives, as revealed through polls, focus groups, and similar techniques – all culminating in the adoption of strategies designed to build a dependable reputation for reliable delivery of service on key policy issues that should maximize votes.[26] That view does provide useful insights, but the conceptualization of the postmodern campaign in this study places greater emphasis on the ways that technological and socioeconomic developments are altering the context of political communications, such as the rise of the Internet, to which all actors (parties, campaign professionals, and journalists) are being forced to respond. After all, polls were available for at least twenty years before they became widely used internally to shape party strategies. Even in recent campaigns, the use of systematic marketing techniques to inform party policies often has been very limited. For example, the British Conservative party commissioned few opinion polls in the run-up to the 1997 campaign, in large part because they were short of funds, and their strategic plan was scrapped when John Major tore up the script the night before an election broadcast and made an impromptu plea for internal unity over Europe. The postmodern conceptualization sees politicians as essentially lagging behind technological and economic changes, and running hard just to stay in place by adopting the techniques of political marketing in the struggle to cope with the more complex news environment – rather than driving these developments.

Instead of being a linear development, the postmodern campaign symbolizes a return to some of the more localized and interactive forms of communication that were present in the premodern period. As shown in Figure 7.3, the new technology allows for forms of political communication that can be located schematically somewhere between the local activism of the premodern campaign (with direct town-hall meetings and political rallies) and the national-passive forms of communication characteristic of the modern television campaign. The development of political discussion groups on the Net and party intranets, the availability of interactive political sites run by government agencies, community associations, or interest groups, and the political use of e-mail or list-serves to mobilize and organize, as well as access to 'traditional' news media on the Web, all represent a midway point in the model. These formats continue to evolve, along with the political uses of the Web.[27] As mentioned earlier, at present, access to the Internet varies widely across postindustrial societies and is particularly low in southern Europe. Nevertheless, as political use of the Internet expands, the postmodern campaign does seem destined to add yet another distinctive layer of communications to the process, supplementing existing channels.

MEDIATING CONDITIONS

The way these changes become manifest in different countries, and the pace of change over time, will be heavily dependent on certain mediating conditions. Postmodern campaigns are exemplified most clearly by contests like the U.S. presidential and congressional elections – characterized by two major catch-all parties, with minimal ideological baggage, in winner-take-all elections, involving an army of hired technical consultants, widespread use of capital-intensive TV ads in a frag-

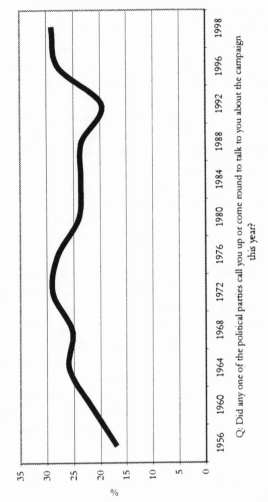

Q: Did any one of the political parties call you up or come round to talk to you about the campaign this year?

Figure 7.3. People contacted by major parties, United States, 1956–98. *Source:* NES, 1956–98.

mented multichannel environment, rapid expansion in the political uses of the Internet, and an electorate with weakened party loyalties. Such an open environment is ideal for an entrepreneurial approach designed to maximize electoral support. In contrast, premodern campaigning continues to characterize many other types of contests, such as British local elections, which are second-order, low-salience contests in which the major parties rely primarily on volunteer grassroots members, activists, and candidates in each local constituency to canvass voters and mobilize partisan support. In those campaigns there is minimal national coverage on television or in newspapers, the chief means of publicity remain handbill displays and printed pamphlets, and financial resources are restricted.

Four major factors can be identified as important mediating conditions affecting the modernization process:

- the *regulatory environment*, including the *electoral system* (whether single-member majoritarian or proportional party list), the *type of election* (including the frequency of elections, the type of office, such as presidential or parliamentary, and whether at a subnational, national, or supranational level), and the *laws* governing campaigning (such as rules on party funding and state subsidies, campaign expenditures, the publication of opinion polls, and access to political broadcasts or ads),
- the *party system*, including the organizational structure, membership, and funding of parties (such as whether elite-led, mass–branch, catch-all, or cartel) and the system of *party competition* (such as one party predominant, two-party, moderate or polarized pluralism),
- the *media system*, including the level of development of the *political-consultant industry* (including the availability of professional market researchers, opinion pollsters, advertisers, and campaign managers) and the *structure and culture of the news media* (such as the contrasts already discussed between newspaper-centric or television-centric systems, between the partisan-leaning or 'objective' models of journalism, and whether broadcasting reflects a public service or commercial ethos),
- the *electorate*, including the patterns of *voting behaviour* (such as whether electors display strong or weak party loyalties, and whether there is limited or extensive electoral volatility).

Previous chapters have discussed some of these factors, so here we can focus on comparing the regulatory framework and party campaign organizations.

The Regulatory Framework

The regulations governing television coverage during elections concern three main areas: the purchase of paid commercial advertisements, the allocation and content of free party political broadcasts, and the rules governing political balance in campaign debates, news coverage, and current affairs. During the era when public-service channels predominated in most countries there were severe restrictions on the ability of political parties to purchase any airtime on television. A comparative survey of Western societies in the late 1970s found that only five of the twenty-one countries had commercial channels, and paid political advertising on television was allowed only in Australia, Canada, Japan, and the United States.[28] By the mid-1990s, following deregulation and the explosive increase in the number of commercial channels already documented, about half of the OECD countries allowed paid political advertising on television (Table 7.2). In practice, the use of that facility has varied substantially among countries, as well as between public-service and commercial channels.[29] In The Netherlands, for example, although political commercials are now allowed, and were used for the first time in 1994, in practice few have been aired, mainly because of the limited financial resources of the Dutch parties.[30] In contrast, in the United States, campaign ads are employed for every level of office, producing capital-intensive campaigns. For example, in recent presidential campaigns, the costs of producing and airing TV and radio commercials have accounted for about 60% of all expenditures.[31]

Following the long tradition of public-service broadcasting, all OECD countries other than America allocate some free airtime to parties, either by law or because of long-standing agreements with broadcasters. The length of these slots varies substantially, from the 30- or 60-second ads common in Italy to 2.5 minutes in Germany, 4 minutes in France, and an allocation of up to 10 minutes (usually only partially used) for British party political broadcasts. Three formulas are commonly used for allocating time among contestants. Strict equality among all parties is used in countries like the Czech Republic and Mexico; in the latter, the Federal Electoral Institute buys 15 minutes per month for advertising on television and radio for each party. Other countries provide allocations based on the results of the preceding

Country	Paid Political Ads on TV	Free TV Airtime to Parties	Fair Balance Rules	Leader Debate Last Election	Ban on Publication of Opinion Polls Prior to Election	U.S. Consultants Involved in Recent Campaign	Direct Funding Subsidy to Parties or Candidates	Contribution Limit
Australia	✓	✓	✓					✗
Austria	✓	✓	✓	✓	✗	✓	✓	
Belgium	✗	✓	✓	✓	✗	✗	✗	✗
Canada	✓	✓	✓	✓		✓	✓	
Denmark	✗	✓	✓	✓	✗	✓	✓	✓
Finland	✗	✓	✓	✓	✗	✓	✓	✗
France	✗	✓	✓	✓	✓	✓	✓	
Germany	✓	✓	✓	✗	✗	✗	✓	
Greece					✗	✓	✓	
Ireland	✗	✓	✓	✓	✗	✓	✓	✓
Italy	✓	✓	✓		✓	✓	✗	✓
Japan	✓	✓	✓	✓		✓	✓	✓
Mexico	✓	✓	✓	✓		✓	✓	✓
Netherlands	✓	✓	✓		✗	✗	✗	✗
NZ	✓	✓	✓	✓	✗	✓		
Norway	✗	✓	✓		✗	✓	✓	
Poland							✗	
Portugal				✓	✓	✗		✓
Spain	✗	✓	✓	✓	✓	✗		✓
Sweden	✓	✓	✓	✓	✗	✗	✗	✗
Switzerland	✗	✓	✓		✓	✓	✓	
Turkey	✗	✓	✓	✓		✓	✓	✓
UK	✗	✓	✗	✗	✗		✓	✓
US	✓	✗	✓	✓			✓	✓
OECD Total	11/21	21/22	18/18	16/18	5/16	13/18	15/20	8/13

Sources: Lawrence LeDuc, Richard G. Niemi, and Pippa Norris (eds.). 1996. *Comparing Democracies: Elections and Voting in Global Perspective.* Thousand Oaks, CA: Sage.

general election. For example, Greek parties are given airtime based on the sizes of their memberships in the preceding Parliament, with modest allocations for parties with no representatives but with many candidates. Lastly, countries like Australia and Britain divide the time according to an agreement among the parties and the broadcasting authorities; in Britain, for example, in line with many previous contests, the allocation in the 1997 campaign was a 5:5:4 ratio whereby the major parties each received five 10-minute party election broadcasts during the campaign, the Liberal Democrats got four slots, and other minor parties with at least fifty candidates got one each, with additional arrangements for the regions.[32]

In addition, all the countries for which we have information have some fair-balance rules, either formally or informally regulating the balance of political coverage on television news, on current-affairs programs, and on leadership debates during election periods. In Britain, for example, the 5:5:4 ratio used for party political broadcasts is also used to allocate the time balance of coverage of the parties on the news, following the 'stop-watch' principle.[33] In the United States, presidential debates have followed a variety of formats and schedules. For example, the questions have been asked either by selected journalists or by members of the public in an invited audience, or by a mix of both. But all debates follow a strict allocation of time designed to be impartial to all candidates.[34]

PARTY CAMPAIGN ORGANIZATIONS AND FUNDING

An extensive literature has documented changes in the structure, membership, and finance of party organizations, including the Katz and Mair party-organization project.[35] Drawing primarily on party documents and reports, Katz and Mair concluded that the role of parties has evolved or adapted since the 1960s in Western democracies, rather than simply weakened. Documenting trends in party membership in ten European countries from the early 1960s to the end of the 1980s, their study recorded a decline in the proportion of electors who were party members in eight nations, ranging from a very modest slippage (in Sweden) down to far sharper falls (in Denmark, from 21.1% of the electorate in the early 1960s down to 6.5% in the late 1980s). The decline was strongest in relative terms, meaning that party membership failed to keep up with the expansion in the population. Studies based on survey evidence in fifteen western European countries have reached similar conclusions about modest long-term erosions of party membership in many established democracies, although the declines were neither steep nor uniform.[36]

In counterbalance, Katz and Mair also found that since the 1960s those countries they studied had experienced substantial increases in the proportion of staff employed by parties, most notably parliamentary party staff paid by state funds, as well as a considerable rise in central party income. Where these personnel and resources are being funded by state subventions, this may signal, they suggest, a shift from mass–branch parties based primarily on voluntary labour towards a 'cartel' party organization, more dependent on public resources.[37] This pattern is clearer in some countries than in others; state subsidies to parties are far more generous in Germany, Sweden, and Norway, for example, than in Ireland, Britain, and The Netherlands, where party income remains more dependent on membership dues. Table 7.2 shows that by the mid-1990s, direct funding provided to parties or candidates had become common; fifteen out of twenty countries provided public funds, although at different levels of subsidy. In some countries, such as Canada, France, and Australia, public subsidies are designed to reimburse some election expenditures, while in others, such as The Netherlands, Ireland, and Denmark, such funds are designed for other purposes, such as general administration, policy research, political education, or to promote participation by young people or women.[38] Public funding is often said to decrease the risk of parties and candidates becoming dependent on large donations or falling under the influence of lobby groups.

The question whether the 'cartel' party represents the emergence of a new and distinctive type of party organization, as seems evident in many countries, remains controversial.[39] There are also important questions concerning the consequences of the decline in party membership, and in particular whether the fall has been concentrated mostly among the less active older members or whether it involves an across-the-board contraction. Nevertheless, what does seem well established by various studies is that many European countries experienced a gradual shrinkage in grassroots party membership from the 1960s to the late 1980s, probably reducing the pool of voluntary labour available for traditional local campaigning. By way of counterbalance, parties have growing numbers of professional staff, employed in parliaments and at central party offices, as well as more generous financial resources from public funds. These developments, accompanied by the technological and economic changes in the news system, have contributed towards the shift from direct to mediated forms of campaigning.

To examine the consequences of these organizational developments for campaign activity, we can compare the most common ways that European voters were contacted directly by parties or received alternative sources of mediated information during campaigns in the twelve member states for the elections to the European Parliament in 1989 and 1994. It should be noted that those European elections were second-order contests, and in that regard the results can best be interpreted as referendums on the performances of the various national governments, rather than reflecting genuine policy divisions over European issues or a reaction to the performance of the EU.[40] As a low-key contest, we would expect the campaigning to have reflected a 'mixed' model, combining elements from both the direct and mediated channels of communication, with the variations between countries reflecting their electoral, political, and media environments, and that is indeed what we find. The European election surveys (EES) asked voters about their activities during the two or three weeks before polling day, how the campaign came to their attention, and also what information sources they found most useful in making up their minds how to vote. Campaign activities can be ranged along a rough continuum from direct forms of communication (such as talking to friends or family about the election, trying to persuade someone how to vote, speaking to a party worker, attending a party rally, reading election materials sent to their homes, and reading election posters) to indirect or mediated forms of communication (reading a political advertisement in a newspaper, reading a newspaper report on the campaign, watching a television program or listening to a radio program on the election).

The results in Table 7.3 show considerable variation across different items. The single most common type of campaign activity was watching a television program about the election, experienced by half the respondents, although this activity proved far more popular in Germany (61%) than in Luxembourg (43%) or Portugal (30%). The other mediated forms of communication tapped smaller audiences, such as reading a newspaper report about the election (26%) or hearing a radio program (16%), and again there were considerable cross-national variations in these activities. Some of the more direct forms of party–voter communication proved popular, including discussing the election with friends or family (38%), reading election posters (22%),

Table 7.3. *Campaign activities, European elections, 1989 (% 'yes')*

	Direct Party-Voter Communications						Mediated Party-Voter Communications			
	Talked to friends, family or workmates	Tried to persuade someone to vote	Spoke to a party worker	Attended a public meeting or rally	Read election material sent to my home	Read an election poster	Read an advertisement in a newspaper	Read a newspaper report about the election	Heard a program on the radio about the election	Watched a TV program about the election
Belgium	19	4	4	3	11	17	16	14	9	30
Denmark	42	6	6	3	14	17	25	33	18	58
France	39	8	5	3	18	25	14	26	19	51
Germany	40	4	9	7	16	35	23	32	19	61
Greece	53	4	6	13	11	11	10	46	28	47
Ireland	36	3	11	4	25	18	17	30	23	48
Italy	47	8	8	11	10	27	17	19	8	48
Luxembourg	40	0	7	7	21	29	21	36	27	43
Netherlands	37	3	4	3	14	14	15	34	12	47
Portugal	26	2	3	4	5	16	8	15	11	55
Spain	31	2	3	3	13	15	10	17	20	48
UK	32	7	4	1	32	11	15	30	18	50
EU-12	38	6	6	5	17	22	16	26	16	51

Note. Q: 'Which of the following did you do during the two or three weeks before the European elections?'
Source. Eurobarometer 31A, European elections, N. 11,819, EU-12, June–July 1989.

Table 7.4. *Most useful sources of information, European elections, 1989 (%)*

	Television	Newspapers and Magazines	Personal Discussions	Radio	Polls
Belgium	26	14	13	7	2
Denmark	54	32	14	12	2
France	44	23	15	14	4
Germany	56	37	26	20	11
Greece	40	39	36	25	5
Ireland	50	29	15	16	5
Italy	47	25	27	6	2
Luxembourg	43	47	21	29	0
Netherlands	51	42	13	14	4
Portugal	45	14	13	12	2
Spain	59	21	10	26	4
UK	53	30	19	12	2
EU-12	*50*	*28*	*20*	*15*	*4*

Note: Q: 'Which of the following sources of information do you consider to be the most helpful for making up your mind at the time of the elections?'
Source: Eurobarometer 31A, European elections, N. 11,819, EU-12, June–July 1989.

and reading election materials sent to people's homes (17%). But the results also show that in these elections few people reported more active forms of personal engagement, such as speaking to a party worker (6%), attending a party meeting or rally (6%), or trying to persuade others how to vote (6%). There were some interesting variations among nations. For example, rallies were more popular than average in Greece and Italy, and campaign leaflets were more common forms of communication in Ireland and in the UK, both characterized in these elections by non-party-list electoral systems. Similar patterns were confirmed in the 1994 European elections, where again few of the electorate (7%) reported being contacted by party workers during the campaign, while at the other extreme almost two-thirds (65%) were aware of the campaign coverage on television and radio.

Voters were also asked about the most useful source of information when making up their minds how to vote in the European elections. The results in Table 7.4 confirm the preeminence of television in most countries, cited as most helpful by half the respondents, although in Luxembourg newspaper coverage was preferred, while in Greece the print press and television coverage were tied. One-fifth of the electorate

regarded personal discussions as useful, with particularly high preferences in Greece and Italy, two countries where we have already noted
the importance of traditional campaign rallies. Radio (15%) and
opinion polls (4%) were seen as the least useful sources. The overall
pattern in the late 1980s confirmed that the traditional forms of campaigning were persisting throughout Europe, but that these channels
were being supplemented by mediated communications, with television
predominant.

CONCLUSIONS: UNDERSTANDING CAMPAIGN CHANGE

Many commentators have noted the transformation of traditional
forms of political campaigning, and a growing literature has begun to
distinguish the key features of these developments. Much of that literature has conceptualized these changes as involving an 'Americanization' of campaigning. Swanson and Mancini have provided one of the
most ambitious theoretical accounts along these lines, suggesting that
the Americanization of campaigning has produced similar developments across postindustrial societies: 'Around the world, many of the
recent changes in election campaigning share common themes despite
great differences in the political cultures, histories, and institutions of
the countries in which they have occurred. Increasingly, we find such
common practices as political commercials, candidates selected in part
for the appealing image they project on television, technical experts
hired to produce compelling campaign materials, mounting campaign
expenses, and mass media moving center stage in campaigns.'[41] The key
features of the 'Americanization' in this account are certain features of
campaigning that are understood to have originated first in U.S. elections and then were exported to other countries. Swanson and Mancini
stressed four major developments: the 'personalization' of politics as
leaders and candidates rise in importance; the 'scientificization' of campaigning as technical experts like opinion pollsters begin to make decisions formerly reserved for party officials; the detachment of parties
from citizens as politicians come to be increasingly reliant on opinion
polls rather than on direct contact with grassroots activists and voters;
and the development of more autonomous structures of communication, as the modern news media are more determined to pursue their
own interests rather than to serve the needs of politicians.

Yet the impact of these practices varies substantially among nations,
depending on the institutional context of an election campaign, such as

the legal rules governing campaigning, the strength of traditional mass–branch party organizations, and the structure of the electorate. Previous chapters have demonstrated the major contrasts between newspaper-centric and television-centric news environments, as well as the differences among broadcasting systems that are predominantly commercial, mixed, or public-service-oriented. As we have seen, the predominance of almost purely commercial television in America is atypical of most democracies. The regulations covering campaign ads and party political broadcasts and the systems of campaign finance also vary substantially cross-nationally.[42] As a result of such structural contrasts, rather than following the American model, election campaigns in different postindustrial societies continue to display striking differences.[43] The diffusion of television-dominated, personality-driven, and money-driven campaigns, often seen as characteristic features of the Americanization of campaigning, probably has progressed further in Italy, Venezuela, and Israel, for example, than in Britain, Germany, and Sweden. National case studies suggest complex and varied patterns of campaigning worldwide, rather than a simple and uniform Americanization of campaigning.[44]

The findings in this chapter indicate that the major developments we have discussed can be understood as a process of *modernization*, with campaigns evolving through the premodern, modern, and postmodern stages. These changes did not displace local constituency activity, as the ritual of canvassing and leafleting continued in many countries characterized by mass–branch party organizations. Dedicated party volunteers and candidates have continued to engage in the day-to-day activities of organizing, canvassing, leafleting, telephone polling, and mobilizing support.[45] Nevertheless, because of new technology, central campaign headquarters can now tightly coordinate even local activities.[46] As mentioned earlier, many of the features of traditional premodern campaigns also continue in America; retail face-to-face politics remains important for presidential candidates in the Iowa caucus and the New Hampshire primary, as well as in local and state races. In the same way, the print press remains a vital channel of political communication, particularly in newspaper-centric societies characterized by high readership. Nevertheless, the primary focus of campaign activities shifted during the 1950s towards national television news, and then subsequently into a wide range of venues like talk shows, Web sites, and cable stations in a more fragmented electronic environment. The shift towards the postmodern campaign has moved towards the permanent campaign, in which the techniques of electioneering become inter-twined with those of governing. To understand this process further, the next chapter considers case studies of the evolution of campaigning in the United States and Britain, as well as the possible consequences of these developments.

CHAPTER 8

The Rise of the Postmodern Campaign?

To understand the implications of these developments and the longer-term changes in campaigning outlined in the preceding chapter, we can turn to detailed case studies of American and British elections in the mid-1940s, just prior to the rise of television and opinion polls, and compare them to campaigns in the 1990s. The techniques of modern campaigning probably have been transformed most radically in America, so a case study of U.S. presidential elections should highlight the extent of the changes and the outlines of the postmodern campaign that is emerging. Comparisons can be drawn with Britain, a country sharing strong cultural bonds with America, with important similarities in party and electoral systems, and therefore perhaps one of the countries most strongly influenced by transatlantic trends. The first section compares party organizations, news environments, and electorates in the 1948 U.S. and 1945 British elections as exemplars of premodern campaigning. The next section goes on to compare the situations in the 1996 American presidential election and the equivalent 1997 British general election and then considers the implications of these changes.

THE PREMODERN AMERICAN CAMPAIGN

The 1948 American presidential campaign represented the last hurrah for the old system. The Truman and Dewey campaign organizations still relied heavily on traditional face-to-face retail politics for getting out the message, with whistle-stop railway tours across the country, meetings with party notables, ticker-tape parades in major cities, and keynote speeches before packed crowds.[1] Politics was very much a public spectacle, not a private event experienced in living rooms, although in the early twenties the incursion of radio had already begun to transform the process. In the United States, the first mass-based party organizations had developed in the Jacksonian era in the early nineteenth century to mobilize support in the states and in cities like New York, Chicago, and Boston.[2] In urban strongholds the Democratic machine continued to organize events and turned out supporters at local and state levels. The presidential candidates relied on only a handful of close advisors: Truman's campaign train had an entourage of only about twenty campaign staff, including speech-writers, secretaries, and security personnel, accompanied by a small group of about forty reporters. Dewey's campaign organization was similar in size, with about one hundred reporters accompanying his whistle-stop trains.

Newspapers, radio, and movie newsreels provided the main sources of mediated news. America had about 1,800 daily newspapers, reaching about a third of the population every day, not including thousands of weekly papers and popular magazines. Early American newspapers were highly partisan, with editors seeing their job as serving as the mouthpiece for different political leaders and factions. The mid-nineteenth century saw the emergence of more commercially oriented mass-circulation tabloid newspapers, with greater political independence because their principal source of revenue was sales, rather than government subsidies. But it was not until the 1920s, following the arrival of Joseph Pulitzer, that journalism started to evolve towards the 'objective' model emphasizing standards such as fairness, impartiality, and avoidance of direct partisan leanings.[3] By 1948 the partisan press had been in decline for many decades, but in their editorial support newspapers were clearly stacked to favour the GOP camp: 771 papers (65% of all papers) endorsed Dewey, compared with only 182 papers (15%) that supported Truman.[4] The Republican edge in terms of circulation figures was even greater, and this imbalance persisted in every election until the 1960s.

Yet newspaper partisanship received a counterbalance from the other media. The 1934 Communication Act regulating the airwaves ensured equal-opportunity access to the airwaves for all bona fide candidates for public office, forbade censorship of political broadcasts on the radio, and regulated radio and television stations through the Federal Communications Commission (FCC). Roosevelt's fireside chats on radio, and later Truman's, reached a national audience, with over 90% of households owning a radio set. Radio carried candidate speeches to a wide audience, in addition to broadcasting paid ads and special political programs throughout the election. During the campaign, two short, ten-minute films of Truman and Dewey played in movie theatres throughout the country, at a time when about sixty-five million people went to the movies every week.

Television was only emerging into the political spotlight: In 1948 the party conventions were covered on TV for the first time, reaching audiences in New York and Washington, DC, and this campaign also saw the first paid television appearances by presidential candidates. But the audience was limited: In 1950, only 9% of American households had a black-and-white television set flickering in the corner of the living room, although the consumer boom of the fifties rapidly transformed that situation. For the few who watched TV, without cable, the three major networks monopolized the airwaves, with each network broadcast providing only fifteen minutes of news in the early evening. The balance between the print press and electronic media was already beginning to shift as early as 1952: When people were asked by the NES about their main sources of election information, 39% reported following the campaign 'regularly' in newspapers, one-third listened to 'a good many' radio speeches or discussions, but already one-third watched 'a good many' programs about the campaign on television.[5]

As mentioned earlier, Paul Lazarsfeld and colleagues in the early 1940s carried out the first systematic studies of media use and voting behaviour in American campaigns.[6] Lazarsfeld emphasized that the main function of the campaign was to reinforce those supporters who already had partisan leanings; those in the 'attentive public' who tuned into campaign speeches on the radio, followed the campaign in newspapers, and discussed politics with friends were already the most committed partisans. The campaign provided information about Truman and Dewey that helped to crystallize voting decisions for Democrats and Republicans. In contrast, the inattentive public, drawn from the less well educated and lower socioeconomic groups, were less exposed to the news media and less likely to vote.

Most commentators predicted that President Truman would be defeated. International problems during the postwar reconstruction had led to divisions among the Allies and the start of the Cold War. At home there were the problems of demobilization. The conversion of the American economy to peacetime production led to high taxes, labour strikes, and rising prices. The race issue was to expose some serious, deep-rooted divisions: Truman was sympathetic to black demands for civil rights, and when the Democratic convention strongly endorsed this plank of the platform, the party split into three factions, with Governor Strom Thurmond heading the states' rights 'Dixiecrats', opposed to reform, while on the left former Vice-President Henry Wallace led a new Progressive party of pacifists, reformers, and New Dealers. When the Republicans, in the first convention covered on television, nominated Governor Dewey again, almost everyone expected him to win. Fifty of the nation's top political writers picked Dewey as the winner. After the election, in the first of the nationwide surveys that eventually became the NES, two-thirds of the public expressed surprise at the outcome.

The conventional wisdom about the result was reinforced by the few available opinion polls. The first systematic opinion polls based on samples of the population were developed in the mid-1930s. But Truman disregarded the polls and relied instead on his close advisors and on the crowds that greeted him at every campaign stop. Dewey was the first presidential candidate to employ a pollster on his staff, but that probably proved a source of unreliable advice; in 1948 the available surveys by George Gallup, Archibald Crossley, and Elmo Roper confidently predicted a comfortable victory for Governor Thomas E. Dewey. Just before the election, *Life* carried a big picture of Dewey with the caption 'The next President of the United States', while the *Chicago Tribune*'s premature headline was 'Dewey Defeats Truman'. Elmo Roper even discontinued polling on 9 September 1948, when he predicted 52.2% for Dewey to 37.1% for Truman; he regarded the result as so inevitable that 'no amount of electioneering' could alter the outcome. In the end, the pollsters, press commentators, and editorial writers suffered a rout: Truman won about 50% of the popular vote and carried twenty-eight states that yielded 303 electoral-college votes, and the Democrats recaptured control of both houses of Congress.

THE PREMODERN BRITISH CAMPAIGN

If we compare the 1948 American campaign with its equivalent in Britain, the similarities are striking. The British general election in 1945 exemplified the premodern campaign, with its decentralized, ad-hoc, uncoordinated organization, its volunteer labour force, and its constituency focus.[7] The end of the wartime coalition government on 21 May 1945 and the dissolution of Parliament two days later brought the first general election in a decade. The process of British campaigning had gradually evolved in the mid-nineteenth century, following the Second Reform Act in 1867, which encouraged the development of mass party organizations registering and mobilizing the newly enfranchised electorate. In local constituencies, most contact was on a face-to-face basis between candidates, and voters, with campaign rallies, hustings, canvassing, and party meetings, as well as coverage through local newspapers. Despite the introduction of wireless broadcasting in the 1920s, that pattern continued in recognizable form in Britain until at least the late 1950s.

The grassroots organization of the local prospective parliamentary candidates, assisted by voluntary helpers within each constituency, remained the bedrock of the Labour, Conservative, and Liberal campaigns. That reflected patterns of constituency party organization that had developed in the mid-Victorian era. The British electorate was small in number prior to World War I: There were about 900 votes per constituency in 1835, 3,500 in 1868, and 5,200 in 1900. With electorates of that size, candidates and their agents could manage local campaigns on a personal basis, contacting many voters directly. The main work of constituency associations lay in maintaining the registration of supporters and battling in the courts over the registration claims of opponents. The Corrupt Practices Act of 1883 put an end to the bribery and treating that had characterized election management. The 1918 Reform Act transformed the electorate, with extension of the franchise to women voters over age thirty, as well as the removal of complex property qualifications. The further expansion of the franchise to all women in 1928 saw a dramatic increase in voting numbers. By 1945 there were almost 40,000 voters per seat. Mobilizing support on that scale required an effective party organization within each constituency.

The Conservative party organization had been allowed to fall into disrepair during World War II: It had been 'mothballed' because partisan activity was seen as unpatriotic, and there was minimal coordination between its different branches. At the grassroots level, each of the 640 constituency associations functioned as an independent unit, with its own funds, officers, candidates, and publicity staff. Above that loose structure were the Central Council and the Executive Committee of the National Union, which tried to coordinate the local party associations, mainly through persuasion. The Central Office also produced a variety of pamphlets, handbills, posters, and material for speeches. Yet, as Lord Wooten summarized the prevailing wisdom of the time, all politics was local: 'Let there be no mistake about it; elections are won in the constituencies and not in the central or area offices. Elections are won on doorsteps of the land, not at great public meetings.' Local parties were gradually transformed from small, informal groups of voters engaged as registration societies to mass-membership organizations with regular meetings and a more bureaucratic structure of officers. Party membership reached its peak in the postwar era, with around 2.8 million in 1953 in the Conservative party and around one million in the Labour party, representing about one in ten voters, given a total electorate of 33.7 million. The membership was mobilized during the campaign to leaflet the constituency, canvass voters, plan the local campaign, and activate supporters on election day. Candidates were often adopted just before the election, having just come home from the war to throw themselves enthusiastically into a hectic round of five or six public meetings a night in village halls, with tours in speaker vans and leafleting during the day.

In 1945 the national campaign and the role of central party head-quarters remained low-key for both major parties. Prior to development of the tools of market research, the party leadership developed their party platform and campaign messages in the light of conference debates, political 'hunches', and informal feedback from the constituencies, but without any input derived from the paraphernalia of survey research, focus groups, and political consultants. The Market Research Society was first organized in 1947, but it was not until 1962–3 that the major British political parties seriously considered those techniques. The few polls published by Gallup during the months leading up to the campaign pointed to a Labour victory, but they were largely ignored. Behind the leadership of Winston Churchill, at the zenith of his long career, the Conservatives remained confident of victory. Under Churchill's leadership, Germany had surrendered, and Japan was about to fall. The party leaders toured the country addressing public meetings. Attlee covered around seven or eight meetings a day around the country, driven by his wife and accompanied by a single publicity officer who dealt with the press. The Labour leader made about seventy speeches in total, mostly extemporary, with minimal notes. Churchill went on a four-day whistle-stop tour around the country in a special train, addressing six to eleven cities every day. Meetings within the constituency were the heart of the local campaign. Activity was reported to have declined with the use of radio broadcasts; nevertheless, one study reported that in one city alone (Glasgow) over 600 school halls had been booked for public meetings during the 1950 campaign.

Media coverage of the campaign was limited compared with today. Although the BBC had resumed regular broadcasting in 1947, television played no role during or after the campaign. The first programs about party politics appeared on television in 1951, but television news did not cover the campaign until 1959. Nevertheless, the first revolution in the electronic media had already created a mass audience and the beginnings of a national campaign. The introduction of radio broadcasting in 1924 permanently altered the way campaigns were fought. Leadership speeches, which previously had reached audiences of only a few thousand, began to be heard night after night by millions. In the 1945 campaign, BBC radio scheduled one (twenty-to-thirty-minute) free party political radio broadcast after the main evening news each weekday evening. By prior agreement, ten broadcasts were allocated to the Conservatives and Labour, four to the Liberals, one each to the Communists and the Common Wealth party. Labour broadcasts were more coordinated and thematic than those of the Conservatives. The opening broadcasts by the party leaders set the tone for the subsequent campaign. According to BBC audience research, the listenership was substantial: Just under half the adult population heard each broadcast, with numbers rising towards polling day. Moreover, just as television later set the agenda for newspapers, so the radio broadcasts were reported at length in the print press.

Newspaper readers had weekday choices among the national tabloids *Daily Mirror* and *Daily Sketch* or one of the seven broadsheet national morning newspapers or one of the many daily regional and local papers. The print media were highly partisan, especially the popular press. Conservative-leaning national newspapers (the *Daily Express*, the *Daily Mail*, the *Daily Sketch*, and the *Daily Telegraph*) had the highest circulation, selling about 6.8 million copies. But the Conservative edge in the national press was not great. The Labour-supporting *Daily Herald* and *Daily Mirror* enjoyed a combined circulation of 6.6 million, and the Liberals received the support of the *News Chronicle* and the *Manchester Guardian*, with a total circulation of 1.6 million. The *Times* remained fairly independent, being traditionally Conservative, although anti-Churchill in that election. Much of the coverage consisted of 'straight' factual reporting, such as the details of constituency contests and of leadership speeches, with more partisan messages in the editorials.

The only newspaper with a systematic opinion poll was the *News Chronicle*, which published polls by the British Institute of Public Opinion, later known as Social Surveys (Gallup Poll) Ltd. These polls showed a twenty-point Labour lead over the Conservatives in February and April 1945. The Gallup survey taken closest to polling day, with fieldwork between 24 and 27 June in 195 constituencies, showed a smaller gap between the parties, with 47% voting Labour, 41% voting Conservative, and 10% Liberal. Nevertheless, most journalistic commentators expected a close result or a Conservative victory, as did most contemporary observers, based largely on Churchill's personal popularity and international stature.

Prior to the first national election surveys, little systematic information is available about the attitudes and values of the British electorate, but the data available at the constituency level, as well as from the earliest Gallup polls, suggest that class was the preeminent cleavage in British politics, the foundation of the two-party system. The period between the Second Reform Act and World War I was characterized by a principal cleavage between supporters of the established church and non-conformists, reinforced and overlain by divisions over Irish home rule versus unionism, and a regional cleavage between core and periphery. Studies suggest that the critical shift that moved the party system from the politics of religion to the politics of class occurred after World War I.[8] The earliest systematic analysis of voting behaviour, based on the series of British election studies by Butler and Stokes, stressed that in the mid-1960s the electorate was anchored for long periods of time, perhaps for their lifetimes, to the Labour or Conservative parties through sectoral cleavages and party loyalties, produced by socialization within the family, school, workplace, and local community, reinforced by the messages of the partisan press.[9]

There was a three-week hiatus between polling day and the announcement of the results, occasioned by the need to collect and count the votes of three million troops abroad. When declared, the results of the 1945 general election proved remarkable in nearly all regards: the largest two-party swing in votes since 1918, the substantial Labour landslide, the size of the Conservative defeat. On 5 July 1945, Labour received 48.3% of the vote, the best result they have ever received, before or since. The number of Labour MPs more than doubled overnight, from 154 to 393. Labour had held two minority administrations in 1924 and 1929, but the 1945 election would yield the first Labour government with a comfortable overall majority (of 147 seats) and with prospects of a full term in office to implement plans for radical economic and social changes. Conservative seats were decimated, from 585 in 1935 to 213 in 1945. That first postwar election can only be regarded as a 'critical election'; it produced a long-term shift in the balance of partisan forces, with Labour developing and consolidating a new policy agenda and establishing the basis for 'normal' two-party politics for successive decades. The 1945 election was a watershed in British politics that gave birth to the Westminster two-party system.

THE EVOLUTION OF THE POSTMODERN
AMERICAN CAMPAIGN

The extent of the revolution in political communications is striking if we contrast those two typical postwar campaigns in America and Britain with the situation that had developed by the mid-1990s. One of the major consequences of developments in the late 1960s and early 1970s was the 'nationalization' of the American presidential campaign, with network news programs broadcasting candidate speeches, party conventions, and election events across the country, unifying America in a common experience.[10] During that period, coverage by CBS, NBC, and ABC, as well as the *New York Times, Washington Post,* and *Wall Street Journal,* defined the focus for the presidential campaign, with anchors, broadcast journalists, and reporters for the major papers appearing to be figures of unchallenged authority. There was a well-established hierarchy among and within news organizations and a clear sense of professional identity and high standards among journalists. Yet the 'golden days' of network news were not to last; soon there would be anxieties about the proliferation of media outlets and messages. The networks in 1970 had no rivals: Only 10% of American homes had cable. By 1980, cable service had reached only 20% of households. But by the late 1990s, almost three-quarters had cable or satellite (72%) and VCRs (77%). As mentioned earlier, not surprisingly, given these developments, the networks' audience share plummeted from 93% in 1977 to less than half in the late 1990s.[11] We have seen how the readership for American newspapers has experienced a steady hemorrhage for decades, which shows no signs of being staunched.

As discussed in the preceding two chapters, competition for viewers has become far more intense, with fragmentation of the television market into narrower and narrower segments. Partial deregulation of the television industry, the growth of cable television systems and satellite services, the rise of new networks, the use of VCRs, and communication via the Internet have splintered the market and escalated the competition for viewers. The developments in digital and broadband technology multiplying television channels, along with new sources of

Internet information, seem likely to accelerate these developments. The growth of 'narrowcasting' means that more and more news sources are reaching increasingly specialized audiences. Although a small group of political aficionados can find ever more detailed information about government, public policy, and campaigns through these sources, simultaneously surfing the Web and watching CNN and C-SPAN during the election, many others may find it easier to tune out political information and watch MTV, HBO, and *Monday Night Football.* The multiplicity of news outlets, stories, and channels has undermined the sense that the network news could ever again sign off with the classic Walter Cronkite phrase: 'And that's the way it is.' The familiar authority figures have gone, replaced by multiple realities.

As a result of these developments, political leaders face greater difficulties in connecting with voters in a news system characterized by increasing fragmentation. Candidates have to run up the down escalator simply to stay in place. In order to do this, America has experienced the evolution of the permanent campaign. The techniques for monitoring the pulse of the public, including focus groups, daily tracking polls, and 'electronic town meetings', have gradually moved beyond the campaign to become integral parts of governing. Starting with John Kennedy, but developed particularly under Richard Nixon, the White House's sensitivity to public opinion has become an enduring institutional feature of the modern presidency. Opinion polling, once fairly ad hoc, has become integral within the White House, part of the routine procedures for monitoring public support.[12] More recent developments have included changes in the techniques commonly used to measure public opinion and greater sensitivity to the polling results in framing and communicating public-policy options. These developments began within the presidency, but subsequently have expanded throughout all levels of government, so that the techniques for winning elections have become increasingly incorporated into the techniques for governing, and the policy debate in Washington has become part of the permanent campaign.

The professionalization of the political-consultant role and the growth of the political-marketing industry in the United States are phenomena that have been widely documented.[13] Many aspects of such trends are not particularly new in American politics: Joe McGinness wrote his classic book *The Selling of the President* more than three decades ago.[14] The use of market research on an extensive scale can be dated to campaigns in the early 1960s. By the mid-1970s, pollsters were already dividing the electorate into segments and regions for targeted messages. The 1980 campaign saw the emergence of several marketing tools that became widely adopted, including hard-hitting negative advertising, direct mail, ready availability of funds from political action committees (PACs), and sophisticated strategic campaign planning. The 1992 campaign brought two main innovations: Focus groups and rolling tracking polls were used extensively to monitor public reactions to the campaign on a day-by-day basis, keeping a finger on the pulse of public opinion. And the forums for political debate widened beyond the old media, such as *Meet the Press*, to live talk shows on television and radio, like *Larry King Live*. With the mass audience deserting the network evening news, candidates searched elsewhere for voters. Today political consulting has grown to such an extent that the major networking organization, the American Association of Political Consultants, established in 1969, now claims 800 active members and a billion-dollar industry. That the industry can now legitimately be called a profession, in the strict sense of the term, can be questioned. Campaign consultants more commonly base their work on experience, craft, and 'folk wisdom' than on any body of well-developed scientific knowledge and expertise that could be easily exported to other contexts, and the industry lacks training qualifications and an enforceable code of ethics.[15] Nevertheless, the sheer size of the U.S. industry in political consultancy makes it a model for many other countries.

In terms of campaigning, the 1996 presidential election was marked less by innovation than by consolidation, for the Clinton and Dole campaigns drew on all of these techniques.[16] After the excitement generated by Clinton's first victory in 1992, and the turmoil associated with the Gingrich revolution in 1994, the 1996 election proved something of a low-key affair. By far the most important developments in campaign communications concerned the growing political use of the Internet. Hill and Hughes remarked as follows: 'In 1994, if a political party or interest group had even a rudimentary Web site, it was a pioneer in the Information Age. . . . In 1996, if a candidate for president had a Web site, he would likely give out the address for it during televised appearances. . . . By 1997, if a party or interest group still did not have a Web site, it was run by a bunch of idiots.'[17] By 1996 the major parties had fairly sophisticated Web sites, as did the presidential candidates, alongside the sites for the traditional news media like CNN, ABC News, and the *New York Times*, but in that race the Web was still a novelty rather than integral to the campaign strategy. But use of the Internet by political organizations continued to proliferate, so that by the time of the 1998 elections almost all gubernatorial candidates, almost three-quarters of all Democratic and Republican Senate candidates, and just over half of the candidates for the House of Representatives had sites, equally divided between the major parties.[18]

Moreover, the size of the Internet user community has been growing exponentially, becoming mainstream. The Pew Center survey in May 1998 estimated that the percentage of Americans regularly getting *news* from the Internet (where 'regularly' is defined as at least once a week) had more than tripled in the preceding two years, rising from 11 to 36 million users, or 20% of all Americans.[19] Similar figures are reported for those who regularly go online to communicate with others via discussion lists and chat groups, while slightly fewer go online for entertainment news (14%) and financial information (10%). Within the space of just a few years the regular audience for online news has become larger than the audiences for many traditional media, such as for mainstream news magazines like *Time* and *Newsweek* (15%) and for listeners to talk radio (13%), let alone for viewers of minority outlets like the PBS *Newshour* and C-SPAN (4%). That pattern was particularly marked among the younger generation; the Pew Center survey in May 1998 found that among eighteen-to-twenty-nine-year-old Americans, more had gone online the previous day (38%) than had read a newspaper (28%) or magazine (35%). It is true that the online users of news and political Web sites proved most likely to see the Internet as a supplementary source rather than a new source of information, because they were already more likely to pay attention to politics in the traditional news media.[20] Nevertheless, the rapid expansion of the Internet in the United States and its increasing convergence with the traditional media of radio, television and newspapers seem likely to add another layer of complexity to the political communication process within the next decade.

THE EVOLUTION OF THE POSTMODERN BRITISH CAMPAIGN?

British parties have also been transformed by the gradual evolution of the permanent campaign in which the techniques of spin-doctors, opinion polls, and professional media management are increasingly applied to routine everyday politics. Nevertheless, although the professionalization of British party communications has increased in recent years, as has the fragmentation of news media, neither process has yet reached the levels evident in the United States. In Britain, a few trusted experts in polling and political marketing are influential during the campaign in each party, such as Maurice Saatchi, Tim Bell, and Gordon Reece at Conservative Central Office, but their roles continue to be as part-time outside advisors, not integral to the process of government, nor even to campaigning, which is still essentially run by politicians. Unlike in the United States, the political-marketing industry has been limited, mainly because the only major clients are the Labour and Conservative parties. The minor parties have modest resources, and parliamentary candidates run retail campaigns based on shoe leather, grassroots helpers, and tight budgets. But the effect of television during elections has been to shift the primary focus of the campaign from unpaid volunteers and local candidates towards the central party leadership, flanked by paid, although not necessarily full-time, professionals.[21]

Labour's election machine in 1997 was commonly regarded as widely effective.[22] The high-tech developments in media management at Millbank Tower were widely discussed in the press. Supposedly modeled on the 'war room' in the Clinton campaign, the Millbank organization had a tight inner core, including Peter Mandelson, Gordon Brown, the press secretary Alastair Campbell, the pollster Philip Gould, Blair's personal assistant Anji Hunter, Lord Irvine of Lairg, and Jonathan Powell. The interior circle was surrounded by about two hundred staffers connecting via fax, modem, and pagers to key shadow spokespersons and candidates in marginal constituencies. Briefings were sent out nightly, sometimes twice a day. The Labour party included a rebuttal unit ready for rapid responses to anticipated attacks.

After 1992, Labour realized that elections are not usually won or lost in the official campaign, and they subsequently designed their strategy for the long haul. For two years before polling day, a Labour task force was planned in an attempt to change the minds of 5,000 voters in each of ninety targeted marginal seats. People identified as potential Labour converts in those seats were contacted by teams of volunteers at their doorsteps, as well as by a canvassing operation run from twenty telephone banks around the country, coordinated from Millbank during the campaign. In January 1997, get-out-the-vote letters were sent to the targeted voters, and young people received a videotape of Tony Blair. Information from the canvassing operation, especially issues of concern raised by voters, was also fed back to Philip Gould, to help shape

Labour's presentations. All the major parties maintained Web sites, providing information about activities and policies, as well as how to join, although few of the features were truly interactive.[23]

Opinion polling was carried out regularly from late 1993, and Philip Gould and Deborah Mattinson conducted a program of focus-group research to monitor reaction to Labour's policies. Strategy meetings were conducted almost daily from late 1994, tackling Labour's weaknesses on taxation, trade unions, and crime well before the official campaign began. A manifesto, *New Labour: Because Britain Deserves Better*, was designed to focus on specific pledges. The main theme of Labour's advertising was 'Britain Deserves Better', fairly bland and safe, if unmemorable. To highlight the message, Tony Blair visited 60 constituencies, traveling about 10,000 miles by road, rail, and air, and providing controlled photo opportunities rather than press conferences for the media. The membership drive launched by Blair was also part of that long-term strategy, increasing grassroots membership by almost two-thirds, up from 261,000 in 1991 to a peak of 405,000 in January 1998.

In Britain, the major parties once had been able to campaign assured of largely sympathetic coverage by newspapers with a traditional Labour or Conservative leaning. Hence, in an election, Labour could always campaign counting on fairly favourable coverage in the popular *Daily Mirror*, while the Conservatives could be assured of positive editorials in the *Daily Mail*. But in the 1997 campaign both major parties experienced weakening of press–party linkages, not just among the Conservative press. Content analysis of the front pages of six major national newspapers during the April 1997 campaign found that, compared with 1992, more coverage fell into the 'mixed' category, neither favourable nor unfavourable to any of the three major parties.[24] Therefore trends in Britain seem to have followed those in many other European countries that once had strongly partisan wings of the press, such as The Netherlands, but where political coverage was coming to be driven more strongly by an autonomous 'media logic' in the fierce competition for readers, rather than by traditional allegiances or by the politics of their proprietors. 'Modern media are more powerful, more independent, and more determined to pursue their own interests through a professional culture of their own making.'[25] Press–party dealignment has increased the complexity and uncertainty of media management for the parties, which can no longer rely on getting their message out through a few sympathetic sources.

The electronic media have not yet been fragmented as much in Britain as in the United States. In the 1997 campaign, the major flagship news programs on British television continued to be BBC1's *6 O'Clock News* and *9 O'Clock News*, ITN's *News at Ten*, Channel 4's *7 P.M. news*, and BBC2's 10:20 *Newsnight*, along with weekly current-affairs programs like *Panorama*. Nevertheless, cable, satellite, and the Internet have begun to make inroads into this world, and the new digital and broadband channels that will be available by the time of the next general election will exacerbate this process further. The first satellite services in Britain became available from Sky TV in February 1989, followed by BSB the next year. By 1992, about 3% of homes had access to cable TV, while 10% had satellite dishes. In contrast, by 1997 almost a fifth of all households could tune in to more than fifty channels on satellite and cable. In those homes, more than a third of all viewing was on the new channels. During the campaign, some 10–15% of the audience usually watched cable and satellite programs every evening. Occasionally, when there was wall-to-wall election news on the terrestrial channels, such as on Thursday, 24 April 1997, a week before the election, the proportion of cable and satellite viewers jumped to almost a quarter of the audience. Moreover, Sky News, CNN, News 24, Channel 5, and BBC Radio's *Five Live* have altered the pace of their news to brief headlines on the hour every hour.

The Internet also promises to transform news habits. In 1997 the availability of the BBC's *Election '97*, *ITN Online*, the online headlines from the Press Association and Reuter's, and party home pages, as well as electronic versions of the *Times* and the *Telegraph*, dramatically accelerated the news cycle. The BBC's *Online*, with easy access to RealAudio broadcasts of its major political programs and live parliamentary coverage, suggests the shape of things to come.[26] With 24-hour coverage, the acceleration of the news cycle has dramatically increased the need for parties to respond quickly to a suddenly shifting agenda, or else get knocked off their feet. By spring 1998, one-fifth of all British citizens had access to the Internet (see Table 5.7). Thus the national news media continue to be far more important in Britain than in America. The major parties still depend on getting their messages out via the major national television news programs and the national newspapers. Yet the fragmentation of the electronic media does seem likely to increase in Britain, as well as in the rest of Europe.

Moreover, major changes have also become evident among the electorate. The most comprehensive study of the 1997 election, based on the series of British election surveys (BES), concluded that the 1997 election revealed a more instrumental electorate.[27] Voters proved to be less closely tied to many of the traditional bedrocks of party support, mainly because of political developments and the way that Labour moved towards the center ground of British politics. The most consistent evidence suggests a pattern of continuing secular dealignment in the British electorate. In particular, in response to Labour's center shift, class voting reached its lowest level since the BES series began in the early 1960s. Regional cleavages also began to fade, with further closure of the north–south divide. And strong partisan loyalties, already eroded in a series of elections during the 1970s, weakened further. The 'old' politics of ideological divisions over the virtues of the market versus public ownership declined in importance for Labour voting, while the 'new' issues of Europe increasingly cut across the old patterns of voting behaviour. The weakening of partisan identities and the increased instrumentality of voting characteristic of the late twentieth century are making all electoral groups more open to competitive appeals. As a result, the potential impact of political communication to influence the electorate becomes greater, although, at the same time, if all the major parties professionalize their campaign communications, then, rather like a high-tech *Star Wars*, developments in one party are likely to be neutralized as others adopt similar strategies.

CONCLUSIONS: THE CONSEQUENCES OF
THE MODERNIZATION PROCESS

On the basis of this comparison we can conclude that despite major differences in their political systems, campaigns in Britain and in the United States have many common features. In the postwar era, if Truman had campaigned in Britain, or Attlee in America, they would have encountered familiar environments. At the end of the twentieth century, certain common trends were affecting both American and British practices. Elections were becoming increasingly professionalized in both countries. For example, Tony Blair's Labour party adopted many of the techniques common in the Clinton campaign: a campaign war room, a rapid-response unit, and daily focus groups. There was also considerable interchange of campaign advisors and politicians between the two camps, as pollsters like Philip Gould visited the Clinton team, while Stan Greenberg polled for Tony Blair.[28] The news media remain more national-oriented in Britain than in the United States, but because of satellite, digital, and broadband stations the British electronic media are already heading down the path towards greater fragmentation of outlets and levels. And the electorate clearly has become more dealigned from traditional party and social loyalties in both countries.

This does not mean, however, that British campaigns have become 'Americanized', as some claim, in terms of the role of money and an increase in negative political coverage. Considerable contrasts remain because of legal regulations and structural constraints. During the past forty years, the United States has experienced the rise of the candidate-centered campaign,[29] characteristically capital-intensive, heavily television-driven, and run by an industry of full-time campaign consultants. In contrast, although British general elections have adopted some off-the-shelf American techniques, Britain still exemplifies the party-centered campaign, as do most European democracies. Politicians remain in the driver's seat, assisted by their advisors. The party leadership may have become more visible within the campaign, because of the rise of television, but this does not mean that parliamentary candidates have followed suit. America has experienced the rise of the candidate-centered campaign, but in Britain the contest is still essentially about party; for example, in the 1997 election half the electorate could not name a single candidate correctly.[30] In both countries the heart of the election campaign is the battle to dominate the news headlines. But the structure and ethos of British television mean that election coverage is far more balanced and extensive than in America. British newspapers, despite dealignment, remain more partisan than those in the United States. Above all, capital-intensive television advertising, the mother's milk of American politics, remains unknown in Britain. We can therefore conclude that modernization has transformed the process of electioneering in both countries. The defining features of postmodern campaigns in both countries are the professionalization of campaign consultants, the fragmentation of the news-media system, and the dealignment of the electorate. But because of differences in structural conditions, many of the features commonly regarded as characteristic of American campaigns are absent from Britain.

What are the consequences of the modernization process for the linkages between parties and citizens in a democracy? The postmodern campaign can be seen to represent a new openness and tolerance for alternative views and multiple forms of understanding, as well as a source of anxiety and disorientation as the familiar standards are swept away. As a result of the fragmentation of the news media, politicians seem to be struggling ever harder to retain control of their messages through the older channels, while the familiar ground is shifting under their feet, producing a pervasive mood of angst. Some have regarded the fragmentation of the old media as a positive development, increasing the plurality of outlets and opening alternative avenues for politicians and voters to communicate with each other. Rather than being locked into the ideological blinders of one or two partisan newspapers, or being limited to the evening news on one or two television channels, many voters now have greater opportunities to access different channels, styles, and formats for news in the electronic media. Focus groups and opinion polls can be seen as effective means by which parties can stay in touch with public opinion – means that may be more representative of the general electorate than is reliance on the opinions of local party activists.

Alternatively, the evolution of modern and postmodern campaigns can be seen as threatening the democratic process, widening the gap between citizens and their representatives. If parties and candidates adopt whatever message seems most likely to resonate with focus groups, if pollsters, consultants, and advertisers rather than politicians come to determine the content of campaigns, and if 'spin' begins to outweigh substance, then the serious business of government may be replaced by the superficial manipulation of images. 'Packaging politics,' Bob Franklin argues, 'impoverishes political debate by oversimplifying and trivializing political communications.'[31] Such a process may thereby exacerbate public cynicism about the electoral process and undermine the democratic legitimacy of representative bodies. Some fear that the shift in campaign techniques may have a direct impact on civic engagement, with voters becoming passive spectators to symbolic events staged in TV studios, rather than active participants in local party meetings and community campaigns.[32] As discussed earlier, the most common concern is that postmodern campaigns will turn off voters because of the decline in face-to-face communications and the rise of practices such as emphasis on negative news highly adversarial to government, horse-race journalism, and trivialization of campaign discourse. These criticisms are heard most commonly concerning developments in the United States, but similar concerns are increasingly expressed elsewhere. To evaluate these alternative interpretations, the next section of this book goes on to examine the consequences of political communications for citizens.

PART III

The Impact on Democracy

CHAPTER 9

Negative News, Negative Public?

Earlier chapters have focused on major changes in the processes of political communication within the news media and parties. Theories of media malaise emphasize that modern developments have transformed the content of news, with the growth of 'infotainment', 'negative' news, and 'tabloidization', contributing towards widespread cynicism about government and political leaders. To examine these claims, we need systematic evidence about the content of news coverage and the public's responses. We are concerned here with public attitudes, understood as political preferences towards the major policy issues facing the polity, as distinct from levels of knowledge and information, which will be dealt with in subsequent chapters. This chapter assumes that three interrelated conditions must be met if the news media are to have an impact sufficient to change public attitudes at the aggregate level:

(1) The news media need to provide reasonably extensive coverage of each issue.
(2) The coverage that is provided needs to display a consistent directional bias.
(3) The public needs to be attentive to news cues, as compared with other types of information, such as those provided by parties, political leaders, specialist consultants, social and political groups, interpersonal communications, objective conditions, and personal experiences.[1]

The reasoning is that if news coverage of an issue proves fleeting and ephemeral, then in a complex world of rapidly changing information this is unlikely to have much impact on public awareness. So quickly do events follow one another that impressions of one event will be swept away by the next, leaving no residue in a world of flux. If the first condition is met and there is persistent coverage, but it proves to be largely balanced, either internally within a news outlet or externally between different news sources, then it will be unlikely to shift public opinion in a consistent direction. If positive and negative stories are roughly equal, termed by Zaller 'two-sided' information flows,[2] then the effects are likely to cancel each other out at the aggregate level. People are most likely to be swayed if a series of stories strongly and persistently reinforces one side or another of a debate. Lastly, if the public is presented with a consistent stream of stories, such as a series of reports headlining a political scandal like the Lewinsky affair, but they prefer to rely on other sources for their opinion cues, sources that perhaps they trust more than the media, then the third condition fails to be met. In this regard we need to distinguish between the effects of opinion cues transmitted via the press, such as official government briefings, party leadership speeches, or commentary from scientific authorities, and the independent effects of news-media reporting per se. To examine these factors, we need information about the amount of coverage, the direction of coverage, and its influence on the collective public.

This chapter examines these issues within the context of the European Union (EU). If most news about the Community is overwhelmingly negative – for example, if there is a steady stream of Euroskeptic headlines about the inefficiency and incompetence of the European Commission bureaucracy, the failure and waste of EU policies like the Common Agricultural policy, and the excessive burden of the budget on member states – and the public takes its cues from the news media, then that plausibly could contribute towards a growing disconnect between European leaders and the public. The first sections of this chapter describe the context and the data used in this study. We then examine the evidence regarding the three conditions that need to be met for the news media to influence public support for the EU: Is information about the European Union and its policies easily available in newspapers and television news? Is the direction or tone of news coverage overwhelmingly negative or more balanced? And what is the association between trends in negative coverage in the news media and public disillusionment with the EU? The conclusion summarizes the major findings and considers how far we can generalize from the European Union to other contexts.

EVIDENCE AND DATA

The European Union provides a suitable case in which to test theories of media malaise, for in recent years many have expressed concern about a growing 'democratic deficit' within the Community and the contribution of the news media to this problem. Many factors may have contributed towards problems of democratic legitimation in the EU, including the structure of EU institutions, the continuing weakness of the European Parliament *vis-à-vis* the European Commission, the lack of transparency of decision-making within the Council of Ministers, and the unwillingness of parties to contest European Parliament elections on the basis of European issues.[3] Although we lack systematic evidence, news coverage about the EU plausibly may be contributing to this problem, exacerbating the lack of public awareness of the European Union, at best, and fuelling public hostility, at worst.[4] As one commentator expressed this view, when explaining record low voting turnouts in the June 1999 European elections, 'the media hasn't really got to grips with communicating the very complicated and complex things which happen in Europe, which just compounds people's general misunderstanding. We go from the tabloid's scare reporting of straight bananas through to the jargon-laden language of some of the high-brow media. It's a turn-off and people lose interest.'[5] Anderson and Weymouth have used discourse analysis to present a convincing case for the pervasive Euroskeptic bias across about three-quarters of the British press, with a few exceptions like the *Financial Times* and the *Guardian*.[6]

Studies of public opinion have suggested that the news media may be more likely to shape perceptions of foreign policy than perceptions of domestic politics.[7] The reason is that in our daily lives we often have direct experience of the impact of taxes, prices, and crime that can counterbalance and perhaps outweigh information from the media. People have had personal contact with public agencies like unemployment offices, schools, and hospitals. Yet, despite its public information campaigns, the European Union seems to remain disconnected from the lives of most citizens. The public may not regard the EU as responsible for programs like regional aid or training subsidies, because such initiatives are implemented through national legislation and local bodies. In one study, when asked about their sources of information about the EU, only 3% of the public had contacted the EU directly within the preceding three months, whereas in contrast, three-quarters of the public had seen something on television news, and over half had heard something on the radio or read about the EU in a newspaper.[8] Thus the news media have the potential to be particularly influential in framing public perceptions of EU institutions and policies, in the same way that their coverage may shape people's views of issues like Kosovo and perceptions of NATO.

These propositions can be tested with systematic evidence from regular Eurobarometer and Europinion tracking surveys of public opinion and monthly content analyses of news coverage of the European Union in its fifteen member states, with data provided by the European Commission.[9] As discussed in detail in the Technical Appendix, data were derived from *Monitoring Euromedia*, a unique monthly report measuring coverage of the European Union and its policies in newspapers and television news. Those reports covered a thirty-three-month period spanning important developments in European politics, from the enlargement of the EU in January 1995 to include Sweden, Finland, and Austria to the signing of the Amsterdam treaty in autumn 1997. The research design involves a three-stage process: first, to determine which issues received extended coverage during the period under review; second, to examine the direction of coverage of these issues; third, to focus on the impact of the news coverage of these issues on aggregate public opinion.

THE VISIBILITY OF THE EU IN THE NEWS

To establish baseline trends, the first task is to analyze how much news about the European Union and its policies was reported in newspapers and television news. We can draw a simple distinction between 'routine' news on a monthly basis and 'event-driven' news when coverage peaked around biannual meetings of national ministers at the European Council.

The pattern of routine news about the EU is drawn from the monthly *Monitoring Euromedia* reports that provide an overview of the hundreds of news stories about the EU generated in all member states. This indicates the typical amount of coverage 'of the EU and its policies', counting the total number of stories per country and classifying the contents into twenty-one different issue topics. This process allows us to filter out those stories that prove ephemeral and of passing interest: announcement of the appointment of a particular commissioner, a meeting of the European Council, or a new initiative on competition or trade policy. Many topics fell into that category,[10] such as disputes about fisheries policy, the Schengen agreement on open borders, 'mad-cow' disease (bovine spongiform encephalopathy, BSE), and the plight of the Kurds in Turkey. These types of stories were excluded from the second stage of analysis because they were not featured heavily or consistently in the news headlines throughout the selected period. As argued earlier, if coverage should prove fleeting, then we would not expect such stories to have much impact on public attitudes towards Europe, for good or ill, and therefore such issues fail to meet the first condition in our model of media influence.

Routine television news was monitored in a monthly time-series analysis in six countries (Belgium, Italy, France, Germany, the United Kingdom, and Spain) from 1995 to 1997. Overall, 576 news programs were analyzed by *Monitoring Euromedia* during that period. They included 487 items referring to the European Union and its policies, representing on average almost one item (0.85) per program.[11] As a proportion of the schedule, we can estimate that 3.4% of the evening news was devoted to EU affairs, representing about 4.2 minutes of news per day. Of course, that underestimates total European coverage, because this figure does not include news about the EU available on the many other bulletins and current-affairs programs shown on different channels and at different times throughout the day. We have already noted the proliferation and diversification of news outlets, from discussion programs to twenty-four-hour news on cable and satellite stations, not to speak of sources like newspapers, radio, and the Internet, none of which were counted in the estimate.[12] Routine coverage was fairly low-key throughout all member states, although there were some cross-national variations. For example, during this period, Spanish and British television news devoted about twice as much time to the EU as did French and Italian TV.

Critics may regard this amount of news coverage of European affairs as far too limited, but there is no simple and universally agreed yard-stick to evaluate adequacy, because judgments depend on political priorities and news values. There can be endless unresolved debate of the 'half-empty, half-full' variety. Press officers, politicians, and officials working within the European Parliament or European Commission may well feel that their work is getting far too little attention: One study found that many British MEPs were clearly dissatisfied with the volume and quality of coverage given to the European Parliament in the national and local press.[13] There is some survey evidence that many members of the public sympathize with this view: When asked to evaluate the availability of coverage of European Union affairs, more than a third of the public (38%) thought there was 'too little' television news, only 9% complained that there was 'too much', and almost half the public (45%) believed coverage was 'about right'.[14]

If we accept the view that news about the EU has been too limited, the most important point for the argument here is that this fact in itself restricts the ability of television news to shape anti-European or pro-European sentiments, because people watching regular news programs most of the time will encounter relatively little about the activities in Brussels, Luxembourg, and Strasbourg. Only a few exceptional issues, such as the launch of the euro, have become sufficiently visible over a longer period to meet the first condition specified in our model of media influence. Inadequate reporting of EU affairs can certainly influence levels of knowledge and interest about Europe, but it should minimize the media impact on political attitudes.

Certain European issues and events have attracted more extended treatment on television, whether measured by the proportion of stories or by time (Figure 9.1).[15] There was a pronounced cyclical pattern, with news peaking around the biannual meetings of national ministers at the European Council. That was evident in June 1995 (with the Cannes Council focusing on unemployment and aid for the Mediterranean region), at Christmas 1995 (when the new currency was christened the 'euro' by the Madrid Council), in the spring of 1996 (with the Turin IGC looking at institutional reform), in midsummer of 1997 (around the time of the Florence Council and the beef row), at Christmas 1996 (around the time of the Dublin Councils I and II), and in midsummer of 1997 (concerning the third stage of the EMU, the Amsterdam Council's decisions on the 'Stability and Growth Pact', and the convergence criteria that member states had to meet to participate in the eurozone). This regular cycling suggests that the routine daily grind of European Parliament debates, European Commission business, and presidential initiatives remains largely invisible to the public, but key summits, where government leaders meet every six months at the European Council, provide a sense of heightened drama that attracts the international media. More than 3,000 journalists from around the world usually travel in the wake of European Council summits.

The monthly trends in newspaper coverage, shown in Figure 9.2, have somewhat flatter peaks and troughs, but they confirm the importance of key summits in attracting heightened news coverage of

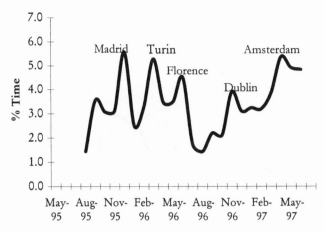

Figure 9.1. Trends in TV coverage of the EU: The figures represent the proportions of news broadcasts about the European Union and its policies in six countries (Italy, Belgium, Germany, France, UK, Spain) from May 1995 to July 1997. The correlation between percentage of time and percentage of stories is 0.66. *Source:* Calculated from *Monitoring Euromedia,* 1995–97. Brussels: European Commission.

European affairs. The average number of stories fluctuated throughout 1995, but never rose above 6,000 per month. Coverage rose sharply, however, at the time of the Turin IGC in the spring of 1996, discussing institutional reform, and it soared again to over 12,000 for the Dublin Councils in December 1996.

The patterns of newspaper coverage also varied substantially among member states.[16] By far the highest proportions of stories were found in the German and British press, whereas there were relatively few stories in newspapers in the smaller member states like Greece, Luxembourg, and Ireland (Figure 9.3). Such cross-national differences could have resulted from many factors, including party debates over Europe and the salience of the EU on the national political agendas. Greater coverage in the German press may have been due to Chancellor Kohl's pivotal leadership in mobilizing support for the euro during that period. The British press devoted extensive front-page coverage to Europe because of the controversy over the BSE crisis and the British opt-out clause from the EMU that John Major had negotiated at Maastricht, deeply dividing the governing Conservative party into irreconcilable factions of Euroskeptics and Europhiles.

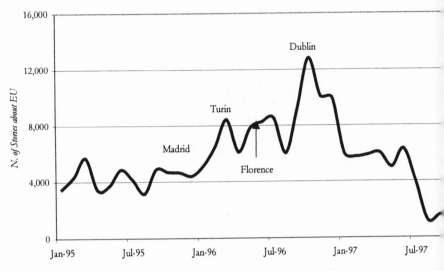

Figure 9.2. Trends in newspaper coverage of the EU-15, January 1995 to September 1997.

THE ISSUE AGENDA

So far we have examined general trends in television and newspaper coverage, but which EU policies were featured in these stories? The peaks and troughs that we have already observed suggest a tendency for the news agenda to focus on dramatic developments, such as the BSE health crisis and the launch of the euro-zone, and events like European Council summits. But did journalists also inform the public about more routine policy initiatives, such as debates about environmental protection, employment programs, and competition policy? The stories in our study were assigned two or three different *topic* codes, because most covered more than one subject. The twenty-one categories included issues such as foreign policy, agricultural policy, and EU institutions (see the Technical Appendix for the full list).

THE NEWSPAPER AGENDA

Economic and monetary policy was the single most important topic on the newspaper agenda during these years, accounting for just over one-quarter of the stories (Figure 9.4). The category of 'EU develop-

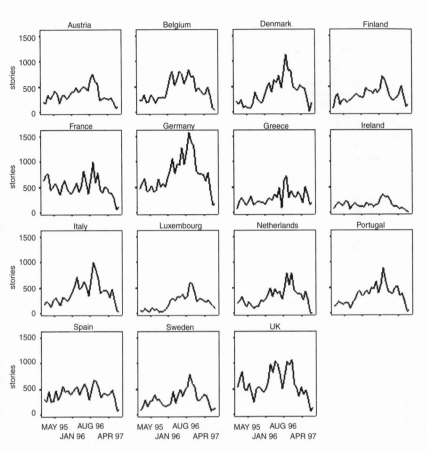

Figure 9.3. Amount of coverage of the EU: monthly numbers of stories, 1995–97. Lines show means.

ment', including reports about the IGC, EU expansion, and reform of the decision-making process, received about one-fifth of the press coverage. The next topics, in order of decreasing rank, were foreign policy (including conflict in Bosnia), agriculture (including the BSE story, at least in part),[17] EU institutions (such as reports about the presidency, Council, Commission, and Parliament), and social policy (including employment and health). Although there was a scattering of stories on the other topics, none of the other policy areas, such as transport or the environment, garnered more than 5% of the press coverage.[18]

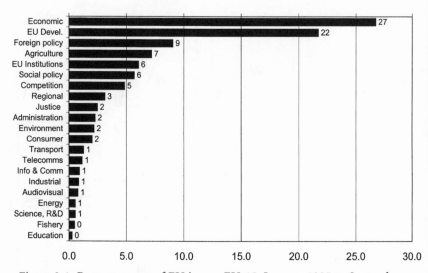

Figure 9.4. Press coverage of EU issues: EU-15, January 1995 to September 1997. *Source:* Calculated from *Monitoring Euromedia,* 1995–97. Brussels: European Commission.

The Television Agenda

The range of issues on mainstream television news shows a slightly different pattern (Figure 9.5), partly because the data cover television news in only six countries in the period from May 1995 to May 1996. Foreign policy emerged as the top issue on television, reflecting the dramatic conflict in the Balkans. The development of the European Union proved almost as important, accounting for one-fifth of all items, followed by TV coverage of EU institutions, and economic and monetary policy, in that order. One difference between television and press coverages was that agriculture was not a major story on television news because the BES crisis hit the headlines only in late March 1996. Many of the more routine but still important policy issues where the EU has been active, such as regional aid, competition policy, and environmental protection, received little attention on TV.

Given the premises of this argument, we can disregard those issues that did not receive much coverage in the news media in the period under review. Two topics were selected for further analysis: the ambitious and far-reaching project of Economic and Monetary Union (EMU) and the issue of EU development. Each of these issues provides a robust test of the media malaise thesis. If extensive negative news

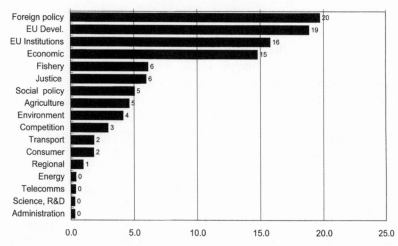

Figure 9.5. TV coverage of EU issues: Belgium, Italy, Germany, UK, France, Spain, May 1995 to July 1997. Source: Calculated from *Monitoring Euromedia*, 1995–97. Brussels: European Commission.

about these topics has had little or no impact on public opinion, then we would expect more fleeting issues to have even less influence.

EMU

Throughout this period, the project on European Economic and Monetary Union (EMU) was high on the agenda.[19] The most important development concerned the single currency. In 1989 the Delours committee recommended moving towards EMU via a three-step plan involving closer economic and monetary coordination, a single currency, and a European Central Bank. In July 1990 the first stage of EMU began with the free movement of capital. In December 1991 the European Council agreed to EMU, with subsequent opt-out agreements with Britain and then Denmark. In November 1993 the Maastricht Treaty went into effect.

In December 1995 the new currency was officially termed the 'euro' by the Madrid Council. The following two years brought discussions of the convergence criteria for membership and speculation about which countries would manage to meet those criteria in order to join the euro-zone. Plans for monetary union continued to advance at the March 1996 Turin Council and the June 1996 Florence Council. In June 1997 the Amsterdam Council adopted the Stability and Growth Pact, defining the conditions for participation in the third stage of EMU, such as the need for sound government finances, sustainable growth, and stable prices. The uncertainty about EMU was resolved in May 1998 at a special meeting of the European Council where it was decided that eleven member states qualified for entry, not including Britain, Denmark, Sweden, and Greece. The euro was launched into the world market on 1 January 1999, with monetary policy coming under the direction of the European Central Bank. In the following six months the euro steadily lost ground against its initial value in trading on world currency markets. If all goes according to plan, the use of euro notes and coins is due to begin in the euro-zone in 2002. Therefore EMU, which initially was one of the most abstract and technical issues of European politics, has come to affect the daily lives of all its citizens. Because of this, the Commission launched information campaigns to inform the public about the consequences of the single currency for matters like the transition to new notes and coins, charges for currency conversion, and retail prices. Since the euro represents a new issue, which the public had not encountered before during their lifetimes, this provides an exceptionally good 'natural experiment' to test learning effects from the information provided by the news media and other sources.

The importance of EMU in press coverage of Europe over the whole period under review is illustrated in Figure 9.6. There were some substantial fluctuations in the numbers of stories about this issue, caused by particular initiatives or events. Press reports about economic and monetary policy accounted for 12–16% of all European stories in the spring of 1995, and that rose sharply to almost one-third of all EU coverage in January 1996, after the Madrid Council christened the euro. Reports on EMU fluctuated sharply in the spring of 1996, then rose again from the autumn of 1996 to the time of the Amsterdam Treaty in June 1997. The cyclical pattern of European coverage that we saw earlier is also evident for this issue.

EU DEVELOPMENT

The second issue selected for extended analysis concerns EU development, including the proposed enlargement of the EU to embrace some central and eastern European states and the potential reform of EU governance to promote greater accountability and efficiency. The 1993 Copenhagen Council agreed on a number of criteria that countries wanting to join the EU had to meet, including respect for democracy and human rights, a level of economic development close to those in the

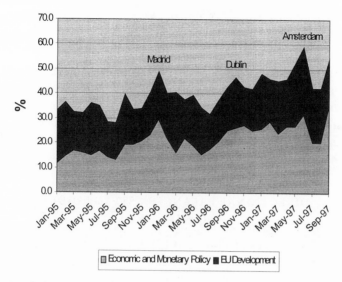

Figure 9.6. Percentage press coverage of selected issues: EU-15, January 1995 to September 1997. *Source*: Calculated from *Monitoring Euromedia*, 1995–97. Brussels: European Commission.

existing member states, and protection of the environment. In the spring of 1998, accession negotiations commenced with the Czech Republic, Cyprus, Estonia, Hungary, Slovenia, and Poland, and the Commission set up accession partnerships with Bulgaria, Latvia, Lithuania, Romania, and Slovakia. There was also discussion of membership by Turkey and Malta. Most of the debate has revolved around the economic and political conditions for accession. The consensus in the Community is that European decision-making and budgeting processes need to be reformed before engaging upon further enlargement.

These years also saw heated debate about the institutional development of the EU. The issue of the 'democratic deficit' has long generated arguments about inadequate mechanisms for accountability, transparency, and representation in the EU policy-making process. Equally important, there has been much concern about the efficiency of the Community decision-making process as the scope and complexity of EU policy has grown, along with the range of players due to enlargement from the original EU-6 to the current EU-15. Many of the debates about institutional reform involve fairly technical although important issues, such as the principle of subsidiarity concerning who should make the decisions in areas transcending national borders, the European Parliament's sharing of decision-making powers with the Council of Ministers, and the veto powers of member states within the council. These discussions progressed at several events, including the March 1996 Turin IGC, the June 1996 Florence Council, the September–October Dublin Council I, and the December 1996 Dublin Council II, and several institutional reforms expanding the powers of the European Parliament were agreed to in the 1997 Amsterdam Treaty. The news coverage about EU development reflected that debate, with peaks and troughs in coverage throughout this period.

DIRECTIONAL BALANCE: A STEADY DIET OF NEGATIVE NEWS?

Given that the issues of EMU and EU development received extensive coverage in news about Europe, we can examine whether that coverage met the second condition of our model: Did the media coverage of those issues display a consistent directional bias? If news about Europe should prove to have been overwhelmingly negative, as some believe, then we would expect to find a succession of 'bad-news' headlines high-lighting quarrels between member states, the sluggishness of the euro, inefficiency, red tape, and extravagance in Brussels, and so on, which would have fed Euroskepticism among the public. On the other hand, if the coverage should prove to have been fairly neutral, then the influence of some critical stories about Europe should have been counter-balanced by more positive reports. *Directional balance* is measured by whether stories are positive or negative from the perspective of each political actor – for example, whether the introduction of the euro was regarded as a good development, or whether an article expressed approval of the actions of the Commission or the president.[20] As described in detail in the Technical Appendix, the directional code ranged from very negative (−2.0) to very positive (+2.0).

NEWSPAPER DIRECTIONAL BIAS

The results show that newspapers usually adopted a Euroskeptic tone on most issues, although the degree of negative bias remained limited. Out of twenty-five separate issues, the coverage for all but four leaned in a negative direction (Figure 9.7). The classification of newspaper coverage shows that the most highly critical stories concerned the European Commission, the EU policy towards the Kurds in Turkey, the audit of EU finances, Bosnian policy, the fisheries dispute, the Schengen

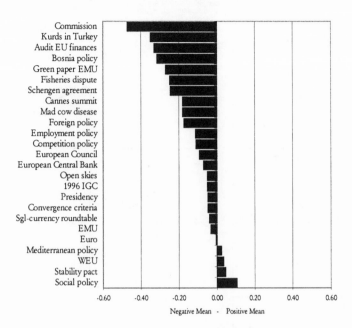

Figure 9.7. Direction of press coverage of the EU. *Source:* Calculated from *Monitoring Euromedia*, 1995–97. Brussels: European Commission.

agreement on open borders, and the Cannes summit. All of these reports were rated as significantly negative (defined as stories rated greater than –0.20). The only exceptions that leaned in a slightly positive direction concerned the issues of social policy (including health and jobs), the stability pact, the Western European Union, and Mediterranean policy. If we take the average tone of press coverage of all EU issues per month, the direction fluctuated slightly but clearly fell within the negative zone throughout this period, with the single exception of the month of December 1995, which saw a positive blip having to do with the Madrid Council.

TELEVISION DIRECTIONAL BIAS

We might expect that given the public-service ethos emphasizing political impartiality, television news would have provided more balanced coverage than the more partisan press. The available evidence for the directional bias of TV news in six countries suggests that, contrary to expectations, in fact the tone of television news proved consistently more negative towards Europe than did that of the press. As shown in Figure 9.8, the most highly critical news about the EU was shown on

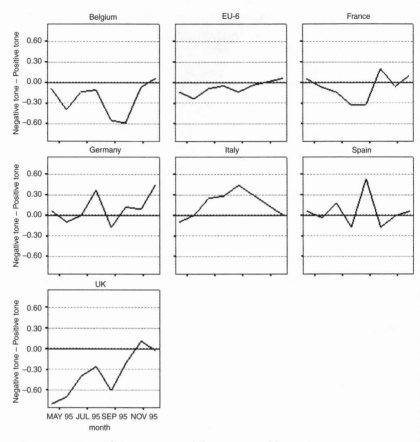

Figure 9.8. Tone of TV coverage of the EU: monthly stories, 1995. Lines show means.

the BBC, especially in midsummer 1995, with stories that reflected the Euroskeptic position of leading spokespersons within the governing Conservative party. Belgian news was also strongly negative, but German television coverage proved more neutral, and Italian TV was more positive. The trends show a significant correlation between the overall directions of coverage in newspapers and television ($R = 0.66$, $P = 0.01$), increasing confidence in the consistency and reliability of the indicators.

Overall, the coverage of the European Community in newspapers and on television news therefore often proved anti-Europe. Newspaper headlines commonly highlighted issues such as lax financial control and cronyism in the Commission, sluggish economic growth, profligate agricultural subsidies, the euro's slide on world markets, the failure of Europe to act in the Balkans conflict independently of American leadership, and deep-seated quarrels over the pace and extent of European integration. Negative coverage was perhaps most evident in the Euroskeptic British press, which produced a series of headlines about mythical Brussels demands to introduce straight bananas, ban British bangers, and outlaw Women's Institute jam – stories that have become enshrined in popular folklore.[21] If an endemic 'bad-news' or Euroskeptic frame characterized most EU coverage, drowning out positive news about progress on budgetary reform or European defense, then plausibly that may have fuelled public disillusionment with Europe.

THE INFLUENCE ON THE PUBLIC

This leads us to the last and most important issue concerning the association between news coverage and public opinion. The effect of bad news on public disaffection is widely assumed but rarely demonstrated. As argued earlier in Chapter 3, trend analysis at the aggregate level is open to many criticisms on methodological grounds. The most important factor concerns the interaction between the media coverage and public opinion, including the classic chicken-and-egg question of who leads and who follows. On the one hand, coverage of the EU by television and the press may drive public support towards Europe. But, equally plausibly, the broader political culture may influence journalists and help frame media reports. Spurious correlations may be produced by independent factors. For example, political leaders may act as cue-givers, influencing both reporters and the public. For all these reasons, trend analysis at the aggregate level is inherently more subject to flaws and more difficult to interpret than individual-level approaches, as analyzed in subsequent chapters. Nevertheless, this approach allows us to test the common media malaise claim that the steady drumbeat of negative media messages was correlated with public opinion at the national level.

We can examine the impact of press coverage about the EU on public opinion using three dependent variables. The news media could influence either 'diffuse' support, meaning general orientations towards the European Union and its institutions, or 'specific' support, meaning orientations towards particular policies.[22] *Diffuse support* for the EU is measured by the standard indicators of *membership* and *benefit* that have been widely employed since the start of the Eurobarometer series.[23]

Specific support is measured according to agreement or disagreement with the following statement about the euro:[24] 'There has to be one single currency, the euro, replacing the [national currency] and all other national currencies in the European Union.' The responses allow us to monitor diffuse and specific support for the EU every month in each country using the Europinion tracking surveys. To increase the reliability of the analysis, the study compared measurements of press coverage and public opinion per country every month, producing 180 observation points for analysis.

Two independent variables were used to monitor the direction of news coverage, focusing on the selected issues of monetary union and EU development. Throughout 1995 the tone of newspaper stories about EMU showed a highly negative tendency, with a stepped descent, reaching its nadir in October 1995. Coverage subsequently moved into the neutral zone for 1996. It was only at the very end of the series, in the summer of 1997, that coverage started to move in a more positive direction (Figure 9.9). The direction of news about EU development was measured by coverage of the 1996 IGC, which focused on the enlargement of EU membership and institutional reforms to the decision-making process. The tone of the news about the IGC fluctuated, and treatment over the whole thirty-three-month period was occasionally neutral or even briefly positive, but the predominant coverage was persistently in the negative zone. Most people reading articles about the debate over EU development would have received critical coverage of these issues.

Simple bivariate correlations were run to analyze the impact of monthly trends in the tone of press coverage on European support. The results of these correlations confirmed that *the tone of news about monetary union was strongly and significantly related to diffuse support for EU membership and to specific support for the euro* (Table 9.1). In contrast, negative press coverage of the IGC was not associated with public support for the EU.

Regression models were run to see if the tone of press coverage continued to prove significant after introducing controls for the 'nation' variable. The results in Table 9.2 confirm the pattern found with simple correlations, namely, that the tone of press coverage towards EMU continued to be predictive of public support for the euro and diffuse support for EU membership (although not EU benefits). The national variables performed as expected. For example, that for Ireland proved relatively positive, and that for the UK negative, across all three indica-

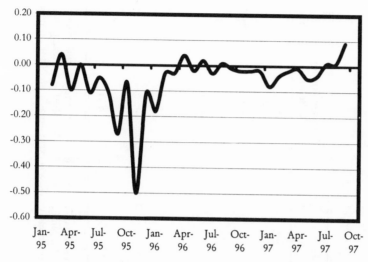

Figure 9.9. Direction of press coverage of EMU: EU-15, January 1995 to October 1997. *Source*: Calculated from *Monitoring Euromedia*, 1995–97. Brussels: European Commission.

Table 9.1. *Bivariate correlation between tone of press coverage and public support for the EU*

Public Support	Tone Press EMU			Tone Press IGC/EU Development		
for the Eu	R	Sig.	N.	R	Sig.	N.
Support for Euro	0.387	***	132	0.160		132
EU Membership	0.362	***	167	0.071		180
EU Benefit	0.103		165	0.051		180

Note: For the correlation between public support and the tone of press coverage, the observational unit is the 'country-month'. See text for details.
Source: Calculated from *Monitoring Euromedia*, 1995–97. Significance: ***$P = 0.01$. Brussels: European Commission.

tors of European support, with the overall models explaining a high proportion of the variance in the dependent variables. More formal modeling supported that conclusion. Although the results are not reported here, several time-series models were estimated to test whether or not the tone of each month's news about EMU related to measurable changes in diffuse public support and specific public support. The results from these models confirmed a significant relationship.

Table 9.2. *Models predicting specific and diffuse support for the EU*

	Predictors of Support for the Euro	Sig.	Predictors of Support for EU Membership	Sig.	Predictors of Support for EU Benefit	Sig.
Constant	48.0		51.3		45.2	
Tone of Press Coverage of Euro	0.24	**	0.17	**	−0.03	**
Austria			0.07	*	−0.13	**
Belgium	0.30	**	0.13	**	0.15	**
Germany	−0.09	*	0.27	**	0.01	
Denmark	−0.08	*	−0.04		0.11	**
Greece	0.41	**	0.09	*	−0.04	
France	0.41	**				
Finland	−0.07					
Ireland	0.65	**	0.61	**	0.33	**
Netherlands						
Portugal	0.15	**	0.37	**	0.33	**
Sweden	0.10	**	0.02		0.50	**
UK	−0.19	**	−0.38	**	−0.39	**
R^2	0.82		0.79		0.81	

Note: The figures represent standardized beta coefficients predicting aggregate EU support based on ordinary least-squares regressions models. The dependent variables are the mean national monthly support for the euro, EU membership, and EU benefit, as described in the text. Countries are coded as dummy variables. Significance: ** $P > 0.01$; * $P > 0.05$. The Luxembourg dummy variable is excluded as a predictor in these models. There are 180 observational units in total (nation-months).

Why should we find a relationship between press coverage and public opinion concerning the euro, but no impact from the coverage of European development? Many reasons plausibly could have accounted for this difference. It might be that the issue of 'EU development' was too complex and abstract, encompassing many different elements within that single category. People plausibly may have favoured institutional reform, for example, but still may not have wanted to enlarge membership to central and eastern European states. A wide range of complex and technical reforms fall under the broad heading of 'EU development'. Alternatively, perhaps the measures that we were using were insufficiently sensitive to gauge subtle shifts in public opinion towards these issues; ideally we should have had monthly data monitoring specific support for enlargement and for institutional reform. Nevertheless, the fact that we have demonstrated a significant link between trends in negative news coverage of the euro and the level of public support towards a single European currency is important. In principle, the methodology could be extended and applied to other types of issues in other contexts. Such a process would help us to understand the conditionality of media effects, both when the news media can and cannot influence mass attitudes.

CONCLUSIONS: NEGATIVE NEWS, TURNED-OFF PUBLIC?

There has long been concern that a steady diet of negative news has contributed to public disillusionment with government and political leaders. This issue is believed to affect many postindustrial societies, from the United States to Japan, but perhaps it can best be examined systematically within the context of the European Union. European citizens cannot be expected to care much about European elections, to feel connected to MEPs, or to know much about their rights within the EU if there is minimal news coverage of the European Parliament debates in Strasbourg, if major initiatives concerning aid for the Balkans, monetary union, and employment programs go unreported in the press, and if the only coverage that is widely available is generally hostile towards European Community institutions and policies.

In the early years of the Community it was assumed that there was a 'permissive consensus' about the future development of Europe and that decisions by the Council of Ministers and Commission were broadly in line with public opinion. The public displayed passive acquiescence towards Europe, delegating and legitimating the decisions of

European policy-makers in Brussels, Luxembourg, and Strasbourg.[25] In recent years, the increases in the powers and responsibilities of European institutions have been considerable, through the Single European Act and the Maastricht Treaty, as well as through the enlargement of EU membership to Austria, Sweden, and Finland. With a population of almost 300 million, the EU is now the world's largest trading bloc and one of the three most important players on the global economic scene, alongside the United States and Japan. Many believe that the processes of representation and accountability have not kept pace with that expansion. The resignation of the entire European Commission in March 1999, following a scathing report on mismanagement, underscored the need for greater democratic control over the Brussels bureaucracy.

Over the past decade, while the scope and responsibilities of the European Community have grown, there has been a significant erosion of public support. Behavioural indicators like turnout for European elections, reaching record lows of under half the electorate (49.2%) in June 1999, suggest profound apathy, or possibly even growing alienation, from the European project. Although institutional arrangements play a large role in explaining cross-national variations in turnout, these factors are less satisfactory in explaining the downward trend.[26] Attitudinal indicators can gauge whether people think that their country's membership in the European Union is a good thing ('membership') and whether people believe that the EU has benefited their own country ('benefited').[27] These indicators, which were stable or rising during the 1980s, fell from 1990 to 1997. In 1998, just over half (54%) of the public believed that European membership was a good thing, well down from the peak in the spring of 1990, when almost three-quarters expressed approval. Euroskepticism is most widespread among the latecomers to the Community, including Sweden, Austria, and Finland, as well as the UK.

That situation is compounded by the fact that the institutions of European governance remain so distant from the lives of most European citizens, and the decision-making processes usually occur behind closed doors. Citizens are linked to EU governing institutions via two primary channels of representative democracy.[28] In the *intergovernmental model*, citizens convey their preferences over Europe via established channels of democracy within the nation-state, through parties, parliaments and governments to European institutions, for example when national ministers meet behind closed doors in the European

Council. In the *federal model*, the electorate express their policy choices directly to the European Parliament, and indirectly to other levels of European governance. Yet there are major flaws with both routes. The activities of the European Parliament, the most democratic forum in EU politics, often appear only weakly related to the public they represent. Without any direct experience of European politics, most people have to rely on other sources of information for their knowledge and evaluations of EU institutions and policies. Europe therefore provides a strong test case for the media malaise thesis: If the people take their cues from the news media, then we would expect that negative messages in the press and television would decrease public support for the EU.

MAJOR FINDINGS

To summarize the results of this analysis, we assumed that the news media could influence aggregate public opinion under three conditions: (1) if there was extensive media coverage of an issue, (2) if this coverage displayed a consistent directional bias, and (3) if the public was willing to take its cues from the news media.

In terms of the *amount* of coverage, the evidence shows that *most European issues received minimal coverage in the news media*. Routine news about EU affairs was limited, although there was a cyclical pattern, with newspaper and television coverage regularly peaking around the biannual meetings of the European Council. If the coverage by the news media was ephemeral and sporadic, with only a few occasional stories about issues like competition or trade policy, then we would not expect that coverage to have had much impact.

The news media devoted most coverage to the two topics selected for further analysis, namely, monetary union and EU development. These issues raised important questions about widening and/or deepening the EU. Monetary union provoked a heated debate that recurred throughout the period under review. The development of a single currency probably was the most controversial and important issue in Community politics, and ultimately it will affect the future direction of Europe and the lives of all its citizens. The issue about reform of EU institutions is at the heart of the European agenda. If news about these issues failed to sway public attitudes, then it seems legitimate to assume that people were influenced even less by coverage of issues further down the news agenda, such as EU policies on energy, consumer affairs, and education.

In terms of the *direction* of coverage, we found that *when the media reported about the EU, though sometimes the news was neutral, the coverage usually was given a negative-leaning slant.* Although the bias was only modest, it proved fairly consistent. The attentive public reading about Europe in newspapers or watching TV news received a steady diet of 'bad' news. That can be criticized from a normative standpoint. As argued earlier, for the news media to provide an effective civic forum, European citizens should be able to hear the pros and cons concerning controversies about the future development of the European Community. If political leaders are divided over the euro and enlargement, and people can read or watch only one side of the argument, then that potentially impoverishes public debate.

Lastly, and most importantly, in terms of *effects*, did the news coverage influence public opinion? We have established that *extensive and sustained negative coverage of the euro was significantly associated with lowered levels of diffuse and specific public support for Europe.* At the aggregate level, negative news about the monetary union was associated with lower levels of public support for EU membership in general, and for the euro in particular.

If we can generalize further from those findings, and if we assume that the direction of influence runs from the news media to the public, this implies that when issues receive extensive coverage that is also predominantly negative in direction, then the public does not remain immune from media messages. Negative news about the euro plausibly may have contributed to public disaffection with Europe. The pattern that we have established here seems likely to hold in many other contexts, particularly in regard to issues like conflict in Kosovo and the dangers of global warming with which the public has little or no direct personal experience to counterbalance the media messages.

That being said, there is an important qualification to this argument. *We still cannot establish the direction of causality in the relationship.* There is a significant *association,* but that, in itself, does not demonstrate causality. One interpretation is that a critical press, with headlines constantly casting doubt on the viability and effects of a single European currency, had the capacity to influence public perceptions of the European Union and the desirability of monetary union. Alternatively, the press may have taken its cues from a broader political reality, shaped by the complex interactions of party elites, interest groups, and political cultures. For example, the British press may have been so strongly Euroskeptic in part because of the predominance of the anti-European faction within the governing Conservative party, as well as the strength of anti-European feeling in grassroots public opinion, which hostility long predated the issue of monetary union. Aggregate-level analysis is simply unable to settle the question of whether public opinion led media coverage or media coverage led public opinion, in their complex tango. The most plausible interpretation probably is a pattern of complex interactions, rather than any single causal direction. Journalists are players in a broader political culture and are not immune to its influences. And the political culture and system are, in turn, shaped and moulded by, among other things, the long-term patterns of media coverage. In order to test the media malaise thesis further, we can go on to see if the findings in this chapter are confirmed at the individual level when we examine the effects of media exposure on citizens' political knowledge, political trust, and civic engagement.

CHAPTER 10

Knows Little? Information and Choice

To assess what the public learns from the news media, we need to establish suitable benchmarks for political knowledge. Three perspectives are common in the literature. The 'civics' approach assumes a single narrow type of 'ideal' information about government and public policy that all citizens need to know. The 'relativist' stance acknowledges that people have a limited reservoir of political information but suggests that this is sufficient for people to cast a meaningful ballot. A preferable strategy would be to understand what practical knowledge citizens need in order to make informed judgments about the consequences of their actions in multiple roles, for example, as claimants of welfare benefits, as consumers of genetically modified food, or as activists concerned about global warming, in addition to their role as electors. Some judgments involve daunting information hurdles; for others the demands are fairly minimal. Some arise sporadically, like voting, and others involve people's daily lives.

On the basis of this conceptualization we can explore the roles of newspapers, radio, and television in contributing to the practical knowledge that European citizens acquire, using five different contexts that are progressively more abstract: public awareness of social issues such as the personal health risk from skin cancer; economic issues such as the single European currency (the euro); citizens' rights within the European Union; general knowledge about the institutions and functions of the European Union; and understanding of party policies in elections to the European Parliament. When asked where they looked for information about the European Union, people most commonly cited television (60%), newspapers (41%), and radio (24%). Far fewer said that they acquired information from sources like personal discussions, public libraries, and information centers (Figure 10.1).

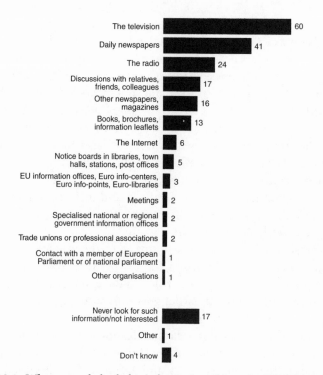

Figure 10.1. Where people look for information about the EU (EU-15).
Source: Eurobarometer 50.0, fieldwork, October–November 1998.

The study demonstrates that the public does indeed learn from the news in many important ways, even after controlling for factors like prior education and political interest. Europeans who used the news media acquired more practical information across all five dimensions of political knowledge, and Chapter 12 confirms that similar patterns are evident in the United States. Far from 'dumbing-down' the public, as media malaise theories suggest, the analysis shows that the news media contribute positively to civic education.

THE CIVICS FALLACY

To develop this argument, we can start by considering how we conceptualize and measure political knowledge. The most common view, derived from classical liberal theories of representative government, defines 'political' rather narrowly, as restricted to the governmental or electoral context. This view assumes that in order to make rational electoral decisions, voters need some general understanding about the rules of the game and how the political system operates, information about the major policy proposals by the main contenders for office, and familiarity with the government's record.[1] A long tradition in cognitive psychology has explored what voters learn from election campaigns in general and from the news media in particular. Following the earliest scientific polls of public opinion and the pioneering work of Paul Lazarsfeld,[2] much of the literature has stressed the breadth and depth of people's ignorance about public affairs and their minimal retention of factual political knowledge from exposure to the news,[3] although more recent work has revised this picture.[4]

The most recent comprehensive survey of the available research in the United States, by Delli Carpini and Keeter, focused on three dimensions of political knowledge: the rules of the game (what government is), the substance of politics (what government does), and people and parties (who embodies the government). The study demonstrated that most people 'failed' against standard 'civics' tests, such as correctly identifying the name of the speaker of the House of Representatives, the role and powers of the Supreme Court, and the term of office served by U.S. senators.[5] Moreover, despite substantial increases in educational levels attained and much greater availability of mass media, that study found American citizens to be no better informed about politics today than were those half a century ago. There was also a significant 'knowledge gap', reflecting major disparities between the information-rich and the information-poor, with the latter concentrated among poorer groups. Knowledge of foreign policy is usually particularly low, as indicated by such measures as being able to identify international leaders or even other countries.[6] A study in another context examined what the public had learned during the year-long campaign preceding the 1997 British general election, in terms of identifying the party most strongly in favour of six different policy issues such as electoral reform and independence for Scotland, and it found that the public had acquired no information about these issues, despite extensive media coverage of politics during the year-long campaign.[7]

On the basis of such findings, many commonly assume that the news media are largely to blame for public ignorance. The problem, some suggest, lies in neglect of substantive policy issues in favour of stories about opinion polls and campaign strategy,[8] the personal characteristics of political leaders, and editorial punditry. Lichter and Smith's critical conclusions about the news coverage of the 1996 U.S. presidential election exemplifies that view: 'The results of this study raise disturbing questions about the nature and quality of the political reporting provided by television network news. . . . Although coverage of the 1996 primary campaign was extensive, it was dominated by discussion of the horse race and other non-substantive topics. Reports featuring policy issues were relatively uncommon and tended to be both brief and superficial, with discussions far more likely to include an interpretation of the political implications of a candidate's platform than any details about its specific nature or substantive effects. . . . Far from aiding the democratic process, it [the coverage] may further erode public confidence in the political process and in mainstream journalism as well.'[9]

But this common view involves the fallacy of regarding the news media as analogous to a third-grade civics teacher. The relevant question concerns the level of practical knowledge necessary to cast an 'informed' ballot.[10] As argued earlier in Chapter 2, the capacity to make reasoned electoral choices does not require encyclopedic information about every detail of each party's manifesto policies and the government's record, nor does it necessarily require comprehensive knowledge of textbook civics. People do not need to be able to recite each party's detailed proposals on matters like health care, nor the names of government ministers, nor even the names of their local candidates. Citizens would quickly sink from information overload if they attempted to meet these conditions. It may be intrinsically worthwhile to know about such matters, but the principles of analytical knowledge concerning the causes of phenomena, which are widespread in scholarship, are not the same as the standards for practical knowledge about the consequences of decisions, as required in the political world. Just as drivers do not need to know the principles of mechanics, or even how a spark plug works, to accelerate a car, so citizens do not need to plumb the depths of how a bill becomes law to understand the probable consequences of their political decisions.

THE RELATIVIST FALLACY

Recognizing widespread public ignorance about the basic facts of political life, recent work by John Zaller and Samuel Popkin has focused on the role of cognitive shortcuts such as ideology or 'schema' that can reduce the time and effort required to monitor the candidates and allow a reasoned choice with imperfect information.[11] In this view, citizens are capable of making good low-information decisions because the costs of keeping fully informed are high, while the rewards for engaging in politics in contemporary democracies are low. Others have emphasized the limited but still significant acquisition of information about candidates and issues derived from exposure to the news in an election campaign, so that gains in knowledge, even if modest, may be sufficient to allow voters to cast meaningful ballots. Neuman, Just, and Crigler have argued that people use the messages they receive from the news media to construct political meanings that allow them to play the roles of active and informed citizens: 'They [voters] actively filter, sort, and reorganize information in personally meaningful ways in the process of constructing an understanding of public issues.'[12]

But if citizens can construct meanings from the campaign, that does not necessarily mean that they thereby possess political knowledge, unless these constructions bear some resemblance to 'reality'. The danger of the relativist notion is to assume that any beliefs that voters use to help them come to judgments, whether true or false, are the equivalent of knowledge. The distinction between knowledge and belief needs to rest on the Popperian understanding that the latter has to be subject to some external test of verifiability or falsifiability.[13] If voters believe, for example, that crime statistics are rising, when trends show that the number of incidents is actually falling, or if they think that the British Labour party is more likely to support independence for Scotland than the SNP,[14] or if they believed that in the 1992 election President Clinton was more experienced in foreign affairs than Senator Dole, then in all likelihood voters are probably factually wrong in their judgments, and not just in trivial ways.[15] One American survey in midsummer 1999 found that most people were unaware that rates of violent crime and teenage pregnancy had fallen in recent years, and nearly half the country did not know that the economy was growing.[16] The pollster Humphrey Taylor attributed such American misperceptions of social and economic trends to local TV: 'A nightly diet of crime and other bad news on local TV has created a badly misinformed public who just do not recognize how good these times are.'[17] If people evaluate the performances of the candidates and parties in elections on that basis, their misperceptions can lead to serious errors of judgment.

PRACTICAL KNOWLEDGE

So if the 'civics test' and the 'relativist notion' are flawed conceptions of political knowledge in a democracy, what is the alternative? The argument advanced here assumes that in its role as civic forum, the news media system needs to provide information sufficient to enable citizens to estimate the probable risks and benefits of their decisions. In this view, people need practical knowledge that can help them to connect their political and social preferences to the available options.[18]

Practical knowledge is situational, so the type of political information that will prove most useful will depend on the context. For example, information about the government's record and the parties' policies on the major issues can prove essential in general elections. But in other contexts, such as presidential primaries, the most useful information may concern the personal characteristics of the candidates. Faced with referendum proposals, voters may need issue information to assess the risks and benefits of complex policy options. Yet in other situations, opinion-poll data can prove invaluable, providing information about the relative rankings of the candidates and parties to guide tactical voting choices. Understanding the campaign strategies adopted by parties may help voters to weigh, sift, and evaluate the reliability of manifesto promises. Editorial commentary and partisan cues, rather than simply 'straight news' or factual issue information, may help waverers decide. Commentators often decry the tendency for news to cover 'soft' topics, such as 'the health beat'. But in their daily lives people may need practical information about the health risks from contaminated foods, their welfare rights at benefit offices, or how they can claim legal redress for grievances. In short, citizens' abilities to make informed choices will vary with the context. If we accept that 'the personal is the political', then being deprived of 'soft' information about the danger of cancer from pesticides can be just as important, if not more so, than being deprived of 'hard' information about the government's proposals on welfare reform or distant events in Kosovo. In representative democracies, most people are probably powerless to influence social or foreign policy, outside of casting their votes in the electoral arena every few years, but they can decide which fruits and vegetables to consume every day of their lives.

LEARNING FROM THE NEWS

Given these assumptions, what do people learn in different contexts, and, in particular, what is the role of the news media in this process? We can examine comparative evidence drawn from the fall 1996 Euro-barometer conducted in the fifteen member states. Following the approach of Delli Carpini and Keeter,[19] we assume that people learn about a subject if they have the ability, motivation, and opportunity to do so. Cognitive skills, particularly prior education, should facilitate further learning. The logic is that the more we know, for example about European history, the easier it is to acquire and to make sense of new information, such as events in Kosovo. Motivation drives the desire and willingness to learn, including whether we pay attention to new information provided by conversations with friends, classroom teachers, or newspaper columns. Lastly, the structure of opportunities concerns the availability of information and how easy or difficult it is for a person to learn about a topic, given his or her ability and motivation. The more dense the information environment, with a proliferation of media sources, outlets, and levels, the easier it is to learn. But a mere proliferation of news without any prior cognitive guideposts or interest can produce information overload and a situation of 'blooming, buzzing' confusion. This conceptualization is analytically useful, although it rarely relates in a simple one-to-one fashion with specific characteristics. Civics education, for example, can influence both people's abilities (skills) and their motivations (interest).

We can develop an analytical model predicting political knowledge based on structural, attitudinal, and media-related factors. The *structural variables* include the usual socioeconomic indicators such as age, sex, education, and income. Educational background, in particular, usually is strongly associated with the cognitive and analytical skills required for learning. We noted in earlier chapters how age, gender, and social status relate to distinct patterns of media use, like exposure to television and the Internet. *Attitudinal factors* include left–right ideology, political interest (measured by political discussion with friends and colleagues), and attitudes towards the European Union. We assume that the pro-Europeans will be more interested than Euroskeptics in following EU events and issues. Many researchers have found political interest and involvement to be among the strongest predictors of media use and attention.[20] People interested in public affairs use the available media more purposefully.[21]

Media-exposure factors include regular use of television news, daily newspapers, and radio news, as well as use of the Internet.[22] Newspapers require greater effort than television, and some have suggested they provide more information,[23] although other recent American studies have argued that television news may be a more important source of political learning than the printed press.[24] In this study we draw on a distinction between long- and short-term media effects. Without experiments we are unable to examine the short-term impact of reading a particular story about the euro or watching a television documentary about the European Commission. The evidence from panel surveys that is available, from within the intensive information environment provided by the year-long 1997 British campaign, suggests that short-term exposure to the news media had negligible influence on awareness of public-policy issues.[25] Nevertheless, long-term or cumulative media effects can be analyzed from cross-sectional surveys by comparing differences between groups of media users, such as whether regular readers of the press prove to be more informed than nonreaders, after controlling for factors like prior education and interest. We cannot prove that any persistent differences result from patterns of media attention per se, but, as argued elsewhere, that seems a plausible assumption. Although the more highly educated may possess cognitive skills that can facilitate reading newspapers or watching the news, nevertheless long-term repeated or habitual exposure to the news can be expected to make people better informed, in a virtuous circle. In this regard, the role of the news media is no different from the socialization process experienced in the home, school, workplace, or community. Thus the key issue this study explores is whether long-term patterns of media exposure can help to predict political knowledge, after controlling for a wide range of structural and attitudinal variables. This chapter focuses on the comparative evidence in Europe, and Chapter 12 picks up this question again in the American context.

DIMENSIONS OF POLITICAL KNOWLEDGE

Given our broad conceptualization, five measures of knowledge were selected from the 1996 Eurobarometer survey to represent distinct contexts and progressively more abstract types of information. Each can be regarded as broadly 'political', informing different aspects of citizenship, although only some relate more narrowly to government and elections per se. Standardized 100-point scales were used for comparability across dimensions.

SOCIAL ISSUES: THE RISK OF CANCER

The first measure concerns public awareness of social issues that are important for personal health and well-being, such as those featured in information campaigns about the risk of AIDS, food safety, drugs in the workplace, the link between smoking and cancer, and the consumption of alcohol before driving. Information about such issues is both important and practical, as it affects everyday lives. The issue tested in the 1996 survey concerned levels of public knowledge about the effects of exposure to the sun on skin cancer. The EU had been conducting an information campaign around this issue, called 'Europe Against Cancer', through paid media and the press. If political communication is understood as a two-way process in which political leaders are trying to influence the public at the same time that citizens are seeking to influence government, then we need to explore whether government information campaigns actually can make a difference. The question we can explore is whether the people who were most attentive to the news media proved to be the best informed about this issue. Knowledge of the risk of skin cancer was tested by twenty-seven items monitoring whether people were aware of the risk related to sun exposure. People were asked whether they agreed or disagreed with the following types of statements: 'Some moles can develop into skin cancer.' 'The sun is most dangerous for people with fair complexions.' 'If the sun is covered by clouds, there is no risk of being exposed or getting sunburnt.' (See Appendix 10A for details.)

ECONOMIC ISSUES: THE EURO

Knowledge of economic issues can encompass a wide range of indicators, ranging from the most abstract (information about GATT, or the role of the World Bank) down to the most prosaic (information about whether everyday prices are rising or falling in the shops). In this study, information about the economy was examined in terms of awareness of the single European currency. As discussed in Chapter 9, the issue of economic and monetary union had received extensive coverage in the news media in the period before the Eurobarometer survey. The previous year, in December 1995, the new currency had been officially termed the 'euro' by the Madrid Council. There was widespread debate in the press about the budgetary and economic conditions for membership and speculation about whether weaker countries like Italy and Greece would meet the standards necessary to enter the euro-zone. Plans for monetary union continued at the March 1996 Turin Council and the June 1996 Florence Council. The issue of monetary union has many dimensions, some very abstract, but at a practical level the public needs to be aware of the implications of the new notes and coins due to be introduced in January 2002, including information about such matters as bank charges for exchanging old currency, the rate of exchange, the schedule for the changeover, and the implications for comparing prices and purchasing goods in another EU member state. The switch to the euro will eventually reach into the lives of everyone in the EU, especially those living in the eleven-member euro-zone. Knowledge about monetary union is also important in terms of public participation in the policy process in countries like the UK and Sweden, where the issue of eventual membership in the euro-zone remains under debate. The evidence from Europinion tracking surveys shows that in the spring of 1996 less than half the public (46%) could correctly identify the 'euro' as the name of the single currency, but by the spring of 1998 over three-quarters (78%) could do so.[26] Knowledge of the name of the currency proved twice as high (87%) in the EU-11 countries that joined the euro-zone as in member states that stayed out (44%). The Eurobarometer survey monitored practical knowledge about the euro using five factual items, such as whether the euro would have to be converted into the currency of another participating member state in order to pay for goods and services in that country (see Appendix 10A).

Citizenship Rights

The dimension of citizenship rights represents another form of practical knowledge. The Eurobarometer survey examined whether citizens knew about their legal rights, using a series of ten true/false items concerning issues like the rights to work, travel, study, and claim benefits in another EU member state, as well as to travel around Europe without showing a passport or identity card. The survey also included ten items monitoring whether people had heard of matters like the right to reimbursement for urgent medical expenses anywhere in the EU, to equal treatment at work without sex discrimination, to health and safety at work, and to vote or stand as a candidate in local and European elections for residents in any EU country. If people are unaware of such rights, that limits their ability to seek legal redress. Much of the work of the EU has focused on such issues. The 1992 Single European Act was intended to eliminate physical, technical, and fiscal frontiers between member states, reduce regional inequalities, harmonize rules governing working conditions, strengthen research and development programs, protect the environment, and facilitate monetary coopera-tion. The Maastricht Treaty in 1992 and the Amsterdam Treaty in 1996 were intended to strengthen political as well as economic union. Wide-spread ignorance about the rights established by these treaties will limit the practical effects of these initiatives.

EU INSTITUTIONS

At an even more abstract level, some grasp of EU institutions is required if people are to understand the relationships among the EU Parliament, Commission, and Council of Ministers, as well as the linkages between EU governance and the national governments. By the 'civics' standard, ideally people should be able to identify certain factual statements correctly, like the name of the president of the Commission and their country's commissioners, the locations of most EU institu-tions, and the number of EU member states. Ten typical institutional items were included in the spring 1996 Eurobarometer (see Appendix 10A). Unfortunately, the complexities and lack of transparency within the EU policy-making process, as well as the lack of direct elections for the leadership positions, pose high hurdles for anyone seeking to under-stand the roles of EU institutions and its leaders. The only occasion on which the public has any direct opportunity to influence the EU policy-making process is during elections for the European Parliament, and even then their influence is limited because of the continuing weakness of the Parliament as an institution, and because parties usually fail to contest European elections primarily on EU issues.[27] Consequently, for most people, most of the time, there is no practical incentive to learn about EU institutions. This can be deplored from a traditional 'civics' standpoint, because robust citizenship should involve awareness of the growing powers, scope, and responsibilities of the EU. But from the perspective of practical political knowledge, that is, information that can be used to do something, such matters as learning mundane de-tails about the roles of economic and social committees or about the Common Agricultural Policy (CAP), or even knowing who heads the European Commission, are of low priority on rational grounds. In contrast, if people are unaware that exposure to the sun risks skin cancer for their children, or that they have a right to work in another country, or what the euro means for retail prices, this matters to their lives, producing higher learning incentives.

Party Policies

Lastly, the most challenging aspect of political knowledge, with perhaps the highest information hurdles to be overcome, concerns the extent to which people were found to be well informed about party policies during elections to the European Parliament. Much of the literature in cognitive psychology has defined political knowledge in similar terms. Classical theories of rational voting suggest that to cast informed ballots, electors need to understand the major issue differences between the contending parties so that they can link their policy and ideological preferences to their ballot choices. If voters lack accurate perceptions of what political parties stand for, they may unintentionally cast their ballots for policies they disagree with. One major difficulty in assessing this issue concerns how we determine the accuracy of voters' perceptions. When dealing with simple factual statements like the number of EU member states (fifteen), there is no ambiguity about the correct response. With assessments of party policies, however, perceptions often are more matters of judgment than of fact. One benchmark that can be used to determine the accuracy of voters' perceptions of party policies is available from the 1994 European election study, which asked electors to place the parties in their country on four 10-point scales: on the issues of the single European currency, national border controls, employment programs, and left–right ideological position (see Appendix 10A). The median assessments for each party by the electorate can be compared with where the candidates for the European Parliament placed their own parties on the same scales (from the 'European Candidates Study' in 1994), taken as a fairly accurate indicator of party policy. Previous research had suggested that there might well be a systematic perceptual bias in how voters and candidates perceived party positions,[28] but nevertheless European Parliament candidates could be regarded as well informed about the policy positions taken by their parties. The key question in this study is not the relative proximity or distance of voters' perceptions from party policies, as analyzed elsewhere,[29] but whether those most attentive to the news media proved most accurate in their judgments.

The strategy employed to explore these issues first examined the dependent variables, in terms of the distribution of political-knowledge scales. Descriptive cross-tabulations were used without any controls to examine the simple bivariate association between exposure to each of the news media and the five scale measures of knowledge. The final step examined these relationships using ordinary least-squared regression models controlling for demographic factors (gender, age, education, and household income) and attitudinal factors (political interest, pro-EU attitudes, and left–right ideology).[30] These models used a media scale that combined uses of television news, newspapers, and radio. Given the contextual differences in news environments that we have already documented, region and nation were included as dummy variables in the regression models. In all cases a positive coefficient indicated that greater exposure to the news media was associated with higher knowledge.

THE IMPACT OF THE NEWS MEDIA ON
POLITICAL KNOWLEDGE

What was the evidence that the public was well informed about these different types of issues, and, in particular, did those who were most exposed to news prove the most knowledgeable? Table 10.1 shows the simple distribution of percentages of correct responses to the items measuring knowledge of the risk of cancer, the euro, EU rights, and EU institutions.

The results show quite a wide spread for these items, especially in the last two columns. On the institutional scale, for example, while two-thirds were aware that most EU institutions were in Brussels or Luxembourg, and half knew that the European flag had a blue background and yellow/gold stars, nevertheless on the more 'civics' end of the scale less than a fifth could name the leading spokesperson for the EU (Jacques Santer, as president of the European Commission), and in the fall of 1996 only one in twenty realized that the euro notes and coins were going to be in their pockets by the year 2002. In general, there tended to be far greater awareness of the social issues of the risk of cancer from exposure to the sun, which most directly affects people's lives, and least knowledge about the more distant and abstract institutional items that had little practical relevance. People can still grasp many of the most important aspects of the European Union without memorizing such facts as the number and names of the commission-

	Cancer Risks	Euro	EU Rights	EU Institutions
Knows too much sun contributes to aging of the skin	90			
The sun is most dangerous for people of fair complexion	88			
Knows some moles can develop into skin cancer	88			
Knows can study in any EU state			81	
Knows can seek work in another EU state			80	
Knows euro will be the only official EU currency		65		64
City of most EU institutions is Brussels or Luxembourg				64
Knows euro is worth the same in all member states		61		
Knows colours of the EU flag are blue/yellow				59
Knows euro is the same as the ecu		53		
Knows if the sun is covered by clouds, there's still a risk of sunburn	51			
Euro will not need to be converted		50		
Can name the new currency (euro)				46
Knows no need to change driving license if move			46	
Knows can travel without passport/id			43	
Getting brown before the holidays does not protect you efficiently from the harmful effects of the sun	43			
Knows no need to use customs for EU goods			41	
Knows do not need work permit in another EU state			39	
Knows can vote in local elections in another EU state			39	
Knows right to receive unemployment benefit if seeking work in another EU state			34	
Can identify the name of a commissioner				33
Common emergency number			27	
Can identify the correct number of member states (15)				26
Can identify the nation holding the presidency of EU				26
Can identify the value of ecu				23
Can identify the number of commissioners				19
Can identify the name of the Commission president				13
Can identify the year euro notes/coins will be introduced (2002)		10		

Note: Items recoded into a consistent direction to represent the 'correct' response.
Sources: Knowledge of cancer risk, euro, and EU rights from Eurobarometer 46.0, fall 1996, *N*. 16,248, weighted EU-15; knowledge of EU institutions from Eurobarometer 45.0, spring 1996; knowledge of EU party policies from Eurobarometer 41.1, fall 1994.

Table 10.2. *Patterns of media use and knowledge (% correct)*

	Cancer Risks	Euro	Know EU Rights	Heard of EU Rights	EU Institutions
All	66.5	47.7	48.6	36.6	34.2
TV News					
Never	63.8	42.2	44.1	31.2	27.1
Sometimes	65.1	45.9	47.9	35.0	32.4
Every Day	67.1	48.8	49.1	37.5	35.1
Newspaper					
Never	66.4	42.2	53.9	28.9	21.5
Sometimes	65.8	48.2	48.5	36.7	32.8
Every Day	66.8	50.2	50.9	40.2	39.8
Radio News					
Never	66.6	44.5	46.2	30.6	26.9
Sometimes	64.7	47.6	48.3	36.6	34.7
Every Day	67.3	49.6	50.0	39.6	38.4
Zero-order correlation between media use and knowledge scale (R)	0.05**	0.13**	0.15**	0.13**	0.30**

Note: See Appendix 10A for details of all scale items. The scales have been standardized to 100 points for comparability across columns; $**p = 0.01$.
Sources: Knowledge of cancer risk, euro, and EU rights from Eurobarometer 46.0, fall 1996, N. 16,248; weighted EU-15; knowledge of EU institutions from Eurobarometer 45.0, spring 1996; knowledge of EU party policies from Eurobarometer 41.1, fall 1994.

ers from their country, which, as government appointments, they were powerless to influence.

The issue at the heart of this chapter is the role of the news media in cognitive awareness. An examination of the bivariate relationship between use of television news, newspaper, and radio news and the proportion of correct answers on the first four dimensions shows that in nearly every case the most regular users of the news media were more likely to prove the most politically knowledgeable across all dimensions (Table 10.2). The differences between those who used the media every day and other groups usually were fairly modest, but on the more demanding items the knowledge gap proved more substantial, for example in terms of hearing about citizenship rights within the EU. Moreover, despite the many different items used in the scales, the knowledge gap concerning the euro, citizenship rights, and EU institutions was consistent. This gap was less surprising among regular newspaper readers, but, contrary to the media malaise thesis, it was also evident among viewers of TV news.

Of course, one possible explanation could be that those who were drawn to the news were disproportionately from the more affluent and better-educated social groups, in addition to those who were already most motivated to follow politics and European affairs because of their prior inclinations and interests. Prior involvement in politics often has been found to be one of the strongest predictors of media use.[31] As mentioned earlier, it is difficult to resolve such issues through cross-sectional survey data. Nevertheless, Table 10.3 examines whether use of the news media continued to prove significant on the first four dimensions of political knowledge after controlling for the structural and attitudinal variables discussed earlier, as well as national controls. The regression models show a fairly consistent pattern across each dimension. In every case, as expected, the more knowledgeable usually proved to be well educated, more affluent, younger, and usually male,[32] in addition to those who were most interested in politics and more pro-European in their leanings.

The strength of the relationship between attention to the news media and the political-knowledge scales weakened once controls for those factors were introduced, suggesting that people who were better educated or more pro-European would prove both more attentive to the news media and more knowledgeable about EU affairs. Yet at the same time, and this is the important point, even after structural and attitudinal controls were introduced, exposure to the news media still continued to exert a significant independent effect on political knowledge.

What is the relationship between use of the news media and the last and most demanding dimension of knowledge, the ability of voters to identify party policies with some degree of accuracy? In theories of representative party government, this is the most critical type of information for voters. If people are unaware of where the parties stand on the major issues of the day, they are unable to cast informed ballots based on prospective policy platforms. We can examine the correlation between attention to the news media in the 1994 European election campaign and the public's ability to place each national party accurately on ten-point scales measuring party positions on the single currency, national borders, the European employment program, and general left–right ideology. This represents a strong test of the thesis, because

Table 10.3. *Predictors of knowledge, EU-15, mid-1990s*

	Risks of Cancer	Sig.	Euro	Sig.	EU Rights	Sig.	EU Institutions	Sig.	Operationalization
STRUCTURAL									
Education	0.02		0.09	**	0.09	**	0.19	**	Age finished full-time education
Gender: Male	−0.12	**	0.06	**	0.07	**	0.17	**	Male (1) Female (0)
Age	0.04	**	−0.01	**	−0.13	**	0.07	**	Age in years
Household Income	0.01		0.03	**	0.07	**	0.09	**	Harmonized income scale
ATTITUDINAL									
Political Discussion	0.01		0.10	**	0.07	**	0.14	**	How often discuss: never, occasionally, freq.
Pro-EU Attitudes	0.11	**	0.08	**	0.11	**	0.11	**	Member + benefit scale
Left-Right Ideology	0.03	**	0.01	**	0.01	**	0.01		10-point scale: From left (1) to right (10)
USE OF NEWS MEDIA									
Media News Use	0.06	**	0.11	**	0.05	**	0.17	**	15-point use of TV news + paper + radio news

NATION								
Austria	-0.17	**	0.05	**	0.02		0.12	**
Belgium	-0.14	**	0.01		0.02		0.03	**
Denmark	0.01		-0.15	**	0.14	**	0.08	**
Finland	-0.08	**	-0.07	**	0.15	**	0.04	**
France	-0.04	*	-0.04	**	0.11	**	-0.01	
Germany	-0.14	**	0.08	**	0.07	**	0.07	**
Ireland	-0.08	**	0.02		0.01		-0.01	
Italy	-0.01		-0.12	*	0.02	*	-0.01	
Luxembourg	-0.03	**	0.02	**	0.05	**	0.08	**
Netherlands	-0.12	**	-0.26	**	0.14	**	-0.04	**
Portugal	-0.08	**	-0.04	*	0.01		-0.01	
Spain	-0.06	**	-0.02	**	-0.03	**	-0.04	**
Sweden	-0.08	**	-0.05	**	0.14	**	-0.04	**
UK	-0.02		-0.18	**	0.07	**	-0.12	**
Constant	66.9		28.4		28.4		17.7	
R^2	0.06		0.17		0.16		0.28	
N.	16,247		16,247		16,247		65,178	

Notes: Columns report the standardized beta coefficients predicting knowledge based on ordinary least-squares regression models. The dependent variable is the 100-point scale measuring knowledge. See Appendix 10A for details. Significance: $\star\star P > 0.01$; $\star P > 0.05$. In the national dummies, Greece is excluded.

Sources: Knowledge of cancer risk, euro, and EU rights from Eurobarometer 46.0, fall 1996, *N.* 16,248; weighted EU-15; knowledge of EU institutions from Eurobarometer 44.2 bis, January–March 1996; weighted EU-15.

Table 10.4. *Correlation between media use and knowledge of party policies*

	Low Media Use in Campaign	High Media Use in Campaign
Left-Right Scale	0.894	0.892
Euro	0.653	0.699
National Borders	0.567	0.712
Employment Program	0.675	0.710

Note: Correlation at national party level (*N.* 60) between voters' perceptions of party positions on 10-point scales and the actual positions of party policies, as assessed by candidates for the European Parliament. All coefficients are significant at 0.01 or above. *Sources*: European Representation Study, 1994; Eurobarometer 41.1, the European Election Study.

at least two of these issues (borders and jobs) were of low salience to the European public. The 'accurate' rating for each party position on these scales, establishing the benchmark, is estimated on the basis of where candidates for the European Parliament placed their own parties on these scales. The correlations between the public perceptions and the 'actual' positions of parties were measured at the national party level for sixty different European parties.

The general results in Table 10.4 show that the public proved relatively well informed on most issues: There was a strong correlation between public perceptions and the actual positions of parties across all items, but particularly on the ideological scale. As previous studies had found,[33] despite the low interest in European elections and the complexities of party policies on these issues, most voters knew reasonably well where the different parties stood on matters like the euro and national borders. This may well surprise those who have been contending that the public remains ignorant of many major issues of public policy. But what is most important for my argument is that those who paid greatest attention to the news media proved consistently more accurate in their assessments of party policies on the three policy issues than did the inattentive.[34] On the general ideology scale there was no difference; because the left–right dimension is one of the commonest ways of understanding differences in European party politics, most voters could assess party positions irrespective of media cues. Contrary to the media malaise thesis, the results suggest that the information provided by the news media helped voters understand the party choices they faced on some of the key issues facing the European Union.

CONCLUSIONS: PRACTICAL INFORMATION AND CITIZENSHIP

Two alternative perspectives for conceptualizing political knowledge are common in the literature. On the one hand there is the 'civics' approach, which holds up an ideal of textbook knowledge that most voters fail to achieve. On the other hand there is the 'relativist' view, in which whatever voters 'know' is deemed sufficient for electoral choice. My aim is to steer a middle course between these two positions, arguing that citizens need practical knowledge to evaluate the consequences of their actions.

What does this conceptualization of practical political knowledge imply for the role of the news media as a civic forum? Critics commonly castigate the news media for failing to provide serious coverage of policy issues and public affairs. If we accept that knowledge is contextual and multidimensional, it follows that citizens need a variety of different types of practical political information – about personal health as well as politics, polls as well as policies, evaluations of character as well as party strategy, editorial commentary as well as campaign debates, and vox pop as well as the leadership speeches. If politics is understood to be part of our daily lives, involving everyday decisions about our health, lifestyles, and community, it is just as important for us to learn about a breakthrough in the search for an AIDS cure, or the danger of dioxin in eggs, or problems of sexual harassment in the workplace, as it is to learn about European parliamentary debates over the CAP or a meeting of the G8. Given this understanding, it is therefore incorrect to assume, as some critics do, that the civic function of news is limited to coverage of government and the public-policy process. Instead, in this view the news environment most conducive to public learning is one that provides a wide range of political information (broadly defined), in different formats and at different levels, so that citizens can select the types of practical information most useful to them.

What does the public learn from the news media? The evidence from this study suggests that levels of awareness of the issues under comparison vary substantially. The public tended to know more about the social issue of skin cancer, which could affect their daily lives, than about the more abstract and distant issues of EU institutions and leaders. Studies claiming that the public is fairly clueless about politics often have been based on 'civics' tests, but such studies fail to show why it matters whether people can identify the capital of Iceland, or can name the head of the United Nations, or can say how many members are elected to Congress. There is no rational incentive to memorize facts that have no practical relevance to citizens' multiple political roles.

The conclusions from this analysis are that, even after controlling for prior educational levels and political interest, exposure to the news media contributes positively to what European citizens learn, whether about everyday social matters like personal health or about more abstract and distant issues of party politics within the European Union. Whether the American pattern is similar or different will be discussed in Chapter 12. Of course, with cross-sectional analysis we can never demonstrate conclusively that the associations we found were due to the process of reading newspapers or watching television; that would require time-series panel studies. Yet, as argued elsewhere, given the controls in our models, it seems most plausible to believe that over the long term there is a virtuous circle; people with higher cognitive skills and greater political interest are most likely to pay attention to the news media, and in turn, the process of media exposure is likely to add to anyone's store of political knowledge. The reason is that if people already understand something about the role of the Commission and the functions of the European Parliament, they are better prepared to process new information about implementation of the euro, or the appointment of Roman Prodi as president of the Commission, or debate over enlargement. In a nutshell, the more one knows, the more one can learn. But if people do learn from the news media, and the messages, as we saw in Chapter 8, tend to be negative, do they also perhaps learn to become more wary and mistrustful of government and political leaders? Does an unduly cynical media produce a cynical public? We need to go on to examine this issue.

APPENDIX 10A: QUESTIONS IN SCALE MEASURES

EUROBAROMETER 46.0, FALL 1996

KNOWLEDGE OF THE EURO. Q32: I am going to read out a number of statements. For each one of them, could you please tell me whether you think it is true or false? The single currency, the euro, in which some countries will take part in 2002 . . .

(a) will be the only official currency in the European Union and will be used to pay for goods and services in all participating member states. (*True*/False/Don't know)

(b) will still need to be changed into the currency of another participating Member State in order to pay for goods and services bought in that Member State. (True/*False*/Don't know)

(c) will be worth the same whatever the participating Member State, that is, if you change a euro used in your country into dollars, you will receive the same amount as if you had changed into dollars a euro used in another country. (*True*/False/Don't know)

(d) is exactly the same as the ecu, only the name is different. (*True*/False/Don't know)

Q28: Notes and coins in the European currency, that is in euro, may be introduced some time after exchange rates are. In December this year designs for the European currency's banknotes will be chosen. When do you think these notes and coins will be introduced?

Before 1999/In 1999/In 2000/In 2001/*In 2002*/In 2003/In 2004/In 2005/Later/Never/Don't know.

KNOWLEDGE OF EUROPEAN RIGHTS. For each of the following statements, please tell me whether you think they are true or false.

(a) You have to have a work permit in order to be able to work in another European Union member country. [False]

(b) You are allowed to vote in local elections in another European Union country, if you are resident there. [False]

(c) You are allowed to seek work placement with firms in other European countries. [True]

(d) You have no right to receive unemployment benefit from (OUR COUNTRY) if you go to another European Union country to look for work. [False]

(e) There is a common telephone number for emergency services in all European Union countries. [False]

(f) You are not allowed to have a savings account with a bank or buy insurance in another European Union country to look for work. [False]

(g) You are allowed to travel around the European Union without showing your passport or identity card. [True]

(h) You are allowed to study in any European Union country. [True]

(i) You have to go through customs when you bring home goods that you have bought in another European Union country for your own personal use. [True]

(j) You have to change your driving license when you move to another European Union country. [False]

AWARENESS OF EU RIGHTS. Q69a: Have you heard, over the last few years, about the rights and opportunities you have, as a citizen of the European Union, to . . .

(a) go and live in any European Union country?

(b) go and work or start up a business in any other European Union country, under the same conditions as the citizens of that country?

(c) go and study in any European Union country?

(d) buy goods for your personal use in any other European Union country and bring them back home, without going through customs?

(e) be reimbursed for any urgent medical attention you may need in another European country?

(f) be guaranteed adequate health and safety standards in the workplace anywhere in the European Union?

(g) be guaranteed equal treatment at work, without discrimination based on sex, anywhere in the European Union?

(h) borrow and invest from banks anywhere in the European Union?

(i) take out an insurance policy anywhere in the European Union?

(j) if you live in another European Union country, to vote and stand as a candidate in local elections there?

(k) if you live in another European Union country, to vote and stand as a candidate in European elections there?

KNOWLEDGE OF EU INSTITUTIONS. Do you happen to know . . .

(a) the current number of states in the European Union? [15]

(b) the name of the President of the European Commission? [Jacques Santer]

(c) the number of [NATIONALITY] Commissioners? [2 or 1 depending upon member state]

(d) the name of one [NATIONALITY] Commissioner? [Name]

(e) the recently chosen name of the European currency? [the euro]

(f) the country which holds the Presidency of the European Union since January 1 and until end of June 1996? [Italy]

(g) the current value of the ecu in [NATIONAL CURRENCY]?
(h) the city in which most of the European Union institutions are located? [Brussels or Luxembourg]
(i) one of the two colours of the European flag? [yellow/gold or blue]
(j) the year when notes and coins in the European currency will be introduced? [2002]

KNOWLEDGE OF CANCER RISK. Examples of some of the items: Q17: For each of the following statements, could you please tell me if you tend to agree or tend to disagree?

(a) Too much sun contributes to the development of skin cancer.
(b) Too much use of sun beds contributes to the development of skin cancer.
(c) Too much sun contributes to the aging of skin.
(d) Too much use of sun beds contributes to the aging of skin.
(e) If the sun is covered with clouds, there is no risk of being over-exposed or getting sunburnt.
(f) Some moles can develop into skin cancer.
(g) Sunburn is more dangerous for children than adults.
(h) Getting brown before the holidays protects you efficiently from the harmful effects of the sun.

EUROBAROMETER 41.1, SUMMER 1994

KNOWLEDGE OF PARTY POLICIES. Q44: Some people think it would be best for [OUR COUNTRY] to keep its own currency and make it more independent from the other European currencies. Others think the best thing would be to create a common European currency.

More independent							New common		
national currency							European currency		
1	2	3	4	5	6	7	8	9	10

Where would you place yourself on this scale? And where would you place the [OUR COUNTRY] parties on this scale?

Q45: Another important problem for the European Union is unemployment. The President of the European Union has proposed to raise funds for a massive employment program in order to fight unemployment. Others argue that the competition of the Single European Market alone will promote economic growth and will be the best remedy for the current problem of unemployment. What is your opinion? [Same 10-point scale as above]

Q46: Still another issue with the European Union has to do with national borders. What do you think? Should the European Union continue to remove national borders and let people move freely between countries, or should we reintroduce tighter border controls in order to be better able to fight crime in [OUR COUNTRY]?

CHAPTER 11

Cares Less? Cynical Media, Cynical Public?

Much of the concern about the role of the news media in society has been generated by the long-term slide in public confidence in the core institutions of representative democracy, including parliaments, the legal system, and parties. Many accounts have exaggerated the depth and breadth of the problem; there is little evidence of any widespread 'crisis of democracy'. Yet many postindustrial societies have experienced a growth in the number of 'critical citizens'. Public faith in democracy as an ideal form of government remains widespread, but at the same time citizens have become increasingly dissatisfied with the performance of representative institutions.[1] This phenomenon may be caused by many factors, including the failure of government performance set against expectations, the growth of new cultural values challenging traditional forms of authority, and problems of institutional effectiveness.[2] Recently, as discussed in Chapter 1, a wide range of journalists and scholars in the United States have blamed the news media for growing public cynicism, while in Europe many believe that the development of professional political marketing by parties has also contributed towards public mistrust. Perhaps an endless diet of stories about government corruption and public sector incompetence, coupled with excessive use of party spin-doctors and glossy television marketing in election campaigns, has eroded public faith in the political process.

We can identify two claims of the media malaise thesis. The weaker version holds that negative news erodes support for specific leaders or policies. For instance, news media criticism may have reduced President Clinton's popularity and affected evaluations of his administration. This version seems plausible; in Chapter 9 we saw that press coverage of the European Union displayed a systematic bias, providing a steady diet of negative news. Monthly trends in news coverage were significantly related to variations in the level of public support for the euro. But does negative news have more profound consequences, for example, fuelling deeper disenchantment with the European Community? The stronger version of the thesis holds that a systematic pattern of political reporting, based on deep-rooted news values, undermines diffuse-level confidence in the political system. This chapter aims to examine the systematic evidence for that stronger claim.

THE CONCEPTUAL FRAMEWORK AND MEASURES

In analyzing the effects of the mass media, we need to distinguish between television and newspapers. Most concern about media malaise has centered on television; for example, in the United States, as mentioned earlier, Robinson concluded that certain common themes and predilections used in portraying public affairs on TV news were responsible for political cynicism among the public in the aftermath of Watergate.[3] Miller and associates found a similar effect among newspaper readers.[4] In Europe, as discussed earlier, considerable concern has also focused on the techniques of political communication used by parties and the decline in direct voter–party linkages. Political communication is therefore broadly conceived in this study in order to allow examination of the effects of messages emanating from both parties and the news media during campaigns.

Evidence is drawn from the 1989 and 1994 European election surveys, the 1996 Eurobarometer, and the 1997 British election campaign panel study (BES). Attention to campaign coverage by newspapers and TV and radio news, as well as party communications, in the 1994 European elections was measured on the basis of the following question:

'At the European elections we have just had, the parties and candidates campaigned for votes. Did their campaign come to your attention in any of the following ways?

- Party worker called at your home to ask for votes.
- Election leaflets put in your letterbox or given to you in the street or in shopping centers, etc.
- Advertising on behalf of the candidates or parties.
- Coverage of the campaign in newspapers.

- Coverage of the campaign on TV and radio.
- Family or friends or acquaintances discussing the European election.'

Because there were strong similarities among those who used information from canvassing by party workers, campaign leaflets, and party advertising, these items were collapsed into a single scale of party-communication activity.[5] The spring 1996 Eurobarometer was also used, both to replicate and confirm the results and because this survey also measured Internet use. To analyze the effects of the news media on political support, regression models were used, controlling for the usual structural and attitudinal variables already discussed in previous chapters, as well as national dummies representing societal-level variations.[6]

We need to clarify the central concepts used as the dependent variables. Studies commonly refer to 'political trust' as if it were all of one piece, so that standard measures, such as to what extent Americans trust public officials, are said to provide insights into a range of attitudes towards the political system. But, as argued elsewhere, there is convincing evidence that the public often distinguishes between different levels or objects of support.[7] People may well be critical of particular political leaders, such as President Clinton, without necessarily losing confidence in the institution of the presidency. Or they may become disenchanted with the current government's performance without losing faith in democratic ideals. We therefore need to disentangle public attitudes towards these different components of the political system.

Expanding on the classic Eastonian framework, we can distinguish theoretically among support for the political community, support for the regime (including regime principles, performance, and institutions), and support for political actors (Figure 11.1). This framework can be conceptualized as ranging from the most diffuse support down through successive levels to the most concrete and specific. Widespread erosion of identification with the community, such as challenges from breakaway ethno-nationalist movements, or deep-rooted conflict over the core principles of the regime, is a particularly serious development that can dissolve the 'glue' binding the polity together. On the other hand, short-term fluctuations in people's evaluations of government performance, institutions, and leaders represent a routine part of the democratic process. To see whether this conceptual framework was

Type of Political Communications Independent Variables	Objects of Political Support Dependent Variables
Attention to Television News	Political Community
	Regime Principles
Attention to Newspapers	Regime Performance
	Regime Institutions
Party Communications	Political Actors

Figure 11.1. Conceptual framework of political support.

reflected in political attitudes, principal-component factor analysis was employed to examine the intercorrelations between survey items in the 1994 European election study, discussed later, and the results in Table 11.1 served to confirm these theoretical distinctions.

NATIONAL TRUST

In the conceptual framework used in this chapter, the most diffuse level of support concerns identification with the political community, meaning a general willingness among citizens to cooperate together politically. The boundaries usually are conceived in terms of the nation-state, but a community can be defined at the supranational level, in terms of a sense of European identification, or at subnational level, such as in terms of Basque or Scottish identities. If there is a general sense of community within the European Union then we would expect that European citizens would show considerable trust towards people in other member states, so that Germans would trust the Greeks, British, and Italians, and so on, more than they would trust nationals in countries outside the European Community, such as the Americans, Japanese, and Russians. News coverage can be expected to play a major role in how much people believe that they can trust those from other countries, given the role of world news in transmitting images of other societies.[8]

Levels of 'trust in people' in fifteen nations were compared in the 1994 European election study, and factor analysis was used to examine the intercorrelations underlying these attitudes (Table 11.1). Three

Table 11.1. *Dimensions of political support*

	Political Community			Regime Performance	Regime Institutions		Political Actors Like Leaders
	Trust Northern Europeans	Trust Southern Europeans	Trust G8	European Union	National Government	EU and National	
Trust Dutch	0.823						
Trust Luxembourgers	0.809						
Trust Belgians	0.806						
Trust Danes	0.801						
Trust British	0.571		0.415				
Trust Germans	0.545						
Trust Greeks		0.762					
Trust Portuguese		0.736					
Trust Spaniards		0.714					
Trust Italians		0.462					
Trust French		0.443					
Trust Japanese			0.730				
Trust Americans			0.617				
Trust Russians		0.491	0.506				
EU Dissolve				0.738			
EU Member				0.730			
EU Unify				0.690			
EU Benefit				0.662			
EU Demo				0.457	0.511		

Table 11.1 *(cont.)*

	Political Community			Regime Performance	Regime Institutions		
	Trust Northern Europeans	Trust Southern Europeans	Trust G8	European Union	National Government	EU and National	Political Actors Like Leaders
Rely Nat Demo					0.798		
Rely Nat Govnt					0.678	0.503	
Rely Nat Parl					0.656	0.528	
Rely Euro Parl						0.817	
Rely Euro Council						0.807	
Rely Commission						0.785	
Rely Euro Court						0.774	
French Leader							0.715
Spanish Leader							0.592
German Leader							0.569
British Leader							0.522
% of Variance	23.8	6.6	3.9	5.3	4.5	11.8	3.8

Note: The coefficients are derived from factor analysis using principal-component analysis with varimax rotation. Coefficients below 0.40 are suppressed. See Appendix 11A for the exact wording of the items. In total, the items explained 59.8% of the variance.
Source: European Election Study 1994, Eurobarometer 41.1.

dimensions clearly emerged from the analysis: trust in northern Europeans (citizens of Luxembourg, Denmark, Ireland, Germany, The Netherlands, Belgium, and France), trust in southern Europeans (Spain, Portugal, Greece, and Italy, and this factor also loaded on France), and trust in nationals in the larger G8 world powers (Japan, Russia, America, Germany, and Britain). Most strikingly, after the end of the Cold War, trust in Russians and Americans fell into one category among Europeans, rather than being divided by east and west.[9]

The results from the regression models, in Table 11.2, show a fairly consistent pattern across all three dimensions. Those who proved more trusting included the more affluent and better-educated social strata, men, and younger generations, and political interest proved one of the strongest indicators of national trust. The country-level dummy variables often proved significant and in the expected direction, that is to say, those who lived in northern Europe proved more trusting of their neighbours, and less trusting of residents in Mediterranean Europe. Lastly, after including these controls, attention to news on television and radio and in the papers failed to predict national trust, whereas people who relied on party channels of communication proved slightly more trusting. At the most diffuse level, therefore, a sense of European community, indicated by trust in people from other member states, was not significantly related to use of the news media.

SUPPORT FOR DEMOCRATIC IDEALS

Support for regime principles concerns approval of the core values of the political system. In democratic states this dimension can be termed the 'idealist' definition of democracy, derived from classic liberal theory. Surveys can tap agreement with specific democratic values, like freedom or equality,[10] or more commonly can measure general agreement with the idea of democracy as the best form of government. Because no suitable items were included in the 1994 European Election Study, we turned to the equivalent 1989 study, where support was gauged by the single four-point item tapping whether people were for or against democracy as an idea. If news coverage commonly has a negative bias towards the political process and public affairs, then according to the media malaise thesis those most exposed to that steady barrage of messages should prove most cynical about democratic principles. The regression models in Table 11.3 confirmed that attention to the news media was significantly correlated with support for democracy, but, contrary to media malaise claims, the direction proved

Table 11.2. *Predictors of national trust*

Trust in . . .	Northern Europeans	Sig.	Southern Europeans	Sig.	G8 Nationals	Sig.	Operationalization
STRUCTURAL							
Education	0.05	**	0.02		0.04	*	Age finished full-time education
Gender	0.05	**	0.01		0.03	*	Male (1) Female (0)
Age	−0.04	**	−0.07	**	−0.06	**	Age in years
Income	0.11	**	0.05	**	0.10	**	Harmonized household income scale
ATTITUDINAL							
Political Interest	0.15	**	0.11	**	0.14	**	Interest in politics (4-pt scale).
Left-Right Ideology	0.01		−0.04	*	0.03	*	Scale: From left (1) to right (10)
ATTENTION TO							
TV/Radio News	−0.02		−0.01		0.01		Yes (1) No (0)
Newspapers	0.02		0.02		0.02		Yes (1) No (0)
Party Communications	0.03	*	0.04	*	0.03	*	
NATION							
Belgium	0.14	**	−0.07	**	0.07	**	
Denmark	0.18	**	−0.08	**	0.16	**	
Germany	0.13	**	−0.10	**	0.16	**	
Ireland	0.01		−0.13	**	0.03		
UK	0.02		−0.09	**	0.06	**	
Luxembourg	0.08	**	−0.02		0.05	**	
Netherlands	0.18	**	−0.05	**	0.14	**	
Italy	−0.03		−0.08	**	0.09	**	
Portugal	−0.01		−0.01		0.01		
Spain	−0.01		−0.02		0.02		
Constant	12.4		9.5		8.8		
R^2	0.16		0.05		0.11		
N.							

Notes: The figures represent OLS standardized regression coefficients (betas). Q2: 'I would like to ask you a question about how much trust you have in people from various countries. For each please tell me whether you have a lot of trust, some trust, not very much trust, or no trust at

Table 11.3. *Predictors of support for democratic principles and the performance of the European Union*

	Support for Democracy as an Ideal (i)	Sig.	Support for EU Performance (ii)	Sig.
STRUCTURAL				
Education	0.08	**	−0.02	
Gender	0.01		0.06	**
Age	0.05	**	−0.03	
Income	0.09	**	0.10	**
ATTITUDINAL				
Political Interest	−0.01		0.29	**
Left-Right Ideology	−0.02		0.04	*
ATTENTION TO				
TV/Radio News	0.04	**	0.04	*
Newspapers	0.09	**	0.04	*
Party Communications	0.04	**	0.05	*
NATION				
Belgium	−0.12	**	−0.03	*
Denmark	−0.02		−0.14	**
Germany	−0.08	**	−0.16	**
Ireland	−0.08	**	0.04	*
Italy	−0.08	**	0.04	*
Luxembourg	0.01		0.03	*
Netherlands	−0.05	**	0.01	
Portugal	0.06	**	−0.06	**
Spain	−0.08	**	−0.03	
UK	−0.03	*	−0.15	**
Constant	3.2		5.1	
R^2	0.08		0.18	
N.				

Notes: The figures represent OLS standardized regression coefficients (betas). See Appendix 11A for scales. France is excluded from the dummy variables. $**p > 0.01$; $*p > 0.05$.
Source: (i) European Election Study 1989; (ii) European Election Study 1994, Eurobarometer 41.1.

positive: The more people watched and read, the more they had faith in democratic principles.

EVALUATIONS OF REGIME PERFORMANCE

The third level concerns evaluations of regime performance, meaning support for how government works at the level of the European Union. We used the standard indicators, including the conventional measures of 'membership' and 'benefit' discussed earlier, as well as items on unification and the dissolution of the EU widely employed in previous research. In Eurobarometer surveys these items can be supplemented by 'satisfaction with the performance of democracy in the EU', that is, how well democracy is perceived to function in practice as opposed to the ideal.[11] The selected five items clustered together as a distinct dimension in the factor analysis presented in Table 11.1, confirming the conceptual distinction. Media malaise theory suggests that systematic patterns of news coverage of EU performance blaming Brussels bureaucrats and Strasbourg politicians for sluggish economic growth, the devaluation of the euro, or lack of a defence policy in Kosovo, as documented in Chapter 9, should reinforce public disenchantment with Europe. The simple version of the thesis is that those most exposed to the news coverage should prove most critical of the performance of the European Union. Yet, in line with the previous model, in fact we find that attention to the news media during the European campaign was positively associated with evaluations of EU performance: Those who watched or read more about European affairs proved the most pro-European (Table 11.3).

CONFIDENCE IN REGIME INSTITUTIONS

The studies in *Critical Citizens* found that support for democracy as an ideal proved widespread in established and newer democracies, but that many postindustrial societies have experienced substantial erosion of public confidence in traditional political institutions, particularly parliaments. As one of the primary linkage mechanisms between citizens and the state, this development has worrying implications. Previous studies, such as those by Lipset and Schneider, compared confidence in a range of public institutions, such as the legal system and the police, the state bureaucracy, political parties, and the military.[12] This approach seeks to measure generalized support for political institutions – such as approval of the functioning of the White House, rather than support for President Clinton – although in practice the dividing line between the office and incumbent can often prove fuzzy. Institutional confidence was measured in the Eurobarometer by how far people felt that they could rely on decisions made by European agencies, including the European Parliament, the European Commission, the European Court, and the Council of Ministers. Similar questions tapped confidence in the decisions of national parliaments and national governments, and the responses to these latter items were intercorrelated with levels of satisfaction with the performance of democracy at the national level.

We examined the relationship between use of the news media and these indicators of institutional confidence, and Table 11.4 shows that regular users of television and radio news, newspapers, and the Internet were more likely than average to feel they could rely on European and national institutions. In regard to national parliaments, the 'confidence gap' was around 10 percentage points for the groups most and least attentive to TV news and newspapers. In all cases the zero-order correlations proved significant and positive. In regression models controlling for structural, attitudinal, and national variables, the structural variables performed as expected (Table 11.5). Above-average institutional confidence tended to be found among more affluent, better-educated men. The country-level variables reflected long-standing differences in attitudes towards government. For example, the Italians displayed low trust in their own government. Lastly, and most importantly, uses of television and radio news, newspapers, and the Internet proved consistently significant, although weak, predictors of positive institutional confidence.

SUPPORT FOR POLITICAL ACTORS

At the most specific level, we compared levels of support for specific political actors, measured by feelings towards national leaders like the German chancellor, Helmut Kohl, and the French president, François Mitterrand. Leadership popularity can be expected to ebb and flow over time; the regular midterm 'blues' have been widely observed in many countries as part of the regular electoral cycle. Dissatisfaction with leaders and policies is part of run-of-the-mill politics that may not necessarily lead to disenchantment with the political system as a whole. It is only when support for party and leadership remains persistently low over successive elections, for example in predominant one-party systems like Japan and Mexico, where the same party rules for decades irrespective of elections, that public discontent can be expected to erode confidence in the broader institutions of government and generate the feeling that the public is powerless to influence public affairs.

The regression model run to test the effects of media attention on the popularity of national political leaders showed that none of the coefficients proved significant (Table 11.6). The most plausible reason would be that the available measures of leadership popularity were too limited to capture that dimension satisfactorily, and other factors

Table 11.4. *Political communications and institutional confidence*

% 'Can rely upon . . .'	European Commission	European Parliament	Council of Ministers	National Government	National Parliament
All	39	40	37	43	46
TV News					
Never	32	32	29	35	37
Sometimes	35	36	33	40	42
Every Day	41	41	38	44	47
Newspaper					
Never	35	36	33	39	39
Sometimes	40	41	38	41	44
Every Day	40	41	38	46	49
Radio News					
Never	38	40	36	39	41
Sometimes	38	38	35	42	45
Every Day	41	41	38	46	49
Online User					
No	39	40	36	43	45
Yes	45	44	41	46	53
Zero-order correlation between media use and confidence scales (R)	0.05**	0.04**	0.05**	0.08**	0.10**

Notes: Q: 'Many important decisions are made by the European Union. They might be in the interests of people like yourself, or they might not. To what extent do you feel you can rely upon each of the following institutions to make sure that the decisions taken by this institution [are] in the interests of people like yourself? Can rely on it/Cannot/Don't know.' **$P > 0.01$.
Source. Spring 1996 Eurobarometer 44.1bis, N. 65,178; weighted EU-15.

Table 11.5. *Predictors of institutional confidence*

Can rely upon institutions of . . .	European Union	Sig.	National Government	Sig.
STRUCTURAL				
Education	0.05	**	0.02	*
Gender	0.05	**	0.05	**
Age	−0.01		0.04	**
Income	0.03	**	0.02	*
ATTITUDINAL				
Political Discuss	0.04	**	0.01	**
Left-Right Ideology	0.04	**	0.05	**
ATTENTION TO				
TV News	0.04	**	0.03	**
Radio News	0.02	*	0.02	**
Newspapers	0.04	**	0.03	**
Internet	0.02	*	0.02	*
NATION				
Austria	−0.11	**	0.01	
Belgium	−0.02	*	−0.03	**
Denmark	−0.10	**	0.03	**
Finland	−0.10	**	−0.01	
Germany	−0.26	**	−0.10	**
Greece	0.01		0.03	**
Ireland	0.01		0.03	**
Italy	−0.05	**	−0.10	**
Luxembourg	0.01		0.05	**
Netherlands	0.01		0.10	**
Portugal	−0.07	**	0.01	
Spain	0.02	*	−0.01	**
Sweden	−0.15	**	−0.04	**
UK	−0.16	**	−0.08	**
Constant	0.49		0.34	
R^2	0.09		0.06	

Notes: Q: 'Many important decisions are made by the European Union. They might be in the interests of people like yourself, or they might not. To what extent do you feel you can rely upon each of the following institutions to make sure that the decisions taken by this institution [are] in the interests of people like yourself? Can rely on it/Cannot/Don't know.' The figures represent OLS standardized regression coefficients (betas). France is excluded from the national dummies. See Appendix 11A for measures. **$p > 0.01$.

Source: Spring 1996 Eurobarometer 44.1 bis, N. 65,178; weighted EU-15.

Table 11.6. *Predictors of support for political leaders*

	Political Leadership Scale	Sig.
STRUCTURAL		
Education	0.02	
Gender	0.01	
Age	0.11	**
Income	0.04	*
ATTITUDINAL		
Political Interest	0.06	**
Left-Right Ideology	0.06	**
ATTENTION TO		
TV/Radio News	−0.01	
Newspapers	0.03	
Party Communications	0.01	
NATION		
Belgium	0.03	*
Denmark	−0.02	
Germany	0.11	**
Ireland	0.06	**
Italy	−0.05	**
Luxembourg	0.02	
Netherlands	0.01	
Portugal	−0.06	**
Spain	−0.06	**
UK	−0.05	**
Constant	−1.3	
R^2	0.06	

Notes: The figures represent OLS standardized regression coefficients (betas). See Appendix 11A for scales. ** $p > 0.01$; * $p > 0.05$.
Source: European Election Study 1994, Eurobarometer 41.1.

probably were influencing the evaluations, such as nationality and perceptions of government performance.

THE CLASSIC CHICKEN-AND-EGG ISSUE OF CAUSALITY

On the basis of this evidence we can conclude that attention to television and radio news, newspapers, and party communications either was positively related to indicators of political support (in terms of support for democratic ideals, evaluation of regime performance, and institutional confidence) or else proved neutral (in terms of national trust and political leaders). At no stage across this battery of indicators did we find any evidence that media attention was significantly associated with political cynicism. The pattern is consistent with other recent research based on survey data in the United States and other postindustrial societies that has served to question the media malaise thesis.[13]

Yet the correlations we have identified fail to address, still less resolve, the direction of causality in this relationship. This is the classic chicken-and-egg issue that plagues communications research based on cross-sectional surveys. Following this line of reasoning, it could be argued that we still have not disproved the media malaise case. The argument so far has implicitly assumed that people who consume more news develop a more positive orientation towards the political system. But, equally plausibly, it could be that those who are politically trusting pay more attention to news about public affairs.

When examining the effects of major structural variables, such as parental class and educational qualifications, we can safely assume that the factors furthest from the 'funnel of causality' are independent of the political attitudes and behaviour we are seeking to explain, such as voting choice. Over the long term, habitual use of the media can be expected to shape political views. For example, over the years, regular readership of the partisan press can be expected to reinforce party choices. Some people still may habitually read the same newspapers and watch the same programs for years, but where a more competitive market has developed, media loyalties probably have become increasingly fickle in recent decades. We have already seen that until the 1980s, usually there were only two or three television channels available in most postindustrial societies. Newspapers often had restricted local or regional distribution networks. Because of technological developments, including simultaneous printing in different cities, today in most countries people will choose a paper based on the front-page headlines they see at the newsstand, and they can more easily surf to another channel when the news is broadcast. Over the short term, therefore, in this situation we would expect to find increased reciprocity, or a virtuous circle, between media attention and political attitudes. People can more easily choose whether to read about politics or sports, celebrities, or fashion.

We lack time-series data to explore this issue on a comparative basis, but we can turn to the 1997 British election study (BES) campaign panel survey that monitored changes in media attention and political trust during the course of the twelve-month 'long' campaign.[14] The same people in the panel were re-interviewed four times: first in May 1996

Table 11.7. *Changes in political trust by media attention, Britain, 1997*

Media Use/Attention	Political Trust			
	Wave A Spr 96	Wave B April 97	Wave D May 97	A:D Change
ALL	6.8	7.3	8.2	1.4
ATTENTION TO TV NEWS				
Attentive to political news	7.5	8.4	9.2	1.7
Not attentive	6.6	7.2	7.9	1.3
ATTENTION TO NEWS IN PAPER				
Attentive to political news	7.8	8.5	9.2	1.4
Not attentive	6.7	7.0	8.1	1.4

Notes: Cell entries are mean scale scores. The scale ranges from 1 to 15. Only respondents in all waves (ABCD) are included (*N*. 1,422). Questions on trust in politicians and parties were asked of only one-third of the sample in wave A.
Source: British Campaign Panel Survey, 1997.

(wave A), in early April 1997 (wave B), in late April 1997 (wave C), and immediately after polling day (1 May 1997) (wave D). The survey monitored trust in political actors, at the specific level, measured on a fifteen-point scale based on agreement with three statements about parties and politicians:

- 'Generally speaking those we elect as MPs soon lose touch with people pretty quickly.'
- 'Parties are only interested in people's votes, not in their opinions.'
- 'It doesn't really matter which party is in power, in the end things go much the same.'

In Britain, the public's responses to these measures remained fairly stable from the mid-1970s until the early 1990s, but from 1991 to 1996 the parties and politicians were increasingly seen as out of touch with the needs of the electorate.[15] To what extent does blame for this phenomenon lie in political coverage by the news media, such as the extensive press coverage of financial scandals and sexual shenanigans that afflicted the British government during these years?

Table 11.7 shows that political attitudes became more positive during the British campaign: As polling day approached, more people came to believe that parties and politicians were responsive to public concerns. The changes were similar for those most and least attentive to the news,

Table 11.8. *Who turned off, Britain, 1997*

	Political Trust	
Change in % who ...	Low	High
Watched TV news yesterday	−1	−7
Read newspaper yesterday	−7	−4
N	1,135	285

Note: Only respondents in all waves (ABCD) are included (*N.* 1,422). Political trust – high: Respondents who scored 8 or more on the political-trust scale in wave B. Political trust – low: Respondents who scored 7 or less on the political-trust scale in wave B. The change is from wave B (early April) to wave C (late April).

Source: British Campaign Panel Survey, 1997.

which suggests that the cause lay in the event itself: As the election approached, more people came to believe that parties and politicians were concerned about listening to the public. Changes in political trust during the campaign were independent of news habits. Nevertheless, just as in the Eurobarometer data, the attentive public showed levels of political trust that were consistently higher than average.

Is there any evidence from the BES panel that the direction of causality flows from political trust to media use? After all, people who feel that the parties and politicians can be believed have greater incentive to pay attention to them in the news. The respondents were divided into two groups based on their levels of trust during the early stages of the official British general election campaign. We then examined the change during the official campaign in the proportion of each group who said that they read a newspaper or watched television news 'the previous day'. We knew from aggregate figures that news use declined during the campaign,[16] and indeed that was what we found (Table 11.8).

Yet the overall findings proved mixed. It is true that newspaper readership did decline slightly more during the campaign among those with lower trust. But with television the opposite pattern was evident: News viewership fell slightly more for people with greater trust. The most plausible interpretation to be drawn from these results is that the relationship between media use and trust in politicians probably is reciprocal, in a virtuous circle.

If we can extrapolate from these findings to the European context, it seems plausible to suggest that people who read or viewed more news about the campaign for the European Parliament developed a stronger understanding and support for the European Union. In contrast, those who saw and read little European news were less likely to believe that they could trust bureaucrats and politicians in Brussels, Luxembourg, and Strasbourg. This pattern is likely to be self-reinforcing: People who know the least about the EU, and have minimal trust, probably will pay little attention to the news about European affairs, on rational grounds.

CONCLUSIONS: THE VIRTUOUS CIRCLE

The process of drawing together what was known from the earlier literature suggested three conditions that guided this research design. First, we have argued elsewhere that the concept of 'political trust' is multidimensional, and so we examined the impact of the news media on diffuse and specific levels of support. Moreover, the effects of media exposure can be expected to vary by outlet, and so we distinguished the attentive public for television, newspapers, and the Internet, as well as between mediated and direct forms of traditional party–voter linkages. Lastly, a rigorous test of the media malaise theory required both cross-sectional and panel data. The former allowed us to see whether media use was correlated with political support, in a positive or negative direction, in many countries. Panel data, available for Britain, allowed us to disentangle the causal relationship underlying the association. One reason that previous studies had reported somewhat contradictory and inconclusive results may have been their failure to distinguish these different conditions.

The weaker version of the media malaise case suggests that if the public is attentive to news cues, then extensive coverage by the media, in a consistent direction, will have the power to shape the public's evaluations of the performances of the government and its leaders. This version does seem plausible, on the basis of the available evidence, as reviewed in Chapter 9, but on the other hand, this claim raises few serious concerns. So long as there is a plurality of viewpoints in the media and society, then this process is just part of the regular checks and balances in democratic politics. The stronger version of the media malaise thesis claims that a systematic pattern of news coverage is capable of generating widespread disillusionment with the political system. In this view, if journalists commonly highlight issues like the incompetence of the European Commission, the waste and extravagance of the European Parliament, and the problems of the European monetary union, then people exposed to this coverage plausibly may become more mistrustful of the European Community, EU institutions, and the principle of integration.

Yet the stronger media malaise claim does not seem to be supported by the evidence presented in this chapter: The attentive public exposed to the most news consistently displayed the most positive orientation towards the political system, at every level. We cannot determine the direction of causality on the basis of cross-sectional surveys, any more than could many previous studies using this method. But the panel survey data available from the 1997 BES allow us to trace the process of attitudinal change over time. The most plausible conclusion from the panel analysis is that attention to campaign communications and feelings of political trust are mutually reinforcing, producing a virtuous cycle.

The evidence we have considered leads us to conclude that the stimulus–response model at the heart of the media malaise theory, in which negative news produces a cynical public, is too simplistic. Rather than being passive recipients of media messages, due to selective perception readers and viewers are actively screening, filtering, and surfing for news that is consistent with their prior political preferences. As a result, during the campaign for the European Parliament, the people who proved most disenchanted with politics screened out coverage, whereas those who already sympathized with the European project and who trusted politics were more attentive to news about EU affairs. Experimental research, discussed elsewhere, reinforces this conclusion. In a rigorous test, negative news about politics during the 1997 British campaign was found to have no short-term impact, whereas positive news did significantly boost party support.[17]

Applying this argument more broadly, theories of selective perception are hardly new; indeed, they reflect the traditional view of political communications. But perhaps today they are more relevant than ever before. As recently as the 1960s and 1970s most people in most countries got most of their news from one or two national television stations and from one or two newspapers. We have already established that, in contrast, postmodern communications are characterized by a rich proliferation of alternative news sources, formats, and levels, with newspaper readership supplemented, not replaced, by an increasing range of television and radio stations, as well as the Internet. In competitive newspaper markets, traditional loyalties towards particular papers often appear to have declined. As a result, consumers have more opportunities than ever before to find news sources most congruent with their prior interests and political predilections. The power of the news media to influence the public is therefore limited and counter-balanced by the growing power of media users to select their preferred information sources.

The cross-sectional and panel evidence we have presented therefore provides no convincing support for the stronger claim in the media malaise case. At the individual level, users of the news media were no different than average, or on balance slightly more positive in their attitudes towards the political system.

Of course, it could be argued that focusing on users of the news media may still miss the mark, for there could well be some diffuse effects from pervasive negative messages in the mass media that affect society as a whole. As George Gerbner argues, it is possible that the images projected by the mass media produce a 'mean world' effect, in which the continuous streams of images from movies, television and the popular press convey a broad picture of corrupt public officials, a violent, crime-ridden society, and a conflictual world.[18] If the long-term effects of the media on popular culture are pervasive, all-encompassing, like the air we breathe, then everyone may become equally polluted, not just the news users.

This argument is considered in detail in Chapter 13, which examines trends in civic engagement in the United States. But it is difficult to test such claims in a satisfactory manner. In the same vein, if pornography, violent movies, and tobacco advertising corrupt society as a whole, not just those who see them, then it is unclear how we can ever hope to refute these claims, short of creating an idyllic society free of pornography, violent movies, and tobacco advertising. At this abstract level, the logic of media malaise theory, like Marxism or religion, becomes more a matter of faith than fact. While such claims may suit the arguments of those who favour banning pornography or violent movies or cigarette ads, that approach would represent a profoundly illiberal philosophy. The more skeptical perspective would argue that if effects cannot be demonstrated at the individual level, it is incumbent on proponents of the media malaise thesis to demonstrate media influence at the societal level, if they can. And if the influence of the mass media on society is as diffuse as the air we breathe, so that the impact falls equally on the attentive and inattentive, as rain falls equally upon the just and unjust, then perhaps it would be more satisfactory to look for alternative and more plausible explanations for the phenomenon of the growth of critical citizens in postindustrial societies.

Appendix 11A. *Measuring political support in the EU*

Object	Indicators and Measures
Political Community: National Trust	*'How much do you trust [NATIONALITY]? Do you have a lot of trust, some trust, not very much trust, or no trust at all?'* [Italians, Germans, etc.]
Regime Performance: EU and National Governments	Approval of the performance of the EU: *'Are you for or against efforts being made to unify Western Europe?'* *'Do you think your country's membership in the EU is a good thing or a bad thing?'* *'Would you say your country has benefited or not from being a member of the European Community?'* *'If you were told tomorrow that the European Community has been scrapped, would you feel very sorry about it, indifferent or relieved?'* *'How satisfied are you with the way democracy works in the EU?'*
Regime Institutions	Confidence in institutions: *'To what extent do you feel you can rely upon [NAME OF INSTITUTION] to make sure that the decisions taken by this institution [are] in the interests of people like yourself?'* *European Institutions* • The European Commission • The Council of Ministers • The European Parliament *National Institutions:* • National parliament • The national government *'How satisfied are you with the way democracy works in your country?'*
Political Actors	Popularity of political leaders: *'Here's a question about the British Prime Minister, John Major. Would you say you quite like him, or you don't particularly like him?'* • The British Prime Minister, John Major • The Spanish Prime Minister, Filepe Gonzales • The French President, François Mitterrand • The German Chancellor, Helmut Kohl

CHAPTER 12

Stays Home? Political Mobilization

D o newspapers, television and the Internet serve to mobilize voters? Or, instead, do these media reinforce activism? Or even damage civic engagement? The literature remains divided. After outlining the theoretical framework for understanding political participation, this chapter examines the evidence for two issues: What is the impact of traditional political communications on electoral turnout? And, given the explosive increase in the use of new technology, does the Internet have the capacity to play a positive role in civic engagement? The conclusion to this chapter considers the broader implications of the findings.

UNDERSTANDING POLITICAL PARTICIPATION

Explanations of political participation have focused on four sets of factors. The institutional perspective stresses the importance of the legal context, including the extent of political rights and civil liberties, the type of electoral system, the facilities for registration and voting, the extension of the franchise, the frequency, level, and timing of elections, and the competitiveness of electoral politics.[1] In one of the most thorough comparative studies, Jackman and Miller examined voter participation in twenty-two democracies and found that political institutions and electoral laws were the factors that figured most prominently in the most plausible explanation for variations in voter turnout, including levels of electoral participation and proportionality, multi-partyism, and compulsory voting.[2] Franklin, Van der Eijk, and Oppenhuis have argued that the variations in participation in European elections can be attributed in large part to differences in systemic factors, notably the use of compulsory voting, the proportionality of the electoral system, and the temporal proximity of European elections to national elections.[3] In the United States, as well, the legal hurdle of the registration requirement and the frequency of elections are widely believed to depress voter turnout.[4]

At the individual level, the cultural perspective, based on survey analysis, has emphasized the importance of individual *resources*, such as education, age, socioeconomic status, and time, combined with *motivation*, meaning the attitudes people bring to the electoral process, such as a sense of efficacy, political interest, and party identification. Almond and Verba have stressed the importance of 'civic values' learnt through the early socialization process.[5] In a long series of studies, Verba has demonstrated how various forms of participation make different demands in terms of skills, money, and time, so that political participation can best be understood as a multidimensional phenomenon.[6] That is, people who regularly donate money to campaigns or contact their representatives are not necessarily involved in other dimensions like party work or community activism. There are different costs and benefits associated with different types of participation. The main categories distinguished by Verba and his colleagues concern voting, campaign work, communal activity, and contact specialists. In addition, a few citizens are active across all dimensions, while some are involved in none.

Lastly, the organizational perspective has stressed the role of *mobilizing agencies*, referring to the campaigning functions of party and candidate organizations, group networks like churches, voluntary associations, and trade unions, social networks of families, friends, and colleagues, and the role of the news media.[7] Putnam has argued that the decline of dense networks of local associations and community organizations has reduced social capital and contributed towards long-term erosion of American voter turnout among the postwar generations. Verba found that churches and voluntary organizations provided networks of recruitment, so that those drawn into the political process through such associations tended to develop the organizational and communication skills that would facilitate further activity.[8] In the United States, Aldrich and Wattenberg have suggested that the decline of party organizations, and their replacement by entrepreneurial candidates, has been critical to the low voter turnout.[9]

The processes of political communication via parties and the news media fall into this latter category of factors. Parties act as mobilizing agencies through direct communication with voters, including traditional grassroots activities such as canvassing, leafleting, and contacting voters, in addition to holding party meetings and campaign rallies and using national advertising and party political broadcasts. The news media serve this function by providing information about parties, candidates, and policies that can help to crystallize voting choices, and the partisan press, in particular, has long been thought to help reinforce party support. Through such activities, involving positive messages, both parties and the news media can serve to increase party and candidate support among electors and the propensity to turn out, or they can convey negative messages that function to depress participation.

The literature is divided about the effects of media activity. In the traditional 'Columbia' model, partisan-leaning newspapers and party campaigns were seen as playing vital roles in reinforcing support and getting out the vote: 'The more that people read about or listened to the campaign on the mass media, the more interested they became in the election and the more strongly they came to feel about their candidate. . . . Media exposure gets out the vote at the same time that it solidifies preferences. It crystallizes and reinforces more than it converts.'[10] The 'Michigan' model conceptualized attention to political communication somewhat differently, as itself a minor form of activism, instead of an independent factor capable of influencing turnout. This perspective became so influential that it developed into the mainstream view in studies of political participation, which rarely treated the media as important causal factors in their models.[11] Several more recent studies have credited the media with boosting public participation.[12]

In contrast, as discussed in Chapter 1, in recent years many popular commentators have suggested that the public has become disengaged because of negative messages. There are two separate issues here. One concerns the effects of negative or 'attack' ads, wherein candidates and party campaigns criticize their opponents on the basis of character or record.[13] In the United States, Ansolabehere and Iyengar have provided some of the most convincing experimental evidence that negative or attack television campaign ads criticizing opponents have the capacity to turn off American voters at the ballot box. 'Negative advertising drives people away from the polls in large numbers. . . . Negative advertising breeds distrust of the electoral process and pessimism about the value of an individual's own voice.'[14] Yet it is difficult to know how far we can generalize from such findings more broadly, in part because of the different institutional contexts of advertising in European and American campaigns.[15] As discussed in Chapter 7, commercial political advertising has come late to most European countries. In some, like Austria, negative advertisments are banned by law. In others, like The Netherlands, although ads are allowed, few are aired, because parties have limited financial resources. And in still others, like Britain, it is difficult to compare the effects of a five-to-ten-minute party political broadcast, shown once per channel, with the effects of the repetitive thirty-second ads common in the United States. Lacking systematic comparative data on exposure to negative ads, we cannot pursue the issue further here.

A second concern relates to practices common in the news media, which we can examine, such as when headlines and stories routinely emphasize political scandals, government incompetence, and partisan conflict.[16] For example, Patterson has suggested that American voters are turned off by the media's routine emphasis on the 'game' schema, characterized by horse-race journalism (who's ahead, who's behind) and extensive coverage of opinion polls.[17] He has argued that changes in journalism in the 1960s produced a shift towards game-immersed news, strengthening voters' mistrust of the candidates and reducing their sense of involvement. According to Cappella and Jamieson, the use of a strategic frame for political news activates cynical responses to politicians, governance, and campaigns.[18] Yet others have argued that a strategic focus and horse-race polls function in a positive way, by increasing the American public's attention to issue information and political knowledge. Zhao and Beske have concluded that coverage of opinion polls is complementary to issue coverage, stimulating rather than displacing attention.[19] It seems equally plausible that what matters for electoral participation is *what* the polls report, not the extent of poll coverage per se. In Britain, for example, Heath and Taylor found that the closeness of the race, as monitored by reported opinion polls, was one of the best predictors of turnout.[20] Neck-and-neck contests increased the incentive to vote. In addition, the effects of negative news are not well established. In the British context, for example, large-scale experiments in the 1997 election demonstrated that exposure to negative television news about the major parties had no influence on party images or the propensity to vote, whereas positive news did have a significant impact on voters.[21]

Therefore, we need to go further to understand the effects of political communication on public participation. Since most of the research has been conducted within the context of American campaigns, which are atypical of those in most established democracies, it is useful to reexamine the evidence from a broader range of postindustrial societies. This chapter focuses on political participation in European elections and explores the effects of campaign communications in the 15 member states, controlling for some of the major cultural and structural factors already discussed. In Chapter 13 we consider whether there are similar or different effects of media use on campaign participation in American midterm elections. Political participation involves many different types of activities, from contacting representatives to becoming active in community organizations, political parties, and interest groups. In this study we focus on comparing voter turnout, one of the least demanding forms of activity, but also one of the most universal. For many people, casting the ballot provides their only form of political expression. This measure is also comparable across established democracies, unlike involvement in parties or interest groups that may mean very different things in different institutional settings.

POLITICAL COMMUNICATION AND
ELECTORAL TURNOUT

Many have assumed that there has been a general decline in voter participation in the established democracies, but in fact the levels of turnout have remained fairly stable during the past two decades; 71% of the voting-age population participated in elections in established democratic countries in the 1990s, down only 3% from the 1970s.[22] Despite similar socioeconomic and political developments in postindustrial societies, there are persistent cross-national disparities in levels of electoral participation. Some countries, like Switzerland, France, and The Netherlands, have experienced substantial long-term falls (Figure 12.1). In the American presidential election in 1996, less than half (47.2%) of the voting-age population cast ballots, down from almost two-thirds (63.1%) in 1960. If we calculate the average percentage turnout for each of 171 countries worldwide, in all national elections from 1945 to 1998, Switzerland ranks 137th, the United States ranks 138th, and Mexico ranks 139th.[23]

Problems of turnout are particularly relevant in elections to the European Parliament. The level of voting participation fell from almost two-thirds (63%) of the electorate in the first direct elections in 1979 to just under half (49.2%) of European citizens in June 1999, its historical nadir (Figure 12.2). The decline over successive elections is particularly clear in The Netherlands and Portugal, as well as in Austria, Finland, and Sweden, which saw a sharp drop after their first 'founding' European elections. There are also stark national differences. In the

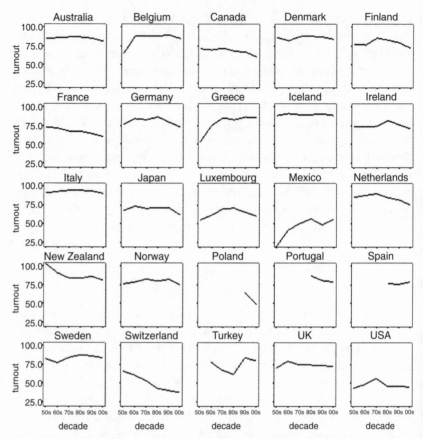

Figure 12.1. Postwar mean turnout per decade, 1950s to 1990s: percentages of voting-age populations. Lines show means. *Source:* IDEA.

most recent elections, 90% of Belgian citizens voted, compared with only one-quarter (23%) of the British electorate (Table 12.1). As Franklin and his colleagues have argued,[24] the institutional systems of electoral laws provide much of the explanation for those persistent systemic differences, notably the use of compulsory voting (in Belgium, Luxembourg, and Italy), Sunday polling day (Austria, Belgium, Finland, France, Germany, Greece, Italy, Luxembourg, Portugal, Spain, and Sweden), and the majoritarian first-past-the-post electoral system (used in mainland Britain until the 1999 contests).

But within this context, can the news media or party campaigns be blamed for the downward trend in European participation? If news headlines highlighted corruption at the European Commission,

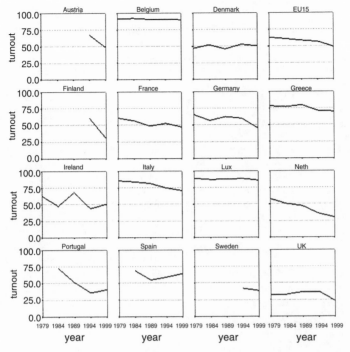

Figure 12.2. Turnout in EU elections, 1979–99. Lines show means.

bureaucratic overregulation in Brussels, and junkets for the European Parliament, it would not be surprising if voters had shunned the polling stations. Yet if we compare the sources of campaign information seen and heard by those who reported voting in the 1994 European elections, then, contrary to the media malaise thesis, a positive relationship is evident: Those who saw something about the campaign in newspapers and on television, or who received an election leaflet or saw party advertising, were more likely to cast a ballot (Table 12.2). All the zero-order correlations (with the exception of being contacted by a party worker) proved significant. In many cases the gap between voters and non-voters proved modest, but in the case of newspaper readers the gap reached 10 percentage points.

To see if those relationships held up under multivariate analysis, regression models were run for 1989 and 1994, predicting voting turnout using the standard structural, attitudinal, and national-level controls employed throughout this book. They included education, age, and income (the latter as a proxy for socioeconomic status), which have

Table 12.1. *Turnout in European elections, 1979–99*

Country	1979	1984	1989	1994	1999	Chg 1994–99	Notes
Austria				67.7	49.0	−18.7	[1995]
Belgium	91.6	92.2	90.7	90.7	90.0	−0.7	
Denmark	47.1	52.3	46.1	52.9	50.4	−2.5	
Finland				60.3	30.1	−30.2	
France	60.7	56.7	48.7	52.7	47.0	−5.7	
Germany	65.7	56.8	62.4	60.0	45.2	−14.8	
Greece	78.6	77.2	79.9	71.2	70.1	−1.1	[1981]
Ireland	63.0	47.6	68.3	44.0	50.5	6.5	
Italy	85.5	83.9	81.5	74.8	70.8	−4.0	
Luxembourg	88.9	87.0	87.4	88.5	85.8	−2.7	
Netherlands	57.8	50.5	47.2	35.7	29.9	−5.8	
Portugal		72.2	51.1	35.5	40.4	4.9	[1987]
Spain		68.9	54.8	59.1	64.3	5.2	[1987]
Sweden				41.6	38.3	−3.3	[1995]
UK	31.6	32.6	36.2	36.4	23.0	−13.4	
EU-15	*63.0*	*61.0*	*58.5*	*56.8*	*49.2*	*−7.6*	

Source: http://europa.eu.int.

Table 12.2. *Political communications and voting participation*

% Who said campaign came to their attention via . . .	Did Not Vote	Voted	Zero order correlation [R]	Sig.
Discuss with friends/family	18	30	0.13	**
Newspapers	35	45	0.10	**
Television/radio	59	67	0.07	**
Party advertising	35	40	0.05	**
Election leaflet	38	41	0.03	**
Party worker called at home	6	7	0.01	

Note: $**p > 0.01$.
Source: European Election Study 1994, Eurobarometer 41.1, *N*. 13,095.

most commonly been found to be associated with turnout, along with political interest. The results in Table 12.3 confirm the patterns we have already observed in both elections. As many previous studies have found, age and income proved strong predictors of turnout, along with political interest. The younger generations were particularly prone to stay home. In contrast, the gender gap in turnout has shrunk over the

Table 12.3. *Predictors of voting participation*

	Voted in the European Elections 1989	Sig.	Voted in the European Elections 1994	Sig.
STRUCTURAL				
Education	−0.04	*	0.01	
Gender	−0.01		0.01	
Age	0.21	**	0.24	**
Income	0.04	**	0.05	*
ATTITUDINAL				
Political Interest	0.10	**	0.17	**
Left-Right Ideology	−0.02		0.01	**
ATTENTION TO				
TV News	0.13	**	0.04	**
Newspapers	0.11	**	0.04	**
Party Communications	0.07	**	0.10	**
NATION				
Belgium	0.13	**	0.06	*
Denmark	−0.04	**	−0.11	**
Germany	0.02		−0.08	**
Ireland	0.06		−0.15	**
Italy	0.11	**	0.03	**
Luxembourg	0.08	**	0.05	**
Netherlands	−0.02		−0.16	**
Portugal	−0.05	*	−0.13	**
Spain	0.01		−0.01	
UK	−0.10	**	−0.21	**
Constant	0.29		0.17	
R^2	0.16		0.18	

Note: The figures represent OLS standardized regression coefficients (betas). ** $p > 0.01$; * $p > 0.05$.
Sources: European Post-Election Survey, June–July 1989, Eurobarometer 31A; European Election Study 1994, Eurobarometer 41.1, *N*. 13,095.

years to become insignificant, and education (measured on a restricted scale) proved an inconsistent indicator. National factors also proved important, with below-average reported turnouts in Britain, The Netherlands, Portugal, and Ireland, a pattern already shown in official aggregate figures in Table 12.1. As noted earlier, the legal and institutional contexts, such as the use of compulsory voting, provide by far the most convincing explanation for these national contrasts. After controls for those factors were included, all the forms of political communication proved significant and positive, including use of newspapers, television, radio, and party campaign activity. The strengths of these factors did vary across the models, in part because of the use of functionally equivalent but different measures of media attention, but all pointed in the same direction. The replication seen with these models in the two elections increases our confidence in the results in the European context. We shall return to consider whether there were similar patterns in American midterm elections, which were comparable low-salience contests, in later chapters.

Yet interpretation of these findings is subject to the same issue of causality that we have observed in Chapter 11. Does media attention to the campaign lead to turnout? Or does a general propensity to turn out lead to media attention (because I intend to vote, I seek out information about the parties and candidates)? Or is there, as seems most plausible, a virtuous circle, where watching the news activates existing predispositions to vote and, simultaneously, the predisposition to vote prompts people to seek out more news. What we find no evidence for is the claim that those most attentive to news coverage during the campaign were demobilized by the experience.

These issues cannot be resolved with cross-sectional data, but to explore some of the reasons behind this pattern we can look at how people evaluated a series of statements concerning television coverage of a campaign. Table 12.4 shows that, compared with those who did not turn out, voters were significantly more likely to report that TV coverage showed them where their party stood on Europe, helped make up their minds how to vote, and highlighted party differences. This supports the idea advanced by Paul Lazarsfeld fifty years ago: that the attentive use the information on the news to help crystallize their voting choices. In contrast, non-voters more often reported that news coverage left them feeling confused or bored. If we can generalize from those findings, they suggest that campaign communications may reinforce the division between those who tune in and tune out from public affairs. Some people will have more civic skills, social networks, and interest in finding out about events in Brussels or Luxembourg, and they will tend to vote. The institutional context also seems important in determining electoral turnout, and devices like compulsory voting and Sunday polling days can raise levels of participation. But the evidence here suggests that coverage of public affairs in the traditional news media should not be blamed for low voter turnout, but rather the broader

Table 12.4. *Evaluations of TV campaign news by turnout*

% Mentioned agreement with statement . . .	Did Not Vote	Voted	R	Sig.
It showed me where my party stands on European questions	6	18	0.16	**
It helped me make up my mind how to vote	3	12	0.14	**
It helped me think about the future of Europe	10	15	0.07	**
It brought out the differences between parties on European matters	6	10	0.07	**
It told me how the European Commission is run	5	8	0.07	**
It told me about the relationship between (my country's) parties and those in other countries	5	9	0.07	**
It didn't tell me about the advantages . . . of being in the EU	16	16	0.01	
It didn't show me why I should care about the European Parliament	13	12	−0.01	**
It left me feeling rather confused	19	15	−0.04	**
It all seemed rather boring	21	15	−0.06	**

Note: Q: 'Thinking especially how the campaign was covered on television, which of these statements would you say you agree with?'R: zero-order correlation between TV use and statement.
Source: European Post-Election Survey, June–July 1989; Eurobarometer 31A.

inequalities in educational skills and socioeconomic resources common throughout postindustrial societies.

THE INTERNET AND POLITICAL PARTICIPATION

But what will be the impact of new technology? In particular, will the Internet play a distinctive role in expanding political participation? Opinion remains divided on this issue. The mobilization theories reviewed in Chapter 6 assume that use of the Net will facilitate and encourage new forms of political activism.[25] The strongest claims of mobilization theories are that Net activism represents a distinctive type of political participation that differs in significant ways from conventional activities like working for political parties, organizing grassroots social movements, and lobbying elected officials. By sharply reducing the barriers to civic engagement, leveling some of the financial hurdles, and widening the opportunities for political debate, the dissemination of information, and group interaction, it is thought that more people will become involved in public life. For enthusiasts, the Net promises to provide new forms of horizontal and vertical communication that will facilitate and enrich deliberation in the public sphere.

Yet, in contrast, reinforcement theories suggest that use of the Net will strengthen, not radically transform, existing patterns of civic involvement. From this more skeptical perspective, despite the new technology and the interactive potential of the Net, the effects of the new media are expected to be very similar to those of television and newspapers that we have already observed.[26]

Both the mobilization and reinforcement theories may be plausible, but despite all the conjecture, it is difficult to find systematic comparative evidence that can throw light on this debate. Given the remarkable expansion in the use of the Web in just a few years, as in the early television age, it would be foolish to attempt predictions about the direction of future developments. Much will depend on political and economic conditions, such as the extent to which Net access becomes available to the various social strata. In this chapter we focus on patterns of Net activism in American campaigns, as it is one of the countries with high levels of Internet access, and then consider whether similar trends are becoming evident in Europe.

Analysis of the 1996 and 1998 American election campaigns demonstrates that Net activists are among the most motivated and best-informed groups in the electorate. In this sense, the new capacities for interactive communication do hold promise for strengthening the process of political communication. As argued in Chapter 7, the typical campaign uses of the new media can be located between the traditional sort of face-to-face activism of premodern communications, characterized by town-hall meetings, party rallies, and personal candidate–voter contacts, and the more passive and distant campaigns conducted by national party leaders across the airwaves. The use of party Web sites, especially intranet linkages that facilitate interactive horizontal communication within parties, as well as Internet discussion groups and the use of e-mail, arguably could be seen as a return to some of the older forms of campaign communications (Figure 7.2). Nevertheless, the available survey evidence indicates that at present, politics on the Internet reinforces the activism of the activists, much as in the traditional media, rather than magically transforming the apathetic into engaged citizens.[27]

Chapter 6 examined how many people used the Internet and found that, according to the latest estimates, in the spring of 1999 about 20%

of Europeans had Internet access, with highest access in Denmark, Sweden, and Finland. In the United States, about one half of the public is now online, with explosive growth since the mid-1990s. The social profile for European users has confirmed the familiar disparities by age, education, socioeconomic status, and gender found in America. The most important indication that any of those factors might affect political activism in the future concerns the generational pattern. Younger people are least likely to use the traditional news media, but their preponderance among Net users may have important consequences.

The extent of the news revolution caused by the growth of Internet use in the United States becomes apparent if we compare regular users of conventional and online media. Estimates of the use of Internet news have varied over time, as both news events and the way people think about Internet 'news' continue to change. Nevertheless, Pew Center surveys suggest that the percentage of Americans regularly getting news from the Internet (where 'regularly' is defined as at least once a week) more than tripled over two years, rising from eleven million users in June 1995 to thirty-six million in May 1998, or 20% of all Americans. As shown in Table 12.5, similar levels of use are evident among those who regularly go online to communicate with others via discussion lists and chat groups, while slightly fewer go online for entertainment news (14%) or financial information (10%). Within the space of just a few years, the regular audience for online news in America has become larger than those for many traditional media, such as mainstream news magazines like *Time* and *Newsweek* (15%), and larger than that for talk radio (13%), let alone minority news outlets like the PBS *Newshour* and C-SPAN (4%).

The growth of the Net in America is providing a major rival for traditional news media outlets. The most common activities, engaging about two-thirds of all Americans, continue to be reading daily newspapers and watching the local evening TV news. The majority also regularly catch radio news at some time during the day, and listenership has expanded during the past decade. In contrast, network news has suffered a dramatic hemorrhage of viewers because of the fragmentation of cable and satellite stations and the Balkanization of the television audience: Today, just over a third (38%) regularly tune in to watch Jennings, Brokaw, and Rather. To some extent this merely reflects the dispersion of the network audience to cable and satellite, as people find MSNBC or CNBC more convenient for their schedules than netwotk news at 6:30 P.M. But this phenomenon, combined with the growth of

Table 12.5. *Regular use of the news media, United States, 1998*

% of all Americans who regularly . . .	(%)
Read Daily Newspaper	68
Watch Local Evening TV News	64
Listen to Radio News	52
Watch Network TV News (CBS, ABC or NBC)	38
Watch TV News Magazines (e.g., *60 Minutes, Dateline*)	37
Watch Weather Channel	33
Go online at least once a week(*)	→25
Watch Morning TV News (e.g., *Today Show*, CBS *This Morning*)	23
Watch Cable News Network (CNN)	23
Go online to get news at least once a week	→20
Go online to use discussion lists/chat groups (*)	→20
Read News Magazines (e.g., *Time, U.S. News, Newsweek*)	15
Listen to National Public Radio (NPR)	15
Watch TV Tabloids (e.g., *Hard Copy, Inside Edition*)	14
Go online to get information about entertainment (*)	→14
Watch Daytime TV Talk Shows (e.g., *Jerry Springer*)	13
Listen to Talk Radio	13
Watch CNBC	12
Watch Daytime TV Talk Shows	10
Go online to get financial information (*)	→10
Watch MSNBC	8
Watch Court TV	6
Watch MTV	6
Listen to Rush Limbaugh's Radio Show	5
Read Business Magazines (e.g., *Forbes, Fortune*)	5
Watch PBS *Newshour* with Jim Lehrer	4
Listen to Howard Stern's Radio Show	4
Watch C-SPAN	4
Read Print Tabloids (e.g., *National Enquirer, The Sun*)	3

Note: Q: 'Now I'd like to know how often you watch (or listen to or read) . . . Regularly, Sometimes, Hardly ever, Never.' For online sources (*) the question was 'Please tell me how often, if ever, you engage in each of the following online activities. . . .' Regular use is defined as at least once a week.
Source: The Pew Research Center for the People and the Press, Media Consumption Survey using a nationwide sample of 3,002 adults, fieldwork 24 April to 11 May 1998.

the Net, clearly is posing greater competition for the major American networks.

WHY DO PEOPLE USE THE INTERNET?

In America, in terms of the *size* of its total audience, the Internet can increasingly claim to be a mass medium. But is there a common experience of the Net, such that we can talk about the effects of participating online, in the same way that we discuss the influences of network news, violent movies, or talk radio? If so, then it is legitimate to generalize, as both sides of the debate often do, about the experience and attitudes of 'online users'. Yet because of the fragmentation of the news audience and the segmentation of the Internet into the myriad uses that it can serve, perhaps we need a more cautious approach. Given the host of choices about where to go and what to do in the digital world, the question arises whether we have a shared experience of the Web at all, and therefore whether it constitutes a mass medium in the conventional sense.

The need to refine our conception of online users may be particularly important for the various types of Net political activism. As argued earlier, political participation can best be understood as a multidimensional phenomenon. Thus participation in virtual democracy on the Net can be understood to involve many different kinds of activities. A person clicking to the Europa home page, or getting news from BBC *Online*, for example, might be seen as engaging in a quite different sort of activity than someone discussing *l'affaire* Lewinsky in a user group, or e-mailing colleagues about the time of a community meeting. To explore the dimensions of Net use, the Pew Center surveys asked American online users how often, if at all, they engaged in a wide variety of activities, such as getting information about movies, travel, or the Dow Jones, chatting with people in online forums, and engaging in political discussion. People were questioned about ten types of activities in the 1998 survey, and the overall pattern was mapped using factor analysis.

As shown in Table 12.6, the analysis revealed two distinct dimensions or types of activities on the Net. On the one hand, *general users* were most interested in using the Net for news about current events, entertainment-related information about movies and hobbies, financial information, sending e-mail messages, buying goods online, finding practical information about health, and communicating via online discussion groups. Just as various people turn first to the sports pages or television listings or stock-market results in traditional newspapers, so people seek a wide range of 'news', usually apolitical, on the Web. Although some of that activity may put people in touch with public affairs as they click from one topic to another, the process is more accidental than purposive. In contrast, during the 1998 campaign, *political activists* who used the Internet more often went online to engage in

Table 12.6. *Factor analysis of online activities, United States, 1998*

% of online users who . . .	General Users	Political Activists
Go online for news/information on current events, public issues, or politics	0.77	
Go online for news	0.76	
Get entertainment-related information, e.g., movies, hobbies	59	
Get financial information such as stock quotes	57	
Send or receive e-mail	0.52	
Purchase goods or services online	0.49	
Get health or medical information	0.46	
Communicate with others through online forums, discussion lists	0.39	
Engage in online discussions about politics		0.85
Contact or e-mail groups or officials about political issues		0.82
Went online for information about the 1998 elections		0.55
% Variance	26	17

Note: The model uses principal-component factor analysis with varimax rotation and with Kaiser normalization suppressing coefficients below 0.35. See the Technical Appendix for questions.
Source: The Pew Center for the People and the Press, 1998 Technology and On-line Use Survey, *N.* 1993, fieldwork November 1998.

political discussions, to contact officials or groups about an issue, or to get specific information about the campaign. Therefore, political activists who go online to seek political information or communication can be categorized as a distinct group within the Internet community, as in society.

Are Net political activists a small minority? If we compare the most common general types of Net activity, defined as those that occurred 'at least once a week', among online users during the 1998 campaign, the pattern (Table 12.7) shows that the most popular general uses included e-mail (regularly used by almost three-quarters of Net users) and work-related research (regularly used by almost half). Searching for information about politics and current events was the next most popular activity, involving 38% at least once a week. The more active forms of online civic engagement were pursued by far fewer Net users in the 1998 campaign, such as political discussion (used by 4%) and contacting officials or groups about politics (4%). Comparison of the 1996 and 1998 campaigns shows that the greatest increase in use was in e-mailing, and there

Table 12.7. *Frequency of activities among all online users, United States, 1996–98*

% of all online users who . . .	% At Least Once Every Week 1996	% At Least Once Every Week 1998
Send e-mail	64	72
Do research for work	48	47
Get news on current events, public issues, and politics	39	38
Get entertainment-related information, e.g., movies, hobbies	30	35
Get financial information	23	28
Communicate via online forums, discussion lists, chat groups	23	22
Do research for school	22	14
Go online for information about elections	12	10
Get travel information	10	12
Engage in online political discussions	4	4
Contact groups and officials about political issues	2	4

Sources: The Pew Center for the People and the Press: 1996 Technology and On-line Use Survey, *N.* 1,003, fieldwork October 1996. 1998 Technology and On-line Use Survey, *N.* 1,993, fieldwork November 1998.

was also some increase in use of the Net to get entertainment-related and financial information. In contrast, the proportions engaged in the more political types of activities hardly changed. Wider access to the Web has expanded the audience for general-interest subjects, such as information about the weather and movies, much more than the audience for political or international news.

The evidence shows a strikingly similar profile in Europe. The 1997 Eurobarometer asked people if they would be interested in using a series of online services. Groups were also classified into *actual users* (who already accessed the Internet), *potential users* (who did not currently use the Internet but remained interested in doing so), and *non-users* (who did not use and were not interested in using the Net). The results in Table 12.8 show that across all groups the most popular uses of the Internet were for education and e-mail. One-third or fewer Europeans expressed interest in using the Internet to read newspapers, get health information, or go online for banking and financial services. In terms of broadly political activities, the most popular were consulting local

Table 12.8. *European interest in uses of the Internet, EU-15, 1997*

% of each group interested in using internet to . . .	Use Internet	Do Not Use Internet but Interested	Do Not Use Internet and Not Interested
Follow a training program from home	59	56	46
E-mail	41	34	16
Read news and magazines	36	27	17
Get a doctor's advice on a health problem	35	38	38
Banking and finance	35	36	25
Consult local town or council services	28	31	28
Travel information	28	28	25
Consult employment offices	22	28	25
Museum tour	21	20	15
Get consumer information on products	20	21	14
Take part in group discussion	16	15	9
Contact a politician and take part in political debates	10	10	8

Note: Q: 'I am going to name several examples of services you could have access to by using one of these communication networks, for example, the Internet. For each of these services could you please tell me if it interests you or not?'
Source: Eurobarometer 47.0, January–February 1997, *N*. 16,362.

town or council services for information (27%) and reading newspapers online (22%). In contrast, relatively few Europeans expressed any interest in the more demanding forms of political engagement, such as participating in group discussions or using the Internet to contact politicians.

If we compare EU member states, Table 12.9 shows significant differences in the potential interest expressed in the different forms of political activity. Some variations probably reflected different national experiences. For example, many Scandinavians expressed interest in online newspapers, and that is a region where we have already observed relatively high readership of the traditional print sector. Yet potential interest did not necessarily reflect actual experience of Internet use. For example, about a third of those living in Portugal, Spain, and Greece expressed interest in consulting their local councils through Net channels, far more than in Scandinavia, despite extremely low levels of access in the Mediterranean region.

Table 12.9. *Interest in political uses of the Internet, EU-15, 1997*

% of pop. interested in using Internet to . . .	Consult Local Town or Council Services	Read Newspapers and Magazines	Contact Politicians
Austria	36	22	14
Belgium	20	18	6
Britain	18	17	6
Denmark	25	35	12
East Germany	34	12	8
Finland	27	32	5
France	21	21	7
Greece	38	19	11
Ireland	14	10	5
Italy	29	19	7
Luxembourg	34	32	14
Netherlands	20	24	5
Northern Ireland	15	15	7
Portugal	37	25	20
Spain	33	25	8
Sweden	19	33	8
West Germany	33	14	10
All	27	22	9

Note: See Table 12.8 for details of the question.
Source: Eurobarometer 47.0, January–February 1997, *N*. 16,362.

What do we know about the minority of all Internet users in America (15%) who went online specifically to get political information during the 1996 and 1998 U.S. elections? If we look more closely at the types of activities among that select group, we find that the most popular activities included getting information about a candidate's voting record, participating in an online poll, sending e-mail supporting or opposing candidates, downloading election information, and sending information such as e-mail messages and mailing addresses (Table 12.10). But in all cases such activity involved less than 5% of the total Internet community, and obviously an even smaller proportion of the general electorate.

The Internet community differs socially from the general public, as we have seen, but does it also differ politically? If reinforcement theories were correct, we would expect to find that Net users would be drawn from among the most politically knowledgeable and engaged. Table 12.11 compares the political attitudes of all Net users with those of Net

Table 12.10. *Online election activities, United States, 1996–98*

	1996	1998
Get information about a candidate's voting record		30
Participate in an online poll	34	26
Get or send e-mail supporting or opposing a candidate for office		22
Download election information	56	20
Provide information such as your e-mail/mailing address	31	18
Participate in online discussions	31	13
Get information about where and when to vote		12

Note: Percentages of those who went online to get news or information about the 1998 elections via various routes (15% of the online user community). Q80: '*When you went online to get information about the elections, do/did you do any of the following?*'
Source: The Pew Center for the People and the Press: 1996 Technology and On-line Use Survey, *N.* 1,003, fieldwork October 1996; 1998 Technology and On-line Use Survey, *N.* 1,993, fieldwork November 1998.

Table 12.11. *Political profile for American online users, 1998*

% of each group who . . .	All Online Users 1998	Net Political Activists	Association	Sig.
Read the paper yesterday	70	76	0.15	**
Watched the TV news yesterday	63	68	0.11	**
Listened to radio news yesterday	47	51	0.09	**
Voted in 1998	56	78	0.46	**
Voted Republican 1998	42	44		
Voted Democrat 1998	41	40	0.04	
Know GOP Hold House	62	80	0.41	**
Social Trust: High	42	45	0.04	
Political Trust: High	28	26	0.02	

Notes: 'Net political activists' are defined as those who engaged in online discussions about politics, contacted or e-mailed groups or officials about political issues, or went online for information about the 1998 elections. The coefficient of the association was measured by gamma. $**p > 0.01$; $*p > 0.05$.
Source: Pew Research Center Online Technology Survey, November 1998.

political activists during the 1998 American midterm election. Net activists were higher-than-average consumers of all types of media news, including television and radio. Net activists also reported particularly high rates of voting turnout, confirming the association that we have already observed with users of traditional news media. That pattern also was clearly reflected in levels of political knowledge: When asked which party had control of the House of Representatives, Net political activists were more likely than average Net users to get the answer right. There were no significant differences between Net activists and general Net users in terms of levels of political and social trust. In the 1996 and 1998 American elections, the group of Net activists proved similar to the Net community as a whole in terms of their House votes. Nevertheless, there was a significant difference between the online community and the general electorate in terms of approval of House Republicans, with Net users showing greater approval. Moreover, the pro-Republican partisanship of Net users was not simply a product of the gender, income, and educational biases among the user community, because approval of congressional Republicans remained a significant factor in predicting online news use even after controlling for social background.

Are similar patterns evident among the Internet community in Europe? The first two columns in Table 12.12 show the mean scores for the online community in Europe using a range of ten indicators of political attitudes, including scales for trust in government, trust in EU institutions, trust in the news media, satisfaction with democracy in one's own country and within the EU, left–right ideology, political efficacy, support for the EU, voting participation, and political knowledge.[28] The next column in Table 12.12 shows the zero-order correlations between online use and the attitudinal scales. The last column shows the standardized coefficients (betas) for regression models monitoring the effects of Net use on political attitudes, controlling for prior education, gender, income, and age. The aim in the analysis was not to develop a comprehensive causal model explaining these political attitudes, which would have required many additional factors, but rather to examine whether the political characteristics of Net users proved distinctive on a wide range of indicators even after controlling for some of the social factors that distinguished this group.

The findings indicate that across all the mean scores, those who went online were more likely to display positive attitudes towards the political system, including greater trust, efficacy, participation, and knowl-

Table 12.12. *Political characteristics of online users, EU-15, 1999*

Attitudinal Scales	Online Users (Mean) (i)	Non-Users (Mean)	Zero order correlations [R] (ii)	Sig.	Standardized beta coefficients (β) (iii)	Sig.
Political Efficacy	5.07	4.29	0.138	**	0.086	**
Knowledge of EU Institutions	6.03	5.14	0.136	**	0.033	*
Trust in Government Institutions	2.76	2.33	0.085	**	0.049	**
Satisfaction with Democracy in Own Country	2.83	2.67	0.079	**	0.051	**
Trust in EU Institutions	3.74	3.20	0.066	**	−0.025	*
Trust in News Media	2.08	1.89	0.064	**	0.026	*
Support for EU	4.19	4.07	0.049	*	−0.011	
Left-Right Ideology	5.40	5.20	0.038	*	0.061	**
EU Voting Participation	3.09	2.96	0.036	*	0.002	
Satisfaction with Democracy in EU	2.43	2.48	−0.029	**	−0.075	**

Notes: (i) Mean scores on the scales, comparing online users and non-users. (ii) Zero-order coefficients between online use and dependent variables without any controls. (iii) Standardized regression coefficients (betas) with prior controls for education, age, gender, and household income. $**p > 0.01$; $*p > 0.05$.
Source: Eurobarometer 51.0, spring 1999.

edge. The mean differences between Net users and non-users were often only modest, but in most cases (with the exception of satisfaction with democracy in the EU) they were in the positive direction for the online community, and the zero-order correlations (without any controls) confirmed a significant relationship. Lastly, after controls for social factors were introduced, the pattern became more mixed. Nevertheless, Net users proved significantly more positive towards the political system on six out of ten indicators, they were more significantly negative on two, and there was no difference on the remainder. Such findings suggest that, just as in the United States, the online community in Europe is drawn from the pool of those already most predisposed to be relatively positive towards the political system. The pattern of the traditional news media serving to further activate the active, which we saw earlier, also seems evident in the online community.

CONCLUSIONS: ACTIVATING ACTIVISM

The media malaise thesis is far from new, as there have always been those who have feared that the press, and then television, and now the Internet, will have pernicious effects on the public. But the 1990s have witnessed another wave in which this view has again become fashionable, strongly reflecting the pervasive mood of skepticism about the political process in the United States, as well as increasing concern about cynicism towards democracy in Europe. The popular claim is that the typical coverage of public affairs provided by newspapers and television has reduced public trust in traditional sources of authority in government and served to disengage the electorate. The new media are often regarded as the saviours of democracy, galloping to the rescue to attract groups who might otherwise be uninvolved in conventional forms of activism, especially the younger generations who traditionally have shown low levels of voting turnout and civic engagement and those who have felt alienated from mainstream society.

The analysis presented in this chapter suggests that both the worst fears of the media malaise claims and the inflated hopes of the new media proponents are misplaced and exaggerated. The evidence we have reviewed indicates that the people who pay the greatest attention to campaign coverage in newspapers and television, as well as the messages from parties, are more likely to participate in the political process. And the findings from our analysis of Net users confirm a strikingly similar pattern. Admittedly, access to the Web is expanding by leaps and bounds, but most of those people are checking their stocks or paying their bills or reading their e-mail from friends or downloading music, not engaging in public affairs, even by a generous definition. The people most likely to be motivated to seek out election information on party Web pages, or to communicate and organize via the Net, are those who would be most engaged in traditional forms of political activism in parties, discussion groups, and lobbying activities. The news media thereby serve primarily to further activate activism. There is little support for either the optimistic belief that the media can generate civic engagement or the pessimistic view that can dampen it down.

Clearly, any attempt at a definitive prognosis would be foolhardy at this stage, as use of the Net in the next few years will evolve further, broadening its user base, and will normalize in subsequent elections. As in the early years of radio and television, Internet access will widen.

Just as we are seeing rapid evolution of e-commerce, parties and candidates will develop new ways to communicate interactively via the Web. It seems likely that the passive Web page, where people get vertical access to 'top-down' information, much as they would from conventional political leaflets, will gradually be superseded by more active formats allowing horizontal communication among networks of citizens and 'bottom-up' feedback into the political process. Parties may find that the most valuable uses will concern 'intranets' connecting different levels and bodies within their organization, as much as Internet communication with the outside public. Interactivity seems likely to appeal most to the small group of mobilized and interested activists, rather than reaching citizens with lower levels of political efficacy and interest. Internet access and use have certainly expanded sharply in the past few years and will expand further, but the pool of Net political activists remains small. The proportions of Americans and Europeans currently involved in any form of online election activity strongly suggest the need for caution in forecasting any transformative capacity of the Web for democracy, at least in the short term.

CHAPTER 13

American Exceptionalism?

The case presented so far in this book rests heavily on comparative evidence derived from aggregate data across OECD countries and the Eurobarometer surveys available for the fifteen member states of the EU. It could be argued, however, that the evidence we have presented thus far misses the point if media malaise turns out to be a case of 'American exceptionalism'. Many accounts of media malaise have focused on specific aspects of the news media and campaigns in the United States, and it may be that these propositions and findings cannot be generalized more widely to other systems. This potential criticism needs to be addressed because there are many plausible reasons why the pattern seen in the United States could prove different from the patterns observed in other postindustrial societies, including the nature of the media environment, political system, and historical culture.[1] This chapter considers these reasons and then explores the evidence for specific and diffuse media malaise effects in the American context. Far from indicating American exceptionalism, the findings suggest the positive effect from the news media that we have already observed in Europe.

REASONS FOR AMERICAN EXCEPTIONALISM?

There are many reasons why the media malaise theory may be applicable to America. The political system and institutions in the United States have many features that may produce distinctive patterns of political communication unlike those in other established democracies. These features include, inter alia, the extreme fragmentation of powers among and within institutions; the permeability of the system, allowing multiple opportunities for pressure-group bargaining, input, and blocking; the weakness of national party organizations and the

279

predominance of one of the few remaining two-party systems; the unique number, frequency, capital-intensive, candidate-centered, and professionalized nature of American election campaigns; and the judicialization of the policy-making process.[2] Some Latin American countries have emulated certain features of the U.S. Constitution, notably the presidential system, with a division of powers among the executive, legislature, and judiciary.[3] Yet, as Wilson observed, 'nothing is more distinctive about the United States than its institutions. Parliamentary democracies are a dime a dozen. . . . In contrast, no stable First World democracy is based on the institutions of the United States.'[4] The extreme fragmentation of authority among government institutions and the permeability of those institutions, combined with the weakness of parties as the 'glue' holding the political system together, may allow the news media (especially network TV news, the major newspapers, and a handful of policy-oriented monthlies) to play a much more powerful role in the policy-making process than in most other established democracies.

American culture has also played an important role in shaping a distinctive set of fundamental values and beliefs about politics and government. Louis Hartz and Seymour Martin Lipset have long argued that the liberal political tradition established by the founders of the American republic has shaped a political culture far more distrustful of government power – especially that of the central government – than is common in European welfare states or in other English-speaking nations.[5] The United States is unique among industrialized democracies in never having had a strong social-democratic movement or a socialist party with a widespread popular following. A recent review of the evidence from public-opinion polls concluded that Americans do subscribe to the 'liberal tradition' in the abstract, although not necessarily when it comes to discussing specific policies or problems.[6] American attitudes towards the role of the news media also tend to be distinctive, with stronger adherence to the ideal of an 'objective' rather than a 'partisan' press, although few differences have been found in terms of some other indicators of civil liberties, such as attitudes towards freedom of publication.[7] The particular wrenching events in American politics in the mid-1960s and early 1970s – assassinations, Vietnam, and Watergate – only weakly echoed in the countercultures on the streets of London, Paris, and Bonn, are regarded by many as having been critical in the growth of a more adversarial news culture.[8]

Lastly, to recap just some of the key contrasts in the news industries, as discussed in earlier chapters, the United States has been far more television-centric than most countries, with higher-than-average TV viewing and lower newspaper readership. The American newspaper industry is characterized by lack of market competition, the absence of a strong tabloid sector, and falling sales. Moreover, American television is far more commercially dominated than any of the other systems we have been comparing. Historically, most postindustrial societies have had public-service television monopolies. When commercial channels became more widely available throughout Europe in the 1980s, the tradition of television had already become well established. The strict regulation of political balance common in public-service television, along with an ethos committed to providing serious coverage of news and public affairs, is still evident in the news culture in European television. The fragmentation of channels via cable, satellite, and broadband TV has gone further in the United States than in most OECD countries, although others have been quickly catching up. For all these reasons, the negative impact of the news media – and particularly television – on civic engagement may perhaps prove to be another case of American exceptionalism.

EVIDENCE FOR AMERICAN EXCEPTIONALISM?

How can we test this thesis? As discussed in Chapter 3, various studies have examined both individual-level survey data and aggregate time-series data about public-opinion trends.

The most common approach, established in the 1970s by Robinson and by Miller and associates, has emphasized that we should expect those most attentive to television news and newspapers to display the highest levels of political mistrust and disengagement.[9] This can be termed the *specific* version of the media malaise thesis, because the effects are expected at the individual level. This approach suggests a significant association between various habitual patterns of media use, such as groups of people who watch much or little TV news, and indicators of civic malaise. The most recent American NES data can be used to test this thesis. If we find that use of the news media is associated with civic malaise in the United States, in contrast to the positive picture that we have seen in Europe, then that possibly could be accounted for by systematic differences in the political systems or cultures, such as those we have already discussed.

In contrast, trend analysis can be used if we expect a media malaise effect to be evident at *diffuse* level. Here we need to look at long-term indicators of civic engagement to see if any systematic changes relate to developments in the news media. As in 'cultivation' theory, it is the diffuse influence of a steady stream of media messages displaying a systematic bias, not the specific impact of exposure to particular media on particular audiences, that is believed to be important.[10] The literature suggests two hypotheses, based on cultural or structural changes in journalism, that can be examined.

One perspective suggests that the American news culture was altered in the late 1960s and early 1970s in response to Vietnam and Watergate, producing a more adversarial journalism–government relationship, more negative campaign news, and a stronger focus on strategy in election campaigns.[11] If so, then like an airborne virus, the effects may have spread beyond those who were most attentive to the news to infect the broader American political culture in this era. We lack direct evidence of the content and direction of news in the 1960s and 1970s. But as a working hypothesis we can assume that American campaign news did become more negative, strategic, and adversarial in the late 1960s and early 1970s, following these events, and then examine whether the timing of any decline in civic engagement fits this thesis. If we should find either a period-specific stepped shift in civic engagement in the late 1960s and early 1970s or a secular trend downward that started in this era (with a modest lag), then this would provide prima facie support for the Vietnam/Watergate hypothesis. Of course, we still cannot disentangle the effects of actual events surrounding Vietnam and Watergate from the possible impact of any changes in the news culture subsequent to those events. But if we should find a pattern of either trendless fluctuations around the mean or stable trends, or if the timing of any fall in civic engagement should not fit the Vietnam/ Watergate hypothesis, then this would cast serious doubt on such an explanation.

Along similar lines, the structural account of media malaise by authors like Neil Postman, suggests that the standards of American journalism began to head south in the early 1980s, with the shrinkage of the audience for network news, the blending of entertainment and news values in magazine formats filling the airwaves on cable and satellite stations, and the downsizing of news divisions after they were merged into larger entertainment-oriented corporations.[12] Again, following the same logic, if such a shift in news and current-affairs coverage affected public engagement with the political process, that should be evident from public-opinion trends in the early 1980s.

To examine a wide range of indicators of civic malaise, we draw on the rich legacy of fifty years of survey data from the series of American national election studies stretching from 1948, prior to the television age, until 1998.

AMERICAN MEDIA USE AND CIVIC ENGAGEMENT

We can start by using individual-level survey analysis to see whether use of the news media in America has been associated with civic engagement, as in the patterns we have observed for Europe, using models similar to those employed earlier.[13] The NES items used to measure media use and political attitudes are not identical with those in the Eurobarometer, so we can expect to find only an approximate fit, but to facilitate comparisons we have used functionally equivalent items of attention to campaign media, political knowledge, political trust, and civic engagement. Because the European elections were second-order contests, characterized by low turnout and interest, the 1998 midterm NES data were selected for comparison, with the U.S. congressional election representing an equivalent low-salience campaign. The NES included standard seven-point scales for how many days per week people read newspapers, watched national and local television news, and listened to radio news, comparable to the five-point European measures of attention to the news media. As for the Internet, the NES also monitored whether Americans went online to get information about the campaign. These items were run separately, and because there was much overlap, they were also analyzed as a combined twenty-nine-point media-exposure scale.

POLITICAL KNOWLEDGE

Few items monitoring knowledge were available from the 1998 NES, but open-ended questions asked people if they could name the job or political office held by Al Gore (vice-president), William Rehnquist (chief justice of the Supreme Court), Boris Yeltsin (president or leader of Russia), and Newt Gingrich (speaker of the House). People were also asked if they knew which party had the most members in the House of Representatives and in the U.S. Senate prior to the 1998 elections. These six items, while tapping mostly the 'civics' dimension, provided a consistent and balanced scale reflecting knowledge of political leaders and

Table 13.1. *Knowledge of political leaders and parties by media use,*
United States, 1998

% Correct	All	Paper Not Daily	Paper Daily	National TV News Not Daily	National TV News Daily	Local TV News Not Daily	Local TV News Daily	Internet Campaign News Users No	Internet Campaign News Users Yes
Proportion of the electorate	100	65	35	65	35	56	44	90	10
Know Gore is vice-president	88	86	94	87	91	89	87	87	99
Know GOP controlled House	67	61	79	62	67	66	69	65	86
Know Gingrich is/was Speaker of the House	60	55	69	57	64	60	60	58	75
Know GOP controlled Senate	56	49	69	50	65	54	58	54	75
Know Yeltsin is president of Russia	50	48	54	48	53	53	46	48	70
Know Rehnquist is chief justice	11	8	16	10	12	12	8	9	27
None correct	8	10	3	9	6	7	8	9	1
1–3 correct	41	45	34	44	36	40	42	43	41
4–5 correct	45	40	54	41	52	45	45	43	61
All correct	6	5	9	6	7	8	5	5	16
Mean score	3.3	3.0	3.8	3.1	3.6	3.3	3.3	3.2	4.3
Zero-order correlation	0.26**	0.19**		0.17**		0.01		0.20**	

Notes: Q: 'Now we have a set of questions concerning various public figures. We want to see how much information about them gets out to the public from television, newspapers and the like. The first name is AL GORE. What job or political office does he now hold?' Q: 'Do you happen to know which party had the most members in the House of Representatives/U.S. Senate before the election (this/last) month?' Daily = use media every day. Not daily = do not use media every day. **$p > 0.01$.
Source: NES, 1998.

parties (with an intercorrelation, measured by Cronbach's alpha, of 0.70). It can be argued that being able to identify the office held by Rehnquist or Yeltsin is of little practical relevance for most people's lives, but understanding which party controls Congress is important for evaluating the legislative branch and for holding parties accountable for their actions. In the open-ended leadership items, a correct answer could not be the result of mere guesswork, although with regard to control of Congress people had a 50% chance of guessing the right party.

Table 13.1 shows that the vast majority of the American public (88%) knew that Al Gore was vice-president of the United States, and two-thirds knew that the Republicans had control of the House. A majority of the public gave correct answers to most of the other items, with the exception of identifying William Rehnquist as chief justice of the Supreme Court, which only one in ten Americans knew. Most people got about half the answers correct; out of six items, the average score was 3.3. At the bottom of the class, a small group (8%) flunked every answer, and in contrast, a few people (6%) got everything right.

The key question for this study was the relationship of media use to these indicators of political knowledge. The simple frequency distributions, without any controls for social factors, showed a clear pattern: Use of Internet campaign news, newspapers, and national television news was consistently and significantly associated with greater knowledge. This pattern was particularly clear on the more demanding indicators, such as identifying which party held the Senate, where there was a fifteen-to-twenty-point knowledge gap between those who did and those who did not regularly watch network news, read a daily newspaper, or surf Net news. At the same time, watching local TV news made no significant difference to political knowledge, which was consistent with its greater emphasis on crime, sports, and weather and its neglect of national politics. The difference by media outlets is important, because it suggests that what makes the difference in political awareness is not simply the profile of the overall TV audience but rather the characteristics of those who tune in to network news. Overall, Internet news users proved the most knowledgeable (getting 4.3 out of 6 right), followed by newspaper readers (3.8) and viewers of national TV news (3.6). Viewers of local TV news scored no better than the average American (3.3).

Regression models were run to see if these relationships were maintained after controlling for the usual indicators used in the models reported in earlier chapters, including social background (age, education, gender, income) and attitudinal indicators (willingness to engage in political discussion, liberal–conservative ideology). The first model used a composite indicator of media use, and the second analyzed each of the different types of media. Table 13.2 shows that, as before, education, gender, age, and income all proved significant predictors of political knowledge, in that order of decreasing importance. Just as many previous studies had found, the well educated, men, and the older generations had better understandings of parties and leaders. The attitudinal factors were also significant. After entering those variables, the composite scale for media exposure continued to prove significant. Use

Table 13.2. *Predictors of knowledge of leaders and parties, United States, 1998*

	Political Leaders and Parties (i)	Sig.	Political Leaders and Parties (ii)	Sig.	Operationalization
STRUCTURAL					
Education	0.31	**	0.27	**	Education scale
Gender: Male	0.22	**	0.19	**	Male (1) Female (0)
Age	0.15	**	0.15	**	Age in years
Household Income	0.07	*	0.05		Household income scale
ATTITUDINAL					
Political Discussion	0.10	**	0.08	**	How often discuss: never, occasionally, freq.
Lib-Con Ideology	−0.07	*	−0.09	*	7-point scale: From liberal (1) to conservative (7)
USE OF NEWS MEDIA					
Media News Use	0.11	**			29-point use of TV news + paper + radio news
Newspaper			−0.04		7-point scale: How often read
National TV News			0.15	**	7-point scale: How often watch
Local TV News			−0.08		7-point scale: How often watch
Radio News			0.01		7-point scale: How often listen
Net Campaign News			0.13	*	Yes (1) No (0)
Constant	0.674		1.47		
R^2	0.25		0.21		

Notes: The columns report the standardized beta coefficients predicting knowledge based on ordinary least-squares regression models. The dependent variable is the 6-point scale measuring knowledge. See Table 13.1 for details. Model (i), with combined media-use scale. Model (ii), with separate scales for each medium. ** $p > 0.01$; * $p > 0.05$.
Source: NES, 1998, N. 1,281.

of the news media was positively associated with what Americans know about political leaders and parties, even after controlling for the prior backgrounds of readers and viewers. In the second model, breaking out the different types of media, most strikingly it was use of network television news and Internet news that proved the strongest predictors of political knowledge. Such findings lend further support to recent reviews of the literature that have concluded that the conventional wisdom in the 1970s was wrong. Rather, recent studies are suggesting that television news does provide American voters with important information about politics.[14]

Most importantly, these overall findings from an independent data set confirm that the pattern found earlier regarding practical knowledge of EU affairs (see Table 9.3) was not solely applicable to Europe; strikingly similar findings are evident in the United States. As with any cross-sectional survey analysis, taken as a snapshot at one moment of time, we cannot hope to pin down the direction of causality in this relationship. We know that the better educated are more likely to use the news media, as shown earlier. But the most plausible interpretation to be drawn from these results is that habitual attention to the news media – reading about congressional politics, hearing political analysts, following foreign affairs on national TV news – continues to add to our sum of knowledge about public affairs, in an interactive virtuous circle. The more we know, the more we watch or read. The more we watch or read, the more we come to know. And the virtuous circle holds for TV news. These findings lend further confirmation to the conclusions of Michael Delli Carpini and Scott Keeter's exhaustive study of the components of political knowledge in the United States, which also found media attention to exert a positive influence on what Americans know.[15] The results suggest that if the public lacks knowledge of public affairs – if many Americans remained unaware that Boris Yeltsin was president of Russia, or that William Rehnquist was chief justice on the Supreme Court – we should not blame the news media per se for this sorry state of affairs.

POLITICAL TRUST

Yet the heart of media malaise theory is less about cognitive learning than about the public's orientation towards the political system. Is there evidence that any journalistic cynicism towards government resonates more strongly among American readers and viewers than among Europeans? The 1998 NES included the standard index used for forty years to gauge trust in government, including the extent to which people say they can trust government in Washington to do what is right, how many public officials are believed to be 'crooked', how much government is run by a 'few big interests', and how much tax is wasted by people in government. The internal political-efficacy scale, tapping people's sense of their own ability to influence the system, included four standard items: 'officials don't care what people like me think', 'people like me don't have any say in what government does', 'sometimes politics seems so complicated that a person like me can't understand what's going on', and whether elections make government 'pay attention to what people like me think'.

As is well known, the indicators of trust in government plummeted sharply and steadily from the mid-1960s until the early 1970s, bottomed

Table 13.3. *Political mistrust and media use, United States, 1998*
(percentages who agree)

% Agree with the Mistrusting Response	All	Paper Not Daily	Paper Daily	National TV News Not Daily	National TV News Daily	Local TV News Not Daily	Local TV News Daily	Internet Campaign News Users No	Internet Campaign News Users Yes
'Quite a few in Government are crooked'	40	46	31	42	37	43	38	41	36
'Government wastes a lot of tax'	62	64	58	61	63	61	62	62	60
Government does what is right 'Only some of the time/never'	60	62	57	61	59	63	56	61	56
'Government is run by a few big interests'	67	67	66	67	67	67	66	67	63
Zero-order correlation media use and political-trust scale		0.07*		0.01		0.06		0.03	

Note: Daily = use media every day. Not daily = do not use media every day. $*p > 0.05$.
Source: NES, 1998.

out, then experienced a slight recovery in the mid-1980s under Reagan's watch, experienced another fall from the mid-1980s to the mid-1990s, then recovered slightly again in recent years. The long-term fall has caused widespread concern and fuelled much of the current revival in attention to media malaise theories. Many writers have coupled the decline of public trust in government and politicians with the rise of more cynical news media. But are these factors related? Table 13.3 examines the relationship at the individual level between attention to different news media and trust in American government. The results confirm the pattern found in Europe, presented in Chapter 11, namely, that attention to the news media proves to be either neutral or positively related to political trust. In the multivariate regression model in Table 13.4, none of the social or attitudinal variables, except for media use, was significantly related to political trust. The model predicting political efficacy shows a slightly different pattern, with most of the social and attitudinal factors proving significant (with the exception of

Table 13.4. *Predictors of political trust and efficacy, United States, 1998*

	Trust in Government	Sig.	Political Efficacy	Sig.	Operationalization
STRUCTURAL					
Education	0.02		0.28	**	Education scale
Gender: Male	0.05		0.05		Male (1) Female (0)
Age	0.03		−0.08	**	Age in years
Household Income	0.01		0.09	**	Household income scale
ATTITUDINAL					
Political Discussion	−0.02		0.11	**	How often discuss: never, occasionally, freq.
Lib-Con Ideology	−0.05		−0.07	*	7-point scale: From liberal (1) to conservative (7)
USE OF NEWS MEDIA					
Media News Use	0.11	**	0.05		29-point use of TV news + paper + radio news
Constant	6.7		5.6		
R^2	0.02		0.15		

Notes: The columns report the standardized beta coefficients predicting trust and efficacy based on ordinary least-squares regression models. See Table 13.3 for details.
$**p > 0.01$; $*p > 0.05$.
Source: NES, 1998, *N.* 1,281.

gender). After these controls were introduced, media use remained positively related to efficacy, but statistically insignificant at the conventional 0.05 level. The findings on political trust provide further confirmation of the findings in previous research by Bennett and associates,[16] who examined the associations between media *exposure* (including use of local and national TV news, entertainment television, and newspapers) and media *attention* (to campaign news and to talk radio), and trust in politicians, using the 1996 NES survey. Their study concluded that none of the media-exposure variables proved significant, although attention to campaign news was positively related to trust. Far from demonstrating a case of American exceptionalism, the results in this chapter replicate and thereby increase our confidence in the earlier patterns observed in Europe.

POLITICAL ACTIVISM AND PARTICIPATION

Does use of the news media produce passive couch potatoes, with the illusion rather than the reality of civic engagement, as Hart suggests?[17] And does watching television damage face-to-face community activism and social capital, as Putnam argues?[18] Campaign activism was measured in the NES by a battery of six items monitoring whether people had contributed money to candidates and parties, worked for a candidate or party, persuaded others how to vote, attended a candidate meeting, or displayed a campaign button. The items were intercorrelated and formed a consistent activism scale.[19] These measures, designed in an earlier era, are rather old-fashioned: When was the last time Americans actually wore campaign buttons, as opposed to snapping them up as collector's items? The newer forms of engagement, like Internet discussion groups, were excluded. But the scale still tapped some of the most common conventional forms of electoral participation.

The first model in Table 13.5 shows that all the demographic indicators were associated with campaign activism, especially education, which many have found to be one of the strongest predictors of political participation. Even after controlling for background and attitudes, use of the news media emerged as one of the strongest positive predictors of campaign activism. Far from disengaging, those most attentive to campaign news were more likely to become involved, such as to contribute time or money to the campaign. In the second model, we examined the separate effects of the different types of media, and again it was use of national TV news and the Internet that proved most strongly linked to activism.

Moreover, these patterns extended more widely to forms of civic engagement outside of the campaign. An earlier study had compared attention to general television, TV news, and current-affairs programs with a wide range of different dimensions of political participation in America, ranging from voting and campaign activism to protest politics, organizational membership, and community mobilization.[20] In each dimension, increasing numbers of hours devoted to watching TV (including mostly entertainment) did have a consistently depressing effect (Figure 13.1), and that pattern was found in other established democracies as well.[21] The amount of leisure time that people devote to television entertainment does seem to detract from their involvement in politics and community affairs, lending some weight to Gerbner's argument that it is television watching, not TV news, that causes malaise.[22] But we cannot blame journalism per se, because the effect of

Table 13.5. *Predictors of campaign activism, United States, 1998*

	Campaign Activism (i)	Sig.	Campaign Activism (ii)	Sig.	Operationalization
STRUCTURAL					
Education	0.13	**	0.04		Education scale
Gender: Male	0.09	**	0.04		Male (1) Female (0)
Age	0.08	*	0.03		Age in years
Household Income	0.08	*	0.15	**	Household income scale
ATTITUDINAL					
Political Discussion	0.12	**	0.11	**	How often discuss: never, occasionally, freq.
Lib-Con Ideology	0.01		0.06		7-point scale: From liberal (1) to conservative (7)
USE OF NEWS MEDIA					
Media News Use	0.13	**			29-point use of TV news + paper + radio news
Newspaper			0.08		7-point scale: How often read paper
National TV News			0.11	*	7-point scale: How often watch
Local TV News			−0.01		7-point scale: How often watch
Radio News			0.05		7-point scale: How often listen
Net Campaign News			0.12	*	Yes (1) No (0)
Constant	−0.82		−1.01		
R^2	0.10		0.08		

Notes: The columns report the standardized beta coefficients predicting campaign activism based on ordinary least-squares regression models. The participation variable is the 6-point scale measuring attending a candidate meeting, working for a candidate or party, donating money to a candidate or party, displaying a campaign button, and talking to others for or against a candidate. Model (i), with combined media-use scale. Model (ii), with separate scales for each medium. **$p > 0.01$; *$p > 0.05$.
Source: NES, 1998, N. 1,281.

attention to TV news and current affairs consistently has a positive relationship with all types of civic engagement (Figure 13.2).[23] That relationship remained significant in multivariate analysis after the usual battery of controls.

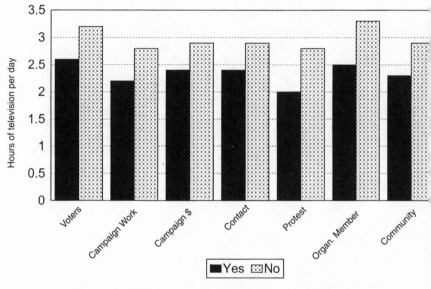

Figure 13.1. Watching TV and participation, United States, 1990.
Source: American Citizen Participation Study, 1990.

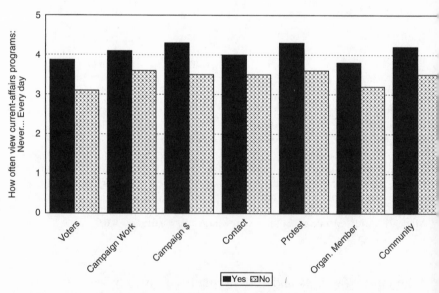

Figure 13.2. Watching current-affairs TV and participation, United States, 1990. *Source*: American Citizen Participation Study, 1990.

Therefore, exposure to negative ads by politicians may demobilize the American electorate, as Ansolabehere and Iyengar suggest.[24] People who choose to spend their evenings watching TV are less likely to join organizations and to go to community meetings, as Putnam argues, which may reduce the overall stock of social capital.[25] But attention to news journalism is consistently and positively associated at the individual level with a wide range of indicators of political knowledge, political trust, and civic engagement, in both Europe and the United States. Although there were many plausible reasons to suspect that we might find different patterns on both sides of the Atlantic, that turned out not to be the case.

LONG-TERM TRENDS IN AMERICAN CIVIC ENGAGEMENT

Thus far we have examined the individual-level associations between groups of media users and their attitudes and behaviours. We have found little support for the media malaise claims, but it could be argued that the effects of news coverage are far more diffuse, affecting all the American public, not just the most attentive viewers and readers. We tend to rely on many overlapping sources of news, not just one, and we learn about events from discussions with colleagues and friends. As a result, perhaps public opinion is being shaped by the host of well-publicized events in popular culture, like the Lewinsky affair or the death of John F. Kennedy, Jr., without the public paying much attention to any particular medium.

Some proponents of the media malaise thesis suggest that cultural decline is the most plausible way to understand long-term changes in American politics. Cultural accounts suggest that following the events of Vietnam and Watergate, American election news became more negative, strategically oriented, and adversarial, across all media, with the result that in the late 1960s and early 1970s the public became increasingly turned off by campaign coverage. 'If Vietnam and Watergate marked a time when the press turned against the politicians', Patterson suggests, 'the recent period represents a time when the press turned on them.'[26] Alternative structural accounts by Postman and others suggest that changes in the news industry created a more entertainment-oriented journalism, or 'news lite', which began to occur in the early 1980s with the widespread proliferation of cable TV and the erosion of network news and was accelerated in the 1990s. If changes in American

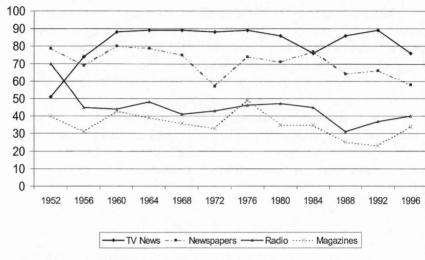

Figure 13.3. Attention to campaign media, United States, 1952–96. *Source*: NES 1952–96.

campaign journalism had a diffuse effect on American public opinion in these eras, that should be evidenced by period-specific effects, or by the start of a secular trend, across different indicators of civic engagement, including political interest, government trust, and electoral activism.

TRENDS IN CAMPAIGN INTEREST

If campaign journalism did become more negative in the 1960s and early 1970s, the first impact might be expected to have been that the American public decided to switch off in droves, preferring baseball, movies, and sitcoms to election news. Yet if we examine the long-term trends in American attention to campaign news, the pattern that emerges most strongly from the NES data since the 1960s is one of stability, rather than any steady linear decline. In this comparison we focus on presidential elections, to remove the fluctuations caused by midterm contests, although congressional elections displayed a similar pattern. Figure 13.3 shows that from 1952 to 1960, television shot into first place as the medium most popular among Americans for following election news, causing a fall in the use of radio news and the print media. But from the 1960 election onwards, attention to television, newspapers, radio, and magazines proved fairly stable, with the exception of a few random fluctuations like the temporary dip in the use of newspapers in

1972, which could have been the result of measurement error. Reliance on TV news did not fall consistently over successive elections in the post-Vietnam and post-Watergate era. The only major temporary dips in the use of TV news occurred in 1984 (counter-intuitively, under the sunny 'Morning Again in America' Reagan campaign), before recovering in 1988 (equally ironically, under the 'revolving door/Willie Horton' negativism of Bush versus Dukakis). Those blips were in the opposite direction to the media malaise thesis. Another dip in TV use occurred in 1996, but it is too early to determine if that represented another temporary fluctuation or the start of a new trend, and the use of radio and magazines experienced a slight surge in these years. If we compare American uses of the campaign media during the past fifty years, there is no consistent major slide across all indicators.

Of course, it still could be the case that despite the aggregate trends, some Americans have become progressively more disengaged from the campaigns, and others have become more involved. There is considerable concern that poorer groups, ethnic minorities, and the less educated have become effectively disenfranchised by American elections. Media malaise effects could be turning off the politically marginalized, rather than mainstream America. To examine the evidence, regression models were run to predict attention to campaign news in successive American presidential elections, examining the strength of predictors for the major demographic variables (age, education, income, gender, and race), as well as political interest. The standardized betas were then plotted by year to examine trends from 1952 to 1996.

The data in Figure 13.4 show a mixed pattern. Sharp fluctuations in the 1950s can plausibly be attributed to the rapid spread of TV ownership from the affluent elite to mainstream America. Since the 1960s, the clearest trend has been by age, where, although the pattern is far from linear, interest in the campaigns has become progressively more concentrated among the older age groups. This may be a life-cycle effect, for we have already established that because of their more sedentary lifestyles, older people usually watch far more television (and TV news) than younger groups. We have seen that in Europe, age proved one of the strongest predictors of attention to TV news, although that pattern has remained stable, not strengthened, during the past thirty years. Alternatively, if that is a generational effect rather than a life-cycle effect, as Miller and Shanks have suggested in their exhaustive study, it represents a genuine cause for concern.[27] This pattern can be linked to diffuse theories of media malaise, and Putnam has argued that such findings

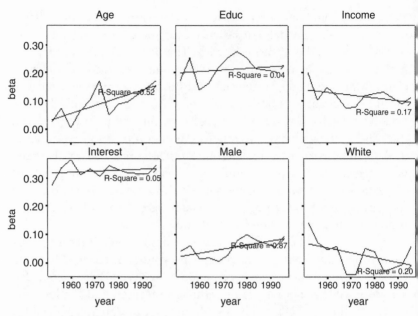

Figure 13.4. Predictors of attention to campaign news, United States, 1952–96 (linear regression).

reflect the development of a 'post-civic' baby-boom generation that grew up in the television era.[28] It remains to be seen if the Internet generation will surf to alternative sources of political information.

Other findings in Figure 13.4 provide less support for the media malaise thesis. The effects of income and race show modest downward slopes, indicating that the audience for campaign news has slightly widened in these regards over time. The fluctuations in campaign attention for African-Americans can plausibly be traced to the salience of racial issue in particular elections, as in 1968 (civil-rights issues) and 1984 (the presidential candidacy of Jesse Jackson). The coefficients for education and gender fluctuate quite sharply around the mean, with slight upwards slopes. Despite closure over the years, and the reversal of the gender gap in electoral turnout, even today women continue to display slightly less interest and activism in many conventional forms of political participation in many countries. For reasons that remain unclear, the effects of education rose sharply from the early 1960s to the 1976 election, and then fell again over successive elections. Lastly, the effect of political interest on media attention has remained stable and has been the strongest predictor of news use. What the general pattern suggests is that some fluctuations over time probably were caused by measurement error, such as slight differences in question wording and sampling in successive NES data sets, but overall, attention to American presidential campaigns has not become progressively more concentrated among demographic groups, with the important exception of the effect of age.

Other indicators of civic engagement concern whether the wider American public followed the campaigns and public affairs. If election coverage became more negative in the 1960s and early 1970s, then plausibly people could have switched off from politics. Figures 13.5 and 13.6 show the long-term trends for those indicators in presidential and midterm elections. The data show that interest in the campaigns became slightly stronger in successive elections from 1952 to 1976, and then fell to a lower level from 1978 to 1998 (with the exception of the 1992 election, when attention rose again). The pattern is far from uniform. For example, interest in the 1956 campaign proved similar to that in 1996. Variations over time plausibly could have been produced by many factors, including the closeness of the races, whether or not an incumbent president was standing for reelection, competition from third-party candidates, the salience of the political issues, and so on.[29] The decline in political interest indicates a period-specific shift, but this change seems to have occurred between 1976 and 1978, later than the Vietnam/Watergate thesis would suggest and earlier than the proposition of structural changes in the news industry. Of course, Vietnam/Watergate plausibly could have produced a lagged shift, as the journalistic culture gradually changed, but that still should have been evident, all other things being equal, in the 1976 race. In addition, the decline in political interest possibly could be attributable to many things beyond changes in the news culture. For example, the aggravated generational and racial tensions in American politics could have increased political interest during the 1960s.

Trends in attention to government and public affairs, rather than campaigns, present a slightly different picture (Table 13.6). The proportion of Americans who followed government and public affairs either 'most' or 'some' of the time in the 1990s was similar to that in the early 1960s. Like a rat in a python, the main exceptions to the overall trend concern heightened attention in the 1964, 1972, 1974, and 1976 election campaigns. As many have observed, the events of these years stimulated political awareness – events such as conflict over civil rights and the consequent urban riots, demonstrations against the Vietnam

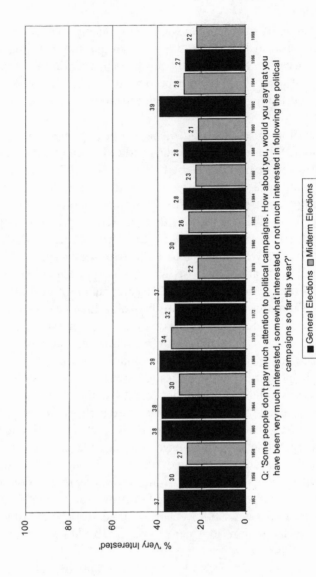

Q: "Some people don't pay much attention to political campaigns. How about you, would you say that you have been very much interested, somewhat interested, or not much interested in following the political campaigns so far this year?"

■ General Elections ▨ Midterm Elections

Figure 13.5. U.S. interest in campaigns, 1952–98. *Source:* NES, 1948–96.

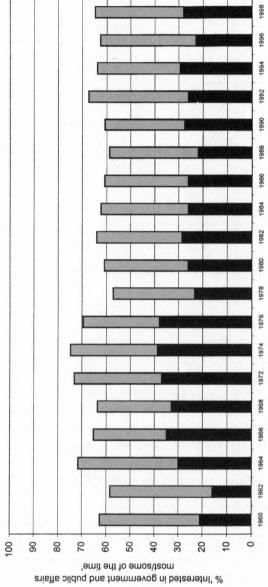

Figure 13.6. U.S. interest in government and public affairs, 1960–98. *Source:* NES.

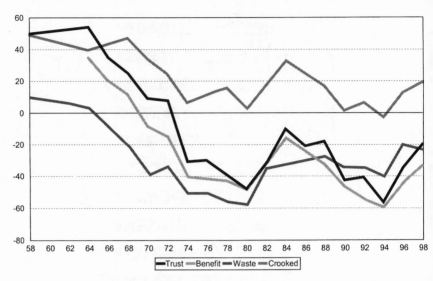

Figure 13.7. Trends in American political trust, 1958–98. *Source:* NES Percentage Difference Index.

War, political assassinations, the rise of second-wave feminism, generational culture wars, and the aftermath of Watergate. From 1976 to 1998, attention returned to the 'normal' level evident in the early 1960s. There was no linear decline of interest in American politics. The 1992 Bush versus Clinton versus Perot election, for example, registered the fifth highest level of interest in the entire series. The common assumption that Americans have become increasingly bored with government and turned off from public affairs in recent years, and that this can be attributed to increasingly negative, trivial, or strategic coverage in the news media, receives no support from this evidence.

TRUST IN GOVERNMENT AND POLITICIANS

Yet any effects of a more cynical culture in journalism should be evident more directly in indicators of political trust in American government and politicians. After all, much of the concern about growing alienation has been generated by the long-term slide in the standard NES indicators of civic malaise. The key question here is whether the timing of the decline in political trust coincided with the events that are alleged to have transformed the news culture.

Figure 13.7 maps the trends in the standard NES indicators of trust in government, discussed earlier, from 1958 until 1998. The pattern confirms relatively high levels of trust during 1958–64, a sharp plunge from 1964 to 1974, a modest slide until 1980, then a revival under Reagan's first term in the early 1980s, a slide again from 1984 to 1994, and then a distinct revival during Clinton's second term. Whereas earlier observers saw only a linear decline, the most recent figures suggest a far clearer pattern of trendless fluctuations. The key question for this study is the extent to which these patterns can be related to the timing of any assumed changes in the news industry and culture. The Vietnam/Watergate hypothesis certainly receives some support from the trends in the early 1970s, although it should be noted that the slide started in 1964–66, before journalists began to provide highly critical coverage of the American involvement in Vietnam.[30] But the subsequent pattern in the 1980s and 1990s, with the rise and fall and rise in American political trust, strongly suggests that rather than a secular phenomenon, driven by cultural or structural trends in American journalism, we should expect to find an events-driven or performance-driven political explanation.[31] If 'negative' campaign coverage increased in the early 1980s, as Patterson has suggested, that may have been associated with the popularity of presidential candidates, but it was unrelated to broader trends in American political trust, which became more positive during this era. Of course, we cannot assume that there was any simple and direct link between attitudes towards the political system and the broader pattern of news coverage, because multiple factors can influence political trust. But at the same time, if the timing of trends in these indicators of civic engagement fails to match the timing of any hypothetical change in the culture of the news media, even with lags, then there is no convincing evidence for those hypothetical effects at a diffuse level.

POLITICAL MOBILIZATION

There remains the issue of falling turnout and campaign activism, generating much concern. Even if interest and trust are unrelated to the pattern of campaign coverage in the news media, it still could be that more negative news demobilizes the public. Is there any evidence that the trends in American political participation support the diffuse version of the media malaise argument?

In Chapter 12 we noted that postwar voter turnout in established democracies has generally remained fairly constant, down only 3% from 1970 to 1990 in the countries under comparison. Yet turnout in the United States has remained far lower than in most other comparable postindustrial societies and has slid further. The postwar trends shown in Figure 13.8 confirm that voting turnout peaked at 63.1% of the voting-age population in the 1960 presidential election. In contrast, in the 1996 presidential election, less than half (47.2%) of the voting-age population cast ballots. As discussed in Chapter 12, many factors may have contributed to the particularly low turnout in the United States: the barriers posed by institutional procedures for registering and voting; the exceptional frequency of American elections; the erosion of partisanship; the two-party system, limiting electoral choice; the fragmentation of power in the U.S. system of government, reducing the salience of elections; and the weakness of party organizations as mobilizing agencies.[32] But what was the role of the news media?

Voter turnout in presidential contests proved moderate throughout the quiescent 1950s, followed by a peak in the 1960s, and then in recent decades a return to the levels common in the 1950s. Rather than a long-term linear decline in turnout for presidential elections since the early 1970s, the pattern shows a plateau in the 1960s, with trendless fluctuations around the mean. Again, turnout, like interest, can suddenly bounce back. For example, the 1992 election had the fifth highest voting participation in the series. Such volatility strongly points to political explanations, not secular trends. It is only for the midterm elections that there has been a more consistent fall in turnout; it began in 1974 and has persisted at about the same level, rather than sliding further, in successive elections to date. The contrast between the patterns for general elections and midterm elections suggests that we should look more closely at the reasons for American disengagement from congressional politics, rather than at broader changes in the news industry or culture. The fluctuations in presidential-level turnout plausibly could be explained by systematic differences in the choices facing American voters in the various elections: the presence of third parties, the closeness of the race, the strength of the incumbent, the effectiveness of get-out-the-vote drives, and the salience of hot-button election issues, rather than by a long-term shift towards more negative media coverage of campaigns 'turning off' the American public.

Yet turnout itself can be the product of many institutional factors. What of the other indicators of conventional political participation and campaign mobilization? The NES battery of items, already used at the individual level, monitors whether Americans have become less engaged in campaigns. If campaign coverage has become more negative, that should certainly be turning off voters. Yet the evidence from the long series of general elections (Figure 13.9) shows that the proportion of

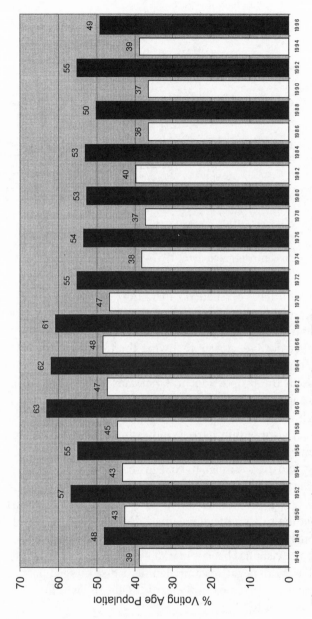

Figure 13.8. U.S. voting turnout, 1946–96. *Source:* IDEA.

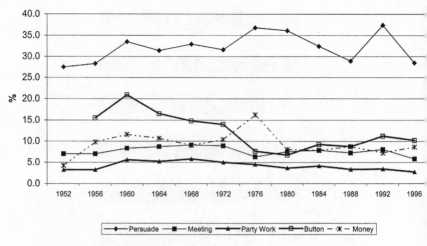

Figure 13.9. U.S. campaign activism, 1952–96. *Source:* NES.

Americans who have persuaded others how to vote by discussing the candidates, arguably the least demanding form of participation, has remained fairly high. The pattern shows trendless fluctuations rather than a secular decline, closely following the trends for the other indicators of campaign interest that we have already observed. The sharpest decline was in the proportion of Americans wearing buttons or displaying bumper stickers, both minor activities that have become unfashionable. Since the 1960s there has also been a modest long-term decline in activism within parties, indicating erosion of the grassroots party organizations, although the proportion of party workers active in the late 1990s was similar to that in the 1950s. As Rosenstone and Hansen have found, the proportion of Americans engaged in other types of campaigning has remained fairly stable, such as contributing money or going to a political meeting.[33] Despite concern about declining civic engagement, and dramatic changes in the nature of American campaigns, activism has been remarkably stable over the past fifty years. The idea that more negative campaign news discouraged participation, either in the early 1970s or in the early 1980s, receives little confirmation from the trends.

AMERICAN NON-EXCEPTIONALISM

It turns out that despite all the possible reasons why America may be different from other democracies, in fact the evidence seems to point towards remarkably similar patterns in the United States and in Europe. At the individual level, when testing the effects of exposure to the American news media on particular groups of users, the effects proved consistently positive or occasionally neutral, but, as in Europe, in no case did we find negative relationships. These generalizations appear to be sufficiently robust to withstand multiple tests in independent data sets across many different years, media environments, and political systems, increasing confidence in the results. No single piece of evidence can be regarded as decisive, but the sheer weight of findings points in a consistent direction. The only exception that might lend some credibility to Gerbner's theory of media malaise was the finding that use of TV *entertainment* was associated with slightly lower levels of political participation. This pattern might be the result, as Gerbner suggests, of a 'mean-world' syndrome that develops from watching TV dramas about cops, courtrooms, and crime. Yet, equally plausibly, the association might be attributable primarily to leisure patterns. Perhaps people who are less sociable, for whatever reason, choose to stay home and watch *Friends* and *ER* rather than attend community meetings in drafty town halls or volunteer to help with local initiatives and campaigns. The many theories suggesting that *journalism* in general and TV news in particular contribute to public cynicism and disengagement receives no support from the individual-level survey evidence.

The long-term trends in American civic engagement raise many puzzles, requiring further analysis. This chapter has sketched only some of the possible explanations. But the attempt to blame the news media for changes in American political interest, trust, and participation must fail, for the timing of any adverse developments in journalism does not fit sufficiently well with the timing of these trends to prove convincing. American journalism may or may not have changed as a result of the experiences of Vietnam and Watergate in the late 1960s and early 1970s or the rise of entertainment values in the news industry in the 1980s. But if so, these events did not have any discernible impact on the American public, according to the indicators we have examined.

Equally important, even the general 'declinism' thesis that has become so pervasive in accounts of American democracy receives little support from the evidence. Yes, there have been important shifts over time in American civic engagement, but the patterns in political interest, trust, and voter turnout reflect '1960s exceptionalism', a bump in the road, rather than a steady secular decline. As always, with any analysis of trends, the selection of starting and ending points is critical. It would be disingenuous and misleading to take the peak of voter turnout, in 1960, as the starting point for any analysis, rather than to examine the continuous NES series available from the early 1950s. Arguably, most Americans would willingly opt for the more quiescent politics of the 1950s and the 1990s, rather than the heated and conflictual, if more participatory, politics of the 1960s. At the beginning of the twenty-first century it appears that American democracy and the American news media are far healthier than many naysayers would have us believe.

Conclusions

CHAPTER 14

A Virtuous Circle?

This final chapter highlights the major findings of this study and offers an alternative interpretation of the evidence whereby the process of political communication can be understood as a 'virtuous circle', a ratcheting process that over the long term gradually reinforces the activism of the active. This interpretation remains theoretical, for we lack direct proof, but it does make sense of the consistent patterns found throughout this study. The conclusion echoes an earlier era of political-communication research of the Columbia school, unfashionable in recent years, when the news media were widely believed to exert a positive force in democracy.

The media malaise theories discussed in this book claim that coverage of public affairs by the news media contributes to civic disengagement, including ignorance of public affairs, disenchantment with government, and political apathy. In understanding such accounts of media malaise, it helps to draw a clear distinction between the explanans and explanandum. Various authors agree about the *effects* of media malaise but differ regarding the reasons for that phenomenon.

The modern idea of media malaise originated with the Langs in the 1960s, developed with the work of Michael Robinson in the mid-1970s, and gained credibility as it was subsequently expanded, with variations on the theme, by several American and European scholars in the 1990s. That idea spread more widely because it fed a mood of self-doubt and angst in contemporary American journalism. In recent years, dissenting voices in the literature have been overwhelmed by the current popularity of media malaise theories. Many accounts imply a general pattern that, if true, should be evident across postindustrial societies. Others provide a narrower focus, suggesting a more purely American phenomenon. Many stress the distinct roles of television journalism (Robinson) and newspapers (Miller). Yet another perspective, not directly examined in this book, looks even more broadly at the associations among watching television entertainment, social trust, and engagement in voluntary associations and community affairs (Putnam). Another strand in the literature criticizes the political-marketing techniques used by politicians, spin-doctors, image consultants, and pollsters. As stressed in Chapter 1, although the term originated with Robinson, there was no single canonical theory of media malaise that influenced all subsequent writers. Rather, there are multiple perspectives in the literature. But by the 1990s a broad consensus had emerged that some, or all, practices in political communication have contributed to public disenchantment with civic life.

Understanding media malaise matters because concern about the impact of the news media has rippled out well beyond a small circle of scholars to become fashionable among policy-makers, journalists, and broadcasters. In the United States there is much self-doubt within the industry; the majority of American journalists believe, for example, that the press pays too little attention to complex issues, blurs the distinction between reporting and commentary, is out of touch with the public, and is too cynical. 'A large majority of news professionals sense a degradation of the culture of news,' Kovach and Rosensteil suggest, 'from one that was steeped in verification and a steadfast respect for the facts, towards one that favours argument, opinion-mongering, haste and infotainment.'[1] Instead of covering political events, such as the Lewinsky affair or gun violence or the GOP primaries, American journalism seems increasingly transfixed by American journalism, looking at itself obsessively in an endless hall of mirrors. As night follows day, the first wave of stories concerns the 'real' event, and the second bemoans how poorly the news media covered the event. In Europe, too, although the debate seems more muted, there are periodic bursts of angst about the standards of journalism, often surrounding coverage of particular events by the more aggressive paparazzi and checkbook tabloids. Concern about the news media has also spread to the public.[2] According to the 1995–97 World Values survey, less than a third of the public had any confidence in the press in Britain, Sweden, Denmark, The Netherlands, Austria, and Germany, and similar proportions trusted television in Switzerland, Germany, Australia, and the United States.

THE EMERGENCE OF POSTMODERN COMMUNICATIONS

Before evaluating how well the news media carry out their democratic functions, we need to agree on some common normative standards. Some theories of representative democracy suggest that the news media should provide a civic forum in which to hear serious and extended political viewpoints from all voices in society, that they should perform a watchdog role to check abuses of civil and political liberties, and that they should serve as mobilizing agents to encourage learning, stimulate interest, and promote participation in public affairs. To analyze whether the news media perform these functions, we can draw distinctions among the production, content, and effects of political communication. The central thesis of this book is that although the structure of the news industry and the process of political campaigning undoubtedly have been altered almost beyond recognition since the postwar era of wireless airwaves, inky linotype, and town-hall meetings, it is far less clear that those developments have eroded the standards of political coverage, still less contributed to political malaise. Instead, I argue that in Europe and in the United States, because of a 'virtuous circle', attention to the news media gradually reinforces civic engagement, just as civic engagement prompts attention to the news.

THE NEWS INDUSTRY

Part II of this book has described how the structure of the news industry has been transformed in recent decades by technological, economic, and political developments common to postindustrial societies. Rather than new media displacing the old, these developments have led to proliferation and diversification of news sources, formats, and levels. There is widespread concern that serious, in-depth reporting about government, public-policy issues, and international affairs has been increasingly displaced by 'infotainment' and 'tabloidization', with more and more human-interest stories about popular celebrities, consumer affairs, and scandal.

Yet the most plausible interpretation of the evidence is that many postindustrial societies have seen diversification in the channels, levels, and formats of political communication that have broadened the scope of news and the audience for news, at both highbrow and popular levels. Newspaper sales have not declined in postindustrial societies; the proportion of regular readers of European newspapers has doubled in the past three decades, and the social profile for readers has broadened. If the definition of 'news' and the scope of 'news' stories have expanded along with the proliferation of diverse news outlets, so that today we often see less coverage of events in the White House, No. 10, and the Kremlin, and more about the latest cancer research and developments in the popular arts, the concern about that tendency may arise primarily from the fact that it poses a challenge to old-fashioned (male?) assumptions about what constitutes 'real' or hard news. The amount of news shown on public-service TV in OECD countries has tripled over the past thirty years, not contracted. Three-quarters of all Europeans watch TV news every day, up from half three decades earlier. Even in the United States, the country where criticism of the quality of journalism has been harshest, C-SPAN coexists with MTV, the *New York Times* with the *New York Post*, the *Jerry Springer* show with *Nightline*, and the *Atlantic Monthly* with *Playboy*. The diversification of the market has meant that in many sectors, quality journalism, serious electoral news, and thoughtful coverage of policy debates have remained strong and flourishing, along with the tabloid trash.

POSTMODERN CAMPAIGNING

Campaigns have been transformed by these changes in the news industry and also by the widespread adoption of professional political marketing. As with developments in the media, new forms of electioneering essentially supplement, rather than replace, older techniques.

This book conceptualizes the evolution of these developments as stages, representing the premodern, modern, and postmodern eras of campaigning. The traditional techniques of door-to-door party canvassing, town meetings and local hustings, volunteer grassroots labour, community mobilization, and leadership tours with standard stump speeches, supplemented by a partisan-leaning press, were the primary forms of campaign communication at least until the 1950s and the rise of the television age.

The modern campaign, which predominated from the early 1960s until the late 1980s, was characterized by greater professionalization as more specialist advisors were employed by central party headquarters and the techniques of public-opinion polling and market research were brought into political marketing. The campaigns lengthened and costs rose as volunteer labour was displaced by hired guns. The central focus of attention became the publicity generated in television studios. The development of political-marketing techniques raised fears of a widening rift, with the politicians, surrounded by a coterie of professional advisors, increasingly isolated from direct contact with the voters.

The growth of postmodern campaigning, which began in many countries with the rise of the Internet and other new media in the 1990s, has the potential to restore some of the older forms of campaign interactivity. Innovations such as party intranets, online discussion groups, party Web sites, e-mail, and even 'old' media in new guises, such as talk radio, can be characterized as located somewhere between the traditional and modern forms of campaigning. The new types of interactivity are still in their development stages, and such channels have progressed much further in those societies that are more fully wired, such as the United States, Sweden, and Finland, than in others like Italy and Portugal. But analysis of Internet users suggests that the newer forms of campaign communication are supplementing the older ones, rather than replacing them. Even in the United States, the proportion of citizens active in the traditional forms of campaigning has remained remarkably stable in the postwar era. Political uses of the Internet, while primarily further empowering the most active, add another layer of complexity to elections.

The Impact on Civic Engagement

How have structural developments in political communications influenced political knowledge, trust, and mobilization? The more pessimistic scenario suggests that the news media in general, and television news in particular, have fuelled political disenchantment. Much of the literature, however, has focused on changes in the news industry without looking directly at public opinion.

The analysis in this book suggests two main conclusions. The weaker version of the media malaise thesis claims that a consistent pattern of negative news erodes *specific* support for particular leaders, governments, and policies – for example, that extensive coverage of violent crime can increase support for the death penalty, or that bloody pictures of school shootings can diminish support for the National Rifle Association. From the evidence reviewed here, that weaker claim does seem convincing. Chapter 9 has shown that a persistently Euroskeptic press did damage early public confidence in the euro. News coverage of European Community affairs usually was quite limited, and most of the routine European Union business went unreported. When EU affairs were covered, however, newspapers and television tended to provide a steady diet of bad news about Brussels. The extent of the bias was by no means large, but it was consistent. When the public read stories about the EU, they were more likely to be accounts of inefficiency, incompetence, and failure than of European cooperation and good governance. Moreover, that influenced the public: The monthly fluctuations in the direction of news coverage of the euro were significantly related to public opinion on the issue. Negative news probably reduced public support for the new currency.

But does attention to the news media appear to produce any deeper signs of civic malaise in Europe or in the United States? After all, public support for particular issues, leaders, and governments can be expected to rise and fall as part of 'normal' politics, without thereby undermining people's deep-rooted faith in the political system. The stronger version of the media malaise argument claims that news coverage directly harms public engagement – for example, that strategic frames and negative news activate political cynicism.

The second major conclusion from this study runs contrary to the media malaise thesis. The survey evidence from the United States and western Europe consistently fails to support the claim that attention to the news media in general, and television news in particular, contributes to deep-rooted indicators of civic malaise and erosion of diffuse support for the political system.

Successive tests have established that those most exposed to the news media and party campaigns consistently proved more knowledgeable, not less; more trusting towards government and the political system, not less; and more likely to participate in election campaigns, not less. These positive associations were found in a succession of models, in Europe and in the United States, despite a battery of structural and attitudinal controls for factors that plausibly could have affected media use and civic engagement. The association between use of the news media and civic engagement often was only modest. Given the limited measures available to gauge news exposure, however, the fact that the results proved significant and remarkably consistent across different data sets, in different years, in different countries, and with different dependent variables, increases our confidence in the reliability of the results. No single finding can be regarded as decisive, for there is no elegant and succinct way to test media malaise, but the weight of the cumulative evidence was ultimately persuasive.

Therefore, even if we accept, as a working assumption, the media malaise claim that the structures in the news industry and the patterns of political coverage have changed in recent decades, that still does not mean that the news media contribute to civic malaise. Let us assume the worst, namely, that political news has become more negative, that campaign stories commonly adopt a strategic frame, that the popular press and tabloid TV devote more attention to gaudy sensationalism than to serious public affairs, and that the Internet has far more sites devoted to porn than politics. Yet, even if we go along with the multiple criticisms of modern journalism, the survey evidence demonstrates that attention to the news media is not associated with public ignorance, political cynicism, and electoral apathy. If there have been systematic changes in journalism, they have not had the dismal effects on civic engagement that so many fear.

A VIRTUOUS CIRCLE?

Certain potential criticisms of this argument deserve special attention. One response to the European evidence might be that perhaps the media malaise effect is a case of 'American exceptionalism'. After all, previous studies in Europe had found little empirical support for media malaise.[3] Differences in news systems, historical experiences, and political cultures could perhaps have made the United States different from other postindustrial societies. But a direct examination of survey evidence from the United States has provided no support for the media malaise thesis at the individual level. Those most exposed to the news media and campaigns in America proved to be more politically engaged, not less, a pattern remarkably similar to that in Europe, thus strengthening the conviction that we have uncovered reliable patterns that are sufficiently robust to permit generalizations, and indeed can be found in many postindustrial societies. Attention to the news media proved to be either neutral or positively linked to a wide range of indicators of civic engagement in the United States and Europe. People who regularly watched, read, or surfed for news usually had greater political knowledge, trust, and participation, even after controlling for social background and prior political interest.

Another potential criticism might be that the findings could be due to methodological artifact. It could be argued that we have analyzed only individual-level effects of exposure to the news media among the most regular readers and viewers, whereas there might well be pervasive and diffuse effects on society as a whole. But when long-term trends in American public opinion were examined, they provided no support for the diffuse theories of media malaise that suggest that the news culture became more cynical after the events of Vietnam and Watergate in the late 1960s and early 1970s. Attention to campaign coverage and levels of campaign activism proved largely stable, rather than experiencing a gradual erosion over time, or a sudden decline, in the post-Vietnam years. Americans' trust in government has fluctuated sharply in recent decades, with peaks and troughs, but it has not experienced a steady and continuous fall. Electoral turnout and interest were relatively low in the early 1960s, then experienced a higher plateau in the heated politics of the 1960s, but returned to the status quo ante in subsequent decades. Given the slippery periodization of the diffuse media malaise thesis, some of the trends could perhaps be interpreted as supporting that thesis, but the timing of events remained loose and untidy, and the evidence was far from consistent across all the indicators of civic engagement in America.

The last and potentially most telling criticism of the interpretation presented in this book is that there are serious problems in using cross-sectional surveys to examine the causal direction of dynamic processes. That is true. Correlation, no matter how consistent, does not equal causation. Controlled experiments offer the only satisfactory way to resolve causality, and that probably will be the most productive avenue for further research.

As mentioned in the introduction, the consistent association between use of the news media and civic engagement is open to three alternative explanations. Critics could argue that the associations established in this study could flow in a single one-way direction, because of a *selection effect*, from prior political attitudes to media use. In other words, because some people are interested in public policy and international affairs, they could decide to read the *New York Times* and watch CNN. That is indeed plausible, especially given the range of choices about where to go and what to do in a multichannel multimedia environment.

Alternatively, because of a *media effect*, the direction of causality could flow one-way from habitual news use to civic engagement. Someone who regularly watches the evening news or reads a paper or listens to the radio (for whatever reason) could be expected to learn more about public affairs, reducing the costs of political involvement, such as casting a vote.

But it is unclear theoretically why either of these flows should operate only in a single direction, and it seems more plausible and realistic to assume an iterative and interactive process, with two-way flow. That is to say, we probably do turn on C-SPAN, skim the Sunday papers, catch the radio headlines, or surf for online news because of our prior interest in learning about events in Washington, London, and Brussels, because we are already engaged in the political process, and because of long-standing news habits. But at the same time, over the long term, repeated exposure to the news seems likely to improve our understanding of public affairs, to increase our capacity and motivation to become active in the political process, and thereby to strengthen civic engagement. Far from seeing a negative impact, the most convincing way to account for the persistent patterns emerging from this study is that attention to the news media acts as a virtuous circle: The most politically knowledgeable, trusting, and participatory are most likely to tune in to public-affairs coverage. And those most attentive to coverage of public affairs become more engaged in civic life. This interpretation remains theoretical, for we cannot prove causation, but it is fully consistent with the association we have established between news exposure and positive indicators of civic engagement.

If the actives are further activated by political communications, why are the apathetic not similarly reinforced in their apathy? The simplest answer would be that those less engaged in politics are naturally immunized against the influences of news media messages by a triple process: First, when those who are less interested encounter political news, they are more likely to turn over, turn off, or click to another site. In a multimedia multichannel environment, with a remote or mouse in hand, the idea of a captive audience is as passé as the phonograph. Why listen to pundits and pollsters when there are so many alternative channels and programs? Second, even though some of the disengaged may continue to watch and read simply from routine habit, because they lack prior interest they probably pay little attention to political coverage. Lastly, even if they watch and pay attention, the disengaged are less likely to regard political news as credible, because trust in the news media and in government go hand in hand.[4]

The result is that the ratcheting effect of political communication functions in a positive direction. Focusing only on the structure of the news industry or on the content of coverage, while neglecting the reaction of the audience, leads to many fundamental misconceptions inherent in media malaise accounts. The public is not passively absorbing whatever journalists and politicians tell them, not simply taking everything at face value. Rather, because of increased cognitive skills and greater diversification of media outlets, the public is actively sifting, sorting, and thereby constructing political impressions in line with their prior predispositions. This conceptualization harks back to an earlier tradition that had long emphasized the role of reinforcement in political communication. A virtuous circle represents an iterative process gradually exerting a positive impact on democracy. The causal steps in this process cannot be demonstrated, any more than we can examine the lifelong socialization process whereby the family, workplace, and community shape political attitudes. The effects are understood as diffuse, operating cumulatively over a lifetime of exposure to the news, rather than being specific to the impact of particular media messages. Nevertheless, this theory provides a reasonable interpretation that makes sense of the consistently positive association between use of the news media and civic engagement encountered throughout this study.

This view also receives support from some findings in experimental research in which groups in Britain were exposed to positive and negative television news, with full details about the methodology and results published elsewhere.[5] Only controlled experiments can provide convincing evidence to resolve issues of causality and thus overcome many of the limitations of cross-sectional survey research. Nevertheless, the findings show that, even after applying a battery of controls for social and attitudinal factors, watching *negative* television news had no impact on party preferences, whereas exposure to *positive* news significantly increased that party's support.[6] If we can extrapolate from this context, this strengthens the argument for an interactive two-way virtuous circle, in which prior positive attitudes stimulate attention to the news and campaign messages, and that attention reinforces positive engagement. Through repeatedly reading or watching news about politics and public affairs, broadly defined, people gradually acquire practical information that helps them to make voting decisions, that prompts them to get involved in community organizations, and that encourages them to trust the political process. Through the virtuous circle, the news media serve to further activate those who are already most active. Those who are less predisposed towards political life will be more immune to political messages.

If the pool of activists is gradually shrinking, so that society is dividing between the information-rich and information-poor, then that process legitimately should raise fears about its effects on mass democracy. But if, as argued here, in postindustrial societies the news media have become diversified over the years, in terms of channels, availability, levels, and even the definition of news, this means that today information about public affairs (broadly defined) is reaching audiences over a wider range of societal levels and with more disparate interests. In this situation, the effects of the virtuous circle should gradually ripple out to broader sectors of society. Such an effect is still consistent with other trends in society, such as increasingly critical attitudes among citizens, as discussed elsewhere.[7] A citizenry that is better informed and more highly educated, with higher cognitive skills and more sources of information, may well become increasingly critical of governing institutions, with declining affective loyalties towards traditional representative bodies such as parties and parliaments. But increasing criticism from citizens does not necessarily reduce civic engagement; indeed, it can have the contrary effect.

The conclusions reached here do not diminish the gravity of many major problems that threaten the vitality of democracy in postindustrial societies, whether low levels of electoral turnout in the United States and Switzerland, violent conflict in Northern Ireland and the Basque region, pervasive political cynicism in Italy and Japan, or endemic political corruption in Mexico and Turkey. The multiple hazards facing transitional political systems like Russia, Indonesia, and Nigeria, stranded midway between an authoritarian past and an uncertain future, are even more threatening and intransigent. But these problems can best be understood as rooted in deep-seated flaws within the political systems and institutional arrangements in these societies, rather than as representing general problems common across democracies, still less problems caused by political communication per se. Blaming the news media is easy, but ultimately that is a deeply conservative strategy, especially in a culture skeptical of regulation of the free press, and it diverts attention from the urgent need for real reforms to democratic institutions, which should have our undivided attention.

Technical Appendix

EUROBAROMETER SURVEYS

Eurobarometer surveys for DGX: Public-opinion analysis for the European Commission was conducted by INRA (Europe), a European network of market and public-opinion research agencies.

The basic sample design applied in all member states was a multi-stage random (probability) design. In each EU country, a number of sampling points were drawn, with probability proportional to population size (for the total coverage of the country) and to population density. The points were drawn systematically from each of the 'administrative regional units' after stratification by individual unit and type of area. They thus represented the whole territory of the member states according to EUROSTAT-NUTS II (or equivalent) and according to the distributions of the resident populations of the respective EU nationalities in terms of metropolitan, urban, and rural areas. In each of the selected sampling points, a starting address was drawn at random. Further addresses were selected at every N-th address by standard random-route procedures. In each household, the respondent was drawn at random. All interviews were face-to-face in people's homes and in the appropriate national language. The samples usually involved just over 1,000 respondents per country (except for Luxembourg and Northern Ireland), and mega-surveys increased the number of respondents to just over 3,000 per country.

For all information about Eurobarometer questionnaires, data sets, published reports, and technical fieldwork details, see europa.eu.int. Data are available from the Zentral Archiv (Universität Köln), as well as the ICPSR and Essex data archives.

CONTENT ANALYSIS

The content analysis was published in the monthly *Monitoring Euro-media* reports (no. 1–33) from January 1995 to September 1997. The content analysis was conducted by Report International in Brussels and was commissioned by the Unit for Public Opinion and Research, Directorate General for Information, Communication, Culture and Audiovisual, DG X.A2, European Commission, Brussels.

NEWSPAPER SOURCES

The content analysis was derived from the following sources, selected to come as close as possible to 50% of the daily newspaper circulation in the member states. National newspapers were included in all 15 countries, along with the most important regional papers, based on their geographic spread. During the whole period, the study examined the contents of 189 major newspapers every month, analyzing in total just under 200,000 articles.

BELGIUM
L'Echo
De Standaard
Het Laatste Nieuws
Gazet van Antwerpen
La Derniere Heure
Knack Magazine
Le Vif/L'Express
De Morgen
The Bulletin
Financieel Ekonomische Tijd
Le Soir
La Libre Belgique
Het Volk
Vers l'Avenir
Trends
De Loyd
Het Nieuwsblad
Het Belang van Limburg

DENMARK
Jyllands Posten
Politiken

Berlinske Tidende
Ekstra Bladet
Politiken Weekly
Borsen
BT
Information
Det Fri Aktuelt

FRANCE
Les Echos
Le Figaro
Libération
Le Parisien
Sud-Ouest
L'Est Républicain
L'Humanité
Le Nouvel Economiste
L'Express
Nouvel Observateur
L'Expansion
La Tribune Desfosses
Le Monde
France-Soir
Ouest France
La Voix du Nord
La Croix
Capital
La Vie Française
Le Point
Le Monde Diplomatique
Le Berry Centre France

GERMANY
Handelsblatt
Frankfurter Rundschau
Suddeutsche Zeitung
Sachsische Zeitung
Berliner Zeitung
Stuttgarter Zeitung
Wirschaftswoche
Welt am Sonntag

Der Spiegel
Stern
Blick dursch die Wirtschaft
Capital
Westdeutsche Allgemeine Zeitung
Hannoversche Allgemeine Zeitung
Frankfurter Allgemeine Zeitung
Die Welt
Bild Zeitung
General-Anzeiger
Kölner Stadtanzeiger
TagesZeitung
Die Zeit
Bild am Sonntag
Focus
Manager Magazin
Rheinischer Merkur

UNITED KINGDOM
The Financial Times
The Independent on Sunday
The Sunday Express
The Daily Telegraph
The Scotsman
The Daily Record
The Sun
The Evening Standard
The Economist
The European
The Independent
The Times
The Guardian
The Sunday Telegraph
The Daily Star
The Daily Mirror
The Daily Mail
The Observer
European Business Review
The Spectator

GREECE
Kathimerini
Ta Nea
El Typos
Express
Rizospastis
Eleftherotypia
Ethnos
Economicos Tahidromos
Naftemboriki
Vima

IRELAND
The Irish Times
Comhar
Sunday Business Post
Business and Finance
Sunday Tribune
Sunday Independent

ITALY
Il Sole 23 Ore
La Repubblica
L'Unità
La Nazione
Mondo Economico
L'Expresso
Il Giorno
La Stampa
Corriere della Sera
Il Giornale
Il Resto del Carlino
Panorama
Il Messagero
Il Mondo

THE NETHERLANDS
Het Financieel Dagblad
Het Algemeen Dagblad
De Telegraaf

Het Parool
De Gelderlander
HP De Tijd
Management Team
NRC Handelsblad
De Volkskrant
Trouw
Het Nieuwsblad van het Norrden
Elsevier
Vrij Nederland

SPAIN
El Mundo
El Periodico
Expansion
Diario 16
El Correo Español
Cambio 16
El Pais
La Vanguardia
Cinco Dias
ABC
Tiempo
Gaceta de los Negocios

LUXEMBOURG
Luxembourger Wort
Tageblatt
La Républicain Lorrain
Lundi Matin

PORTUGAL
Diario de Noticias
Jornal de Noticias
Diario Economico
O Primeiro de Janeiro
O Independente
Exame
Semanario
Publico
Correio Da Manha

Semanario Economico
Expresso
O Dia
A Capital

AUSTRIA
Die Presse
Kurier
Neue Kronen Zeitung
Der Standard
Kleine Zeitung

FINLAND
Helsingin Sanomat
Iltalehti
Kauppalehti
Huvudstads Bladet
Turun Sanomat
Ilta-Sanomat
Kaleva
Aamulehti

SWEDEN
Dagens Nyheter
Expressen
Dagens Industri
Sydsvenska Dagbladet
FinasTidnigen
Aftonbladet
Svenska Dagbladet
Goteborgs-Posten
Kvalls Posten

TELEVISION NEWS SOURCES

For monthly trend analysis, the television data were collected from the main evening news and current-affairs programs in six countries: Belgium, France, Germany, Italy, Spain, and the United Kingdom. The study recorded the main news programs in these societies, analyzing almost 600 programs per month. During the course of the thirty-three-month period the study analyzed around 19,000 programs in total, representing about 10,000 hours of broadcasting. The study examined whether news stories in these programs contained information on the European Union and its policies, and almost 500 EU-related stories were coded every month, following the same process used for newspaper articles. The following programs from six countries were included in the content analysis. All programs were daily unless otherwise specified.

BELGIUM
BRTN
   19:30 *Journaal*
   22:00 *Ter Zake*
   20:00 Monday *Laatavond Journal*
   21:50 Wednesday *Op de Koop*
   21:35 Thursday *Panorama*
   11:00 Sunday *De Zevende*
RTBF
   18:30 *Info Première*
   19:30 *Journal*
   20:00 *JT Soir*
   12:25 Saturday *Objectif Europe*
   12:00 Sunday *Mise au Point*

FRANCE
TF1
   20:00 *Journal*
   19:00 Sunday *7 sur 7*
France 2
   20:00 *Journal*
   22:30 Tuesday *Ca se discute*
   12:00 Sunday *Revue de Presse*

GERMANY
ARD
   20:00 *Tagesschau*
   21:00 *Report*
   22:30 *Tagesthemen*
   22:15 Thursday *Was Nun*
   21:30 Friday *Pro + Contra*
   13:15 Saturday *Europa-magazin*
   12:00 Sunday *Presseclub*
   22:35 Sunday *ZAK*

ZDF
  19:00 *Heute*
  21:00 Monday *Auslands-journal*
  21:45 *Heute*
  23:45 *Heute Nacht*
  19:00 Sunday *Bonn Direkt*

ITALY
RAI1
  20:00 *Telegiornale*
  22:10 *Telegiornale*

SPAIN
TVE
  18:00 *Telediario 1*
  21:00 *Telediario 2*
  19:00 Sunday *Cite con la tele Europa*
  19:30 Sunday *Informe Semanal*
  21:45 Sunday *Informativo*

UNITED KINGDOM
BBC1
  18:00 *6 O'clock News*
  21:00 *9 O'clock News*
  23:00 Thursday *Question Time*
  09:30 Sunday *Breakfast with Frost*
BBC2
  23:30 *Newsnight*
  20:00 Saturday/Sunday *News*

SELECTION OF ARTICLES

Articles containing information on the European Union and its policies were selected from these sources. A random selection of 50% of stories was then used for analysis. Each article was coded for source and country and the type of information it contained (facts, opinions, or comment).

ISSUES

Articles were classified into 21 'issues' using multiple codes:

Foreign policy
Economic and financial affairs

Competition policy
Social policy (employment, social affairs, and health)
Industrial policy
Agriculture policy
Transport policy
Administrative matters (e.g., EU personnel)
Audiovisual policy
Information, communication, and cultural policy
Environmental policy
Science, research and development policy
Telecommunications and information technology
Fisheries policy
Regional policy
Energy policy
Education policy
Consumer policy
EU institutions (e.g., the Commission)
Justice and internal affairs
Evolution of the EU (e.g., expansion)

DIRECTION

Selected articles were subsequently coded for 'direction' in terms of evaluative tone, from the perspective of the main European actor, such as the Commission or the Intergovernmental Conference. The directional codes ranged from very negative (1) to very positive (5). The direction was estimated for each separate issue contained in an article. A neutral code was given when positive and negative arguments were in balance or when information was neither positive nor negative.

Notes

Preface

1. Pippa Norris, John Curtice, David Sanders, Margaret Scammell, and Holli A. Semetko. 1999. *On Message: Communicating the Campaign*. London: Sage.
2. Related arguments about the causes of public disenchantment with public affairs were developed earlier: Pippa Norris (ed.). 1999. *Critical Citizens: Global Support for Democratic Governance*. Oxford: Oxford University press.

Chapter 1 The News Media and Democracy

1. See Pippa Norris (ed.). 1999. *Critical Citizens: Global Support for Democratic Governance*. Oxford: Oxford University Press; Susan J. Pharr and Robert D. Putnam (eds.). 2000. *Disaffected Democrats: What's Troubling the Trilateral Countries*. Princeton, NJ: Princeton University Press.
2. Joseph S. Nye, Jr., Philip P. Zelikow, and David C. King. 1997. *Why People Don't Trust Government*. Cambridge, MA: Harvard University Press; Everett Carll Ladd and Karlyn H. Bowman. 1998. *What's Wrong? A Survey of American Satisfaction and Complaint*. Washington, DC: AEI Press; Robert D. Putnam. 2000. *Bowling Alone*. New York: Simon & Schuster.
3. Jack Hayward. 1995. *The Crisis of Representation in Europe*. London: Frank Cass; Svein S. Andersen and Kjell A. Eliassen. 1996. *The European Union: How Democratic Is It?* London: Sage.
4. See Pippa Norris (ed.). 1999. *Critical Citizens: Global Support for Democratic Governance*. Oxford: Oxford University Press.
5. This study focuses on the effects of news journalism and therefore excludes sociological theories that are concerned primarily with the impact of watching television *entertainment* on matters like social trust, community engagement, and voluntary activism. For a discussion, see Robert D. Putnam. 1995. 'Tuning In, Tuning Out: The Strange Disappearance of Social Capital in America.' *PS: Political Science and Politics* 28(4):664–83.
6. James Curran and Jean Seaton. 1991. *Power Without Responsibility: The Press and Broadcasting in Britain*. London: Routledge.
7. See Shearon A. Lowery and Melvin L. DeFleur. 1995. *Milestones in Mass Communications Research*. New York: Longman.

8. Steven Starker. 1991. *Evil Empires: Crusading Against the Mass Media*. London: Transaction.

9. Kurt Lang and Gladys Lang. 1966. 'The Mass Media and Voting.' In *Reader in Public Opinion and Communication*, ed. Bernard Berelson and M. Janowitz. New York: Free Press. According to the Langs, 'television's style in chronicling political events can affect the fundamental orientation of the voter towards his government. . . . The media, we contend, can stir up in individuals defensive reactions by their emphasis on crisis and conflict in lieu of clarifying normal decision-making processes.'

10. Michael Robinson. 1976. 'Public Affairs Television and the Growth of Political Malaise: The Case of "The Selling of the Pentagon".' *American Political Science Review* 70(3):409–32, p. 425.

11. Michael J. Robinson and Margaret A. Sheehan. 1983. *Over the Wire and on TV: CBS and UPI in Campaign '80*. New York: Russell Sage Foundation.

12. Lee Becker, Idowu A. Sobowale, and William Casey, Jr. 1979. 'Newspaper and Television Dependencies: Effects on Evaluations of Public Officials.' *Journal of Broadcasting* 23(4):465–75; Lee Becker and D. Charles Whitney. 1980. 'Effects of Media Dependencies: Audience Assessment of Government.' *Communication Research* 7(1):95–120; Jack McLeod, Jane D. Brown, Lee B. Becker, and Dean A. Ziemke. 1977. 'Decline and Fall at the White House: A Longitudinal Analysis of Communication Effects.' *Communication Research* 4:3–22; Arthur Miller, Edie H. Goldenberg, and Lutz Erbring. 1979. 'Type-Set Politics: The Impact of Newspapers on Public Confidence.' *American Political Science Review* 73:67–84.

13. Michel Crozier, Samuel P. Huntington, and Joji Watanuki. 1975. *The Crisis of Democracy: Report on the Governability of Democracies to the Trilateral Commission*. New York: New York University Press.

14. George Gerbner and Larry Gross. 1976. 'Living with Television: The Violence Profile.' *Journal of Communication* 16(2):173–99; George Gerbner, Larry Gross, Michael Morgan, and Nancy Signorielli. 1982. 'Charting the Mainstream: Television's Contribution to Political Orientations.' *Journal of Communication* 32(2):100–27; George Gerbner, Larry Gross, Michael Morgan, and Nancy Signorielli. 1984. 'Political Correlates of Television Viewing.' *Public Opinion Quarterly* 48(1):283–300; George Gerbner. 1990. 'Advancing on the Path of Righteousness.' In *Cultivation Analysis: New Directions in Media Effects Research*, ed. N. Signorielli and M. Morgan. Newbury Park, CA: Sage.

15. Austin Ranney. 1983. *Channels of Power: The Impact of Television on American Politics*, pp. 86–7. New York: Basic Books.

16. Robert M. Entman. 1989. *Democracy without Citizens: Media and the Decay of American Politics*. Oxford: Oxford University Press.

17. Neil Postman. 1985. *Amusing Ourselves to Death*. London: Methuen.

18. Roderick Hart. 1994. *Seducing America*. Oxford University Press; Roderick Hart. 1996. 'Easy Citizenship: Television's Curious Legacy.' In *The Media and Politics*, ed. Kathleen H. Jamieson. *Annals of the American Academy of Political and Social Sciences*, vol. 546.

19. Neal Gabler. 1998. *Life the Movie: How Entertainment Conquered Reality*. New York: Knopf.

20. Larry Sabato. 1991. *Feeding Frenzy: How Attack Journalism Has Transformed American Politics.* New York: Free Press.

21. Thomas E. Patterson. 1993. *Out of Order.* New York: Knopf; Thomas E. Patterson. 1996. 'Bad News, Bad Governance.' In *The Media and Politics,* ed. Kathleen H. Jamieson. *Annals of the American Academy of Political and Social Sciences,* vol. 546.

22. Michael J. Robinson and Margaret A. Sheehan. 1983. *Over the Wire and on TV: CBS and UPI in Campaign '80.* New York: Russell Sage Foundation.

23. Joseph N. Cappella and Kathleen H. Jamieson. 1996. 'News Frames, Political Cynicism and Media Cynicism.' In *The Media and Politics,* ed. Kathleen H. Jamieson, pp. 71–84. *Annals of the American Academy of Political and Social Sciences,* vol. 546; Joseph N. Cappella and Kathleen H. Jamieson. 1997. *Spiral of Cynicism: The Press and the Public Good.* New York: Oxford University Press.

24. Kenneth Dautrich and Thomas H. Hartley. 1999. *How the News Media Fail American Voters: Causes, Consequences and Remedies.* New York: Columbia University Press.

25. James Fallows. 1996. *Breaking the News: How the Media Undermine American Democracy.* New York: Pantheon.

26. Michael Schudson. 1995. *The Power of News.* Cambridge, MA: Harvard University Press.

27. William A. Hachten. 1998. *The Troubles of Journalism: A Critical Look at What's Right and Wrong with the Press.* Hillsdale, NJ: Lawrence Erlbaum.

28. See, for example, Pippa Norris. 1997. 'News of the World.' In *Politics and the Press: The News Media and Their Influences,* ed. Pippa Norris. Boulder, CO: Lynne Rienner; Hamid Mowlana. 1997. *Global Information and World Communication,* 2nd ed. London: Sage.

29. Marvin Kalb. 1998. 'The Rise of the New News.' Discussion Paper D-34. Cambridge, MA: The Joan Shorenstein Center on the Press, Politics and Public Policy, John F. Kennedy School of Government.

30. William F. Baker and George Dessart. 1998. *Down the Tube.* New York: Basic Books.

31. Pew Research Center for the People and the Press. 1999. *Striking the Balance: Audience Interests, Business Pressures and Journalists' Values.* Washington, DC: Pew Research Center for the People and the Press.

32. Y. Achille and J. I. Bueno. 1994. *Les télévisions publiques en quête d'avenir.* Presses Universitaires de Grenoble.

33. Jürgen Habermas. 1984. *The Theory of Communicative Action.* London: Heinemann; Jürgen Habermas. 1998. *The Structural Transformation of the Public Sphere.* Cambridge, MA: MIT Press; Peter Dahlgren and Colin Sparks. 1997. *Communication and Citizenship.* London: Routledge; Peter Dahlgren. 1995. *Television and the Public Sphere.* London: Sage; Tony Weymouth and Bernard Lamizet. 1996. *Markets and Myths: Forces for Change in the European Media.* London: Longman.

34. Winfried Schulz. 1997. 'Changes in the Mass Media and the Public Sphere.' *Javnost – The Public* 4(2):57–69; Winfried Schulz. 1998. 'Media Change and the Political Effects of Television: Americanization of the Political Culture?' *Communications* 23(4):527–43.

35. Max Kaase. 2000. 'Germany.' In *Democracy and the Media: A Comparative Perspective,* ed. Richard Gunther and Anthony Mughan. New York: Cambridge University Press.

36. Neal Gabler. 1998. *Life the Movie: How Entertainment Conquered Reality*, p. 61. New York: Knopf.
37. James Lull and Stephen Hinerman (eds.). 1997. *Media Scandals*. Cambridge: Polity Press.
38. Richard Davis and Diane Owen. 1998. *New Media and American Politics*, p. 185. New York: Oxford University Press.
39. Graham Murdock and Peter Golding. 1989. 'Information Poverty and Political Inequality: Citizenship in the Age of Privatised Communications.' *Journal of Communication* 39:180–93.
40. Kevin A. Hill and John E. Hughes. 1998. *Cyberpolitics: Citizen Activism in the Age of the Internet*, p. 44. New York: Rowman & Littlefield.
41. David L. Swanson and Paolo Mancini. 1996. *Politics, Media, and Modern Democracy: An International Study of Innovations in Electoral Campaigning and Their Consequences*. New York: Praeger; David Butler and Austin Ranney. 1992. *Electioneering*. Oxford: Clarendon Press; Shaun Bowler and David Farrell (eds.). 1992. *Electoral Strategies and Political Marketing*. London: Macmillan.
42. For a study of this process in Britain, see Pippa Norris, John Curtice, David Sanders, Margaret Scammell, and Holli A. Semetko. 1999. *On Message: Communicating the Campaign*. London: Sage; Pippa Norris. 1997. 'Political Communications.' In *Developments in British Politics 5*, ed. Patrick Dunleavy, Andrew Gamble, Ian Holliday, and Gillian Peele. Basingstoke: Macmillan.
43. See, for example, Nicholas Jones. 1995. *Soundbites and Spin Doctors*. London: Cassell; Martin Rosenbaum. 1997. *From Soapbox to Soundbite: Party Political Campaigning since 1945*. London: Macmillan.
44. Bob Franklin. 1994. *Packaging Politics*. London: Arnold.
45. Dennis Kavanagh. 1995. *Election Campaigning: The New Marketing of Politics*. Oxford: Blackwell; Margaret Scammell. 1995. *Designer Politics: How Elections Are Won*. London: Macmillan.
46. Barbara Pfetsch. 1996. 'Convergence through Privatization? Changing Media Environments and Televised Politics in Germany.' *European Journal of Communication* 8(3):425–50; Karen Siune. 1998. 'Is Broadcasting Policy Becoming Redundant?' In *The Media in Question: Popular Culture and Public Interests*, ed. Kees Brants, Joke Hermes, and Lizbet van Zoonen. London: Sage; Ralph Negrine and Stylianos Papathanassopoulos. 1996. 'The "Americanization" of Political Communications: A Critique.' *Harvard International Journal of Press/Politics* 1(2):45–62.
47. Stephen Ansolabehere and Shanto Iyengar. 1995. *Going Negative: How Political Advertisments Shrink and Polarize the Electorate*. New York: Free Press; Lynda Lee Kaid and Christina Holtz-Bacha. 1995. *Political Advertising in Western Democracies*. Thousand Oaks, CA: Sage; Kathleen H. Jamieson. 1992. *Dirty Politics*. Oxford: Oxford University Press; Kathleen H. Jamieson. 1984. *Packaging the Presidency: A History and Criticism of Presidential Advertising*. New York: Oxford University Press; Karen S. Johnson-Cartee and Gary A. Copeland. 1991. *Negative Political Advertising: Coming of Age*. Hillsdale, NJ: Lawrence Erlbaum.
48. Jay G. Blumler and Michael Gurevitch. 1995. *The Crisis of Public Communication*. London: Routledge. See also Jay Blumler. 1990. 'Elections, the Media and the Modern Publicity Process.' In *Public Communication: The New Imperatives*, ed.

M. Ferguson. London: Sage; Jay G. Blumler. 1997. 'Origins of the Crisis of Communication for Citizenship.' *Political Communication* 14(4):395–404.

49. Pippa Norris. 1996. 'Does Television Erode Social Capital? A Reply to Putnam.' *PS: Political Science and Politics* 29(3); Pippa Norris. 1997. *Electoral Change since 1945.* Oxford: Blackwell; Pippa Norris. 2000. 'Television and Civic Malaise.' In *Disaffected Democrats: What's Troubling the Trilateral Democracies,* ed. Susan J. Pharr and Robert D. Putnam. Princeton, NJ: Princeton University Press; Pippa Norris, John Curtice, David Sanders, Margaret Scammell, and Holli A. Semetko. 1999. *On Message: Communicating the Campaign.* London: Sage.

50. Kenneth Newton. 1997. 'Politics and the News Media: Mobilisation or Videomalaise?' In *British Social Attitudes: The 14th Report,* ed. Roger Jowell, John Curtice, Alison Park, Katarina Thomson, and Lindsay Brook. Aldershot, UK: Ashgate; Kenneth Newton. 1999. 'Mass Media Effects: Mobilization or Media Malaise?' *British Journal of Political Science* 29:577–99.

51. Christina Holtz-Bacha. 1990. 'Videomalaise Revisited: Media Exposure and Political Alienation in West Germany.' *European Journal of Communication* 5:73–85.

52. John Curtice, Rüdiger Schmitt-Beck, and Peter Schrott. 1998. 'Do the Media Matter?' Paper presented at the Annual Meeting of the Midwest Political Science Association, Chicago. The study found that those most attentive to TV news or newspapers proved more likely to be politically interested and engaged in Britain, Germany, Japan, Spain, and the United States.

53. See Stephen Earl Bennett, Staci L. Rhine, Richard S. Flickinger, and Linda L. M. Bennett. 1999. 'Videomalaise Revisited: Reconsidering the Relation between the Public's View of the Media and Trust in Government.' *Harvard International Journal of Press/Politics* 4(4):8–23.

54. See, for example, Frank Esser. 1999. 'Tabloidization of News: A Comparative Analysis of Anglo-American and German Press Journalism.' *European Journal of Communication* 14(3):291–324. See Chapter 4 for a fuller discussion of this point.

55. The surveys of journalists found no consensus about the relative importance of providing analytical coverage, acting as government watchdog, serving public entertainment, and reporting accurately or objectively. For example, the proportion of journalists who thought that their role as watchdog of government was 'very' or 'extremely' important ranged from 33% in Germany to 67% in the United States and 88% in Britain. See David H. Weaver. 1998. *The Global Journalist: News People Around the World,* pp. 466–7. Cresskill, NJ: Hampton Press.

56. Fritz Plassner, Christian Scheucher, and Christian Senft. 1999. 'Is There a European Style of Political Marketing?' In *The Handbook of Political Marketing,* ed. Bruce I. Newman. Thousand Oaks, CA: Sage.

57. Jay G. Blumler and Elihu Katz (eds.). 1974. *The Uses of Mass Communications: Current Perspectives on Gratifications Research.* Beverly Hills, CA: Sage.

Chapter 2 Evaluating Media Performance

1. David Beetham. 1994. *Defining and Measuring Democracy.* London: Sage.
2. Joseph A. Schumpeter. 1952. *Capitalism, Socialism and Democracy,* 4th ed. London: Allen & Unwin. Certain conceptions of the role of the news media draw more

strongly on direct or plebiscitary notions of democracy, particularly the recent public journalism movement in the United States emphasizing that news organizations need to reconnect with their communities to engage citizens in problemsolving. See, for example, Anthony J. Eksterowicz, Robert Roberts, and Adrian Clark. 1998. 'Public Journalism and Public Knowledge.' *Harvard International Journal of Press/Politics* 3(2):74–95. Nevertheless, the public journalism movement can also work within the liberal or representative conception of democracy used in this book.

3. See also Robert A. Dahl. 1956. *Preface to Democratic Theory*. University of Chicago Press; Robert A. Dahl. 1971. *Polyarchy: Participation and Opposition*. New Haven, CT: Yale University Press; Robert A. Dahl. 1989. *Democracy and Its Critics*. New Haven, CT: Yale University Press.

4. For a discussion of the conflict between 'classical' and 'realist' models of democracy and their implications for theories of the press, see Michael Schudson. 1995. 'The News Media and the Democratic Process.' In Michael Schudson. *The Power of News*. Cambridge, MA: Harvard University Press. For an alternative view, see Benjamin Barber. 1984. *Strong Democracy*. Berkeley: University of California Press.

5. Davis Beetham. 1994. *Defining and Measuring Democracy*. London: Sage.

6. See Freedom House. 1998. 'The Comparative Survey of Freedom, 1998.' *Freedom Review*.

7. See Denis McQuail. 1992. *Media Performance: Mass Communication and the Public Interest*. London: Sage.

8. Jürgen Habermas. 1984. *The Theory of Communicative Action*. London: Heinemann; Jürgen Habermas. 1998. *The Structural Transformation of the Public Sphere*. Cambridge, MA: MIT Press.

9. See Peter Dahlgren and Colin Sparks. 1997. *Communication and Citizenship*. London: Routledge; Peter Dahlgren. 1995. *Television and the Public Sphere*. London: Sage.

10. These standards are intended to apply to all the news media available to citizens within a polity, not to specific media outlets. What is important in this understanding is the availability of information and diverse political viewpoints across all channels of newspapers, television, radio, and Internet, rather than diversity of viewpoints within any particular media outlet.

11. Jay G. Blumler and Michael Gurevitch. 1995. *The Crisis of Public Communication*. London: Routledge.

12. Thomas Patterson. 1998. 'Political Roles of the Journalist.' In *The Politics of News: The News of Politics*, ed. Doris Graber, Denis McQuail, and Pippa Norris. Washington, DC: CQ Press.

13. See Christina Holtz-Bacha and Linda Lee Kaid. 1995. 'A Comparative Perspective on Political Advertising' (Table 2.4). In *Political Advertising in Western Democracies*, ed. Lynda Lee Kaid and Christina Holtz-Bacha. Thousand Oaks, CA: Sage.

14. Russell J. Dalton, Kazuhisa Kawakami, Holli A. Semetko, Hiroshisa Suzuki, and Katrin Voltmer. 1998. 'Partisan Cues in the Media: Cross-National Comparisons of Election Coverage.' Paper presented at the annual meeting of the Midwest Political Science Association, Chicago.

15. John Zaller. 1993. *The Nature and Origins of Mass Opinion*. New York: Cambridge University Press.

16. See, for example, George A. Donohue, Phillip Tichenor, and Clarice N. Olien. 1995. 'A Guard Dog Perspective on the Role of the Media.' *Journal of Communication* 45(2):115–28.

17. See the discussion in George A. Donohue, Phillip J. Tichenor, and Clarice N. Olien. 1995. 'A Guard Dog Perspective on the Role of the Media.' *Journal of Communication* 45(2):115–28; Renate Kocher. 1986. 'Bloodhounds or Missionaries: Role Definitions of German and British Journalists.' *European Journal of Communication* 1:43–64.

18. Pippa Norris. 1999. *Critical Citizens: Global Support for Democratic Governance*. Oxford: Oxford University Press.

19. Thomas E. Patterson. 1993. *Out of Order*. New York: Knopf.

20. Our conception is similar to the understanding of political knowledge in Arthur Lupia and Mathew D. McCubbins. 1998. *The Democratic Dilemma*. Cambridge: Cambridge University Press.

21. Paul F. Lazarsfeld, Bernard Berelson, and Hazel Gaudet. 1944. *The People's Choice: How the Voter Makes Up His Mind in a Presidential Campaign*. New York: Columbia University Press.

22. Robert D. Putnam. 1995. 'Tuning In, Tuning Out: The Strange Disappearance of Social Capital in America.' *PS: Political Science and Politics* 28(4):664–83.

23. Denis McQuail. 1992. *Media Performance: Mass Communication and the Public Interest*, p. 17. London: Sage.

24. See, for example, Jay G. Blumler (ed.). 1992. *Television and the Public Interest: Vulnerable Values in West European Broadcasting*. London: Sage.

25. See Michael Gurevitch and Jay G. Blumler. 1990. 'Political Communication Systems and Democratic Values.' In *Democracy and the Mass Media*, ed. Judith Lichtenberg. Cambridge University Press. There is a large literature on the ethical principles for individual journalists, such as issues of libel, privacy, and conflict of interest, but these differ from the broader normative criteria for the appropriate functioning of political communications in a democracy. See, for example, Elliot D. Cohen and Deni Elliott. 1997. *Journalism Ethics*. Santa Barbara, CA: ABC-Clio.

26. Fred S. Siebert, Theodore Peterson, and Wilbur Schram. 1984. *Four Theories of the Press*. Chicago: University of Illinois Press.

27. Denis McQuail. 1992. *Media Performance: Mass Communication and the Public Interest*, p. 17. London: Sage.

28. McBride Commission. 1980. *Communications and Society Today and Tomorrow*. Paris: UNESCO. For the history of that debate and subsequent developments, see UNESCO. 1998. *World Communication Report: The Media and Challenges of the New Technologies*. Paris: UNESCO.

29. David H. Weaver. 1998. *The Global Journalist: News People Around the World*. Cresskill, NJ: Hampton Press; Thomas E. Patterson and Wolfgang Donsbach. 1996. 'News Decisions: Journalists as Partisan Actors.' *Political Communication* 13(4): 455–68; Renate Kocher. 1986. 'Bloodhounds or Missionaries: Role Definitions of German and British Journalists.' *European Journal of Communication* 1:43–64.

CHAPTER 3 UNDERSTANDING POLITICAL COMMUNICATIONS

1. See, for example, the discussion by Jack McLeod, Gerald Kosicki, and Douglas M. McLeod. 1994. 'The Expanding Boundaries of Political Communication Effects.' In *Media Effects*, ed. Jennings Bryant and Dolf Zillmann. Hillsdale, NJ: Lawrence Erlbaum.

2. For a good discussion of the pros and cons of the content-analysis methodology and a comprehensive review of the literature, see Pamela J. Shoemaker and Stephen D. Reese. 1996. *Mediating the Message*, 2nd ed. New York: Longman.

3. Michael J. Robinson and Margaret A. Sheehan. 1983. *Over the Wire and on TV: CBS and UPI in Campaign '80*, pp. 270–85. New York: Russell Sage Foundation.

4. Austin Ranney. 1983. *Channels of Power: The Impact of Television on American Politics*. New York: Basic Books.

5. Jorgen Westerstahl and Folke Johansson. 1986. 'News Ideologies as Moulders of Domestic News.' *European Journal of Communication* 1:133–49; Susan J. Pharr. 2000. 'Officials' Misconduct and Public Distrust: Japan and the Trilateral Democracies.' In *Disaffected Democrats: What's Troubling the Trilateral Democracies*, ed. Susan J. Pharr and Robert D. Putnam. Princeton, NJ: Princeton University Press; Frank Esser. 1999. 'Tabloidization of News: A Comparative Analysis of Anglo-American and German Press Journalism.' *European Journal of Communication* 14(3):291–324.

6. Thomas E. Patterson. 1993. *Out of Order*. New York: Knopf, p. 23.

7. Herbert Gans, for example, suggests that *Time* and *Newsweek* magazines focus on evaluative features, rather than on 'who did what, where and when', so trends in news magazines may well be unrepresentative of changes in the newspapers, let alone network television news: Herbert Gans. 1979. *Deciding What's News: A Study of CBS Evening News, NBC Nightly News, Newsweek and Time*. New York: Pantheon (table 4, p. 16). The *New York Times*, also used by Patterson in *Out of Order*, is also untypical of a broader range of regional newspapers, because Robinson and Sheehan suggest that it functions as an 'agenda-setter' as the paper of record: Michael J. Robinson and Margaret A. Sheehan. 1983. *Over the Wire and on TV: CBS and UPI in Campaign '80*, pp. 270–85. New York: Russell Sage Foundation.

8. Russell J. Dalton, Paul A. Beck and Robert Huckfeldt. 1998. 'Partisan Cues and the Media: Information Flows in the 1992 Presidential Election.' *American Political Science Review* 92(1). For the five-nation comparative study, see also Russell J. Dalton, Kazuhisa Kawakami, Holli A. Semetko, Hiroshisa Suzuki, and Katrin Voltmer. 1998. 'Partisan Cues in the Media: Cross-National Comparisons of Election Coverage.' Paper presented at the annual meeting of the Midwest Political Science Association, Chicago.

9. Shelley McLachlan and Peter Golding. 1999. 'Tabloidization in the British Press: A Quantitative Investigation into Changes in British Newspapers, 1952–1997.' Communication Research Centre working paper no. 9, Loughborough: Loughborough University; Kees Brants. 1998. 'Who's Afraid of Infotainment?' *European Journal of Communication* 13(3):315–35; Frank Esser. 1999. 'Tabloidization of News: A Comparative Analysis of Anglo-American and German Press Journalism.' *European Journal of Communication* 14(3):291–324.

10. David L. Swanson, Ann N. Crigler, Michael Gurevitch, and W. Russell Neuman. 1998. 'The United States.' In *News of the World: World Cultures Look at Television News*, ed. Klaus Bruhn Jensen. London: Routledge.

11. The timing of the Vietnam and Watergate events also provides a poor fit for the trends in negative campaign coverage presented in Patterson's study, even assuming a lagged effect. In mid-1965, media coverage of Vietnam rapidly expanded, and that process increased still further on the eve of the Tet offensive in 1968: Daniel Hallin. 1989. *The Uncensored War: The Media and Vietnam*. Berkeley: University of California Press. If Vietnam had changed the predominant news culture, then we would expect an increase in negativity to have been evident by 1968, when in fact Patterson shows a slight decrease in 'bad' news in the coverage of the presidential candidates. Even if the effects were lagged, the proportion of 'bad news' coverage of candidates in the 1972 campaign was very similar to that evident in 1964. In the same way, negative news declined slightly in 1976, after Watergate, and increased again only in 1980. An events-driven approach seems to provide a poor prima facie match to the Patterson data.

12. Michael J. Robinson and Margaret A. Sheehan. 1983. *Over the Wire and on TV: CBS and UPI in Campaign '80*, p. 282. New York: Russell Sage Foundation.

13. Michael J. Robinson and Margaret A. Sheehan. 1983. *Over the Wire and on TV: CBS and UPI in Campaign '80*, p. 282. New York: Russell Sage Foundation.

14. John Zaller. 1998. 'Monica Lewinsky's Contribution to Political Science.' *PS: Political Science and Politics* 31(2):182–9.

15. W. Lance Bennett. 1998. 'The Uncivic Culture: Communication, Identity and the Rise of Lifestyle Politics.' *PS: Political Science and Politics* 31(4):741–61.

16. Donald T. Campbell and Julian C. Stanley. 1966. *Experimental and Quasi-experimental Designs for Research*. Chicago: Rand McNally; Ronald R. Kinder and Thomas R. Palfrey. 1992. *Experimental Foundations of Political Science*. Ann Arbor: University of Michigan Press.

17. Michael J. Robinson. 1976. 'Public Affairs Television and the Growth of Political Malaise: The Case of "The Selling of the Pentagon".' *American Political Science Review* 70(2):409–32.

18. Kathleen H. Jamieson. 1992. *Dirty Politics*, pp. 159–69. New York: Oxford University Press.

19. Joseph N. Cappella and Kathleen H. Jamieson. 1996. 'News Frames, Political Cynicism and Media Cynicism.' In *The Media and Politics*, ed. Kathleen H. Jamieson, p. 79. *Annals of the American Academy of Political and Social Sciences*, vol. 546; Joseph N. Cappella and Kathleen H. Jamieson. 1997. *Spiral of Cynicism: The Press and the Public Good*. New York: Oxford University Press.

20. Stephen Ansolabehere and Shanto Iyengar. 1995. *Going Negative: How Political Advertisements Shrink and Polarize the Electorate*. New York: Free Press.

21. Pippa Norris, John Curtice, David Sanders, Margaret Scammell, and Holli A. Semetko. 1999. *On Message: Communicating the Campaign*. London: Sage.

22. Michael J. Robinson. 1974. 'The Impact of Televised Watergate Hearings.' *Journal of Communication* 24(2):17–30; Michael J. Robinson. 1975. 'American Political Legitimacy in an Era of Electronic Journalism: Reflections on the Evening News.' In *Television as a Social Force: New Approaches to TV Criticism*, ed. Douglas Cater and R. Adler. New York: Praeger; Michael J. Robinson. 1976. 'Public Affairs

Television and the Growth of Political Malaise: The Case of "The Selling of the Pertagon". *American Political Science Review* 70(2):409–32.

23. Michael J. Robinson. 1974. 'The Impact of Televised Watergate Hearings.' *Journal of Communication* 24(2):17–30; Michael J. Robinson. 1975. 'American Political Legitimacy in an Era of Electronic Journalism: Reflections on the Evening News.' In *Television as a Social Force: New Approaches to TV Criticism*, ed. Douglas Cater and R. Adler. New York: Praeger; Michael J. Robinson. 1976. 'Public Affairs Television and the Growth of Political Malaise: The Case of "The Selling of the Pentagon". *American Political Science Review* 70(2):409–32.

24. Michael J. Robinson and Margaret A. Sheehan. 1983. *Over the Wire and on TV: CBS and UPI in Campaign '80*, pp. 286–7. New York: Russell Sage Foundation.

25. Arthur Miller, Edie H. Goldenberg, and Lutz Erbring. 1979. 'Type-Set Politics: The Impact of Newspapers on Public Confidence.' *American Political Science Review*. 73:67–84.

26. Robert D. Putnam. 1995. 'Tuning In, Tuning Out: The Strange Disappearance of Social Capital in America.' *PS: Political Science and Politics* XXVIII 28(4):664–83; Robert D. Putnam. 1996. 'The Strange Disappearance of Civic America.' *The American Prospect* 24.

27. Robert D. Putnam. 2000. *Bowling Alone*. New York: Simon & Schuster; Robert D. Putnam, Steven Yonish, and David E. Campbell. 1999. 'Tuning In, Tuning Out Revisited: A Closer Look at the Causal Links between Television and Social Capital.' Paper presented at the annual meeting of the American Political Science Association, Atlanta.

28. George Gerbner, Larry Gross, Michael Morgan, and Nancy Signorielli. 1994. 'Growing Up with Television: The Cultivation Perspective.' In *Media Effects*, ed. Jennings Bryant and Dolf Zillmann. 1994. Hillsdale, NJ: Lawrence Erlbaum.

29. Jay G. Blumler and Elihu Katz (eds.). 1974. *The Uses of Mass Communications: Current Perspectives on Gratifications Research*. Beverly Hills, CA: Sage.

30. Pippa Norris. 2000. 'Television and Civic Malaise.' In *Disaffected Democrats: What's Troubling the Trilateral Democracies*, ed. Susan J. Pharr and Robert D. Putnam. Princeton, NJ: Princeton University Press.

31. Pippa Norris. 1996. 'Does Television Erode Social Capital? A Reply to Putnam.' *PS: Political Science and Politics*. September 29(3):474–80.

32. See Stephen Bennett. 1999. 'Trust in Government, Trust in the Media.' *Harvard International Journal of Press/Politics*. Forthcoming. See also Suzanne L. Parker. 1999. 'The Media and Cynicism: The Survey Side of the Question.' Midwest Political Science Association annual meeting, Chicago; Timothy Vercelloti, Marco Steenbergen, Philip Meyer, and Deborah Potter. 1999. 'Help or Hindrance: How Civic Journalism Transforms Public Perceptions of the Media's Role in Politics.' Midwest Political Science Association annual meeting, Chicago.

33. Kenneth Newton. 1997. 'Politics and the News Media: Mobilisation or Videomalaise?' In *British Social Attitudes: The 14th Report*, ed. Roger Jowell, John Curtice, Alison Park, Katarina Thomson, and Lindsay Brook. Aldershot, UK: Ashgate; Kenneth Newton. 1999. 'Mass Media Effects: Mobilisation or Media Malaise?' *British Journal of Political Science* 29:577–99; Pippa Norris. 1997. *Electoral Change since 1945*. Oxford: Blackwell; Christina Holtz-Bacha. 1990. 'Videomalaise Revisited: Media Exposure and Political Alienation in West Germany.' *European Journal*

of Communication 5:78–85; John Curtice, Rüdiger Schmitt-Beck, and Peter Schrott. 1998. 'Do the Media Matter?' Paper presented at the annual meeting of the Midwest Political Science Association, Chicago.

34. Jay G. Blumler, Jack M. McLeod, and Karl Erik Rosengren. 1992. *Comparatively Speaking: Communication and Culture Across Space and Time*, p. 3. London: Sage.

35. See Jay G. Blumler. 1985. 'European–American Differences in Communication Research.' In *The Media Revolution in America and in Western Europe*, ed. Everett M. Rodgers and Francis Balle. Norwood, NJ: Ablex Publishing; Jay G. Blumler, Daniel Dayan, and Dominique Wolton. 1990. 'West European Perspectives on Political Communication: Structures and Dynamics.' *European Journal of Communication* 5:261–84.

36. Michael Gurevitch and Jay G. Blumler. 1990. 'Comparative Research: The Extending Frontier.' In *New Directions of Political Communication: A Resource Book*, ed. David L. Swanson and Dan Nimmo. Newbury Park, CA: Sage.

37. Mattei Dogan and Dominique Pelassy. 1984. *How to Compare Nations: Strategies in Comparative Politics*. Oxford: Blackwell; see also Giovanni Sartori. 1994. 'Comparing Why and How.' In *Comparing Nations*, ed. Mattei Dogan and Ali Kazancigil. Oxford: Blackwell.

38. The logic conforms to Przeworski and Teune's recommendation to convert country names into variables. See Adam Przeworski and H. Teune. 1970. *The Logic of Comparative Social Inquiry*. New York: Wiley.

39. GDP per capita in 1996 was measured by the OECD in U.S. dollars using current exchange rates. If measured according to purchasing-power parities, there is a slightly flatter distribution of national differences in per-capita GDP.

40. See Daniel C. Levy and Kathleen Bruhn. 1995. 'Mexico: Sustained Civilian Rule without Democracy.' In *Politics in Developing Countries*, ed. Larry Diamond, Juan J. Linz, and Seymour Martin Lipset. Boulder, CO: Lynne Rienner. Ergun Òlzbudun. 1995. 'Turkey: Crisis, Interruptions and Reequilibrations.' In *Politics in Developing Countries*, ed. Larry Diamond, Juan J. Linz, and Seymour Martin Lipset. Boulder, CO: Lynne Rienner.

41. For a useful discussion of the classification of party systems adopted in this book, see Alan Ware. 1996. *Political Parties and Party Systems*. Oxford University Press.

42. I am most grateful, in particular, to Anna Melich and Agnes Hubert, to the European Commission's DG10 section for 'Information, Communication, Culture and Audiovisual Unit Public Opinion Monitoring' (X.A2) for release of this data set, without which this book would not have been possible.

43. For a discussion, see Denis McQuail. 1992. *Media Performance: Mass Communication and the Public Interest*. London: Sage.

44. See the literature review by Pamela J. Shoemaker and Stephen D. Reese. 1996. *Mediating the Message*, 2nd ed. New York: Longman.

45. Peter J. Humphreys. 1996. *Mass Media and Media Policy in Western Europe*. Manchester: Manchester University Press.

CHAPTER 4 THE DECLINE of NEWSPAPERS?

1. See, for example, S. H. Chaffee, S. L. Ward, and L. P. Tipton. 1970. 'Mass Communication and Political Socialization.' *Journalism Quarterly* 47:467–79; Thomas E.

Patterson. 1980. *The Mass Media Election: How Americans Choose Their President.* New York: Praeger; John R. Robinson and Mark Levy. 1986. *The Main Source: Learning from TV News.* Beverly Hills, CA: Sage; John Robinson and Dennis K. Davis. 1990. 'Television News and the Informed Public: An Information Processing Approach.' *Journal of Communication* 40(3):106–19. Note, however, that others have argued that the effect of newspapers on learning washes out once controls are introduced for prior cognitive skills. See W. Russell Neuman, Marion R. Just, and Ann N. Crigler. 1992. *Common Knowledge: News and the Construction of Meaning,* p. 98. Chicago: University of Chicago Press.

2. Michael J. Robinson and Margaret A. Sheehan. 1983. *Over the Wire and on TV: CBS and UPI in Campaign '80.* New York: Russell Sage Foundation.

3. See Ben Bagdikian. 1997. *The Media Monopoly,* p. 198. Boston, MA: Beacon Press.

4. Leo Bogart. 1995. *Commercial Culture: The Media System and the Public Interest.* New York: Oxford University Press; William F. Baker and George Dessart. 1998. *Down the Tube.* New York: Basic Books.

5. John H. McManus. 1994. *Market Driven Journalism.* London: Sage; William F. Baker and George Dessart. 1998. *Down the Tube.* New York: Basic Books.

6. Els De Bens and Helge Ostbye. 1998. 'The European Newspaper Market.' In *Media Policy: Convergence, Concentration and Commerce,* ed. Denis McQuail and Karen Siune. London: Sage.

7. Alain Modoux. 1997. *World Communication Report: The New Media and the Challenge of the New Technologies,* p. 120. Paris: UNESCO.

8. Ellis S. Krauss. 2000. 'Japan'. In *Democracy and the Media: A Comparative Perspective,* ed. Richard Gunther and Anthony Mughan. New York: Cambridge University Press; Jung Bock Lee. 1985. *The Political Character of the Japanese Press.* Seoul: Seoul National University Press.

9. Helge Ostbye. 1997. 'Norway'. In *The Media in Western Europe,* ed. Bernt Stubbe Ostergaard. London: Sage.

10. Karl Erik Gustafsson and Olof Hulten. 1997. 'Sweden'. In *The Media in Western Europe,* ed. Bernt Stubbe Ostergaard. London: Sage.

11. Paul Murschetz. 1998. 'State Support for the Daily Press in Europe: A Critical Appraisal.' *European Journal of Communication* 13(3):291–313; Peter J. Humphreys. 1996. *Mass Media and Media Policy in Western Europe.* Manchester: Manchester University Press (table 3.10).

12. For general accounts of the British press, see Colin Seymour Ure. 1996. *The British Press and Broadcasting since 1945,* 2nd ed. Oxford: Blackwell; Ralph Negrine. 1994. *Politics and the Mass Media in Britain,* 2nd ed. London: Routledge.

13. Hans J. Kleinsteuber. 1997. 'Federal Republic of Germany (FRG).' In *The Media in Western Europe,* ed. Bernt Stubbe Ostergaard. London: Sage; Peter J. Humphreys. 1996. *Mass Media and Media Policy in Western Europe.* Manchester: Manchester University Press.

14. Doris Graber. 1997. *Mass Media and American Politics.* Washington, DC: CQ Press (chap. 2).

15. Doris Graber. 1997. *Mass Media and American Politics.* Washington, DC: CQ Press (chap. 2).

16. W. Russell Neuman. 1991. *The Future of the Mass Audience.* Cambridge: Cambridge University Press.

17. Newspaper Association of America. www.naa.org/Info/Facts.
18. For an overview, see, for example, Carlo Sartori. 1996. 'The Media in Italy.' *Markets and Myths: Forces for Change in the European Media*, ed. Tony Weymouth and Bernard Lamizet. See also Lorenzo Vilches. 1996. 'The Media in Spain.' *Markets and Myths: Forces for Change in the European Media*, ed. Tony Weymouth and Bernard Lamizet. London: Longman. See also the chapters on Italy and Spain in Richard Gunther and Anthony Mughan (eds.). 2000. *Democracy and the Media: A Comparative Perspective*. New York: Cambridge University Press.
19. For a discussion, see Panayote Elias Dimitras. 1997. 'Greece'. In *The Media in Western Europe*, ed. Bernt Stubbe Ostergaard. London: Sage.
20. Peter Dahlgren and Colin Sparks. 1997. *Communication and Citizenship*. London: Routledge; Peter Dahlgren. 1995. *Television and the Public Sphere*. London: Sage.
21. For a discussion of the complexities and ambiguities in attempting to define 'tabloidization', see Steven Barnett. 1998. 'Dumbing Down or Reaching Out: Is It Tabloidization Wot Done It?' In *Politics and the Media*, ed. Jean Seaton. Oxford: Blackwell. See also the discussion by Shelley McLachlan and Peter Golding. 1999. 'Tabloidization in the British Press: A Quantitative Investigation into Changes in British Newspapers, 1952–1997.' Communication Research Centre working paper no. 9. Loughborough: Loughborough University.
22. See, for example, Jeremy Tunstall. 1996. *Newspaper Power: The New National Press in Britain*. Oxford: Clarendon.
23. John Langer. 1998. *Tabloid Television: Popular Journalism and the Other News*. London: Routledge.
24. Michael Schudson. 1978. *Discovering the News: A Social History of American Newspapers*. New York: Basic Books.
25. See James Curran and Jean Seaton. 1993. *Power Without Responsibility: The Press and Broadcasting in Britain*, 4th ed. London: Routledge; Matthew Engel. 1996. *Tickle the Public: One Hundred Years of the Popular Press*. London: Gollancz.
26. See Neal Gabler. 1998. *Life the Movie: How Entertainment Conquered Reality*. New York: Knopf.
27. Raymond Williams. 1961. *Culture and Society 1780–1950*. London: Penguin; Raymond Williams. 1970. 'Radical and/or Respectable.' In *The Press We Deserve*, ed. Richard Boston. London: Routledge; R. Stevens. 1998. 'For "Dumbing Down" Read Respectable.' *British Journalism Review* 9(4):32–5; John Hartley. 1996. *Popular Reality: Journalism, Modernity, Popular Culture*. London: Arnold.
28. Knut Hickethier. 1996. 'The Media in Germany.' In *Markets and Myths: Forces for Change in the European Media*, ed. Tony Weymouth and Bernard Lamizet, p. 109. London: Longman.
29. Kees Brants. 1998. 'Who's Afraid of Infotainment?' *European Journal of Communication* 13(3):315–35.
30. Frank Esser. 1999. 'Tabloidization of News: A Comparative Analysis of Anglo-American and German Press Journalism.' *European Journal of Communication* 14(3):291–324.
31. Shelley McLachlan and Peter Golding. 1999. 'Tabloidization in the British Press: A Quantitative Investigation into Changes in British Newspapers, 1952–1997.' Communication Research Centre working paper no. 9, Loughborough University; Shelley McLachlan. 1999. 'Who's Afraid of the News Bunny? The Changing Face of

the Television Evening News Broadcast.' Information and Democracy Research Project, working paper no. 3, Loughborough, Loughborough University.

32. For a discussion, see John Curtice. 1997. 'Is the Sun Shining on Tony Blair? The Electoral Influence of British Newspapers'. *Harvard International Journal of Press/Politics* 2(2):9–26.

33. See Denis McQuail and Karen Siune. 1998. *Media Policy: Convergence, Concentration and Commerce.* London: Sage.

34. See Jeremy Tunstall and Michael Palmer. 1991. *Media Moguls.* London: Routledge; Anthony Smith. 1991. *The Age of Behemoths: The Globalization of Mass Media Firms.* New York: Priority Press; Alfonso Sanchez-Tabernero. 1993. *Media Concentration in Europe: Commercial Enterprises and the Public Interest.* London: John Libbey.

35. Ben Bagdikian. 1997. *The Media Monopoly.* Boston, MA: Beacon Press; Leo Bogart. 1995. *Commercial Culture: The Media System and the Public Interest.* Oxford University Press.

36. Robert G. Picard. 1988. *Press Concentration and Monopoly: New Perspectives on Newspaper Ownership and Operation.* Norwood, NJ: Ablex; Robert G. Picard. 1998. 'Media Concentration, Economics, and Regulation.' In *The Politics of News: The News of Politics,* ed. Doris Graber, Denis McQuail, and Pippa Norris. Washington, DC: CQ Press.

37. Peter J. Humphreys. 1996. *Mass Media and Media Policy in Western Europe,* p. 197. Manchester: Manchester University Press.

38. See Leonard R. Sussman (ed.). 1997. 'Press Freedom 1997.' *Freedom Review.*

39. The 1998 NES was used to gauge media use in the United States, and it used slightly different questions: 'How many days in the PAST WEEK did you read a newspaper?' 'How many days in the PAST WEEK did you watch the national news on TV?' 'How many days in the PAST WEEK did you watch the local news on TV?' and 'How many days in the PAST WEEK did you listen to news on the radio?' The uses of local and national TV news were combined.

40. The low figures for the United States may be due to differences in data sources and question wording.

41. Note that the socioeconomic status is based on the household's occupational group, not the respondent's. The definitions for all measures are listed under Table 4.3.

42. Fred S. Siebert, Theodore Peterson, and Wilbur Schramm. 1956. *Four Theories of the Press.* Chicago: University of Illinois Press.

43. Denis McQuail. 1994. *Mass Communication Theory.* London: Sage.

44. William A. Hachten. 1996. *The World News Prism.* Ames: Iowa State University Press.

45. See Leonard R. Sussman (ed.). 1997. 'Press Freedom 1997.' *Freedom Review.*

46. For an attempt at revising the normative theories of Siebert et al., see John C. Nerone (ed.). 1995. *Last Rights: Revisiting Four Theories of the Press.* Urbana: University of Illinois Press.

47. If we compare the EU-15 and the United States at the national level, the zero-order correlation between the proportion of newspaper readers and the level of per-capita GDP was $R = 0.635$ (significance, 0.008). The correlation between newspaper readers and the percentage of the adult population who had completed secondary education was $R = 0.537$ (significance, 0.032).

CHAPTER 5 THE RISE (AND FALL?) OF THE TELEVISION AGE

1. Yves Achille and Jacques Ibañez Bueno. 1994. *Les télévisions publiques en quête d'avenir*. Presses Universitaires de Grenoble.
2. Patrick O'Neill. 1998. *Post-Communism and the Media in Eastern Europe*. London: Frank Cass.
3. Penn Kimball. 1994. *Downsizing the News: Network Cutbacks in the Nation's Capital*. Washington, DC: Woodrow Wilson Center Press.
4. For a discussion of these global developments, see UNESCO. 1998. *World Communication Report: The Media and the Challenges of the New Technologies*. Paris: UNESCO.
5. It is worth noting that Finland had a commercial channel in 1959, but it subsequently became absorbed into the public system, while Italy went commercial from 1976 onward. There are various accounts of recent developments in European broadcasting. For a country-by-country overview, see Bernt Stubbe Ostergaard (ed.). 1997. *The Media in Western Europe*. London: Sage; Anthony Smith (ed.). 1979. *Television and Political Life: Studies in Six European Countries*. London: Macmillan; Anthony Smith. 1980. *Newspapers and Democracy: International Essays on a Changing Medium*. Cambridge, MA: MIT Press; Philip T. Rosen. 1988. *International Handbook of Broadcasting Systems*. New York: Greenwood Press; Roger Wallis and Stanley Baran. 1991. *The Known World of Broadcast News*. London: Routledge; Peter J. Humphreys. 1996. *Mass Media and Media Policy in Western Europe*. Manchester: Manchester University Press; Lynne Schafer Gross. 1995. *The International World of Electronic Media*. New York: McGraw-Hill; James A. Coleman and Brigitte Rollet. 1998. *Television in Europe*. Exeter: Intellect; Kay Richardson and Ulrike H. Meinhof. 1999. *Worlds in Common? Television Discourse in a Changing Europe*. London: Routledge; Karen Siune and Wolfgang Truetzschler (eds.). 1992. *Dynamics of Media Politics: Broadcast and Electronic Media in Western Europe*. London: Sage.
6. Jay G. Blumler. 1992. *Television and the Public Interest: Vulnerable Values in West European Broadcasting*. London: Sage (chap. 2). See also the discussion by Michael Tracey. 1998. *The Decline and Fall of Public Service Broadcasting*. Oxford: Oxford University Press (chap. 2).
7. Dave Atkinson and Marc Raboy. 1997. *Public Service Broadcasting: The Challenges of the 21st Century*. Paris: UNESCO; Eli Noam. 1991. *Television in Europe*. Oxford: Oxford University Press; Serge Robillard. 1995. *Television in Europe: Regulatory Bodies, Statutes, Functions and Powers in 35 European Countries*. London: John Libbey.
8. Hans J. Kleinsteuber. 1997. 'Federal Republic of Germany.' In *The Media in Western Europe*, ed. Bernt Stubbe Ostergaard. London: Sage.
9. Bernard Lamizet. 1996. 'The Media in France'. In *Markets and Myths: Forces for Change in the European Media*, ed. Tony Weymouth and Bernard Lamizet. London: Longman; Michael Palmer and Claude Sorbets. 1997. 'France.' In *The Media in Western Europe*, ed. Bernt Stubbe Ostergaard. London: Sage.
10. See Panayote Elias Dimitras. 1997. 'Greece'. In *The Media in Western Europe*, ed. Bernt Stubbe Ostergaard. London: Sage.

11. Patrick O'Neill. 1998. *Post-Communism and the Media in Eastern Europe*. London: Frank Cass.
12. *European Key Facts: Television 98*. IP.
13. Yves Achille and Jacques Ibañez Bueno. 1994. *Les télévisions publiques en quête d'avenir*. Grenoble: Presses Universitaires de Grenoble.
14. Mediametrie. 1999. *One Television Year in the World: 1998*. Paris: Mediametrie.
15. Stig Hadenius. 1992. 'Vulnerable Values in a Changing Political and Media System: The Case of Sweden.' In *Television and the Public Interest: Vulnerable Values in West European Broadcasting*, ed. Jay G. Blumler. London: Sage.
16. Karl Erik Gustafsson and Olof Hulten. 1996. 'Sweden'. In *The Media in Western Europe*, ed. Bernt Stubbe Ostergaard. London: Sage.
17. Asa Briggs. 1985. *The BBC: The First Fifty Years*. Oxford University Press; Geoffrey Cox. 1983. *See It Happen: The Making of ITN*. London: The Bodley Head Ltd.
18. That body was originally called the Independent Television Authority and then the Independent Broadcasting Authority. The ITC came into being in 1990.
19. Independent Television Commission. *Factfile 1997*. London: ITC.
20. S. W. Head, C. H. Stirling, and L. B. Schofield (eds.). 1994. *Broadcasting in America: A Survey of Electronic Media*. Boston: Houghton Mifflin.
21. See *Statistical Yearbook of the United States*. 1998. Washington, DC: U.S. Bureau of the Census.
22. For a discussion, see William F. Baker and George Dessart. 1998. *Down the Tube*. New York: Basic Books.
23. Pew Research Center for the People and the Press. *Media Consumption Survey*, 24 April to 11 May 1998. no. 3002.
24. Richard Davis and Diane Owen. 1998. *New Media and American Politics*, p. 136. Oxford: Oxford University Press.
25. Penn Kimball. 1994. *Downsizing the News: Network Cutbacks in the Nation's Capital*. Washington, DC: Woodrow Wilson Center Press.
26. Mediametrie. 1999. *One Television Year in the World: 1998*. Paris: Mediametrie.
27. Tod Gitlin. 1983. *Inside Prime Time*. New York: Pantheon; W. Lance Bennett. 1996. *News: The Politics of Illusion*, pp. 15–23. New York: Longman.
28. Tony Weymouth and Bernard Lamizet (eds.). 1996. *Markets and Myths: Forces for Change in the European Media*, p. 214. London: Longman.
29. David K. Scott and Robert H. Gobetz. 1992. 'Hard News/Soft News Content of the National Broadcast Networks, 1972–1987.' *Journalism Quarterly* 69(2):406–12.
30. Ed Diamond. 1982. *Sign Off: The Last Days of Television*. Cambridge, MA: MIT Press; David L. Altheide. 1976. *Creating Reality: How TV News Distorts Events*. Beverly Hills, CA: Sage; David L. Altheide. 1985. *Media Power*. Beverly Hills, CA: Sage.
31. See, for example, Neil Postman. 1985. *Amusing Ourselves to Death*. London: Methuen; Neal Gabler. 1998. *Life the Movie: How Entertainment Conquered Reality*. New York: Knopf; James McCartney. 1997. 'News Lite.' *American Journalism Review* June:18–25.
32. David K. Scott and Robert H. Gobetz. 1992. 'Hard News/Soft News Content of the National Broadcast Networks, 1972–1987.' *Journalism Quarterly* 69(2):406–12.
33. François Heinderyckx. 1993. 'Television News Programmes in Western Europe: A Comparative Study.' *European Journal of Communication* 8:425–50.

34. Kees Brants and Karen Siune. 1998. 'Politicization in Decline?' In *Media Policy: Convergence, Concentration and Commerce*, ed. Denis McQuail and Karen Siune. London: Sage.

35. Barbara Pfetsch. 1996. 'Convergence through Privatization? Changing Media Environments and Televised Politics in Germany.' *European Journal of Communication* 11(4):427–51.

36. L. Canninga. 1994. 'Eeen vergelijkende analyse van di nieuwscultuur in de buitlandse berichtgeving op BRTN, VTM, NOS en RTL.' *Media and Maatschappij* 4(1); H. Hvitfelt. 1994. 'The Commercialization of the Evening News: Changes in Narrative Techniques in Swedish TV News.' *Nordicom Review* 2:33–41; A. Powers, H. Kristjansdottir, and H. Sutton. 1994. 'Competition in Danish Television News.' *Journal of Media Economics* 7(4):21–30.

37. Asa Briggs. 1985. *The BBC: The First Fifty Years*. Oxford University Press; Geoffrey Cox. 1983. *See It Happen: The Making of ITN*. London: The Bodley Head Ltd.

38. Pippa Norris, John Curtice, David Sanders, Margaret Scammell, and Holli A. Semetko. 1999. *On Message: Communicating the Campaign*. London: Sage (chap. 2). If anything, the BBC produced the most negative coverage of the government, not commercial TV news. However, the cancellation of ITN's flagship *News at Ten* in 1999 may change the amount of coverage on commercial channels in subsequent elections.

39. Shelley McLachlan. 1999. 'Who's Afraid of the News Bunny? The Changing Face of the Television Evening News Broadcast.' Information and Democracy Research Project, working paper no. 3, Loughborough University.

40. All the Italian public television stations gave considerable attention to those events, probably because two were in Italy: Turin and Florence.

41. W. Russell Neuman. 1991. *The Future of the Mass Audience*. Cambridge University Press.

42. Mediametrie. 1999. *One Television Year in the World: 1998*. Paris: Mediametrie.

43. See Pippa Norris, John Curtice, David Sanders, Margaret Scammell, and Holli A. Semetko. 1999. *On Message: Communicating the Campaign*. London: Sage.

44. The 1970 data are from the European Community Study, the precursor to the Eurobarometer series.

CHAPTER 6 THE EMERGING INTERNET ERA

1. See, for example, Nicholas Negroponte. 1995. *Being Digital*. New York: Knopf; Iain McLean. 1989. *Democracy and New Technology*. Cambridge: Polity Press; Ian Budge. 1996. *The New Challenge of Direct Democracy*. Oxford: Polity Press; Edward Schwartz. 1996. *Netactivism: How Citizens Use the Internet*. Sebastopol, CA: Songline Studios; Michael Dertouzos. 1997. *What Will Be: How the New Information Marketplace Will Change Our Lives*. New York: Harper & Row; Wayne Rash, Jr. 1997. *Politics on the Nets: Wiring the Political Process*. San Francisco: Freeman; Christopher Harper. 1998. *And That's the Way It Will Be*. New York: New York University Press; Christine Bellamy and John A. Taylor. 1998. *Governing in the Information Age*. Buckingham, UK: Open University; W. Russell Neuman. 1998. 'The Global Impact of New Technologies.' In *The Politics of News: The News of Politics*, ed. Doris Graber, Denis McQuail, and Pippa Norris. Washington, DC: CQ Press; Elaine Kamarck and

Joseph S. Nye, Jr. (eds.). 1999. *democracy.com? Governance in a Networked World.* Hollis, NH: Hollis Publishing.

2. Michael Margolis, David Resnick, and Chin-chang Tu. 1997. 'Campaigning on the Internet: Parties and Candidates on the World Wide Web in the 1996 Primary Season.' *Harvard International Journal of Press/Politics* 2(1):59–78; Michael Margolis, David Resnick, and Joel D. Wolfe. 1999. 'Party Competition on the Internet: Minor versus Major Parties in the UK and the USA.' *Harvard International Journal of Press/Politics*; Michael Hauben and Rhonda Hauben. 1998. *Netizens: On the History and Impact of Usenet and the Internet.* Los Alamitos, CA: IEEE Computer Science Press; Kevin A. Hill and John E. Hughes. 1998. *Cyberpolitics: Citizen Activism in the Age of the Internet.* New York: Rowman & Littlefield; Richard Davis and Diane Owen. 1998. *New Media and American Politics.* New York: Oxford University Press; Richard Davis. 1999. *The Web of Politics.* New York: Oxford University Press; Pippa Norris and David Jones. 1998. 'Virtual Democracy.' *Harvard International Journal of Press/Politics* 3(2):1–4; Pippa Norris. 1999. 'Who Surfs? New Technology, Old Voters, and Virtual Democracy in America.' In *democracy.com? Governance in a Networked World*, ed. Elaine Kamarck and Joseph S. Nye, Jr. Hollis, NH: Hollis Publishing.

3. The European data come from successive Eurobarometer surveys conducted among representative samples of the European public in the 15 EU member states: EB44.2bis (*N*.65,178) in spring 1996; EB47.0 (*N*.16,352) in spring 1997; EB50.1 (*N*.16,201) in fall 1998; and EB51.0 (*N*.16,179) in spring 1999. See the Technical Appendix for details.

   For American data, I am most grateful to Andrew Kohut and the Pew Research Center for the People and the Press for generous release of survey data on Internet users. The Pew Center surveys used in this chapter concern Net users in 1995, 1996, and 1998, the May 1998 survey of the public's media consumption, and the November 1998 election surveys. Trends on Net users were updated by the June 1999 Pew Center survey. For information about Pew Center questionnaires, data sets, published reports, and technical fieldwork details, see http://www.people-press.org/.

4. Edward Schwartz. 1996. *Netactivism: How Citizens Use the Internet.* Sebastopol, CA: Songline Studios.

5. Howard Rheingold. 1993. *The Virtual Community: Homesteading on the Electronic Frontier.* Reading, MA: Addison-Wesley.

6. Lawrence Grossman. 1995. *The Electronic Republic.* London: Penguin.

7. Ian Budge. 1996. *The New Challenge of Direct Democracy.* Oxford: Polity Press.

8. Bill Gates. 1995. *The Road Ahead.* New York: Viking.

9. Richard Davis and Diane Owen. 1998. *New Media and American Politics*, p. 185. Oxford: Oxford University Press.

10. Graham Murdock and Peter Golding. 1989. 'Information Poverty and Political Inequality: Citizenship in the Age of Privatised Communications.' *Journal of Communication* 39:180–93.

11. UNESCO. 1998. *World Communication Report: The Media and Challenges of the New Technologies*, pp. 88–95. Paris: UNESCO.

12. Hamid Mowlana. 1997. *Global Information and World Communication*, 2nd ed., p. 104. London: Sage.

13. The Eurobarometer comparison did not monitor changes in the use of mobile phones and pagers, which, sales figures indicate, had become far more popular in Europe during those years. The 1997 Eurobarometer indicated that over a third of Europeans used mobile telephones outside of work.

14. Pew Research Center for the People and the Press. 1999. *Striking the Balance: Audience Interests, Business Pressures and Journalists' Values*. Washington, DC: Pew Research Center for the People and the Press (Survey 18–21 February 1999).

15. Levels of Internet use in the EU-15 and in the United States were correlated with levels of GDP per capita ($R = 0.457$, sig. 0.075), the proportion of the adult population who completed secondary education ($R = 0.491$, sig. 0.054), and most strongly with the proportion of the adult population with higher education ($R = 0.664$, sig. 0.013).

16. UNESCO. 1998. *World Communication Report: The Media and Challenges of the New Technologies*, p. 95. Paris: UNESCO.

17. The zero-order correlation between national levels of newspaper readership and Net use in the EU-15 and the United States is moderately strong and significant ($R = 0.530$, sig. 0.035).

18. Kevin A. Hill and John E. Hughes. 1998. *Cyberpolitics: Citizen Activism in the Age of the Internet*. New York: Rowman & Littlefield; Richard Davis and Diane Owen. 1998. *New Media and American Politics*. New York: Oxford University Press; Pippa Norris. 1999. 'Who Surfs? New Technology, Old Voters and Virtual Democracy in America.' In *democracy.com? Governance in a Networked World*, ed. Elaine Kamarck and Joseph S. Nye, Jr. Hollis, NH: Hollis Publishing.

19. Sidney Verba and Norman Nie. 1972. *Participation in America: Political Democracy and Social Equality*. New York: Harper & Row; Sidney Verba, Norman Nie, and Jae-on Kim. 1978. *Participation and Political Equality: A Seven-Nation Comparison*. New York: Cambridge University Press; Sidney Verba, Kay Lehman Schlozman, and Henry E. Brady. 1995. *Voice and Equality: Civic Voluntarism in American Politics*. Cambridge, MA: Harvard University Press.

20. Kevin A. Hill and John E. Hughes. 1998. *Cyberpolitics: Citizen Activism in the Age of the Internet*. New York: Rowman & Littlefield; Richard Davis and Diana Owen. 1998. *New Media and American Politics*. Oxford University Press; Pippa Norris. 1999. 'Who Surfs? New Technology, Old Voters, and Virtual Democracy in America.' In *democracy.com? Governance in a Networked World*, ed. Elaine Kamarck and Joseph S. Nye, Jr. Hollis, NH: Hollis Publishing.

21. Pippa Norris. 1999. 'Who Surfs? New Technology, Old Voters and Virtual Democracy in America.' In *democracy.com? Governance in a Networked World*, ed. Elaine Kamarck and Joseph S. Nye, Jr. Hollis, NH: Hollis Publishing.

22. UNESCO. 1998. *World Communication Report: The Media and Challenges of the New Technologies*, pp. 50–1. Paris: UNESCO.

CHAPTER 7 THE EVOLUTION OF CAMPAIGN COMMUNICATIONS

1. For recent accounts of campaigning in different nations, see Frederick Fletcher (ed.). 1991. *Media, Elections and Democracy*. Toronto: Dundurn Press; David Butler and Austin Ranney. 1992. *Electioneering*. Oxford: Clarendon Press; Shaun Bowler and David M. Farrell (eds.). 1992. *Electoral Strategies and Political Marketing*.

London: Macmillan; Richard Gunther and Anthony Mughan (eds.). 2000. *Democracy and the Media: A Comparative Perspective.* Cambridge University Press; Bruce I. Newman (ed.). 1999. *The Handbook of Political Marketing.* Thousand Oaks, CA: Sage.

2. For the debate on Americanization, see Dennis Kavanagh. 1995. *Election Campaigning: The New Marketing of Politics.* Oxford: Blackwell; Ralph Negrine and Stylianos Papathanassopoulos. 1996. 'The "Americanization" of Political Communications: A Critique.' *Harvard International Journal of Press/Politics* 1(2):45–62; David Farrell. 1996. 'Campaign Strategies and Tactics.' In *Comparing Democracies: Elections and Voting in Global Perspective,* ed. Lawrence LeDuc, Richard G. Niemi, and Pippa Norris. Thousand Oaks, CA: Sage; David L. Swanson and Paolo Mancini (eds.). 1996. *Politics, Media, and Modern Democracy: An International Study of Innovations in Electoral Campaigning and Their Consequences.* New York: Praeger; Margaret Scammell. 1997. 'The Wisdom of the War Room: U.S. Campaigning and Americanization.' *The Joan Shorenstein Center Research Paper* R-17. Cambridge, MA: Harvard University.

3. Seymour Martin Lipset and Stein Rokkan. 1967. *Party Systems and Voter Alignments.* New York: Free Press.

4. Paul F. Lazarsfeld, Bernard Berelson, and Hazel Gaudet. 1944. *The People's Choice: How the Voter Makes Up His Mind in a Presidential Campaign.* New York: Columbia University Press; Bernard Berelson, Paul Lazarsfeld, and William N. McPhee. 1954. *Voting: A Study of Opinion Formation in a Presidential Campaign.* Chicago: University of Chicago Press.

5. V. O. Key. 1964. *Public Opinion and American Democracy.* New York: Knopf.

6. Angus Campbell, Philip Converse, Warren E. Miller, and Donald E. Stokes. 1960. *The American Voter.* New York: Wiley.

7. David Denver and Gordon Hands. 1997. *Modern Constituency Campaigning.* London: Frank Cass.

8. Scott C. Flanagan, Shinsaku Kohei, Ichiro Miyake, Bradley M. Richardson, and Joji Watanuki (eds.). 1991. *The Japanese Voter.* New Haven, CT: Yale University Press.

9. John Aldrich. 1995. *Why Parties? The Origin and Transformation of Party Politics in America.* University of Chicago Press. On caucuses, see, for example, William G. Mayer. 1996. 'Caucuses: How They Work, What Difference They Make.' In *In Pursuit of the White House,* ed. William G. Mayer. Chatham, NJ: Chatham House.

10. Robert Huckfeldt and John Sprague. 1995. *Citizens, Politics, and Social Communications.* Cambridge: Cambridge University Press.

11. David L. Altheide and Robert P. Snow. 1979. *Media Logic.* Beverly Hills, CA: Sage; Gianpietro Mazzoleni. 1987. 'Media Logic and Party Logic in Campaign Coverage: The Italian General Election of 1983.' *European Journal of Communication* 2(1):81–103.

12. Val Lorwin. 1971. 'Segmented Pluralism: Ideological Cleavages and Political Cohesion in the Small European Democracies.' *Comparative Politics* 3:141–75; Kees Brants. 1985. 'Broadcasting and Politics in The Netherlands: From Pillar to Post.' *West European Politics* 8:104–21; Cees Van der Eijk. 2000. 'The Netherlands.' In *Democracy and the Media: A Comparative Perspective,* ed. Richard Gunther and Anthony Mughan. New York: Cambridge University Press.

13. David L. Swanson and Paolo Mancini (eds.). 1996. *Politics, Media, and Modern Democracy: An International Study of Innovations in Electoral Campaigning and Their Consequences.* New York: Praeger.

14. Although it should be noted that Israel now has direct elections for prime minister, making it a semi-presidential system.

15. For example, there is evidence in Britain that coverage of the main party leaders more than quadrupled from 1970 to 1997, as measured in Nuffield studies by the numbers of times they were quoted on BBC1 or ITN television news during the campaign. This is calculated from the data of David Butler and Michael Pinto-Duschinsky. 1971. *The British General Election of 1970*, p. 208. London: Macmillan. David Butler and Dennis Kavanagh. 1997. *The British General Election of 1997.* London: Macmillan (table 8.4).

16. See the literature review by Ian McAllister. 1996. 'Leaders.' In *Comparing Democracies: Elections and Voting in Global Perspective*, ed. Lawrence LeDuc, Richard G. Niemi, and Pippa Norris. Thousand Oaks, CA: Sage.

17. Fritz Plassner, Christian Scheucher, and Christian Senft. 1999. 'Is There a European Style of Political Marketing?' In *The Handbook of Political Marketing*, ed. Bruce I. Newman. Thousand Oaks, CA: Sage.

18. See, for example, Thomas E. Patterson. 1980. *The Mass Media Election: How Americans Choose Their President.* New York: Praeger; Wilson Carey McWilliams. 1995. *The Politics of Disappointment: American Elections 1976–94.* Chatham, NJ: Chatham House; Larry Sabato. 1981. *The Rise of Political Consultants.* New York: Basic Books; Dan Nimmo. 1990. *Mediated Political Realities.* New York: Longman; Frank I. Luntz. 1988. *Candidates, Consultants and Campaigns.* Oxford: Blackwell; Matthew D. McCubbins. 1992. *Under the Watchful Eye.* Washington, DC: CQ Press.

19. See, for example, Larry Sabato. 1981. *The Rise of Political Consultants.* New York: Basic Books; Barbara G. Salmore and Stephen A. Salmore. 1989. *Candidates, Parties and Campaigns.* Washington, DC: CQ Press; Frank I. Luntz. 1988. *Candidates, Consultants and Campaigns.* Oxford: Blackwell; John Aldrich. 1995. *Why Parties? The Origin and Transformation of Party Politics in America.* Chicago: University of Chicago Press.

20. Angelo Panebianco. 1988. *Political Parties: Organization and Power.* Cambridge: Cambridge University Press.

21. Fritz Plassner, Christian Scheucher, and Christian Senft. 1999. 'Is There a European Style of Political Marketing?' In *The Handbook of Political Marketing*, ed. Bruce I. Newman. Thousand Oaks, CA: Sage; Philippe J. Maarek. 1995. *Political Marketing and Communications.* London: John Libbey. See also Margaret Scammell. 1995. *Designer Politics: How Elections Are Won.* London: Macmillan; Dennis Kavanagh. 1995. *Election Campaigning: The New Marketing of Politics.* Oxford: Blackwell; Nicholas J. O'Shaughnessy. 1990. *The Phenomenon of Political Marketing.* New York: St. Martin's Press; Nicholas Jones. 1995. *Soundbites and Spin Doctors.* London: Cassell; Margaret Scammell. 2000. 'Political Marketing: Lessons for Political Science.' *Political Studies.*

22. Russell J. Dalton, Scott C. Flanigan, and Paul Beck (eds.). 1984. *Electoral Change in Advanced Industrial Democracies.* Princeton, NJ: Princeton University Press; Mark Franklin. 1992. *Electoral Change.* Ann Arbor: University of Michigan Press; Ivor

Crewe and David Denver (eds.). 1985. *Electoral Change in Western Democracies*. London: Croom Helm.

23. See Geoffrey Evans and Pippa Norris. 1999. *Critical Elections: British Voters and Elections in Long-Term Perspective*. London: Sage. For the earliest attempt to conceptualize the catch-all party, see Otto Kirchheimer. 1966. 'The Transformation of Western Party Systems.' In *Political Parties and Political Development*, ed. J. La Polambara and M. Weiner. Princeton, NJ: Princeton University Press.

24. See Jean-François Lyotard. 1979. *The Post-Modern Condition*. Minneapolis: University of Minnesota Press; Jean Baudrillard. 1983. *Simulations*. New York: Semiotext; Jürgen Habermas. 1987. T*he Philosophical Discourse of Modernity*. Cambridge, MA: MIT Press; Krishan Kumar. 1995. *From Post-Industrial to Post-Modern Society*. Oxford: Blackwell.

25. David L. Swanson and Paolo Mancini (eds.). 1996. *Politics, Media, and Modern Democracy: An International Study of Innovations in Electoral Campaigning and Their Consequences*. New York: Praeger.

26. Margaret Scammell. 2000. 'Political Marketing: Lessons for Political Science.' *Political Studies*.

27. See Elaine Kamarck and Joseph S. Nye, Jr. (eds.). 1999. *democracy.com? Governance in a Networked World*. Hollis, NH: Hollis Publishing; Richard Davis and Diane Owen. 1998. *New Media and American Politics*. New York: Oxford University Press; Kevin A. Hill and John E. Hughes. 1998. *Cyberpolitics: Citizen Activism in the Age of the Internet*. New York: Rowman & Littlefield; Edward Schwartz. 1996. *Netactivism: How Citizens Use the Internet*. Sebastopol, CA: Songline Studios; Richard Davis. 1999. *The Web of Politics*. Oxford: Oxford University Press.

28. Anthony Smith. 1981. 'Mass Communications.' In *Democracy at the Polls*, ed. David Butler, Howard R. Pennimann, and Austin Ranney. Washington, DC: AEI Press.

29. See Lynda Lee Kaid and Christina Holtz-Bacha. 1995. *Political Advertising in Western Democracies*. Thousand Oaks, CA: Sage.

30. Cees Van der Eijk. 2000. 'The Netherlands.' In *Democracy and the Media: A Comparative Perspective*, ed. Richard Gunther and Anthony Mughan. New York: Cambridge University Press.

31. Darrell M. West. 1992. *Air Wars: Television Advertising in Election Campaigns, 1952–1992*. Washington, DC: CQ Press. See also Lynda Lee Kaid, Dan Nimmo, and Keith R. Sanders. 1986. *New Perspectives on Political Advertising*. Carbondale: Southern Illinois University Press.

32. For details, see Pippa Norris, John Curtice, David Sanders, Margaret Scammell, and Holli A. Semetko. *On Message: Communicating the Campaign*. London: Sage.

33. See Pippa Norris, John Curtice, David Sanders, Margaret Scammell, and Holli Semetko. *On Message: Communicating the Campaign*. London: Sage.

34. James B. Lemert, William R. Elliott, James M. Bernstein, William L. Rosenberg, and Karl J. Nestvold. 1991. *News Verdicts, the Debates and Presidential Campaigns*. New York: Praeger.

35. Robert Harmel and Kenneth Janda. 1994. 'An Integrated Theory of Party Goals and Party Change.' *Journal of Theoretical Politics* 6:259–87; Richard S. Katz and Peter Mair (eds.). 1992. *Party Organization: A Data Handbook*. London: Sage.

36. Anders Widfeldt. 1995. 'Party Membership and Party Representatives.' In *Citizens and the State*, ed. Hans-Dieter Klingemann and Dieter Fuchs. Oxford: Oxford University Press.

37. Richard S. Katz and Peter Mair. 1995. 'Changing Models of Party Organization and Party Democracy: The Emergence of the Cartel Party.' *Party Politics* 1(1):5–28.

38. Herbert E. Alexander and Rei Shiratori (eds.). 1994. *Campaign Political Finance among the Democracies*. Boulder, CO: Westview. For a useful recent comparative review of practices, see also Neill Report. 1998. *Fifth Report of the Committee on Standards in Public Life: The Funding of Political Parties in the United Kingdom*, vol. 1, chaired by Lord Neill. Cm 4057–I. London: Her Majesty's Stationery Office.

39. Ruud Koole. 1996. 'Cadre, Catch-All or Cartel? A Comment on the Notion of the Cartel Party.' *Party Politics* 2(4):507–24.

40. See Cees Van der Eijk and Mark N. Franklin (eds.). 1996. *Choosing Europe: The European Electorate and National Politics in the Face of Union*. Ann Arbor: University of Michigan Press; Michael Marsh and Pippa Norris (eds.). 1997. 'Political Representation in the European Parliament.' Special issue of the *European Journal of Political Research* 32(2).

41. David L. Swanson and Paolo Mancini (eds.). 1996. *Politics, Media, and Modern Democracy: An International Study of Innovations in Electoral Campaigning and Their Consequences*, p. 2. New York: Praeger.

42. Lynda Lee Kaid and Christina Holtz-Bacha. 1995. *Political Advertising in Western Democracies*. Thousand Oaks, CA: Sage; Herbert E. Alexander and Rei Shiratori (eds.). 1994. *Campaign Political Finance among the Democracies*. Boulder, CO: Westview.

43. David Butler and Austin Ranney (eds.). 1992. *Electioneering*. Oxford: Clarendon Press; Shaun Bowler and David M. Farrell (eds.). 1992. *Electoral Strategies and Political Marketing*. London: Macmillan; Richard Gunther and Anthony Mughan (eds.). 2000. *Democracy and the Media: A Comparative Perspective*. Cambridge University Press.

44. See Dennis Kavanagh. 1995. *Election Campaigning: The New Marketing of Politics*. Oxford: Blackwell.

45. David Denver and Gordon Hands. 1997. *Modern Constituency Campaigning*. London: Frank Cass.

46. Pippa Norris, John Curtice, David Sanders, Margaret Scammell, and Holli A. Semetko. *On Message: Communicating the Campaign*. London: Sage.

CHAPTER 8 THE RISE OF THE POSTMODERN CAMPAIGN?

1. For historical accounts, see Paul F. Boller. 1985. *Presidential Campaigns*. Oxford: Oxford University Press; David McCullough. 1992. *Truman*. New York: Simon & Schuster; Kathleen H. Jamieson. 1984. *Packaging the Presidency: A History and Criticism of Presidential Advertising*. Oxford: Oxford University Press.

2. John Aldrich. 1995. *Why Parties? The Origin and Transformation of Party Politics in America*, chap. 4. Chicago: University of Chicago Press.

3. Darrell M. West. 2000. *The Rise and Fall of the Media*. New York: St. Martin's Press.

4. Harold W. Stanley and Richard G. Niemi. 1995. *Vital Statistics on American Politics*. Washington, DC: CQ Press.

5. Harold W. Stanley and Richard G. Niemi. 1995. *Vital Statistics on American Politics*, p. 66. Washington, DC: CQ Press.

6. Paul F. Lazarsfeld, Bernard Berelson, and Hazel Gaudet. 1944. *The People's Choice: How the Voter Makes Up His Mind in a Presidential Campaign.* New York: Columbia University Press; Bernard Berelson, Paul Lazarsfeld, and William N. McPhee. 1954. *Voting: A Study of Opinion Formation in a Presidential Campaign.* Chicago: University of Chicago Press.

7. For details, see R. B. McCullum and Alison Readman. 1964. *The British General Election of 1945*, 2nd ed. London: Frank Cass. See also Pippa Norris. 1997. *Electoral Change since 1945*. Oxford: Blackwell.

8. Kenneth D. Wald. 1983. *Crosses on the Ballot: Patterns of British Voter Alignment Since 1885*. Princeton, NJ: Princeton University Press.

9. David Butler and Donald E. Stokes. 1974. *Political Change in Britain: The Evolution of Electoral Choice*, 2nd ed. London: Macmillan.

10. Michael Schudson. 1995. *The Power of News*, pp. 169–88. Cambridge, MA: Harvard University Press.

11. See Chapter 6 for details.

12. See Lawrence R. Jacobs and Robert Y. Shapiro. 1995. 'The Rise of Presidential Polling.' *Public Opinion Quarterly*.

13. Larry Sabato. 1981. *The Rise of Political Consultants*. New York: Basic Books; Dan Nimmo. 1990. *Mediated Political Realities*. New York: Longman; Frank I. Luntz. 1988. *Candidates, Consultants and Campaigns*. Oxford: Blackwell; Judith S. Trent and Robert V. Friedenberg. 1991. *Political Campaign Communication: Principles and Practices*, 2nd ed. New York: Praeger; Bruce I. Newman. 1994. *The Marketing of the President: Political Marketing as Campaign Strategy*. Thousand Oaks, CA: Sage.

14. Joe McGinness. 1969. *The Selling of the President*. New York: Trident.

15. See Margaret Scammell. 1997. 'The Wisdom of the War Room: U.S. Campaigning and Americanization.' *The Joan Shorenstein Center Research Paper* R-17. Cambridge, MA: Harvard University.

16. For accounts of the 1996 election, see Gerald M. Pomper (ed.). 1997. *The Election of 1996*. Chatham, NJ: Chatham House; The Institute of Politics. 1997. *Campaign for President: The Managers Look at '96*. Hollis, NH: Hollis Publishing; Paul R. Abramson, John Aldrich, and David Rohde. 1999. *Change and Continuity in the 1996 and 1998 Elections*. Washington, DC: CQ Press; Michael Nelson. 1997. *The Elections of 1996*. Washinton, DC: CQ Press; Lynda Lee Kaid and Dianne G. Bystrom. 1999. *The Electronic Election: Perspectives on the 1996 Campaign Communication*. Hillsdale, NJ: Lawrence Erlbaum.

17. Kevin A. Hill and John E. Hughes. 1998. *Cyberpolitics: Citizen Activism in the Age of the Internet*, p. 133. New York: Rowman & Littlefield.

18. Elaine Kamarck. 1999. 'Campaigning on the Internet in the Elections of 1998.' In *democracy.com? Governance in a Networked World*, ed. Elaine Kamarck and Joseph S. Nye, Jr. Hollis, NH: Hollis Publishing.

19. See Pippa Norris. 1999. 'Who Surfs? New Technology, Old Voters and Virtual Democracy in America.' In *democracy.com? Governance in a Networked World*, ed. Elaine Kamarck and Joseph S. Nye, Jr. Hollis, NH: Hollis Publishing.

20. See Pippa Norris. 'Who Surfs? New Technology, Old Voters and Virtual Democracy in America.' In *democracy.com? Governance in a Networked World,* ed. Elaine Kamarck and Joseph S. Nye, Jr. Hollis, NH: Hollis Publishing.

21. See Bob Franklin. 1994. *Packaging Politics.* London: Arnold; Margaret Scammell. 1995. *Designer Politics: How Elections Are Won.* London: Macmillan; Dennis Kavanagh. 1995. *Election Campaigning: The New Marketing of Politics.* Oxford: Blackwell.

22. For details of the 1997 British election, see Pippa Norris and Neil Gavin (eds.). 1997. *Britain Votes 1997.* Oxford: Oxford University Press; David Butler and Dennis Kavanagh. 1997. *The British General Election of 1997.* London: Macmillan; Anthony King. 1997. *New Labour Triumphs: Britain at the Polls.* Chatham, NJ: Chatham House; Ivor Crewe, Brian Gosschalk, and John Bartle. 1998. *Political Communications: Why Labour Won the General Election Campaign of 1997.* London: Frank Cass; Pippa Norris, John Curtice, David Sanders, Margaret Scammell, and Holli A. Semetko. 1999. *On Message: Communicating the Campaign.* London: Sage; Geoffrey Evans and Pippa Norris (eds.). 1999. *Critical Elections: British Parties and Voters in Long-Term Perspective.* London: Sage.

23. Rachel K. Gibson and Stephen J. Ward. 1998. 'U.K. Political Parties and the Internet: "Politics as Usual" in the New Media.' *Harvard International Journal of Press/Politics* 3(3):14–38.

24. Pippa Norris, John Curtice, David Sanders, Margaret Scammell, and Holli A. Semetko. 1999. *On Message: Communicating the Campaign.* London: Sage (tables 2.2 and 2.3).

25. David L. Swanson and Paolo Mancini (eds.). 1996. *Politics, Media, and Modern Democracy: An International Study of Innovations in Electoral Campaigning and Their Consequences,* p. 15. New York: Praeger.

26. news.bbc.co.uk/

27. See Geoffrey Evans and Pippa Norris (eds.). 1999. *Critical Elections: British Parties and Voters in Long-Term Perspective.* London: Sage.

28. Philip Gould. 1999. *The Unfinished Revolution.* Boston: Little, Brown.

29. Martin P. Wattenberg. 1996. *The Decline of American Political Parties: 1952–1994.* Cambridge, MA: Harvard University Press.

30. Pippa Norris, John Curtice, David Sanders, Margaret Scammell, and Holli A. Semetko. 1999. *On Message: Communicating the Campaign.* London: Sage.

31. See, for example, Bob Franklin. 1994. *Packaging Politics.* London: Arnold.

32. Roderick Hart. 1994. *Seducing America.* New York: Oxford University Press.

Chapter 9 Negative News, Negative Public?

1. These conditions are similar to those specified in seminal accounts of the role of party cues in issue voting. See, for example, the discussion by Philip Converse. 1964. 'The Nature of Belief Systems in Mass Publics.' In *Ideology and Discontent,* ed. David Apter, New York: Free Press; also chapter 13 in David Butler and Donald E. Stokes. 1974. *Political Change in Britain: The Evolution of Electoral Choice,* 2nd ed. London: Macmillan.

2. John Zaller. 1993. *The Nature and Origins of Mass Opinion*, chap. 9. New York: Cambridge University Press.

3. Cees Van der Eijk and Mark N. Franklin (eds.). 1996. *Choosing Europe: The European Electorate and National Politics in the Face of Union*. Ann Arbor: University of Michigan Press; Francis Jacobs, Richard Corbett, and Michael Shackleton. 1992. *The European Parliament*, 2nd ed. London: Longman; Robert Keohane and Stanley Hoffman (eds.). 1991. *The New European Community: Decision-making and Institutional Change*. Boulder, CO: Westview Press; Michael Marsh and Pippa Norris (eds.). 1997. 'Political Representation in the European Parliament.' Special issue of the *European Journal of Political Research* 32(2); Hermann Schmitt and Jacques Thomassen (eds.). 1999. *Political Representation and Legitimacy in the European Union*. Oxford: Oxford University Press; Richard S. Katz and Bernhard Wessels (eds.). 1999. *The European Parliament, the National Parliaments and European Integration*. Oxford: Oxford University Press.

4. The only study linking coverage in the news media with attitudes towards European integration is by Russell Dalton and R. Duval. 1986. 'The Political Environment and Foreign Policy Opinions: British Attitudes towards European Integration, 1972–79.' *British Journal of Political Science* 16:113–34. In addition, for the role of the news media in European elections, see Jay G. Blumler (ed.). 1983. *Communicating to Voters: Television in the First European Parliamentary Elections*. London: Sage.

5. Anne Stevens, quoted in 'UK Turnout: Apathy or Ignorance?' BBC News at http://news.bbc.co.uk. 14 June 1999.

6. Peter J. Anderson and Anthony Weymouth. 1999. *Insulting the Public? The British Press and the European Union*. London: Longman. See also David Morgan. 1994. 'Brussels Media and European Union News.' *European Journal of Communication* 10(3):321–44.

7. See the discussion by Benjamin Page and Robert Y. Shapiro. 1992. *The Rational Public: Fifty Years of Trends in Americans' Policy Preferences*. Chicago: University of Chicago Press; also see William G. Meyer. 1992. *The Changing American Mind*. Ann Arbor: University of Michigan Press.

8. 'Results of Continuous Tracking Surveys of European Opinion,' *Europinion* #13, European Commission, Brussels, November 1997. europa.eu.int.

9. I am most grateful in particular to Anna Melich and Agnes Hubert, as well as to the European Commission's DG10, Information, Communication, Culture and Audiovisual-Unit Public Opinion Monitoring (X.A2) for release of this data set, without which this book would not have been possible.

10. A full chronology of events can be found in the monthly bulletin of the European Union, available at europa.eu.int/abc/doc.

11. It should be noted that multiple codings were used for story topics.

12. In addition, it can be noted, for comparison, that U.S. network news devoted, on average, about 4 minutes per news program to all types of international news during roughly the same period. Pippa Norris. 1997. 'News of the World.' In *Politics and the Press: The News Media and Their Influences*, ed. Pippa Norris. Boulder, CO: Lynne Rienner.

13. David Morgan. 1998. *The European Parliament, Mass Media and the Search for Power and Influence*. Report to the European Commission, DGX, Brussels.

14. Eurobarometer 50, spring 1998. Brussels: European Commission.

15. The measures of the proportion of stories and the proportion of time correlated fairly closely ($R = 0.66$), increasing confidence in the reliability of these measures.

16. Although it should be acknowledged that such a pattern could have been produced by the selection of newspapers used in the content analysis; for example, *Monitoring Euromedia* coded far more British than Irish papers.

17. This may underestimate total coverage of the BSE crisis, which could be classified under 'agriculture' (as it related to the financial problems facing farmers), 'health' (when stories discussed the risks to the human food chain), or even 'consumer affairs' (when stories related to the retail consequences of the crisis, for example for butchers).

18. Unfortunately, we lack any systematic indicator of the priority given to policy issues by the Commission or Parliament that could be compared with this news agenda. Previous studies have commonly analyzed governments' budgets to gauge domestic policy priorities, such as the growth of per-capita spending on welfare services among left-wing and right-wing regimes. Many of the most important issues facing the EU, however, are those of competition, regulation, and governance, without direct spending implications for the EU budget. Agriculture and fisheries, for instance, absorb about two-thirds of all European Community expenditures, but that does not imply that these issues were the most important or controversial matters under debate in the period under comparison. The most difficult agricultural issue in the period under review concerned how the Community should respond to the health risks associated with BSE, an issue that was only in part a matter of financial compensation for farmers. Another independent indicator of policy priorities can be derived from content analysis of the election manifestos of the party or parties in government. See, for example, Hans-Dieter Klingemann, Richard I. Hofferbert, and Ian Budge. 1994. *Parties, Policies and Democracy.* Boulder, CO: Westview Press. But at the Community level, these documents are applicable only in the broadest sense to party groups within the European Parliament, not to the decisions of the European Council or the Commission.

19. There is an enormous literature on this topic. For general background, see, for example, Andrew Duff, John Pinder, and Roy Pryce. 1994. *Maastricht and Beyond.* London: Routledge; Michael J. Baun. 1996. *An Imperfect Union: The Maastricht Treaty and the New Politics of European Integration.* Boulder, CO: Westview Press; Kenneth Dyson. 1994. *Elusive Union: The Process of Economic and Monetary Union in Europe.* London: Longman; Barry Eichengreen and Jeffrey Frieden (eds.). 1994. *The Political Economy of European Monetary Unification.* Boulder, CO: Westview Press.

20. For more detailed discussions of the concepts of balance and bias see Jorgen Westerstahl. 1983. 'Objective News Reporting.' *Communication Research* 10(3):403–24; Denis McQuail. 1992. *Media Performance: Mass Communication and the Public Interest.* London: Sage; Pippa Norris, John Curtice, David Sanders, Margaret Scammell, and Holli A. Semetko. 1999. *On Message: Communicating the Campaign.* London: Sage.

21. A Nexis-Lexis search of non-U.S. newspapers disclosed 130 stories since 1994 referring to the 'straight bananas' story, a claim that seems to have entered the popular

culture in September 1994 when the European Commission proposed banning 'abnormally curved' bananas. See the *Daily Mirror*, 21 September 1994.

22. For a discussion of the concept and measurement of political support, see Pippa Norris (ed.). 1999. *Critical Citizens: Global Support for Democratic Governance.* Oxford: Oxford University Press; see also Oskar Niedermayer and Bettina Westle. 1995. 'A Typology of Orientations.' In *Public Opinion and Internationalized Governance*, ed. Oskar Niedermayer and Richard Sinnott. Oxford: Oxford University Press.

23. The items ask: (*Membership*) 'Generally speaking do you think that (your country's) membership in the European Community is a good thing, a bad thing, or neither good nor bad?' (*Benefit*) 'Taking everything into consideration, would you say that (your country) has on balance benefited or not from being a member of the European Community?'

24. The wording of this item was less than ideal. In particular, people may have felt that the euro *had* to be introduced, as an inevitable step, given their country's membership, without necessarily feeling that it *should* be introduced.

25. Martin Slater. 1982. 'Political Elites, Popular Indifference and Community Building.' *Journal of Commonwealth Studies* 21(1):69–87.

26. Cees Van der Eijk and Mark N. Franklin (eds.). 1996. *Choosing Europe: The European Electorate and National Politics in the Face of Union*, chap. 19. Ann Arbor: University of Michigan Press; Jean Blondel, Richard Sinnott, and Palle Svensson. 1997. 'Representation and Voter Participation.' *European Journal of Political Research* 32(2):273–82.

27. The most comprehensive analysis of public opinion about the EU from the early 1970s until the early 1990s was provided by Oskar Niedermayer and Richard Sinnott (eds.). 1995. *Public Opinion and Internationalized Governance.* Oxford: Oxford University Press. For discussion, see also Svein S. Anderson and Kjell A. Eliassen (eds.). 1996. *The European Union: How Democratic Is It?* London: Sage; Jack Hayward (ed.). 1995. *The Crisis of Representation in Europe.* London: Frank Cass.

28. Jacques Thomassen and Hermann Schmitt. 1999. 'Introduction.' In *Political Representation and Legitimacy in the European Union*, ed. Hermann Schmitt and Jacques Thomassen. Oxford: Oxford University Press.

Chapter 10 Knows Little? Information and Choice

1. See, for example, Jay Blumler and Michael Gurevitch. 1991. 'Political Communications Systems and Democratic Values.' In *Democracy and the Mass Media*, ed. Judith Lichtenberg. Cambridge: Cambridge University Press.

2. Paul F. Lazarsfeld, Bernard Berelson, and Hazel Gaudet. 1944. *The People's Choice: How the Voter Makes Up His Mind in a Presidential Campaign.* New York: Columbia University Press.

3. See, for example, John R. Robinson and Mark Levy. 1986. *The Main Source: Learning from TV News.* Beverly Hills, CA: Sage.

4. Steven H. Chaffee and Joan Schleuder. 1986. 'Measurement and Effects of Attention to Media News.' *Human Communication Research* 13:76–107; Hugh Culbertson and Guido H. Stempel III. 1986. 'How Media Use and Reliance Affect Knowledge Level.' *Communication Research* 13:579–602.

5. Michael Delli Carpini and Scott Keeter. 1996. *What Americans Know about Politics and Why It Matters.* New Haven, CT: Yale University Press. See also Stephen Bennett. 1989. 'Trends in American Political Information, 1967–1987.' *American Politics Quarterly* 17(4):422–35.

6. Using a battery of five questions about international affairs, such as identifying who headed the United Nations or who was president of Russia, Bennett found that knowledge was particularly low in the United States compared with Canada, Britain, Germany, and France. See Stephen Earl Bennett, Richard S. Flickinger, John R. Baker, Staci L. Rhine, and Linda M. Bennett. 1996. 'Citizens' Knowledge of Foreign Affairs.' *Harvard International Journal of Press/Politics* 1(2):10–29.

7. See Pippa Norris, John Curtice, David Sanders, Margaret Scammell, and Holl: A. Semetko. 1999. *On Message: Communicating the Campaign.* London: Sage.

8. See, for example, Thomas E. Patterson. 1993. *Out of Order.* New York: Knopf.

9. Robert Lichter and Ted J. Smith. 1996. 'Why Elections Are Bad News: Media and Candidate Discourse in the 1996 Presidential Primaries.' *Harvard International Journal of Press/Politics* 1(4):15–35.

10. For a discussion, see Doris Graber. 1994. 'Why Voters Fail Information Tests: Can the Hurdles Be Overcome?' *Political Communication* 11(4):331–46.

11. Paul Sniderman, Richard Brody, and Philip Tetlock. 1998. *Reasoning and Choice: Explorations in Political Psychology.* New York: Cambridge University Press; John Zaller. 1993. *The Nature and Origins of Mass Opinion.* New York: Cambridge University Press; Samuel Popkin. 1994. *The Reasoning Voter.* Chicago: University of Chicago Press; Doris Graber. 1988. *Processing the News: How People Tame the Information Tide,* 2nd ed. White Plains: Longman.

12. W. Russell Neuman, Marion R. Just, and Ann N. Crigler. 1992. *Common Knowledge: News and the Construction of Meaning,* p. 77. Chicago: University of Chicago Press; Marion R. Just, Ann N. Crigler, Dean E. Alger, Timothy E. Cook, Montague Kern, and Darrell M. West. 1996. *Crosstalk: Citizens, Candidates and the Media in a Presidential Campaign.* Chicago: University of Chicago Press.

13. Karl R. Popper. 1972. *Objective Knowledge.* Oxford: Clarendon Press.

14. Pippa Norris, John Cartice, David Sanders, Margaret Scammell, and Holli A. Semetko. 1999. *On Message: Communicating the Campaign,* p. 103. London: Sage.

15. For evidence of the inability of many American voters to identify the policy stands of major presidential candidates, see Robert M. Entman. 1989. *Democracy without Citizens: Media and the Decay of American Politics,* p. 25. Oxford: Oxford University Press.

16. Richard Morin. 1999. 'Not a Clue: The Economy's Booming and Crime's Down, but Many Americans Believe It Ain't So.' *Washington Post,* 14 June 1999, p. 34.

17. Quoted by Richard Morin. 1999. 'Not a Clue: The Economy's Booming and Crime's Down, but Many Americans Believe It Ain't So.' *Washington Post,* 14 June 1999, p. 34.

18. For a discussion, see Anthony Downs. 1957. *An Economic Theory of Democracy,* pp. 207–59. New York: Harper & Row; Arthur Lupia and Matthew D. McCubbins. 1998. *The Democratic Dilemma.* Cambridge University Press.

19. Michael Delli Carpini and Scott Keeter. 1996. *What Americans Know about Politics and Why It Matters,* p. 179. New Haven, CT: Yale University Press.

20. Paul F. Lazarsfeld, Bernard Berelson, and Hazel Gaudet. 1944. *The People's Choice: How the Voter Makes Up His Mind in a Presidential Campaign*. New York: Columbia University Press; Angus Campbell, Philip Converse, Warren E. Miller, and Donald E. Stokes. 1960. *The American Voter*. New York: Wiley.
21. Steven H. Chaffee and Joan Schleuder. 1986. 'Measurement and Effects of Attention to Media News.' *Human Communication Research* 13:76–107; Hugh Culbertson and Guido H. Stempel III. 1986. 'How Media Use and Reliance Affect Knowledge Level.' *Communication Research* 13:579–602.
22. Use of the Internet was not included in the fall 1996 Eurobarometer survey, so that was examined separately. It should also be noted that unfortunately we lack measures of news-media attention, which studies suggest may be a better indicator than news-media exposure per se.
23. Fiona Chew. 1994. 'The Relationship of Information Needs to Issue Relevance and Media Use.' *Journalism Quarterly* 71:676–88; Steven Chaffee and Stacey Frank. 1996. 'How Americans Get Political Information: Print versus Broadcast News.' In *The Media and Politics*, ed. Kathleen H. Jamieson, pp. 48–58. *Annals of the American Academy of Political and Social Sciences*, vol. 546.
24. Steven Chaffee and Stacey Frank. 1996. 'How Americans Get Political Information: Print versus Broadcast News.' In *The Media and Politics*, ed. Kathleen H. Jamieson, pp. 48–58. *Annals of the American Academy of Political and Social Sciences*, vol. 546; David Weaver. 'What Voters Learn from Media.' In *The Media and Politics*, ed. Kathleen H. Jamieson, pp. 34–47. *Annals of the American Academy of Political and Social Sciences*, vol. 546.
25. Pippa Norris, John Curtice, David Sanders, Margaret Scammell, and Holli A. Semetko. 1999. *On Message: Communicating the Campaign*, p. 103. London: Sage.
26. European Commission. 1999. *European Public Opinion on the Single Currency*. Brussels: European Commission DG X.A2.
27. Cees Van der Eijk and Mark N. Franklin (eds.). 1996. *Choosing Europe: The European Electorate and National Politics in the Face of Union*. Ann Arbor: University of Michigan Press.
28. See Pippa Norris. 1999. 'New Politicians? Changes in Party Competition at Westminster.' In *Critical Elections: British Parties and Voters in Long-Term Perspective*, ed. Geoffrey Evans and Pippa Norris. London: Sage.
29. See Hermann Schmitt and Jacques Thomassen (eds.). 1999. *Political Representation and Legitimacy in the European Union*. Oxford: Oxford University Press.
30. 'Political interest' was measured by how often the respondent discussed politics with friends and colleagues. Pro-EU attitudes were measured by the combined 'membership' and 'benefit' items already described in Chapter 8. Left–right ideology was gauged by the 10-point self-placement scale.
31. Hugh Culbertson and Guido H. Stempel III. 1986. 'How Media Use and Reliance Affect Knowledge Level.' *Communication Research* 13:579–602.
32. Although it is interesting that on the issue of the risk of cancer the gender relationship reversed, with women proving more knowledgeable than men.
33. Wouter Van der Brug and Cees Van der Eijk. 1999. 'The Cognitive Basis of Voting.' In *Political Representation and Legitimacy in the European Union*, ed. Hermann Schmitt and Jacques Thomassen. Oxford: Oxford University Press.

34. The difference by media use proved modest, but that may be attributable to the limited measure used to gauge news exposure. Instead of the usual items, the European election study (1999) used the following item: 'At the European elections we have just had, the parties and candidates campaigned for votes. Did the campaign come to your attention in any of the following ways? . . . Coverage of the campaign in newspapers (Yes/No). . . . Coverage of the campaign on TV and radio (Yes/No).'

CHAPTER 11 CARES LESS? CYNICAL MEDIA, CYNICAL PUBLIC?

1. See Pippa Norris (ed.). 1999. *Critical Citizens: Global Support for Democratic Governance.* Oxford: Oxford University Press.
2. On government performance, see Ian McAllister, 'The Economic Performance of Governments,' and also Arthur Miller and Ola Listhaug, 'Political Performance and Institutional Trust,' both in *Critical Citizens: Global Support for Democratic Governance,* ed. Pippa Norris. Oxford: Oxford University Press. In the same source, for the evidence on cultural change, see Ronald Inglehart, 'Postmodernization Erodes Respect for Authority, but Increases Support for Democracy.'
3. Michael J. Robinson. 1974. 'The Impact of Televised Watergate Hearings.' *Journal of Communication* 24(2):17–30; Michael J. Robinson. 1975. 'American Political Legitimacy in an Era of Electronic Journalism: Reflections on the Evening News.' In *Television as a Social Force: New Approaches to TV Criticism,* ed. Douglas Cater and R. Adler. New York: Praeger; Michael J. Robinson. 1976. 'Public Affairs Television and the Growth of Political Malaise: The Case of "The Selling of the Pentagon".' *American Political Science Review* 70(2):409–32.
4. Arthur Miller, Edie H. Goldenberg, and Lutz Erbring. 1979. 'Type-Set Politics: The Impact of Newspapers on Public Confidence.' *American Political Science Review* 73:67–84.
5. The scale proved to be highly intercorrelated using Cronbach's alpha. Equivalent, although not identical, media-use measures were employed in the other surveys.
6. In the regression models, the country closest to the overall mean (France) was excluded.
7. See Pippa Norris. 1999. 'Introduction: The Growth of Critical Citizens?' In *Critical Citizens: Global Support for Democratic Governance,* ed. Pippa Norris. Oxford: Oxford University Press.
8. There is a large literature on the concepts of nationalism and national identity. See, for example, B. Anderson. 1996. *Imagined Communities: Reflections on the Origin and Spread of Nationalism.* London: Verso; Michael Billig. 1995. *Banal Nationalism.* London: Sage; Earnest Gellner. 1983. *Nations and Nationalism.* Oxford: Blackwell. For the most thorough empirical work on orientations within Europe from 1973 to 1990, see Oskar Niedermayer and Richard Sinnott (eds.) 1995. *Public Opinion and Internationalized Governance.* Oxford: Oxford University Press.
9. The factor analysis was replicated in the 1996 Eurobarometer survey, and the broad pattern of national trust was repeated, confirming that it measured stable attitudes.
10. See, for example, Dieter Fuchs. 1999. 'The Democratic Culture of Unified Germany.' In *Critical Citizens: Global Support for Democratic Governance,* ed. Pippa Norris. Oxford: Oxford University Press.

11. This item is open to alternative interpretations, because it could measure both support for 'democracy' as a value (which might be expected to rise gradually over time) and also satisfaction with the incumbent regime (which might be expected to fluctuate over time). In this study, we assume that it taps public evaluation of how democracy works, as it loaded with others measuring regime performance.

12. Seymour Martin Lipset and William C. Schneider. 1983. *The Confidence Gap.* New York: Free Press.

13. Stephen Earl Bennett, Staci L. Rhine, Richard S. Flickinger, and Linda L. M. Bennett. 1999. 'Videomalaise Revisited: Reconsidering the Relation between the Public's View of the Media and Trust in Government.' *Harvard International Journal of Press/Politics* 4(4):8–23. On the United States, see Pippa Norris. 1996. 'Does Television Erode Social Capital? A Reply to Putnam.' *PS: Political Science and Politics* 29(3):474–80. On Germany, see Christina Holtz-Bacha. 1990. 'Videomalaise Revisited: Media Exposure and Political Alienation in West Germany.' *European Journal of Communication* 5:78–85. On Britain, see Kenneth Newton. 1997. 'Politics and the News Media: Mobilisation or Videomalaise?' In *British Social Attitudes: The 14th Report*, ed. Roger Jowell, John Curtice, Alison Park, Katarina Thomson, and Lindsay Brook. Aldershot, UK: Ashgate. For a comparative study, see Pippa Norris. 2000. 'Television and Civic Malaise.' In *Disaffected Democrats: What's Troubling the Trilateral Countries*, ed. Susan J. Pharr and Robert D. Putnam. Princeton, NJ: Princeton University Press.

14. For full details about the design and results of the BES campaign panel survey, see Pippa Norris, John Curtice, David Sanders, Margaret Scammell, and Holli A. Semetko. 1999. *On Message: Communicating the Campaign.* London: Sage. It should be noted that these BES measures can also be termed 'external political efficacy', but within the conceptual framework used in this chapter, for consistency, it seemed preferable to include them as trust in parties and politicians at the specific level.

15. John Curtice and Roger Jowell. 1997. 'Trust in the Political System.' In *British Social Attitudes: The 14th report*, ed. Roger Jowell et al. Aldershot, UK: Ashgate.

16. Pippa Norris, John Curtice, David Sanders, Margaret Scammell, and Holli A. Sematko. 1999. *On Message: Communicating the Campaign.* London: Sage.

17. David Sanders and Pippa Norris. 1999. 'Does Negative News Matter? The Effects of Television News on Party Images in the 1997 British General Election.' In *British Elections and Parties Yearbook, 1998*, ed. Charles Pattie et al. London: Frank Cass.

18. George Gerbner et al. 1980. 'The Mainstreaming of America.' *Journal of Communication* 30:10–29.

CHAPTER 12 STAYS HOME? POLITICAL MOBILIZATION

1. See Ivor Crewe. 1982. 'Electoral Participation.' In *Democracy at the Polls*, ed. Austin Ranney and David Butler. Washington, DC: AEI Press; Arend Lijphart. 1997. 'Unequal Participation: Democracy's Unresolved Dilemma.' *American Political Science Review* 91:1–14.

2. Robert W. Jackman and Ross A. Miller. 1995. 'Voter Turnout in the Industrial Democracies During the 1980s.' *Comparative Political Studies* 27:467–92. See also Richard Katz. 1997. *Democracy and Elections.* Oxford: Oxford University Press.

3. Mark Franklin, Cees Van der Eijk, and Erik Oppenhuis. 1996. 'The Institutional Context: Turnout.' In *Choosing Europe: The European Electorate and National Politics in the Face of Union*, ed. Cees Van der Eijk and Mark N. Franklin. Ann Arbor: University of Michigan Press.

4. Raymond Wolfinger and Steven Rosenstone. 1980. *Who Votes?* New Haven, CT: Yale University Press.

5. Gabriel Almond and Sidney Verba. 1963. *The Civic Culture: Political Attitudes and Democracy in Five Nations*. Princeton, NJ: Princeton University Press.

6. See Sidney Verba and Norman Nie. 1972. *Participation in America: Political Democracy and Social Equality*. New York: Harper & Row; Sidney Verba, Kay Lehman Schlozman, and Henry E. Brady. 1995. *Voice and Equality: Civic Voluntarism in American Politics*. Cambridge, MA: Harvard University Press.

7. See, for example, Steven J. Rosenstone and John Mark Hansen. 1993. *Mobilization, Participation and Democracy in America*. New York: Macmillan.

8. Sidney Verba, Kay Lehman Schlozman, and Henry E. Brady. 1995. *Voice and Equality: Civic Voluntarism in American Politics*. Cambridge, MA: Harvard University Press.

9. John Aldrich. 1995. *Why Parties? The Origin and Transformation of Party Politics in America*. Chicago: University of Chicago Press; Martin P. Wattenberg. 1996. *The Decline of American Political Parties: 1952–1994*. Cambridge, MA: Harvard University Press.

10. Bernard Berelson, Paul Lazarsfeld and William N. McPhee. *Voting: A Study of Opinion Formation in a Presidential Campaign*, pp. 246–8. Chicago: University of Chicago Press.

11. See Angus Campbell, Philip Converse, Warren E. Miller, and Donald E. Stokes. 1960. *The American Voter*, p. 92. New York: Wiley. See also Sidney Verba, Norman Nie, and Jae-on Kim. 1978. *Participation and Political Equality: A Seven-Nation Comparison*. Cambridge: Cambridge University Press; Geraint Parry, George Moser, and Neil Day. 1992. *Political Participation and Democracy in Britain*. Cambridge: Cambridge University Press.

12. Bruce E. Pinkleton and Erica Weintraub Austin. 1998. 'Media and Participation: Breaking the Spiral of Disaffection.' In *Engaging the Public: How Government and the Media Can Invigorate American Democracy*, ed. Thomas J. Johnson, Carol E. Hays, and Scott P. Hays. New York: Rowman & Littlefield; Hugh Culbertson and Guido H. Stempel III. 1986. 'How Media Use and Reliance Affect Knowledge Level.' *Communication Research* 13:579–602. Alexis S. Tan. 1980. 'Mass Media Use, Issue Knowledge and Political Involvement.' *Public Opinion Quarterly* 44:241–8.

13. See, for example, Kathleen H. Jamieson. 1992. *Dirty Politics*. Oxford: Oxford University Press; Kathleen H. Jamieson. 1984. *Packaging the Presidency: A History and Criticism of Presidential Advertising*. New York: Oxford University Press; Karen S. Johnson-Cartee and Gary A. Copeland. 1991. *Negative Political Advertising: Coming of Age*. Hillsdale, NJ: Lawrence Erlbaum.

14. Stephen Ansolabehere and Shanto Iyengar. 1995. *Going Negative: How Political Advertisements Shrink and Polarize the Electorate*, p. 112. New York: Free Press.

15. Lynda Lee Kaid and Christina Holtz-Bacha. 1995. *Political Advertising in Western Democracies*. Thousand Oaks, CA: Sage.

16. Joseph N. Cappella and Kathleen H. Jamieson. 1997. *Spiral of Cynicism: The Press and the Public Good.* Oxford: Oxford University Press.

17. Thomas E. Patterson. 1993. *Out of Order.* New York: Knopf.

18. Joseph N. Cappella and Kathleen H. Jamieson. 1997. *Spiral of Cynicism: The Press and the Public Good,* p. 139. Oxford: Oxford University Press.

19. Xinshu Zhao and Glen L. Beske. 1998. 'Horse-Race Polls and Audience Issue Learning.' *Harvard International Journal of Press/Politics* 3(4):13–34. Philip Meyer and Deborah Potter. 1998. 'Pre-election Polls and Issue Knowledge in the 1996 U.S. Presidential Election.' *Harvard International Journal of Press/Politics* 3(4):35–43.

20. Anthony Heath and Bridget Taylor. 1999. 'Turnout and Registration.' In *Critical Elections: British Parties and Voters in Long-Term Perspective,* ed. Geoffrey Evans and Pippa Norris. London: Sage.

21. See Pippa Norris, John Curtice, David Sanders, Margaret Scammell, and Holli A. Semetko. 1999. *On Message: Communicating the Campaign.* London: Sage (chap. 9).

22. IDEA. *Voter Turnout from 1945 to 1998.* www.int-idea.se, p. 25.

23. IDEA. *Voter Turnout from 1945 to 1998.* www.int-idea.se.

24. Mark Franklin, Cees Van der Eijk, and Erik Oppenhuis. 1996. 'The Institutional Context: Turnout.' In *Choosing Europe: The European Electorate and National Politics in the Face of Union,* ed. Cees Van der Eijk and Mark N. Franklin. Ann Arbor: University of Michigan Press.

25. Nicholas Negroponte. 1995. *Being Digital.* New York: Knopf; Michael Dertouzos. 1997. *What Will Be: How the New Information Marketplace Will Change Our Lives.* New York: Harper & Row.

26. Richard Davis and Diane Owen. 1998. *New Media and American Politics,* p. 185. New York: Oxford University Press.

27. For details of this argument and analysis, see Pippa Norris. 1999. 'Who Surfs? New Technology, Old Voters and Virtual Democracy in America.' In *democracy.com? Governance in a Networked World,* ed. Elaine Kamarck and Joseph S. Nye, Jr. Hollis, NH: Hollis Publishing.

28. The scales were constructed from the following standard Eurobarometer items. Factor analysis (not reproduced here) was used to determine the intercorrelations of items in the institutional-trust scales:

- Satisfaction with democracy scales: On the whole, are you very satisfied (4), fairly satisfied (3), not very satisfied (2), or not at all satisfied (1) with
    the way democracy works in our country?
    the way democracy works in the European Union?'
- Support for EU scale: (membership) 'Generally speaking, do you think that our country's membership of the European Union is a good thing (3), a bad thing (1), or neither good nor bad (2)' (Benefit) 'Taking everything into consideration, would you say that our country has on balance benefited (2) or not (1) from being a member of the European Union?' (5-point Membership + Benefit scale)
- EU voting participation: 'Did you vote in the last elections to the European Parliament in June 1994?' 'Do you intend to vote in the next European elections this June?'

- Left–right scale: 'In political matters people talk of the "left" and the "right." How would you place your views on this scale?' Left (1), right (10).
- Knowledge of the EU: 'Have you ever heard of . . . the European Parliament; the European Commission; the Council of Ministers of the European Union; the Court of Justice of the European Commission; the European Ombudsman; the European Central Bank; the European Court of Auditors; the Committee of the Regions of the European Union; the Social and Economic Committee of the European Union?' (9-point scale)
- Trust in EU institutions: 'And for each of [the institutions listed above], please tell me if you tend to trust it or not to trust it.' (9-point scale)
- Trust in government: 'I would like to ask you a question about how much trust you have in certain institutions. For each of the following, please tell me if you tend to trust it or not to trust it? . . . the national government; the national parliament; the EU; political parties; the United Nations; the civil service.'
- Trust in media: '[Same question as above]: the press, radio, television.'

CHAPTER 13 AMERICAN EXCEPTIONALISM?

1. For a recent thorough discussion of the thesis of American exceptionalism, see Graham K. Wilson. 1998. *Only in America? The Politics of the United States in Comparative Perspective.* Chatham, NJ: Chatham House.
2. See Anthony King. 1997. *Running Scared.* New York: Free Press.
3. Scott Mainwaring and Matthew S. Shugart (eds.). 1997. *Presidentialism and Democracy in Latin America.* Cambridge: Cambridge University Press.
4. Graham K. Wilson. 1998. *Only in America? The Politics of the United States in Comparative Perspective,* p. 103. Chatham, NJ: Chatham House.
5. Louis Hartz. 1955. *The Liberal Tradition in America.* New York: Harcourt, Brace; Seymour Martin Lipset. 1996. *American Exceptionalism: A Double-Edged Sword.* New York: Norton.
6. Graham K. Wilson. 1998. *Only in America? The Politics of the United States in Comparative Perspective,* p. 38. Chatham, NJ: Chatham House.
7. Peter Taylor-Gooby. 1989. 'The Role of the State.' In *British Social Attitudes: Special International Report,* ed. Roger Jowell, Sharon Witherspoon, and Lindsay Brook. Aldershot, UK: Gower.
8. Thomas E. Patterson. 1993. *Out of Order.* New York: Knopf.
9. Michael Robinson. 1976. 'Public Affairs Television and the Growth of Political Malaise: The Case of "The Selling of the Pentagon".' *American Political Science Review* 70(2):409–32; Arthur Miller, Edie H. Goldenberg, and Lutz Erbring. 1979. 'Type-Set Politics: The Impact of Newspapers on Public Confidence.' *American Political Science Review* 73:67–84.
10. George Gerbner, Larry Gross, Michael Morgan, and Nancy Signorielli. 1982. 'Charting the Mainstream: Television's Contribution to Political Orientations.' *Journal of Communication* 32(2):100–27; George Gerbner, Larry Gross, Michael Morgan, and Nancy Signorielli. 1984. 'Political Correlates of Television Viewing.' *Public Opinion Quarterly* 48(1):283–300.

11. Thomas E. Patterson. 1993. *Out of Order*. New York: Knopf.
12. Neil Postman. 1985. *Amusing Ourselves to Death*. London: Methuen.
13. These models are not intended to include all the attitudinal and behavioural variables that might contribute to a comprehensive explanation of civic engagement, but rather to include only the social and attitudinal controls that are strictly comparable across the Eurobarometer and NES. The aim of the analysis is not to 'explain' civic engagement but to see if use of the news media remains significant even after introducing prior controls that might plausibly influence such use.
14. Steven Chaffee and Stacey Frank. 1996. 'How Americans Get Political Information: Print versus Broadcast News'. In *The Media and Politics*, ed. Kathleen H. Jamieson, pp. 48–58. *Annals of the American Academy of Political and Social Sciences*, vol. 546; David Weaver. 'What Voters Learn from Media.' In *The Media and Politics*, ed. by Kathleen H. Jamieson, pp. 34–47. *Annals of the American Academy of Political and Social Sciences*, vol. 546.
15. Michael Delli Carpini and Scott Keeter. 1996. *What Americans Know about Politics and Why It Matters*. New Haven, CT: Yale University Press.
16. Stephen Earl Bennett, Staci L. Rhine, Richard S. Flickinger, and Linda L. M. Bennett. 1999. 'Videomalaise Revisited: Reconsidering the Relation between the Public's View of the Media and Trust in Government.' *Harvard International Journal of Press/Politics* 4(4):8–23.
17. Roderick Hart. 1994. *Seducing America*. Oxford: Oxford University Press.
18. Robert D. Putnam. 1995. 'Tuning In, Tuning Out: The Strange Disappearance of Social Capital in America.' *PS: Political Science and Politics* 28(4):664–83.
19. The Cronbach alpha measuring intercorrelations for the activism scale was 0.69.
20. Pippa Norris. 1996. 'Does Television Erode Social Capital? A Reply to Putnam.' *PS: Political Science and Politics* 29(3):474–80.
21. Pippa Norris. 2000. 'Television and Civic Malaise.' In *Disaffected Democrats: What's Troubling the Trilateral Democracies*, ed. Susan J. Pharr and Robert D. Putnam. Princeton, NJ: Princeton University Press.
22. George Gerbner et al. 1980. 'The Mainstreaming of America.' *Journal of Communication* 30:10–29.
23. Pippa Norris. 1996. 'Does Television Erode Social Capital? A Reply to Putnam.' *PS: Political Science and Politics* 29(3):474–80.
24. Stephen Ansolabehere and Shanto Iyengar. 1995. *Going Negative: How Political Advertisements Shrink and Polarize the Electorate*. New York: Free Press.
25. Robert D. Putnam. 1995. 'Tuning In, Tuning Out: The Strange Disappearance of Social Capital in America.' *PS: Political Science and Politics* 28(4):664–83.
26. Thomas E. Patterson. 1994. *Out of Order*, p. 21. New York: Knopf.
27. Warren Miller and Merrill Shanks. 1996. *The Changing American Voter*. Ann Arbor: University of Michigan Press.
28. Robert D. Putnam. 1996. 'The Strange Disappearance of Civic America.' *The American Prospect* 24.
29. For a discussion, see Steven Rosenstone and John Mark Hansen. 1993. *Mobilization, Participation and Democracy in America*, p. 179. New York: Macmillan.
30. Daniel Hallin. 1989. *The Uncensored War: The Media and Vietnam*. Berkeley: University of California Press.
31. For a discussion of alternative explanations for these trends, see Joseph S. Nye, Jr.,

Philip D. Zelikow, and David C. King. 1997. *Why People Don't Trust Government*. Cambridge, MA: Harvard University Press. For performance-based explanations, see Ian McAllister, 'The Economic Performance of Governments', and also Arthur Miller and Ola Listhaug, 'Political Performance and Institutional Trust', both in (1999) *Critical Citizens: Global Support for Democratic Governance*, ed. Pippa Norris. Oxford University Press.

32. Arend Lijphart. 1997. 'Unequal Participation: Democracy's Unresolved Dilemma.' *American Political Science Review* 91:1–14; Sidney Verba, Kay Lehman Schlozman, and Henry E. Brady. 1995. *Voice and Equality: Civic Voluntarism in American Politics*. Cambridge, MA: Harvard University Press.

33. For a general discussion of these trends, see Steven J. Rosenstone and John Mark Hansen. 1993. *Mobilization, Participation and Democracy in America*. New York: Macmillan. The temporary increase in donations that occurred in 1976 may have been caused by the new campaign finance reforms regulated by the Federal Election Commission.

CHAPTER 14 A VIRTUOUS CIRCLE?

1. Pew Research Center for the People and the Press. 1999. *Striking the Balance: Audience Interests, Business Pressures and Journalists' Values*. Washington, DC: Pew Research Center for the People and the Press.

2. For example, a 1998 Pew Center survey found that the majority of Americans thought that news stories and reports were 'often inaccurate', up from one-third who believed that a decade earlier. *Striking the Balance: Audience Interests, Business Pressures and Journalists' Values*. Washington, DC: Pew Research Center for the People and the Press.

3. Kenneth Newton. 1997. 'Politics and the News Media: Mobilisation or Videomalaise?' In *British Social Attitudes: The 14th Report*, ed. Roger Jowell, John Curtice, Alison Park, Katarina Thomson, and Lindsay Brook. Aldershot, UK: Ashgate; Pippa Norris. 1996. 'Does Television Erode Social Capital? A Reply to Putnam.' *PS: Political Science and Politics* 29(3):474–80; Pippa Norris. 1997. *Electoral Change since 1945*. Oxford: Blackwell; Christina Holtz-Bacha. 1990. 'Videomalaise Revisited: Media Exposure and Political Alienation in West Germany.' *European Journal of Communication* 5:78–85.

4. Stephen Earl Bennett, Staci L. Rhine, Richard S. Flickinger, and Linda L. M. Bennett. 1999. 'Videomalaise Revisited: Reconsidering the Relation between the Public's View of the Media and Trust in Government.' *Harvard International Journal of Press/Politics* 4(4):8–23.

5. The study was conducted in only one country, but we should be able to generalize from the findings to understand the direction of causality in correlations found elsewhere. The experiments used a before-and-after research design with over 1,000 participants representing a cross section of the London electorate. Party preferences were first measured with a brief questionnaire. Groups were then exposed to 10 minutes of either positive or negative stories about the Labour or Conservative party, embedded within a typical 30-minute evening television news broadcast during the election campaign in April 1997. Attitudes were then measured again. Analysis was based on comparing the changes in party preferences among groups

exposed to different video stimuli. For details, see Pippa Norris, John Curtice, David Sanders, Margaret Scammell, and Holli A. Semetko. 1999. *On Message: Communicating the Campaign.* London: Sage (chap. 9).

6. See Pippa Norris, John Curtice, David Sanders, Margaret Scammell, and Holli A. Semetko. 1999. *On Message: Communicating the Campaign.* London: Sage (chap. 9). The estimated short-term effects of exposure to positive news on levels of party support were considerable: In a 30-minute news program, exposure to 10 minutes of positive news about either the Conservative or Labour party produced a 10% boost in its level of party support, using a pre–post experimental design. For more details, see David Sanders and Pippa Norris. 1998. 'Does Negative News Matter? The Effects of Television News on Party Images in the 1997 British General Election.' In *British Elections and Parties Yearbook, 1998,* ed. Charles Pattie et al. London: Frank Cass.

7. Pippa Norris (ed.). 1999. *Critical Citizens: Global Support for Democratic Governance.* Oxford: Oxford University Press.

Select Bibliography

Abramson, Jeffrey B., Christopher Arterton, and Gary R. Orren. 1988. *The Electronic Commonwealth*. New York: Basic Books.

Aldrich, John. 1995. *Why Parties? The Origin and Transformation of Party Politics in America*. University of Chicago Press.

Alexander, Herbert E., and Rei Shiratori (eds.). 1994. *Campaign Political Finance among the Democracies*. Boulder, CO: Westview.

Almond, Gabriel, and Sidney Verba. 1963. *The Civic Culture: Political Attitudes and Democracy in Five Nations*. Princeton, NJ: Princeton University Press.

Altheide, David L. 1976. *Creating Reality: How TV News Distorts Events*. Beverly Hills, CA: Sage.

Altheide, David L., and Robert P. Snow. 1979. *Media Logic*. Beverly Hills, CA: Sage.

Anderson, Peter J., and Anthony Weymouth. 1999. *Insulting the Public? The British Press and the European Union*. London: Longman.

Ang, Ien. 1991. *Desperately Seeking the Audience*. London: Routledge.

Ansolabehere, Stephen, Roy Behr, and Shanto Iyengar. 1992. *The Media Game: American Politics in the Television Age*. New York: Macmillan.

Ansolabehere, Stephen, and Shanto Iyengar. 1995. *Going Negative: How Political Advertisements Shrink and Polarize the Electorate*. New York: Free Press.

Asaard, Erik, and W. Lance Bennett. 1997. *Democracy and the Marketplace of Ideas*. Cambridge University Press.

Asp, Kent. 1983. 'The Struggle for Agenda: Party Agenda, Media Agenda and Voter Agenda in the 1979 Swedish Election Campaign.' *Communication Research* 10(3):333–55.

Baker, William F., and George Dessart. 1998. *Down the Tube*. New York: Basic Books.

Baran, Stanley, and Dennis Davis. 1995. *Mass Communication Theory*. Belmont, CA: Wadsworth.

Barber, Benjamin. 1984. *Strong Democracy*. Berkeley: University of California Press.

Bartels, Larry M. 1993. 'Messages Received: The Political Impact of Media Exposure.' *American Political Science Review* 87(2):267–85.

Bellamy, Christine, and John A. Taylor. 1998. *Governing in the Information Age*. Buckingham, Open University.

Bennett, Stephen Earl, Staci L. Rhine, Richard S. Flickinger, and Linda L. M. Bennett. 1999. 'Videomalaise Revisited: Reconsidering the Relation between the Public's

View of the Media and Trust in Government.' *Harvard International Journal of Press/Politics* 4(4):8–23.

Bennett, W. Lance. 1996. *The Governing Crisis: Media, Money and Marketing in American Elections.* New York: St. Martin's Press.

Bennett, W. Lance. 1996. *News: The Politics of Illusion.* New York: Longman.

Bennett, W. Lance. 1998. 'The Uncivic Culture: Communication, Identity and the Rise of Lifestyle Politics.' *PS: Political Science & Politics* 31(4):741–61.

Bennett, W. Lance, and Robert Entman (eds.). 2000. *Mediated Politics.* Cambridge University Press.

Berelson, Bernard, Paul Lazarsfeld, and William N. McPhee. 1954. *Voting: A Study of Opinion Formation in a Presidential Campaign.* University of Chicago Press.

Blumler, Jay. 1983. *Communicating to Voters: Television in the First European Parliamentary Elections.* London: Sage.

Blumler, Jay G. 1992. *Television and the Public Interest: Vulnerable Values in West European Broadcasting.* London: Sage.

Blumler, Jay G. 1997. 'Origins of the Crisis of Communication for Citizenship.' *Political Communication* 14(4):395–404.

Blumler, Jay, and Anthony Fox. 1982. *The European Voter: Popular Responses to the First European Community Elections.* London: Policy Studies Institute.

Blumler, Jay G., and Michael Gurevitch. 1995. *The Crisis of Public Communication.* London: Routledge.

Blumler, Jay G., Michael Gurevitch, and Thomas J. Nossiter. 1989. 'The Earnest vs. the Determined: Election Newsmaking at the BBC, 1987.' In *Political Communications: The General Election Campaign of 1987,* ed. Ivor Crewe and Martin Harrop. Cambridge University Press.

Blumler, Jay G., and Elihu Katz (eds.). 1974. *The Uses of Mass Communications: Current Perspectives on Gratifications Research.* Beverly Hills, CA: Sage.

Blumler, Jay G., Jack M. McLeod and Karl Erik Rosengren. 1992. *Comparatively Speaking: Communication and Culture Across Space and Time.* London: Sage.

Blumler, Jay, and Denis McQuail. 1968. *Television in Politics.* London: Faber & Faber.

Blumler, Jay, and Tom Nossiter. 1991. *Broadcasting Finance in Transition: A Comparative Handbook.* Oxford University Press.

Bogart, Leo. 1995. *Commercial Culture: The Media System and the Public Interest.* Oxford University Press.

Bower, Robert T. 1985. *The Changing Television Audience in America.* New York: Columbia University Press.

Bowler, Shaun, and David M. Farrell (eds.). 1992. *Electoral Strategies and Political Marketing.* London: Macmillan.

Boyd, Andrew. 1994. *Broadcast Journalism: Techniques of Radio & TV News.* Oxford: Focal Press.

Boyd Barratt, Oliver, and Teshi Rantana. 1998. *The Globalization of News.* London: Sage.

Brants, Kees. 1985. 'Broadcasting and Politics in The Netherlands: From Pillar to Post.' *West European Politics* 8:104–21.

Brants, Kees. 1998. 'Who's Afraid of Infotainment?' *European Journal of Communication* 13(3):315–35.

Brants, Kees, Joke Hermes, and Lisbet van Zoonen (eds.). 1997. *The Media in Question: Popular Culture and Public Interests.* London: Sage.

Briggs, Asa. 1985. *The BBC: The First Fifty Years.* Oxford University Press.

Brosius, Hans-Bernd, and Christina Holtz-Bacha. 1999. *German Communication Yearbook.* Cresskill, NJ: Hampton Press.

Bryant, Jennings, and Dolf Zillmann (eds.). 1994. *Media Effects.* Hillsdale, NJ: Lawrence Erlbaum.

Budge, Ian. 1996. *The New Challenge of Direct Democracy.* Oxford: Polity Press.

Budge, Ian. 1999. 'Party Policy and Ideology.' In *Critical Elections: Voters and Parties in Long-Term Perspective*, ed. Geoffrey Evans and Pippa Norris. London: Sage.

Budge, Ian, and David Farlie. 1983. *Explaining and Predicting Elections.* London: Allen & Unwin.

Butler, David. 1952. *The British General Election of 1951.* London: Macmillan.

Butler, David. 1955. *The British General Election of 1955.* London: Macmillan.

Butler, David. 1989. *British General Elections since 1945.* Oxford: Blackwell.

Butler, David, and Dennis Kavanagh. 1974. *The British General Election of February 1974.* London: Macmillan.

Butler, David, and Dennis Kavanagh. 1975. *The British General Election of October 1974.* London: Macmillan.

Butler, David, and Dennis Kavanagh. 1980. *The British General Election of 1979.* London: Macmillan.

Butler, David, and Dennis Kavanagh. 1984. *The British General Election of 1983.* London: Macmillan.

Butler, David, and Dennis Kavanagh. 1988. *The British General Election of 1987.* London: Macmillan.

Butler, David, and Dennis Kavanagh. 1992. *The British General Election of 1992.* New York: St. Martin's Press.

Butler, David, and Dennis Kavanagh. 1997. *The British General Election of 1997.* London: Macmillan.

Butler, David, and Anthony King. 1965. *The British General Election of 1964.* London: Macmillan.

Butler, David, and Anthony King. 1966. *The British General Election of 1966.* London: Macmillan.

Butler, David, and Michael Pinto-Duschinsky. 1971. *The British General Election of 1970.* London: Macmillan.

Butler, David, and Austin Ranney (eds.). 1992. *Electioneering.* Oxford: Clarendon Press.

Butler, David, and Richard Rose. 1960. *The British General Election of 1959.* London: Macmillan.

Butler, David, and Donald E. Stokes. 1974. *Political Change in Britain: The Evolution of Electoral Choice*, 2nd ed. London: Macmillan.

Campbell, Angus, Philip Converse, Warren E. Miller, and Donald E. Stokes. 1960. *The American Voter.* New York: Wiley.

Cappella, Joseph N., and Kathleen H. Jamieson. 1996. 'News Frames, Political Cynicism and Media Cynicism.' In *The Media and Politics*, ed. Kathleen H. Jamieson, pp. 71–84. *Annals of the American Academy of Political Science*, vol. 546.

Cappella, Joseph N., and Kathleen H. Jamieson. 1996. 'News Frames, Political Cynicism and Media Cynicism.' In *The Media and Politics*, ed. Kathleen H. Jamieson. *Annals of the American Academy of Political and Social Sciences*, vol. 546.

Cappella, Joseph N., and Kathleen H. Jamieson. 1997. *Spiral of Cynicism: The Press and the Public Good.* Oxford University Press.

Cathcart, Brian. 1997. *Were You Still Up for Portillo?* London: Penguin.

Cayrol, Roland. 1983. 'Media Use and Campaign Evaluations: Social and Political Stratification of the European Electorate.' In *Communicating to Voters: Television in the First European Parliament Elections,* ed. Jay Blumler. London: Sage.

Cayrol, Roland. 1991. 'European Elections and the Pre-Electoral Period: Media Use and Campaign Evaluations.' *European Journal of Political Research* 19:17–30.

Chaffee, Steven, and Stacey Frank. 1996. 'How Americans Get Political Information: Print versus Broadcast News.' In *The Media and Politics,* ed. Kathleen H. Jamieson, pp. 48–58. *Annals of the American Academy of Political and Social Sciences,* vol. 546.

Chaffee, Steven H., and Stacey Frank Kanihan. 1997. 'Learning Politics from the Mass Media.' *Political Communication* 14(4):421–30.

Chaffee, Steven H., and Joan Schleuder. 1986. 'Measurement and Effects of Attention to Media News.' *Human Communication Research* 13:76–107.

Chan, Sophia. 1997. 'Effects of Attention to Campaign Coverage on Political Trust.' *International Journal of Public Opinion Research* 9(3):286–96.

Chew, Fiona. 1994. 'The Relationship of Information Needs to Issue Relevance and Media Use.' *Journalism Quarterly* 71:676–88.

Cohan, Akido A. 1996. *Global Newsrooms: Local Audiences.* London: John Libbey.

Cohen, Bernard. 1963. *The Press and Foreign Policy.* Princeton, NJ: Princeton University Press.

Coleman, James A., and Brigitte Rollet. 1998. *Television in Europe.* Exeter: Intellect.

Comstock, George. 1989. *The Evolution of American Television.* Newbury Park, CA: Sage.

Corner, John. 1995. *Television Form and Public Address.* London: Arnold.

Cox, Geoffrey. 1983. *See It Happen: The Making of ITN.* London: The Bodley Head Ltd.

Crewe, Ivor. 1997. 'The Opinion Polls: Confidence Restored?' In *Britain Votes 1997,* ed. Pippa Norris and Neil Gavin. Oxford University Press.

Crewe, Ivor, and Brian Gosschalk. 1995. *Political Communications: The General Election Campaign of 1992.* Cambridge University Press.

Crewe, Ivor, Brian Gosschalk, and John Bartle. 1998. *Political Communications: Why Labour Won the General Election of 1997.* London: Frank Cass.

Crewe, Ivor, and Martin Harrop. 1989. *Political Communications: The General Election Campaign of 1987.* Cambridge University Press.

Crozier, Michel, Samuel P. Huntington, and Joji Watanuki. 1975. *The Crisis of Democracy: Report on the Governability of Democracies to the Trilateral Commission.* New York University Press.

Culbertson, Hugh, and Guido H. Stempel III. 1986. 'How Media Use and Reliance Affect Knowledge Level.' *Communication Research* 13:579–602.

Curran, James, and Jean Seaton. 1991. *Power Without Responsibility: The Press and Broadcasting in Britain.* London: Routledge.

Curtice, John. 1997. 'Is the Sun Shining on Tony Blair? The Electoral Influence of British Newspapers.' *Harvard International Journal of Press/Politics* 2(2):9–26.

Curtice, John, and Roger Jowell. 1995. 'The Sceptical Electorate.' In *British Social Attitudes, the 12th Report,* ed. Roger Jowell et al. Aldershot, UK: Dartmouth.

Curtice, John, and Roger Jowell. 1997. 'Trust in the Political System.' In *British Social Attitudes: The 14th Report,* ed. Roger Jowell et al. Aldershot, UK: Ashgate.

Curtice, John, Rüdiger Schmitt-Beck, and Peter Schrott. 1998. 'Do the Media Matter?' Paper presented at the annual meeting of the Midwest Political Science Association, Chicago.

Curtice, John, and Holli Semetko. 1994. 'Does It Matter What the Papers Say?' In *Labour's Last Chance?* ed. Anthony Heath, Roger Jowell and John Curtice. Aldershot, UK: Dartmouth.

Dahlgren, Peter. 1995. *Television and the Public Sphere.* London: Sage.

Dahlgren, Peter, and Colin Sparks. 1997. *Communication and Citizenship.* London: Routledge.

Dalton, Russell J. 1996. *Citizen Politics: Public Opinion and Political Parties in Advanced Industrialized Democracies.* Chatham, NJ: Chatham House.

Dalton, Russell J., Paul A. Beck, and Robert Huckfeldt. 1998. 'Partisan Cues and the Media: Information Flows in the 1992 Presidential Election.' *American Political Science Review* 92(1).

Dalton, Russell J., Kazuhisa Kawakami, Holli A. Semetko, Hiroshisa Suzuki, and Katrin Voltmer. 1998. 'Partisan Cues in the Media: Cross-National Comparisons of Election Coverage.' Paper presented at the annual meeting of the Midwest Political Science Association, Chicago.

Dautrich, Kenneth, and Thomas H. Hartley. 1999. *How the News Media Fail American Voters: Causes, Consequences and Remedies.* New York: Columbia University Press.

Davis, Richard. 1999. *The Web of Politics.* Oxford University Press.

Davis, Richard, and Diane Owen. 1998. *New Media and American Politics.* Oxford University Press.

Dearing, John W., and Everett M. Rogers. 1996. *Agenda-Setting.* London: Sage.

De Bens, Els, and Gianpietro Mazzolini. 1998. 'The Media in the Age of Digital Communication.' In *Media Policy: Convergence, Concentration and Commerce,* ed. Denis McQuail and Karen Siune. London: Sage.

Della Porta, Donatella, and Yves Meny. 1997. *Democracy and Corruption in Europe.* London: Pinter.

Delli Carpini, Michael, and Scott Keeter. 1996. *What Americans Know about Politics and Why It Matters.* New Haven, CT: Yale University Press.

Denver, David, and Gordon Hands. 1997. *Modern Constituency Campaigning.* London: Frank Cass.

Denver, David, Gordon Hands, and Simon Henig. 1998. 'A Triumph of Targeting? Constituency Campaigning in the 1997 Election.' In *British Elections and Parties Review,* ed. David Denver et al. London: Frank Cass.

Dertouzos, Michael. 1997. *What Will Be: How the New Information Marketplace Will Change Our Lives.* New York: Harper & Row.

Diamond, Ed. 1982. *Sign Off: The Last Days of Television.* Cambridge, MA: MIT Press.

Diez-Nicolas, Juan, and Holli A. Semetko. 1995. 'La television y las elecciones de 1993.' In *Communicacion Politica,* ed. A. Munoz-Alonso and J. Ignacio Rospir. Madrid: Editorial Universitas, S.A.

Dogan, Mattei, and Dominique Pelassy. 1984. *How to Compare Nations: Strategies in Comparative Politics.* Oxford: Blackwell.

Douglas, Susan J. 1987. *Inventing American Broadcasting, 1899–1922.* Baltimore: Johns Hopkins University Press.

Downs, Anthony. 1957. *An Economic Theory of Democracy.* New York: Harper & Row.

Dunleavy, Patrick, and Christopher Husbands. 1985. *Democracy at the Crossroads*. London: Allen & Unwin.

Engel, Matthew. 1996. *Tickle the Public: One Hundred Years of the Popular Press*. London: Gollancz.

Entman, Robert M. 1989. *Democracy without Citizens: Media and the Decay of American Politics*. Oxford: Oxford University Press.

Esaisson, Peter, and Søren Holmberg. 1996. *Representation from Above*. Aldershot, UK: Dartmouth.

Esser, Frank. 1999. 'Tabloidization of News: A Comparative Analysis of Anglo-American and German Press Journalism.' *European Journal of Communication* 14(3):291–324.

europa.eu.int/

Evans, Geoffrey (ed.). 1999. *The End of Class Politics?* Oxford: Oxford University Press.

Evans, Geoffrey, and Pippa Norris. 1999. *Critical Elections: British Parties and Voters in Long-Term Perspective*. London: Sage.

Fallows, James. 1996. *Breaking the News: How the Media Undermine American Democracy*. New York: Pantheon.

Faucheux, R. (ed.). 1995. *The Road to Victory: The Complete Guide to Winning in Politics*. Washington, DC: Campaigns and Elections.

Finkelstein, Daniel. 1998. 'Why the Conservatives Lost.' In *Political Communications: Why Labour Won the General Election of 1997*, ed. Ivor Crewe, Brian Gosschalk, and John Bartle. London: Frank Cass.

Flanagan, Scott C. 1996. 'Media Exposure and the Quality of Political Participation in Japan.' In *Media and Politics in Japan*, ed. Susan J. Pharr and Ellis S. Krauss. Honolulu: University Press of Hawaii.

Flanagan, Scott C., Shinsaku Kohei, Ichiro Miyake, Bradley M. Richardson, and Joji Watanuki (eds.). 1991. *The Japanese Voter*. New Haven, CT: Yale University Press.

Fletcher, Frederick (ed.). 1991. *Media, Elections and Democracy*. Toronto: Dundurn Press.

Franklin, Bob. 1994. *Packaging Politics*. London: Arnold.

Franklin, Bob. 1997. *Newzak and News Media*. London: Routledge.

Friedrichsen, Mike. 1996. 'Politik- und Parteiverdruss durch Skandalberichterstattung?' In *Medien und Politischer Prozess*, ed. Otfried Jarren, Heribert Schatz, and Hartmut Wessler. Opladen: Westdeutscher Verlag.

Gabler, Neal. 1998. *Life the Movie: How Entertainment Conquered Reality*. New York: Knopf.

Gadir, S. 1982. 'Media Agenda-Setting in Australia: The Rise and Fall of Public Issues.' *Media Information Australia* 26:13–23.

Gans, Herbert. 1979. *Deciding What's News: A Study of CBS Evening News, NBC Nightly News, Newsweek and Time*. New York: Pantheon.

Garment, Suzanne. 1991. *Scandal*. New York.

Gates, Bill. 1995. *The Road Ahead*. New York: Viking.

Gauntlet, David. 1995. *Moving Experiences: Understanding Television's Influence and Effects*. London: John Libbey.

Gavin, Neil, and David Sanders. 1996. 'The Impact of Television News on Public Perceptions of the Economy and Government, 1993–1994.' In *British Elections and Parties Yearbook, 1996*, ed. David M. Farrell et al. London: Frank Cass.

Gavin, Neil, and David Sanders. 1997. 'The Economy and Voting.' In *Britain Votes 1997*, ed. Pippa Norris and Neil Gavin. Oxford University Press.

Geddes, Andrew, and Jon Tonge (eds.). 1997. *Labour's Landslide*. Manchester University Press.

Gelman, Andrew, and Gary King. 1993. 'Why Are American Presidential Election Campaign Polls So Variable when Votes Are So Predictable?' *British Journal of Political Science* 23:409–51.

Gerbner, George, et al. 1980. 'The Mainstreaming of America.' *Journal of Communication* 30:10–29.

Gerbner, George, Larry Gross, Michael Morgan, and Nancy Signorielli. 1984. 'Political Correlates of Television Viewing.' *Public Opinion Quarterly* 48(1):283–300.

Gerbner, George, Larry Gross, Michael Morgan, and Nancy Signorielli. 1994. 'Growing Up With Television: The Cultivation Perspective.' In *Media Effects*, ed. Jennings Bryant and Dolf Zillmann. Hillsdale, NJ: Lawrence Erlbaum.

Gibson, Rachel K., and Stephen J. Ward. 1998. 'U.K. Political Parties and the Internet: "Politics as Usual" in the New Media?' *Harvard International Journal of Press/Politics* 3(3):14–38.

Glasgow Media Group. 1976. *Bad News*. London: Routledge.

Glasgow Media Group. 1980. *More Bad News*. London: Routledge.

Goddard, Peter, Margaret Scammell, and Holli Semetko. 1998. 'Too Much of a Good Thing? Television in the 1997 Election Campaign.' In *Political Communications: Why Labour Won the General Election of 1997*, ed. Ivor Crewe, Brian Gosschalk, and John Bartle. London: Frank Cass.

Golding, Peter. 1996. 'World Wide Wedge: Division and Contradiction in the Global Information Infrastructure.' *Monthly Review* 48(3):70–85.

Golding, Peter. 1998. 'Measuring Tabloidization in the British Press.' Unpublished paper, University of Loughborough.

Gould, Philip. 1998. 'Why Labour Won.' In *Political Communications: Why Labour Won the General Election of 1997*, ed. Ivor Crewe, Brian Gosschalk and John Bartle. London: Frank Cass.

Gould, Philip. 1999. *The Unfinished Revolution*. Boston: Little, Brown.

Graber, Doris. 1988. *Processing the News: How People Tame the Information Tide*, 2nd ed. White Plains: Longman.

Graber, Doris. 1994. 'Why Voters Fail Information Tests: Can the Hurdles Be Overcome?' *Political Communication* 11(4):331–46.

Graber, Doris, Denis McQuail, and Pippa Norris (eds.). 1998. *The Politics of News: The News of Politics*. Washington, DC: CQ Press.

Gross, Lynne Schafer. 1995. *The International World of Electronic Media*. New York: McGraw-Hill.

Grossman, Lawrence. 1995. *The Electronic Republic*. London: Penguin.

Gunter, Barrie. 1994. 'The Question of Media Violence.' In *Media Effects*, ed. Jennings Bryant and Dolf Zillmann. Hillsdale, NJ: Lawrence Erlbaum.

Gunter, Barrie, Jane Sancho-Aldridge, and Paul Winstone. 1994. *Television and the Public's View, 1993*. London: John Libbey.

Gunther, Richard, and Anthony Mughan (eds.). 2000. *Democracy and the Media: A Comparative Perspective*. Cambridge University Press.

Gurevitch, Michael, and Jay G. Blumler. 1990. 'Comparative Research: The Extending Frontier.' In *New Directions of Political Communication: A Resource Book*, ed. David L. Swanson and Dan Nimmo. Newbury Park, CA: Sage.

Habermas, Jürgen. 1984. *The Theory of Communicative Action*. London: Heinemann.

Habermas, Jürgen. 1987. T*he Philosophical Discourse of Modernity*. Cambridge, MA: MIT Press.

Habermas, Jürgen. 1998. *The Structural Transformation of the Public Sphere*. Cambridge, MA: MIT Press.

Hachten, William A. 1998. *The Troubles of Journalism: A Critical Look at What's Right and Wrong with the Press*. Hillsdale, NJ: Lawrence Erlbaum.

Hallin, Daniel. 1989. *The Uncensored War: The Media and Vietnam*. Berkeley: University of California Press.

Hallin, Daniel C. 1992. 'The Passing of "High Modernism" of American Journalism.' *Journal of Communication* 42:14–25.

Harmel, Robert, and Kenneth Janda. 1994. 'An Integrated Theory of Party Goals and Party Change.' *Journal of Theoretical Politics* 6:259–87.

Harper, Christopher. 1998. *And That's the Way It Will Be*. New York University Press.

Harris, Richard Jackson. 1994. 'The Impact of Sexually Explicit Material.' In *Media Effects*, ed. Jennings Bryant and Dolf Zillmann. Hillsdale, NJ: Lawrence Erlbaum.

Harrison, Martin. 1989. 'Television Election News Analysis: Use and Abuse – A Reply.' *Political Studies* 37(4):652–8.

Harrison, Martin. 1997. 'Politics on the Air.' In *The British General Election of 1997*, ed. David Butler and Dennis Kavanagh. London: Macmillan.

Harrop, Martin, and Margaret Scammell. 1992. 'A Tabloid War.' In *The British General Election of 1992*, ed. David Butler and Dennis Kavanagh. London: Macmillan.

Hart, Roderick. 1994. *Seducing America*. Oxford University Press.

Hartley, John. 1996. *Popular Reality: Journalism, Modernity, Popular Culture*. London: Arnold.

Hartz, Louis. 1955. *The Liberal Tradition in America*. New York: Harcourt, Brace.

Hauben, Michael, and Rhonda Hauben. 1998. *Netizens: On the History and Impact of Usenet and the Internet*. Los Alamitos, CA: IEEE Computer Science Press.

Head, S. W., C. H. Stirling, and L. B. Schofield (eds.). 1994. *Broadcasting in America: A Survey of Electronic Media*. Boston: Houghton Mifflin.

Heath, Anthony, Roger Jowell, and John Curtice (eds.). 1994. *Labour's Last Chance? The 1992 Election and Beyond*. Aldershot, UK: Dartmouth.

Heinderyckx, François. 1993. 'Television News Programmes in Western Europe: A Comparative Study.' *European Journal of Communication* 8:425–50.

Hewitt, Patricia, and Philip Gould. 1993. 'Learning from Success – Labour and Clinton's New Democrats.' *Renewal* 1(1):45–51.

Hill, Kevin A., and John E. Hughes. 1998. *Cyberpolitics: Citizen Activism in the Age of the Internet*. New York: Rowman & Littlefield.

Holbrook, Thomas M. 1996. *Do Campaigns Matter?* Thousand Oaks, CA: Sage.

Holtz-Bacha, Christina. 1990. 'Videomalaise Revisited: Media Exposure and Political Alienation in West Germany.' *European Journal of Communication* 5:78–85.

Hovland, Carl I. 1959. 'Reconciling Conflicting Results from Experimental and Survey Studies of Attitude Change.' *American Psychologist* 14:10–23.

Hovland, Carl, Irving Janis, and Harold H. Kelley. 1953. *Communication and Persuasion*. New Haven, CT: Yale University Press.

Hovland, Carl I., Arthur A. Lumsdaine, and Fred D. Sheffield. 1949. *Experiments on Mass Communications*. Princeton, NJ: Princeton University Press.

Huckfeldt, Robert, and John Sprague. 1995. *Citizens, Politics, and Social Communications*. Cambridge University Press.

Humphreys, Peter J. 1996. *Mass Media and Media Policy in Western Europe*. Manchester University Press.

Hutchinson, David. 1999. *Media Policy*. Oxford: Blackwell.

Ingham, Bernard. 1994. *Kill the Messenger*. London: HarperCollins.

Inglehart, Ronald. 1990. *Culture Shift in Advanced Industrial Society*. Princeton, NJ: Princeton University Press.

Inglehart, Ronald. 1997. *Modernization and Postmodernization: Cultural, Economic and Political Change in 43 Societies*. Princeton, NJ: Princeton University Press.

Iyengar, Shanto. 1990. 'Shortcuts to Political Knowledge. The Role of Selective Attention and Accessibility.' In *Information and Democratic Processes*, ed. John A. Ferejon and James H. Kuklinski. Chicago: University of Illinois Press.

Iyengar, Shanto. 1991. *Is Anyone Responsible? How Television Frames Political Issues*. University of Chicago Press.

Iyengar, Shanto, and Donald R. Kinder. 1987. *News That Matters: Television and American Opinion*. University of Chicago Press.

Iyengar, Shanto, and Richard Reeves. 1997. *Do the Media Govern?* Thousand Oaks, CA: Sage.

Jamieson, Kathleen H. 1984. *Packaging the Presidency: A History and Criticism of Presidential Advertising*. Oxford University Press.

Jamieson, Kathleen H. 1992. *Dirty Politics*. Oxford University Press.

Jamieson, Kathleen H. (ed.). 1996. *The Media and Politics*. Annals of the American Academy of Political and Social Sciences, vol. 546.

Jensen, Klaus Bruhn (ed.). 1998. *News of the World: World Cultures Look at Television News*. London: Routledge.

Johnson, Thomas J., Carol E. Hays, and Scott P. Hays. 1998. *Engaging the Public: How Government and the Media Can Reinvigorate Democracy*. Lanham, MD: Rowman & Littlefield.

Johnson-Cartee, Karen S., and Gary A. Copeland. 1991. *Negative Political Advertising: Coming of Age*. Hillsdale, NJ: Lawrence Erlbaum.

Johnson-Cartee, Karen S., and Gary A. Copeland. 1997. *Inside Political Campaigning*. New York: Praeger.

Johnston, Richard, et al. 1992. *Letting the People Decide*. Montreal: McGill-Queen's University Press.

Jones, Nicholas. 1995. *Soundbites and Spin Doctors*. London: Cassell.

Jones, Nicholas. 1997. *Campaign 1997: How the General Election Was Won and Lost*. London: Indigo.

Just, Marion. 1998. 'Candidate Strategies and the Media Campaign.' In *The Election of 1996*, ed. Gerald M. Pomper. Chatham, NJ: Chatham House.

Just, Marion R., Ann N. Crigler, Dean E. Alger, Timothy E. Cook, Montague Kern, and Darrell M. West. 1996. *Crosstalk: Citizens, Candidates and the Media in a Presidential Campaign*. University of Chicago Press.

Just, Marion, Ann Crigler, and Montague Kern. 1998. 'Information, Persuasion and Solidarity: Civic Uses of the Internet in Campaign '96.' Paper delivered at the Western Political Science Association annual meeting, Los Angeles.

Kaid, Lynda Lee, and Christina Holtz-Bacha. 1995. *Political Advertising in Western Democracies*. Thousand Oaks, CA: Sage.

Kaid, Lynda Lee, Dan Nimmo, and Keith R. Sanders. 1986. *New Perspectives on Political Advertising*. Carbondale: Southern Illinois University Press.

Kalb, Marvin. 1998. 'The Rise of the New News.' Discussion paper D-34. Cambridge, MA: The Joan Shorenstein Center on the Press, Politics and Public Policy, John F. Kennedy School of Government.

Kamarck, Elaine, and Joseph S. Nye, Jr. (eds.). 1999. *democracy.com? Governance in a Networked World*. Hollis, NH: Hollis Publishing.

Katz, Elihu, and Paul Lazarsfeld. 1955. *Personal Influence*. Glencoe, IL: Free Press.

Katz, Richard S., and Peter Mair (eds.). 1992. *Party Organization: A Data Handbook*. London: Sage.

Katz, Richard S., and Peter Mair. 1995. 'Changing Models of Party Organization and Party Democracy: The Emergence of the Cartel Party.' *Party Politics* 1(1):5–28.

Kavanagh, Dennis. 1994. 'Changes in Electoral Behaviour and the Party System.' *Parliamentary Affairs* 47(4):596–613.

Kavanagh, Dennis. 1995. *Election Campaigning: The New Marketing of Politics*. Oxford: Blackwell.

Kavanagh, Dennis. 1997. 'The Labour Campaign.' In *Britain Votes 1997*, ed. Pippa Norris and Neil Gavin. Oxford University Press.

Keane, John. 1991. *The Media and Democracy*. Oxford: Blackwell.

Kellner, Peter. 1997. 'Why the Tories Were Trounced.' In *Britain Votes 1997*, ed. Pippa Norris and Neil Gavin. Oxford University Press.

Kepplinger, Hans M. 1996. 'Skandale und Politikverdrossenheit – Ein Langzeitvergleich.' In *Medien und Politischer Prozess*, ed. Otfried Jarren et al. Opladen: Westdeutscher Verlag.

Kerbell, Matthew R. 1994. *Edited for Television: CNN, ABC and the 1992 Presidential Campaign*. Boulder, CO: Westview.

Key, V. O. 1964. *Public Opinion and American Democracy*. New York: Knopf.

Kimball, Penn. 1994. *Downsizing the News: Network Cutbacks in the Nation's Capital*. Washington, DC: Woodrow Wilson Center Press.

Kinder, Ronald R., and Thomas R. Palfrey. 1992. *Experimental Foundations of Political Science*. Ann Arbor: University of Michigan Press.

King, Anthony. 1997. *New Labour Triumphs: Britain at the Polls*. Chatham, NJ: Chatham House.

King, Anthony. 1997. *Running Scared*. New York: Free Press.

Kirchheimer, Otto. 1966. 'The Transformation of Western Party Systems.' In *Political Parties and Political Development*, ed. J. La Polambara and M. Weiner. Princeton, NJ: Princeton University Press.

Klapper, Joseph T. 1960. *The Effects of the Mass Media*. Glencoe, IL: Free Press.

Klingemann, Hans-Dieter, and Dieter Fuchs. 1995. *Citizens and the State*. Oxford University Press.

Klingemann, Hans-Dieter, Richard I. Hofferbert, and Ian Budge. 1994. *Parties, Policies and Democracy*. Boulder, CO: Westview.

Klite, Paul, Robert M. Bardwell, and Jason Salzman. 1997. 'Local TV News: Getting Away With Murder.' *Harvard International Journal of Press/Politics* 2(2):102–12.

Kohut, Andrew, and Robert C. Toth. 1998. 'The Central Conundrum: How Can People Like What They Distrust?' *Harvard International Journal of Press/Politics* 3(1):110–17.

Koole, Ruud. 1996. 'Cadre, Catch-All or Cartel? A Comment on the Notion of the Cartel Party.' *Party Politics* 2(4):507–24.

Kumar, Krishan. 1995. *From Post-Industrial to Post-Modern Society.* Oxford: Blackwell.

Langer, John. 1998. *Tabloid Television: Popular Journalism and the Other News.* London: Routledge.

Lasswell, Harold. 1949. 'The Structure and Function of Communication in Society.' In *Mass Communication*, ed. W. S. Schramm. Urbana: University of Illinois Press.

Lazarsfeld, Paul F., Bernard Berelson, and Hazel Gaudet. 1944. *The People's Choice: How the Voter Makes up His Mind in a Presidential Campaign.* New York: Columbia University Press.

Lemert, James B., William R. Elliott, James M. Bernstein, William L. Rosenberg, and Karl J. Nestvold. 1991. *News Verdicts, the Debates and Presidential Campaigns.* New York: Praeger.

Lewis-Beck, Michael S. 1988. *Economics and Elections: The Major Western Democracies.* Ann Arbor: University of Michigan Press.

Lewis-Beck, Michael, and Tim Rice. 1992. *Forecasting Elections.* Washington, DC: CQ Press.

Lichtenberg, Judith. 1990. *Democracy and the Mass Media.* Cambridge University Press.

Lijphart, Arend. 1997. 'Unequal Participation: Democracy's Unresolved Dilemma.' *American Political Science Review* 91:1–14.

Linton, Martin. 1994. *Money and Votes.* London: Institute for Public Policy Research.

Linton, Martin. 1995. 'Was It *The Sun* Wot Won It?' Seventh Guardian Lecture, Nuffield College, Oxford, October 30.

Lippmann, Walter. 1997. *Public Opinion.* New York: Free Press.

Lipset, Seymour Martin. 1996. *American Exceptionalism: A Double-Edged Sword.* New York: Norton.

Lipset, Seymour Martin, and Stein Rokkan. 1967. *Party Systems and Voter Alignments.* New York: Free Press.

Lipset, Seymour Martin, and William C. Schneider. 1983. *The Confidence Gap.* New York: Free Press.

Lodge, Milton, and Kathleen M. McGraw. 1995. *Political Judgment: Structure and Process.* Ann Arbor: University of Michigan Press.

Lowery, Shearon A., and Melvin L. DeFleur. 1995. *Milestones in Mass Communications Research.* New York: Longman.

Lull, James, and Stephen Hinerman (eds.). 1997. *Media Scandals.* Cambridge: Polity Press.

Luntz, Frank I. 1988. *Candidates, Consultants and Campaigns.* Oxford: Blackwell.

Lupia, Arthur, and Mathew D. McCubbins. 1998. *The Democratic Dilemma.* Cambridge University Press.

Maarek, Philippe J. 1995. *Political Marketing and Communications.* London: John Libbey.

McChesney, Robert W. 1997. *Capitalism and the New Information Age*. New York: Monthly Review Press.

McCombs, Maxwell. 1997. 'Building Consensus: The News Media's Agenda-Setting Roles.' *Political Communication* 14(4):433–43.

McCombs, Maxwell, and George Estrada. 1997. 'The News Media and the Pictures in Our Heads.' In *Do the Media Govern?*, ed. Shanto Iyengar and Richard Reeves. Thousand Oaks, CA: Sage.

McCombs, Maxwell, and D. L. Shaw. 1972. 'The Agenda-setting Function of the Mass Media.' *Public Opinion Quarterly* 36:176–87.

McCubbins, Matthew D. 1992. *Under the Watchful Eye*. Washington, DC: CQ Press.

McCullum, R. B., and Alison Readman. 1964. *The British General Election of 1945*, 2nd ed. London: Frank Cass.

McKee, David. 1995. 'Fact Is Free but Comment Is Sacred; or Was It *The Sun* Wot Won It?' In *Political Communications: The General Election Campaign of 1992*, ed. Ivor Crewe and Brian Gosschalk. Cambridge University Press.

McKie, David. 1998. 'Swingers, Clingers, Waverers and Quaverers: The Tabloid Press in the 1997 Election.' In *Political Communications: Why Labour Won the General Election of 1997*, ed. Ivor Crewe, Brian Gosschalk, and John Bartle. London: Frank Cass.

McLachlan, Shelley. 1999. 'Who's Afraid of the News Bunny? The Changing Face of the Television Evening News Broadcast.' Information and Democracy Research Project, working paper no. 3, Loughborough University.

McLachlan, Shelley, and Peter Golding. 1999. 'Tabloidization in the British Press: A Quantitative Investigation into Changes in British Newspapers, 1952–1997.' Communication Research Centre, working paper no. 9, Loughborough University.

McLean, Iain. 1989. *Democracy and New Technology*. Oxford: Polity Press.

McNair, Brian. 1994. *News and Journalism in the UK*. London: Routledge.

McNair, Brian. 1995. *An Introduction to Political Communication*. London: Routledge.

McQuail, Denis. 1992. *Media Performance: Mass Communication and the Public Interest*. London: Sage.

McQuail, Denis. 1994. *Mass Communication Theory*. London: Sage.

McQuail, Denis. 1997. *Audience Analysis*. London: Sage.

McQuail, Denis, and Karen Siune. 1998. *Media Policy: Convergence, Concentration and Commerce*. London: Sage.

McQuail, Denis, and Sven Windahl. 1993. *Communication Models*. London: Longman.

Margolis, Michael, David Resnick, and Chin-chang Tu. 1997. 'Campaigning on the Internet: Parties and Candidates on the World Wide Web in the 1996 Primary Season.' *Harvard International Journal of Press/Politics* 2(1):59–78.

Margolis, Michael, David Resnick, and Joel D. Wolfe. 1999. 'Party Competition on the Internet: Minor versus Major Parties in the UK and the USA.' *Harvard International Journal of Press/Politics*.

Markovits, Andrei S., and Mark Silverstein (eds.). 1988. *The Politics of Scandal*. New York: Holmes & Meier.

Marsh, Michael, and Pippa Norris (eds.). 1997. 'Political Representation in the European Parliament.' Special issue of the *European Journal of Political Research* 32(2).

Mayhew, Leon H. 1997. *The New Public: Professional Communication and the Means of Social Influence*. Cambridge University Press.

Mazzoleni, Gianpietro. 1987. 'Media Logic and Party Logic in Campaign Coverage: The Italian General Election of 1983.' *European Journal of Communication* 2(1):81–103.

Mediametrie. 1999. *One Television Year in the World: 1998*. Paris: Mediametrie.

Mendelsohn, Paul F., and Garrett J. O'Keefe. 1976. *The People Choose a President*. New York: Praeger.

Merrill, John C. 1995. *Global Journalism: Survey of International Communication*. New York: Longman.

Meyer, Philip, and Deborah Potter. 1998. 'Pre-election Polls and Issue Knowledge in the 1996 U.S. Presidential Election.' *Harvard International Journal of Press/Politics* 3(4):35–43.

Miller, Arthur, Edie H. Goldenberg, and Lutz Erbring. 1979. 'Type-Set Politics: The Impact of Newspapers on Public Confidence.' *American Political Science Review* 73:67–84.

Miller, Warren, and Merrill Shanks. 1996. *The Changing American Voter*. Ann Arbor: University of Michigan Press.

Miller, William L. 1991. *Media and Voters: The Audience, Content, and Influence of Press and Television at the 1987 General Election*. Oxford: Clarendon Press.

Miller, William L., et al. 1991. *How Voters Change*. Oxford: Clarendon Press.

Miller, William L., Neil Sonntag, and David Broughton. 1989. 'Television in the 1987 British Election Campaign: Its Content and Influence.' *Political Studies* 37(4):626–51.

Milne, R. S., and H. C. Mackenzie. 1954. *Straight Fight*. London: Hansard Society.

Mitchell, Jeremy, and Jay G. Blumler. 1994. *Television and the Viewer Interest*. London: John Libbey.

Mowlana, Hamid. 1997. *Global Information and World Communication*, 2nd ed. London: Sage.

Mughan, Anthony. 1996. 'Television Can Matter: Bias in the 1992 General Election.' In *British Elections and Parties Yearbook, 1996*, ed. David M. Farrell et al. London: Frank Cass.

Murdock, Graham, and Peter Golding. 1989. 'Information Poverty and Political Inequality: Citizenship in the Age of Privatised Communications.' *Journal of Communication* 39:180–93.

Mutz, Diana. 1998. *Impersonal Influence: How Perceptions of Mass Collectives Affect Political Attitudes*. Cambridge University Press.

Negrine, Ralph. 1994. *Politics and the Mass Media in Britain*, 2nd ed. London: Routledge.

Negrine, Ralph, and Stylianos Papathanassopoulos. 1996. 'The "Americanization" of Political Communications: A Critique.' *Harvard International Journal of Press/Politics* 1(2):45–62.

Negroponte, Nicholas. 1995. *Being Digital*. New York: Knopf.

Neill Report. 1998. *Fifth Report of the Committee on Standards in Public Life: The Funding of Political Parties in the United Kingdom*, chaired by Lord Neill of Blayden. Cm 4057-I. London: The Stationery Office.

Neuman, W. Russell. 1991. *The Future of the Mass Audience*. Cambridge University Press.

Neuman, W. Russell. 1998. 'The Global Impact of New Technologies.' In *The Politics of News: The News of Politics*, ed. Doris Graber, Denis McQuail, and Pippa Norris. Washington, DC: CQ Press.

Neuman, W. Russell, Marion R. Just, and Ann N. Crigler. 1992. *Common Knowledge: News and the Construction of Meaning.* University of Chicago Press.

Newman, Bruce I. (ed.). 1999. *The Handbook of Political Marketing.* Thousand Oaks, CA: Sage.

Newton, Kenneth. 1991. 'Do People Believe Everything They Read in the Papers? Newspapers and Voters in the 1983 and 1987 Elections.' In *British Elections and Parties Handbook 1991*, ed. Ivor Crewe, Pippa Norris, David Denver, and David Broughton. Hemel Hempstead, UK: Harvester Wheatsheaf.

Newton, Kenneth. 1997. 'Politics and the News Media: Mobilisation or Videomalaise?' In *British Social Attitudes: The 14th Report*, ed. Roger Jowell, John Curtice, Alison Park, Katarina Thomson, and Lindsay Brook. Aldershot, UK: Ashgate.

Newton, Kenneth. 1999. 'Mass Media Effects: Mobilization or Media Malaise?' *British Journal of Political Science* 29:577–99.

Niedermayer, Oskar, and Richard Sinnott (eds.). 1995. *Public Opinion and Internationalized Governance.* Oxford University Press.

Norpoth, Helmut, Michael S. Lewis-Beck, and Jean-Dominique Lafay. 1991. *Economics and Politics: The Calculus of Support.* Ann Arbor: University of Michigan Press.

Norris, Pippa. 1996. 'Does Television Erode Social Capital? A Reply to Putnam.' *PS: Political Science and Politics* 29(3):474–80.

Norris, Pippa. 1997. *Electoral Change since 1945.* Oxford: Blackwell.

Norris, Pippa. 1997. 'Political Communications.' In *Developments in British Politics 5*, ed. Patrick Dunleavy, Andrew Gamble, Ian Holliday, and Gillian Peele. London: Macmillan.

Norris, Pippa. 1997. *Politics and the Press: The News Media and Their Influences.* Boulder, CO: Lynne Rienner.

Norris, Pippa. 1997. 'Anatomy of a Labour Landslide.' In *Britain Votes 1997*, ed. Pippa Norris and Neil Gavin. Oxford University Press.

Norris, Pippa. 1998. 'Blaming the Messenger? Television and Civic Malaise.' Presented at the conference on Public Trust and Democratic Governance in the Trilateral Democracies, Bellagio, June.

Norris, Pippa. 1998. 'The Battle for the Campaign Agenda.' In *New Labour Triumphs: Britain at the Polls*, ed. Anthony King. Chatham, NJ: Chatham House.

Norris, Pippa. 1999. 'Who Surfs? New Technology, Old Voters and Virtual Democracy in America.' In *democracy.com? Governance in a Networked World*, ed. Elaine Kamarck and Joseph S. Nye, Jr. Hollis, NH: Hollis Publishing.

Norris, Pippa (ed.). 1999. *Critical Citizens: Global Support for Democratic Governance.* Oxford University Press.

Norris, Pippa. 2000. 'The Impact of Television Civic Malaise.' In *Disaffected Democracies: What's Troubling the Trilateral Countries*, ed. Susan J. Pharr and Robert D. Putnam. Princeton, NJ: Princeton University Press.

Norris, Pippa, John Curtice, David Sanders, Margaret Scammell, and Holli A. Semetko. 1999. *On Message: Communicating the Campaign.* London: Sage.

Norris, Pippa, and Geoffrey Evans (eds.). 1999. *Critical Elections: British Parties and Voters in Long-Term Perspective.* London: Sage.

Norris, Pippa, and Neil Gavin (eds.). 1997. *Britain Votes 1997.* Oxford University Press.

Norris, Pippa, and David Jones. 1998. 'Virtual Democracy.' *Harvard International Journal of Press/Politics* 3(2):1–4.

NUA. *www.nua.ie/surveys/how_many_online/index.html*

Nye, Joseph S., Jr., Philip D. Zelikow, and David C. King. 1997. *Why People Don't Trust Government.* Cambridge, MA: Harvard University Press.

O'Neill, Patrick. 1998. *Post-Communism and the Media in Eastern Europe.* London: Frank Cass.

Ostergaard, Bernt Stubbe (ed.). 1997. *The Media in Western Europe.* London: Sage.

Panebianco, Angelo. 1988. *Political Parties: Organization and Power.* Cambridge University Press.

Parry, Geraint, George Moser, and Neil Day. 1992. *Political Participation and Democracy in Britain.* Cambridge University Press.

Patterson, Thomas E. 1980. *The Mass Media Election: How Americans Choose Their President.* New York: Praeger.

Patterson, Thomas E. 1993. *Out of Order.* New York: Knopf.

Patterson, Thomas E. 1996. 'Bad News, Bad Governance.' In *The Media and Politics*, ed. Kathleen H. Jamieson. *Annals of the American Academy of Political and Social Sciences*, vol. 546.

Patterson, Thomas, and Wolfgang Donsbach. 1996. 'News Decisions: Journalists as Partisan Actors.' *Political Communication* 13(4):455–68.

Patterson, Thomas, and McClure, R. D. 1976. *The Unseeing Eye: The Myth of Television Power in National Elections.* New York: Putnam.

Pew Research Center for the People and the Press. 1999. *Striking the Balance: Audience Interests, Business Pressures and Journalists' Values.* Washington, DC: Pew Research Center for the People and the Press.

Pfetsch, Barbara. 1996. 'Convergence through Privatization? Changing Media Environments and Televised Politics in Germany.' *European Journal of Communication* 8(3):425–50.

Pharr, Susan J. 1997. 'Japanese Videocracy.' *Harvard International Journal of Press/Politics* 2(1):130–8.

Pharr, Susan J. 2000. 'Officials' Misconduct and Public Distrust: Japan and the Trilateral Democracies.' In *Disaffected Democrats: What's Troubling the Trilateral Countries*, ed. Susan J. Pharr and Robert D. Putnam. Princeton, NJ: Princeton University Press.

Pharr, Susan J., and Ellis S. Krauss. 1996. *Media and Politics in Japan.* Honolulu: University Press of Hawaii.

Pharr, Susan J., and Robert D. Putnam (eds.). 2000. *Disaffected Democrats: What's Troubling the Trilateral Countries.* Princeton, NJ: Princeton University Press.

Philo, Greg. 1999. *Message Received.* London: Longman.

Pinkleton, Bruce E., and Erica Weintraub Austin. 1998. 'Media and Participation: Breaking the Spiral of Disaffection.' In *Engaging the Public: How Government and the Media Can Invigorate American Democracy*, ed. Thomas J. Johnson, Carol E. Hays, and Scott P. Hays. New York: Rowman & Littlefield.

Plassner, Fritz, Christian Scheucher, and Christian Senft. 1999. 'Is There a European Style of Political Marketing?' In *The Handbook of Political Marketing*, ed. Bruce I. Newman. Thousand Oaks, CA: Sage.

Popkin, Samuel. 1994. *The Reasoning Voter.* University of Chicago Press.

Postman, Neil. 1985. *Amusing Ourselves to Death.* London: Methuen.

Price, Vincent, and John Zaller. 1993. 'Who Gets the News? Alternative Measures of News Reception and Their Implications for Research.' *Public Opinion Quarterly* 57:133–64.

Protess, David L., and Maxwell McCombs. 1991. *Agenda-Setting: Readings on Media, Public Opinion and Policymaking*. Hillsdale, NJ: Lawrence Erlbaum.

Przeworski, Adam, and H. Teune. 1970. *The Logic of Comparative Social Inquiry*. New York: Wiley.

Putnam, Robert D. 1995. 'Tuning In, Tuning Out: The Strange Disappearance of Social Capital in America.' *PS: Political Science and Politics* 28(4):664–83.

Putnam, Robert D. 1996. 'The Strange Disappearance of Civic America.' *The American Prospect* 24.

Putnam, Robert D. 2000. *Bowling Alone*. New York: Simon & Schuster.

Putnam, Robert D., Steven Yonish, and David E. Campbell. 1999. 'Tuning In, Tuning Out Revisited: A Closer Look at the Causal Links between Television and Social Capital.' Paper presented at the annual meeting of the American Political Science Association, Atlanta.

Ranney, Austin. 1983. *Channels of Power: The Impact of Television on American Politics*. New York: Basic Books.

Rash, Wayne, Jr. 1997. *Politics on the Net: Wiring the Political Process*. San Francisco: Freeman.

Rheingold, Howard. 1993. *The Virtual Community: Homesteading on the Electronic Frontier*. Reading, MA: Addison-Wesley.

Richardson, Kay, and Ulrike H. Meinhof. 1999. *Worlds in Common? Television Discourse in a Changing Europe*. London: Routledge.

Robinson, John R., and Mark Levy. 1986. *The Main Source: Learning from TV News*. Beverly Hills, CA: Sage.

Robinson, Michael J. 1974. 'The Impact of Televised Watergate Hearings.' *Journal of Communication* 24(2):17–30.

Robinson, Michael J. 1975. 'American Political Legitimacy in an Era of Electronic Journalism: Reflections on the Evening News.' In *Television as a Social Force: New Approaches to TV Criticism*, ed. Douglas Cater and R. Adler. New York: Praeger.

Robinson, Michael J. 1976. 'Public Affairs Television and the Growth of Political Malaise: The Case of "The Selling of the Pentagon".' *American Political Science Review* 70(2):409–32.

Robinson, Michael J., and Margaret A. Sheehan. 1983. *Over the Wire and on TV: CBS and UPI in Campaign '80*. New York: Russell Sage Foundation.

Rosenbaum, Martin. 1997. *From Soapbox to Soundbite: Party Political Campaigning since 1945*. London: Macmillan.

Rosenstone, Steven. 1983. *Forecasting Presidential Elections*. New Haven, CT: Yale University Press.

Rosenstone, Steven J., and John Mark Hansen. 1993. *Mobilization, Participation and Democracy in America*. New York: Macmillan.

Rubin, Alan. 1994. 'Media Users and Effects.' In *Media Effects*, ed. Jennings Bryant and Dolf Zillmann. Hillsdale, NJ: Lawrence Erlbaum.

Sabato, Larry. 1981. *The Rise of Political Consultants*. New York: Basic Books.

Sabato, Larry. 1991. *Feeding Frenzy: How Attack Journalism Has Transformed American Politics*. New York: Free Press.

Salmore, Barbara G., and Stephen A. Salmore. 1989. *Candidates, Parties and Campaigns*. Washington, DC: CQ Press.

Sanders, David, and Pippa Norris. 1998. 'Does Negative News Matter? The Effects of Television News on Party Images in the 1997 British General Election.' In *British Elections and Parties Yearbook, 1998*, ed. Charles Pattie et al. London: Frank Cass.

Särlvik, Bo, and Ivor Crewe. 1983. *Decade of Dealignment: The Conservative Victory of 1979 and Electoral Trends in the 1970s*. Cambridge University Press.

Scammell, Margaret. 1995. *Designer Politics: How Elections Are Won*. London: Macmillan.

Scammell, Margaret. 1999. 'The Wisdom of the War Room: U.S. Campaigning and Americanization.' *Media, Culture and Society* 20.

Scammell, Margaret. 2000. 'Political Marketing: Lessons for Political Science.' *Political Studies*.

Scammell, Margaret, and Martin Harrop. 1997. 'The Press: Labour's Finest Hour.' In *The British General Election of 1997*, ed. David Butler and Dennis Kavanagh. London: Macmillan.

Schoenbach, Klaus, and Holli A. Semetko. 1992. 'Agenda-Setting, Agenda-Reinforcing or Agenda-Deflating? A Study of the 1990 German National Election.' *Journalism Quarterly* 69(4):837–46.

Schudson, Michael. 1995. *The Power of News*. Cambridge, MA: Harvard University Press.

Schulz, Winfried. 1997. 'Changes in the Mass Media and the Public Sphere.' *Javnost – The Public* 4(2):57–69.

Schulz, Winfried. 1998. 'Media Change and the Political Effects of Television: Americanization of the Political Culture?' *Communications* 23(4):527–43.

Schumpeter, Joseph A. 1952. *Capitalism, Socialism and Democracy*, 4th ed. London: Allen & Unwin.

Schwartz, Edward. 1996. *Netactivism: How Citizens Use the Internet*. Sebastopol, CA: Songline Studios.

Scott, David K., and Robert H. Gobetz. 1992. 'Hard News/Soft News Content of the National Broadcast Networks, 1972–1987.' *Journalism Quarterly* 69(2):406–12.

Seaton, Jean (ed.). 1998. *Politics and the Media*. Oxford: Blackwell.

Selnow, Gary W. 1998. *Electronic Whistle-Stops: The Impact of the Internet on American Politics*. Westport, CT: Praeger.

Semetko, Holli A. 1996. 'The Media.' In *Comparing Democracies*, ed. Lawrence LeDuc, Richard Neimi, and Pippa Norris. Thousand Oaks, CA: Sage.

Semetko, Holli A. 1996. 'Journalistic Culture in Comparative Perspective: The Concept of "Balance" in U.S., British and German TV News.' *Harvard International Journal of Press/Politics* 1(1):51–71.

Semetko, Holli. 1996. 'Political Balance on Television: Campaigns in the United States, Britain and Germany.' *Harvard International Journal of Press/Politics* 1(1):51–71.

Semetko, Holli A., Jay G. Blumler, Michael Gurevitch, and David H. Weaver. 1991. *The Formation of Campaign Agendas: A Comparative Analysis of Party and Media Roles in Recent American and British Elections*. Hillsdale, NJ: Lawrence Erlbaum.

Semetko, Holli, Margaret Scammell, and Peter Goddard. 1997. 'Television.' In *Britain Votes 1997*, ed. Pippa Norris and Neil Gavin. Oxford University Press.

Semetko, Holli A., Margaret Scammell, and T. J. Nossiter. 1994. 'Media Coverage of the 1992 British General Election Campaign.' In *Labour's Last Chance? The 1992 Election and Beyond*, ed. Anthony Heath, Roger Jowell, and John Curtice. Aldershot, UK: Dartmouth.

Semetko, Holli A., and Klaus Schoenbach. 1994. *Germany's 'Unity Election': Voters and the Media*. Cresskill, NJ: Hampton Press.

Seymour-Ure, Colin. 1974. *The Political Impact of the Mass Media*. Beverly Hills, CA: Sage.

Seymour-Ure, Colin. 1995. 'Characters and Assassinations.' In *Political Communication: The General Election Campaign of 1992*, ed. Ivor Crewe and Brian Gosschalk. Cambridge University Press.

Seymour-Ure, Colin. 1996. *The British Press and Broadcasting since 1945*. Oxford: Blackwell.

Seymour-Ure, Colin. 1997. 'Editorial Opinion in the National Press.' In *Britain Votes 1997*, ed. Pippa Norris and Neil Gavin. Oxford University Press.

Shoemaker, Pamela J., and Stephen D. Reese. 1996. *Mediating the Message*, 2nd ed. New York: Longman.

Siune, Karen, and Wolfgang Truetzschler (eds.). 1992. *Dynamics of Media Politics: Broadcast and Electronic Media in Western Europe*. London: Sage.

Smith, Anthony (ed.). 1979. *Television and Political Life: Studies in Six European Countries*. London: Macmillan.

Smith, Anthony (ed.). 1995. *Television: An International History*. Oxford University Press.

Smith, Eric. 1989. *The Unchanging American Voter*. Berkeley: University of California Press.

Starker, Steven. 1991. *Evil Empires: Crusading Against the Mass Media*. London: Transaction.

Stevenson, Robert L. 1994. *Global Communication in the Twenty-First Century*. New York: Longman.

Swanson, David L., and Paolo Mancini (eds.). 1996. *Politics, Media, and Modern Democracy: An International Study of Innovations in Electoral Campaigning and Their Consequences*. New York: Praeger.

Tait, Richard. 1995. 'The Parties and Television.' In *Political Communications: The General Election Campaign of 1992*, ed. Ivor Crewe and Brian Gosschalk. Cambridge University Press.

Takeshita, Toshio. 1993. 'Agenda-Setting Effects of the Press in a Japanese Local Election.' *Studies of Broadcasting* 29:194–216.

Takeshita, Toshio, and Shunji Mikami. 1995. 'How Did Mass Media Influence the Voters' Choice in the 1993 General Election in Japan? A Study of Agenda-Setting.' *Keio Communication Review* 17:27–41.

Tan, Alexis S. 1980. 'Mass Media Use, Issue Knowledge and Political Involvement.' *Public Opinion Quarterly* 44:241–8.

Taylor, Bridget, and Anthony Heath. 1999. 'Turnout and Registration.' In *Critical Elections: British Parties and Voters in Long-Term Perspective*, ed. Geoffrey Evans and Pippa Norris. London: Sage.

Teixeira, Ruy A. 1992. *The Disappearing American Voter*. Washington, DC: Brookings Institution.

Thurber, James, and C. Nelson. 1995. *Campaigns and Elections American Style.* Boulder: Westview Press.

Thurber, James, and Candice J. Nelson (eds.). 2000. *The Role of Political Consultants in Elections.* Washington, DC: Brookings Institution.

Toulouse, Chris, and Timothy W. Luke (eds.). 1998. *The Politics of Cyberspace.* London: Routledge.

Tracey, Michael. 1998. *The Decline and Fall of Public Service Broadcasting.* Oxford University Press.

Trenaman, Joseph, and Denis McQuail. 1961. *Television and the Political Image.* London: Methuen.

Trent, Judith S., and Robert V. Friedenberg. 1991. *Political Campaign Communication: Principles and Practices,* 2nd ed. New York: Praeger.

UNESCO. 1998. *World Communication Report: The Media and Challenges of the New Technologies.* Paris: UNESCO.

UNESCO. Annual. *Statistical Yearbook.* Paris: UNESCO.

Valley, Paul, Christian Wolmar, Colin Brown, Steve Boggan, and Barrie Clement. 1998. 'Blair's Long Trek to Victory.' *The Independent* 3:17–18.

Van der Eijk, Cees, and Mark N. Franklin (eds.). 1996. *Choosing Europe: The European Electorate and National Politics in the Face of Union.* Ann Arbor: University of Michigan Press.

Verba, Sidney, and Norman Nie. 1972. *Participation in America: Political Democracy and Social Equality.* New York: Harper & Row.

Verba, Sidney, Norman Nie, and Jae-on Kim. 1978. *Participation and Political Equality: A Seven-Nation Comparison.* Cambridge University Press.

Verba, Sidney, Kay Lehman Schlozman, and Henry E. Brady. 1995. *Voice and Equality: Civic Voluntarism in American Politics.* Cambridge, MA: Harvard University Press.

Wald, Kenneth D. 1983. *Crosses on the Ballot: Patterns of British Voter Alignment since 1885.* Princeton, NJ: Princeton University Press.

Ward, Stephen, and Rachel Gibson. 1998. 'The First Internet Election.' In *Political Communications: Why Labour Won the General Election of 1997,* ed. Ivor Crewe, Brian Gosschalk, and John Bartle. London: Frank Cass.

Wattenberg, Martin P. 1996. *The Decline of American Political Parties: 1952–1994.* Cambridge, MA: Harvard University Press.

Watts, Duncan. 1997. *Political Communications Today.* Manchester University Press.

Weaver, David H. 1998. *The Global Journalist: News People Around the World.* Cresskill, NJ: Hampton Press.

Weaver, David, Doris Graber, Maxwell McCombs, and C. H. Eyal. 1981. *Media Agenda-Setting in Presidential Elections: Issues, Images and Interests.* New York: Praeger.

West, Darrell M. 1992. *Air Wars: Television Advertising in Election Campaigns, 1952–1992.* Washington, DC: CQ Press.

Westerstahl, Jorgen, and Folke Johansson. 1986. 'News Ideologies as Moulders of Domestic News.' *European Journal of Communication* 1:133–49.

Weymouth, Tony, and Bernard Lamizet. 1996. *Markets and Myths: Forces for Change in the European Media.* London: Longman.

Wheeler, Mark. 1997. *Politics and the Mass Media.* Oxford: Blackwell.

Whiteley, Paul. 1997 'The Conservative Campaign.' In *Britain Votes 1997,* ed. Pippa Norris and Neil Gavin. Oxford University Press.

Williams, Raymond. 1961. *Culture and Society 1780–1950*. London: Penguin.

Wilson, Graham K. 1998. *Only in America? The Politics of the United States in Comparative Perspective*. Chatham, NJ: Chatham House.

Worcester, Robert M. 1998. 'The Media and the Polls.' In *Political Communications: Why Labour Won the General Election of 1997*, ed. Ivor Crewe, Brian Gosschalk, and John Bartle. London: Frank Cass.

Wring, Dominic. 1996. 'From Mass Propaganda to Political Marketing: The Transformation of Labour Party Election Campaigning.' In *British Parties and Elections Yearbook 1995*, ed. Colin Rallings et al. London: Frank Cass.

Zaller, John. 1993. *The Nature and Origins of Mass Opinion*. Cambridge University Press.

Zaller, John. 1998. 'Monica Lewinsky's Contribution to Political Science.' *PS: Political Science and Politics* 31(2):182–9.

Zhao, Xinshu, and Glen L. Beske. 1998. 'Horse-Race Polls and Audience Issue Learning.' *Harvard International Journal of Press/Politics* 3(4):13–34.

Zucker, Harold. 1978. 'The Variable Nature of News Influence.' In *Communication Yearbook 2*, ed. Brent D. Ruben. New Brunswick, NJ: Transaction Books.

Author Index

389

Subject Index